SAILBOAT MAINTENANCE

By
ERIC JORGENSEN

JEFF ROBINSON
Editor and Publisher

CLYMER PUBLICATIONS

World's largest publisher of books devoted exclusively to automobiles and motorcycles.

12860 MUSCATINE STREET • P.O. BOX 20 • ARLETA, CALIFORNIA 91331

FIRST EDITION
First Printing April, 1975
Second Printing May, 1977
Third Printing April, 1979

ISBN: 0-89287-068-0

Printed in U. S. A.

Technical illustrations by Stan Sudjian

CONTENTS

CHAPTER ONE

GENERAL INFORMATION

All boats suffer gradual deterioration from a number of causes. Marine growths cling to the hull, reducing performance or damaging the structure. Corrosive atmospheric conditions etch any exposed metal. Galvanic corrosion eats away underwater metal not adequately protected. Normal use works parts of the boat against each other, eventually wearing them down to the point of failure.

To keep your boat serviceable and safe, you must spot deterioration before it becomes serious, identify the cause, and prevent further damage by repairing or replacing damaged parts.

Every boat needs maintenance—some more than others. In the early days of fiberglass, prospective owners were led to believe the new material was virtually "maintenance free." Some actually believed it—for a short time. On the other hand, everyone *knew* wood boats require "a lot" of maintenance. Other materials seemed to fall in between the two extremes.

Recent surveys have verified what fiberglass boat owners soon discovered: Fiberglass boats, like all boats ever made, require maintenance. In fact, the data shows that fiberglass boats require 70-80% as much attention as a comparable wood boat.

Many maintenance jobs are too complex for the average owner. Troubleshooting and repairing most electronic gear is strictly for profes-

sionals. In fact, only Federally licensed technicians can work on radio-telephone equipment. Repairs involving structural parts are, likewise, best left to a boatyard. Jobs such as replacing hull timbers or patching a large hole in fiberglass require special equipment and skills.

This book describes maintenance procedures well within the capabilities of anyone intelligent and dexterous enough to sail a boat. More complex jobs should be entrusted to a reputable boatyard. Also, there are some jobs which the owner *could* do, but which a boatyard can do far more easily and even less expensively.

Chapter Two describes common boat maintenance tools. Many will be familiar to you if you've worked on an automobile or made minor repairs around the house. Others are specialized for marine maintenance.

Chapter Three describes maintenance required to keep the hull and deck surfaces sound and attractive. Complete instructions for painting and refinishing your boat permit you to get professional results with little or no previous experience. All you need is patience and willingness to see the job through.

Chapter Four includes maintenance of spars, rigging, and sails. Exploded views and repair procedures for several popular winches make their repair entirely within the capabilities of nearly anyone. The chapter also describes maintenance of running and standing rigging. The elements of sail care outlined in this chapter will keep your sails in good condition for many years.

Chapters Five and Six describe routine maintenance of outboard and inboard auxiliaries for sailboats. This information permits you to minimize deterioration and get maximum performance from the engine. Major repairs, however, should be referred to a qualified mechanic.

Chapter Seven covers electrical systems found aboard sailboats and includes troubleshooting and repair procedures.

Chapter Eight includes maintenance and repair of most popular stoves including alcohol, kerosene, and LPG/LNG systems.

Chapters Nine and Ten discuss water systems and heads in common use. A knowledge of how these systems work aids immeasurably in troubleshooting them when they don't work.

Chapter Eleven describes most marine electronics systems used aboard small boats. Nearly all maintenance of these units must be performed by a qualified technician. However, some things can be done by the owner.

Chapter Twelve tells how to keep your trailer and tow vehicle in good condition. A poorly maintained trailer is a menace to your boat, your tow vehicle, and your life.

MAINTENANCE SCHEDULE

Much maintenance depends on hours of use. Other jobs should be done seasonally regardless of use.

Table 1 summarizes maintenance required.

Table 1   MAINTENANCE

	Chapter
Auxiliary power generator	Seven
Batteries	Five, Seven
Electronic equipment	Eleven
Galley equipment	Eight
Head	Ten
Hull	Three
Bottom paint	
Topsides and deck finish	
Clean and wax	
Outboard/inboard motors	Five, Six
Potable water system	Nine
Sails	Four
Spars and rigging	Four
Trailer	Twelve
Hitch	
Lights	
Wheels/tires	

LAY-UP/WINTER STORAGE

It is very important to store a boat properly. Many components can be permanently damaged by disuse or freezing temperatures. **Table 2** summarizes which components require attention. Refer to appropriate chapter for specific lay-up and recommissioning procedures.

Table 2   LAY-UP SUMMARY

Exterior hull and deck surfaces	Clean and touch-up, see Chapter Three
Sails	Clean and fold, see Chapter Four
Outboard motor	See Chapter Five
Inboard engine	See Chapter Six
Batteries and electrical	See Chapter Seven
Galley	See Chapter Eight
Water system	Fill system with non-toxic anti-freeze as described in Chapter Nine
Head	See Chapter Ten
Electronic equipment	Remove if theft is possible
Trailer	Clean and touch-up paint. Protect tires as described in Chapter Twelve

CHAPTER TWO

TOOLS AND FASTENERS

Having the right tools on hand when needed can make maintenance chores much more enjoyable. Good tools do the job neater and faster than improvised or poor quality tools.

This chapter describes various hand tools required to perform virtually any repair job aboard your boat. Each tool is described and recommendations as to proper size are made for those not familiar with hand tools.

Besides having the right tool for a job, it is important that you use the proper fastener. The type, size, and material of each fastener used on your boat must be deliberately chosen. The sections on fasteners and corrosion make selection simple.

GENERAL TOOLS

A number of tools are required to maintain a boat in top condition. You may already have some around for other work such as home and car repairs. There are also tools made especially for marine equipment, and you will have to purchase them. In any case, a wide variety of quality tools will make repairs more effective and convenient.

Top quality tools are essential—and also more economical. Poor grade tools are made of inferior materials and are thick, heavy, and clumsy. Their rough finish makes them difficult to clean and they usually don't stand up long.

Quality tools are made of alloy steel and are heat treated for greater strength. They are lighter and better balanced than inferior ones. Their surface finish is smooth, making them a pleasure to work with and easy to clean. The initial cost of quality tools may be relatively high, but longer life and ease of use make them less expensive in the long run.

Some tools are forged from bronze, especially for marine use. They are rust-proof, spark resistant, non-magnetic, and impervious to corrosive salt water and battery acid. Non-sparking tools like these are used with safety in explosive atmospheres like ordinance depots, chemical plants, and marine engine rooms.

It is aggravating to search and search for a certain tool in the middle of a repair, only to find it covered with grime. Keep your tools in a tool box. Keep wrench sets, socket sets, etc., together. After using a tool, wipe off dirt and grease with a clean cloth and replace it in its correct place.

Screwdrivers

The screwdriver is about the most basic tool, but many people don't use it properly and do more damaging than fixing. The slot on a screw has definite dimensions and shape. A screwdriver must be selected to conform to that shape. A small screwdriver in a large screw slot will twist the screwdriver out of shape and damage the slot. A large screwdriver on a small slot will also damage the slot. In addition, since the sides of the screw slot are parallel, the sides of the screwdriver near the tip must be parallel. If the tip sides are tapered, the screwdriver wedges itself out of the slot; this makes the screw difficult to remove and may damage the slot.

Two basic type screwdrivers are required: a common screwdriver and a Phillips screwdriver. Both types are illustrated in **Figure 1**.

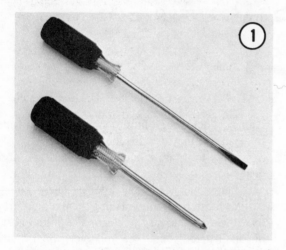

Screwdrivers are available in sets which often include an assortment of common and Phillips blades. If you purchase individual screwdrivers, as a minimum obtain:

   a. Common screwdriver, 5/16 x 6 in. blade

   b. Common screwdriver, ⅜ x 12 in. blade

   c. Phillips screwdriver, size 2, 6 in. blade

Use screwdrivers only for driving screws. Never use a screwdriver for prying or chiseling. In addition, never use a common screwdriver to remove a Phillips or Allen head screw; you can damage the head so that even the proper tool will not remove the screw.

Keep screwdrivers in proper condition and they will last longer and perform better. Always keep the tip in good condition. **Figure 2** shows how to grind the tip to proper shape if it is damaged. Note the parallel sides at the tip.

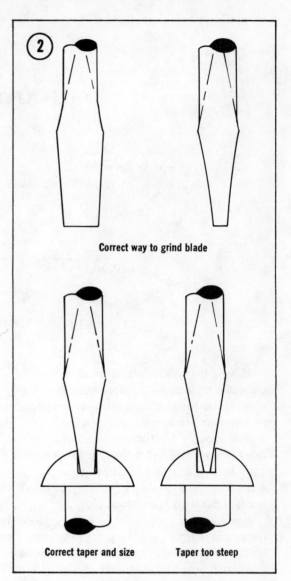

Correct way to grind blade

Correct taper and size   **Taper too steep**

Pliers

Pliers come in a wide range of types and sizes. They are useful for cutting, bending, and crimping. They should never be used to cut hardened objects or to turn nuts or bolts. **Figure 3** shows several pliers useful aboard boats.

Each type of pliers has a specialized function. Channel-lock pliers can be adjusted to hold various size objects; the jaws remain parallel to grip round objects such as piping or tubing. Vise Grips are used as pliers or to grip objects very tightly like a vise. Gas pliers are general purpose and are used mainly for holding things and bending. Needle nose pliers are used to hold or

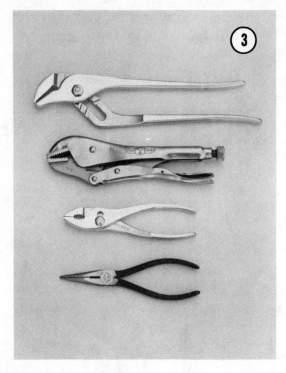

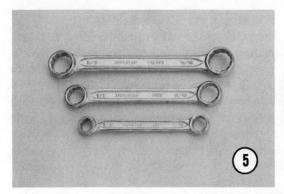

bend small objects. There are many more types of pliers. The ones described here are most suitable for marine repairs.

Box- and Open-end Wrenches

Box-wrenches and open-end wrenches are available in sets or separately in a variety of sizes. See **Figures 4 and 5**. The size stamped near the end refers to distance between 2 parallel flats on a hex head nut or bolt.

European and Asian engines and equipment use metric hardware; English and American engines use English (inch) hardware. Separate wrench sizes are made for metric use and for English use.

Box-wrenches are usually superior to open-end wrenches. Open-end wrenches grip a nut on only 2 flats. Unless it fits well, it may slip and round off the points on the nut. The box-wrench grips all 6 flats. Both 6-point and 12-point openings on box-wrenches are available. The 6-point gives superior holding power; the 12-point allows a shorter swing.

Combination wrenches which are open on one end and boxed on the other are also available. Both ends are the same size.

Adjustable (Crescent) Wrenches

An adjustable wrench (also called a crescent wrench) can be adjusted to fit nearly any nut or bolt head. See **Figure 6**. However, it can loosen or slip, causing damage to the nut. Use only when other wrenches are not available.

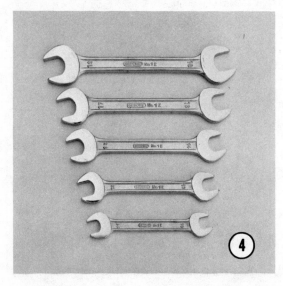

Crescent wrenches come in sizes ranging from 4 in. to 18 in. overall. A 6 in. or 8 in. size is recommended as an all-purpose wrench.

Socket Wrenches

This type wrench is undoubtedly the fastest, safest, and most convenient to use. See **Figure 7**. Sockets which attach to a ratchet handle are available with 6-point or 12-point openings and ¼, ⅜, ½, and ¾ in. drives. The drive size indicates the size of the square drive hole which mates with the ratchet handle. Sockets are available in metric and inch sizes.

Socket wrench sets are relatively expensive. However, they are often indispensable when working in a cramped engine compartment.

Allen Wrenches

These hex-shaped wrenches fit similar shaped recesses in the top of Allen head screws and bolts. See **Figure 8**. Allen head screws are often used to secure winches to the deck and spars. They are occasionally used on engines as well.

Clamps

Clamps come in a variety of sizes and shapes. Selection depends on the job at hand. They are essential for holding things while being glued or screwed together. They are also handy for emergency repairs, making good temporary fasteners.

Figure 9 shows some of the many types available. From top to bottom, they are:

a. Pipe clamp
b. Handscrew
c. C-clamp (sometimes called G-clamp)

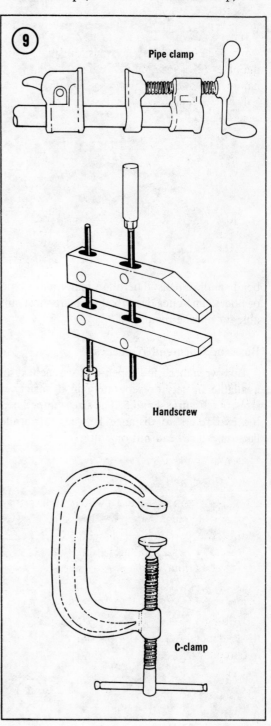

Pipe clamp

Handscrew

C-clamp

Hammer and Mallets

There are many types of hammers made for specialized purposes. Two are most useful for boat maintenance:

    a. Claw hammer

    b. Ball-peen hammer

The claw hammer is mainly for carpentry work. See **Figure 10**. One end is for driving nails, the other (claw) for pulling nails. The ball-peen hammer (Figure 10) is used for metal work. The ball end can be used to shape contours in thin sheet metal.

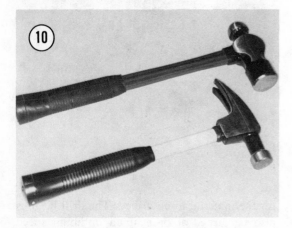

Mallets also come in a variety of types. The hammer heads are usually made of relatively soft material such as:

    a. Wood

    b. Rubber

    c. Plastic (hard)

    d. Lead

Their most important use in boat maintenance is for freeing stuck parts. Where a steel hammer could cause permanent damage to stuck fasteners or cast parts, a mallet will apply good striking force without marring the part.

Drills

Drilling can be accomplished with several tools, depending on the material to be drilled. Most common are:

    a. Hand drill

    b. Electric drill

    c. Brace

Hand drills are very useful aboard boats since they do not require electric power. See **Figure 11**. When used with the proper bit, they can be used to drill any wood and many soft metals such as copper, aluminum, and some iron.

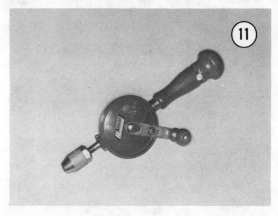

An electric drill is more efficient since it is faster and more powerful than a hand drill. See **Figure 12**. However, there are some disadvantages. Most require a source of AC voltage which is not available on most boats when underway. AC isn't always available at dockside, either. Furthermore AC is potentially very dangerous. The drill must have a 3-prong plug and must be plugged into a 3-prong grounded socket. There are 2 important precautions to heed with any electric tool.

WARNING
*a. Do not use an adapter like the one shown in **Figure 13** to connect a 3-prong plug to a 2-prong socket. Fatal shock is extremely likely.*

b. If you drop the tool overboard while it is connected, stand clear of the connecting cord. Shut off the power to the socket at the main switch before trying to recover the tool. Chances are the circuit breaker or fuse will blow immediately, but don't take any chances.

When using an electric drill, apply gentle but firm pressure. Too light pressure will permit the bit to wander away from the area to be drilled. Too heavy pressure will stall the drill or cause excessive heat which can damage the bit and the material being drilled. Hold the drill firmly and do not let it waver back and forth; this enlarges the hole.

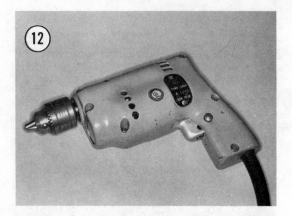

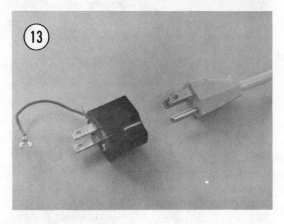

A brace is used when drilling large holes. See **Figure 14**. Naturally, a brace is a type of hand drill. Select the proper bit as described in the next section.

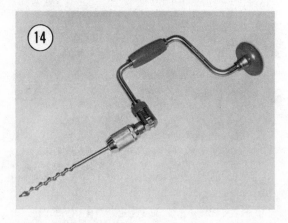

Twist Drill Bits

Twist drills shown in **Figure 15** are commonly used for metal and wood work. In order to work properly, a drill bit must be sharpened properly

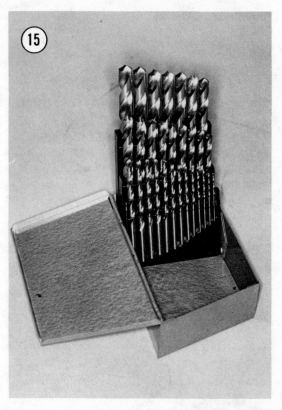

for the material to be drilled. The drill bit must also be turned at or near an optimum speed, determined by the bit size and material to be drilled.

A drill bit must be shaped and sharpened properly to work efficiently to produce the desired hole size. The following should be kept in mind:

a. Cutting edges must be sharp and equal in length.

b. Included angle made by cutting edges is normally about 120°. Regrind as shown in **Figure 16** for harder or softer materials.

c. Clearance must be provided behind cutting edges so the edge can bite into the material. This angle is normally 12°. See Figure 16.

Several inexpensive fixtures which attach to an electric drill are available to regrind and sharpen drill bits.

Auger Bits

Auger bits, used in a common brace, are used for boring large holes in wood. See **Figure 17**.

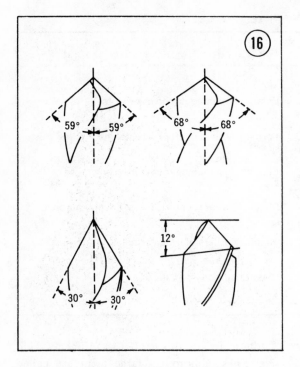

pilot drill. To use it, mount the desired diameter saw in the mandrel. Install the combination in an electric drill. Place the pilot drill in the center of the new hole location. Keep the drill absolutely vertical and cut the hole.

Another type of hole saw is shown in **Figure 19**. Actually, it is more like a specialized bit. It can only be used for wood and soft materials like plastic. Use this saw exactly as you would a bit in an electric drill.

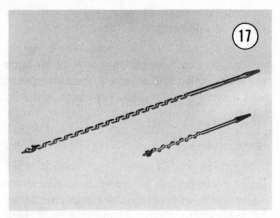

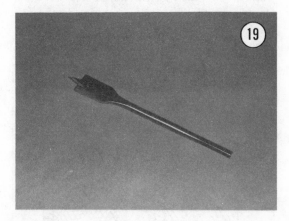

Usually they are available in sizes from ¼-1½ in. (in 1/16 in. increments). The single twist auger is a very rigid, strong tool, capable of very powerful boring. The double twist auger is not as strong as a single twist auger, but produces a very smooth hole; it is strong enough for most cabinet work.

Hole Saws

Hole saws are used when very large holes must be bored in wood or thin, soft metal such as aluminum. Two types are most common. The type shown in **Figure 18** may be used for wood or thin metal. It consists of a mandrel, saw, and

Files

An assortment of files can make repair jobs fast and easy. They come in such a wide variety of types, shapes, and sizes that nearly any shaping or smoothing job can be accomplished.

When shaping with a file, choose a file with a suitable shape. Files are square, triangular, round, half round, flat, and also come in many other specialized shapes. **Table 1** lists common shapes and their intended use.

Table 1   FILES

Types	Cross-section	Use
Square		Enlarging rectangular holes or slots
Triangular (3-cornered)		Forming square corners in rectangular holes
Round (rat-tail)		Enlarging or shaping round or oblong holes
Half-round		Shaping flat or round surfaces; general purpose
Knife-edge		Shaping corners of irregular holes
Flat		General purpose, flat shaping

It is also important to choose a file with the proper teeth. Files can be single cut or double cut. See **Figure 20**. Single cut files have parallel teeth set about 65° to the center line of the file. They are intended for smoothing and finishing. Double cut files have criss-crossing teeth. The resulting diamond teeth cut very fast and are intended for rough work and heavy shaping jobs.

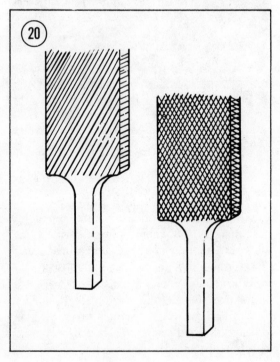

File teeth are also graded as to fineness and size. Files with rough, large teeth are called bastard files; files with relatively smooth teeth are called smooth files.

A rasp is a file with large teeth which tear the material rather than cut it. They are used on wood and other soft materials such as plastic, lead, aluminum, etc. They cut rough, but very rapidly.

Hand Sanders

For many applications, particularly when sanding compound or rounded shapes, sandpaper is used without any block. But when large, relatively flat expanses are sanded, a good block permits more uniform pressure without as much strain.

A small, smooth piece of scrap wood can be used as a block. Simply wrap the sandpaper around it as shown in **Figure 21**.

Commercial sanding blocks are available also. See **Figure 22**. They grip the sandpaper firmly and often have soft padding under the paper. Usually they are easier to hold and less tiring than a simple wood block.

Power Sanders

Several power sanders are available. Most common for boat work are:

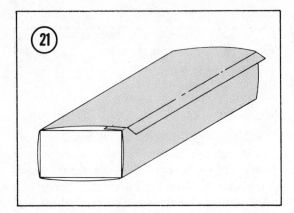

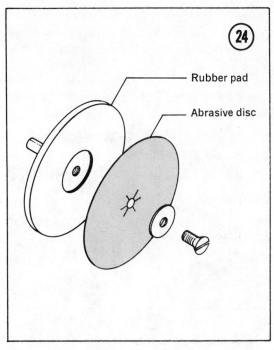

Rubber pad

Abrasive disc

a. Disc sander
b. Vibrating sander
c. Belt sander

A disc sander can be a special power tool made only for sanding (**Figure 23**) or it may be an attachment which can be chucked into an electric drill (**Figure 24**). In either case, an abrasive disc mounts over a hard rubber or foam plastic base.

Disc sanders are useful for paint removal or coarse sanding of wood which will be finished later with finer methods. Circular scoring is unavoidable and can be quite severe if you are careless. With care, scoring can be removed with an orbital sander or heavy hand sanding.

Vibrating sanders (see **Figure 25**) are used for finish work. Attachments are made to convert power drills to vibrating sanders, but they are not very good. Invest in a good quality vibrating sander as it is an often-used tool that will last for years. Some vibrating sanders can be set to produce an orbital motion or a back-and-forth motion. Standard size sandpaper or abrasive sheets can be cut with scissors to fit the sander.

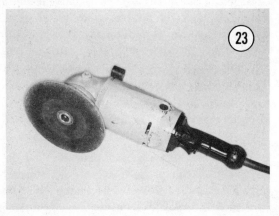

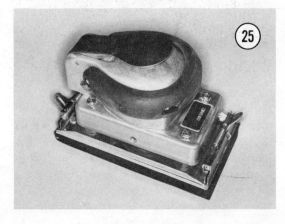

Belt sanders (see **Figure 26**) are used for very large expanses where heavy cutting is necessary. Special belts designed for the sander must be used. This sander must be held firmly and flatly or the belt edges can severely score the surfaces. Use it for rough sanding large areas, then finish with an orbital sander or hand sanding.

All of these sanders, plus very heavy duty industrial sanders, are available from rental centers for a modest fee. Because small, good quality disc and vibrating sanders are relatively inexpensive and so often used, it is well worth purchasing them. However, if you have a lot of rough sanding to do at one time, it will be more economical to rent a belt or industrial duty disc sander.

MECHANIC'S TIPS

Removing Frozen Nuts and Screws

When a fastener rusts and cannot be removed, several methods may be used to loosen it. First apply penetrating oil such as Liquid Wrench (available at any hardware store). Apply it liberally. Rap the fasteners several times with a small hammer; don't hit it hard enough to cause damage.

For frozen screws, apply oil as described, then insert a screwdriver in the slot and rap the top of the screwdriver with a hammer. This loosens the rust so the screw can be removed in the normal way. If the screw head is too chewed up to use a screwdriver, grip the head with Vise Grip pliers and twist the screw out.

For a frozen bolt or nut, apply penetrating oil, then rap on it with a hammer. Twist off with the proper size wrench. If the points are rounded off, grip with Vise Grip pliers as described for screws.

Stripped Threads

Occasionally, threads are stripped through carelessness or impact damage. Often the threads can be cleaned up by running a tap (for internal threads on nuts) or die (for external threads on bolts) through the threads. See **Figure 27**.

Broken Screw or Bolt

When the head breaks off a screw or bolt, several methods are available for removing the remaining portion.

If a large portion of the remainder projects out, try gripping it with Vise Grips. If the projecting portion is too small, try filing it to fit a wrench or cut a slot in it to fit a screwdriver. See **Figure 28**.

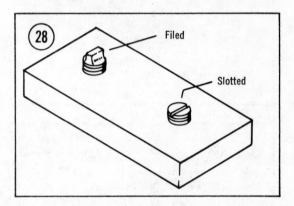

If the head breaks off flush, try using a screw extractor. To do this, center punch exact center of remaining portion of screw or bolt. Drill small hole into screw and tap extractor into the hole. Back screw out with a wrench on the extractor. See **Figures 29A and 29B**.

TOOLS FOR PAINTING AND REFINISHING

Nearly anyone with care, patience, and the proper tools can produce a professional paint job. This section helps you choose the tools you will need and explains their use.

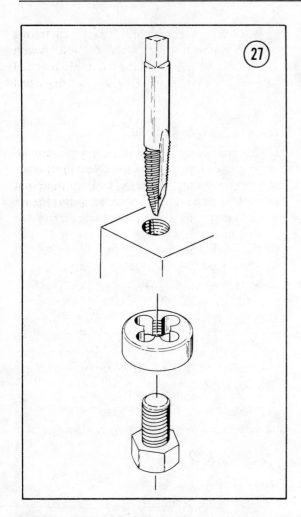

(27)

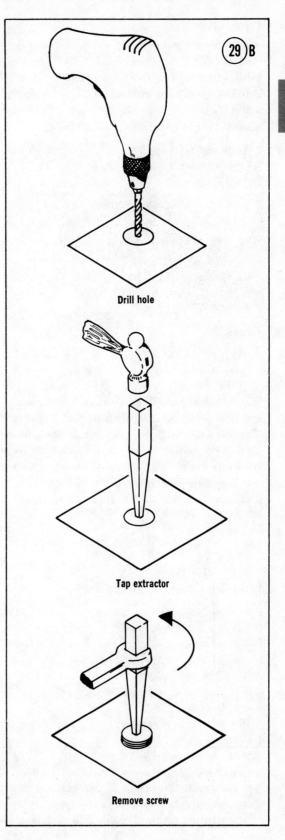

(29) B

Drill hole

Tap extractor

Remove screw

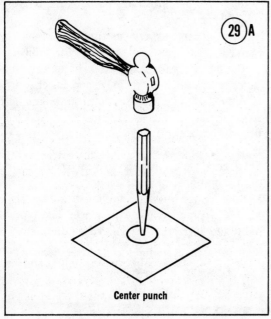

(29) A

Center punch

Paint Brushes

You must have good quality brushes to do a professional job. Poor quality brushes lose bristles and do not spread the finish smoothly. Brushes may have natural animal bristles or nylon filaments. A good brush has bristles which taper slightly from the butt to the tip.

Brushes are shaped for a number of specialized purposes. The following are most useful for boat use.

    a. 4 in. wall brush—bottom painting

    b. 3 in. wall brush—topsides, decks, etc.

    c. 1 in. oval sash brush—small areas, close quarters

    d. Badger bristle brush with full chisel point—varnish

Brush Care

By proper cleaning and storage, a good brush will last for many years.

If the same brush and paint will be used again the next day, hang the brush in a can containing 2 parts raw linseed oil and 1 part turpentine. The ferrule should be just above the level of the liquid and the tips of the bristles should be clear of the bottom. Drill a small hole through the brush and suspend it as shown in **Figure 30**.

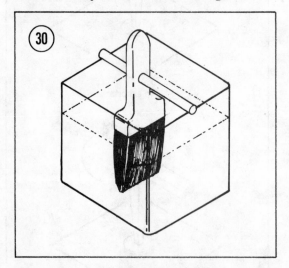

The next day, remove the brush and tap it gently against the inside of the can to remove excessive liquid. Wipe the brush carefully on a newspaper to remove the remaining liquid.

CAUTION
Do not slap the brush on a board or other surface to shake out liquid. This damages the bristles.

If a brush is to be stored or used for a different paint, the brush must be cleaned thoroughly. First wipe the brush on a newspaper to remove excess paint. Soak and clean brush in a solvent or thinner recommended on the paint label. Use turpentine or mineral spirits for oil paints or enamel. Use denatured alcohol for shellac products. Other special materials such as epoxy resin and vinyl resin require special solvents; read the manufacturer's label.

After cleaning with solvent, wash the brush thoroughly in soapy water. Wrap the clean brush in several thicknesses of newspaper and lay it flat for storage. Do not stand the brush on end.

Hardened paint is difficult to remove from a brush. Several brush cleaning liquids on the market will soften the paint so that it can be removed. A painter's comb or wire brush may also help. It is a tedious, messy job which can be avoided by proper cleaning in the first place.

Spray Guns

Spray painting usually does a quicker and better job than brushing, particularly on relatively large areas.

Spray equipment may use pressure or suction guns. Pressure systems are used for industrial work and rarely for boatyard or home use. Suction systems are less expensive and easier to use.

A suction system consists of a spray gun with refillable paint container, compressor, and connecting hose. See **Figure 31**. Compressors vary in size from very small portable ones to large fixed ones. They may be driven by an electric motor, gasoline, or diesel engine.

Finding the proper spraying technique is a matter of practice and experience. The type of paint and surface to be painted determine:

    a. How much thinner to add (see paint label)

    b. How fast to move gun

    c. How close to surface

    d. Proper nozzle tip

Practice on an old board to be sure the gun is properly adjusted and the paint sufficiently thinned.

After each use, empty the paint container and refill with a small quantity of thinner compatible with the paint type. Flush the gun out with the thinner several times. Disassemble the nozzle and container and clean all parts thoroughly with the thinner. Allow parts to dry before reassembly.

WARNING
Never spray anti-fouling paints containing mercury or arsenic compounds. The fine particles are easily inhaled by the worker and anyone nearby.

Paint Rollers

Paint rollers (**Figure 32**) are much faster than brushes for large flat areas. Different rollers are recommended for relatively flat paint such as metallic bottom paint and glossy surface paint. Rollers will not work in close where the surface turns sharply such as between the doghouse and deck, nor will a roller work well around fittings. In these cases, work as close as possible and tie in gaps with a small brush.

Rollers can be cleaned and reused. However, they soak up a great deal of paint and are very messy to clean. Fortunately, they are relatively inexpensive and can be discarded after use. The roll holders are expensive, though, and should be cleaned thoroughly in a suitable solvent.

Paint Bucket

Professional painters always use a paint bucket. Disposable paper ones are very inex-

pensive. See **Figure 33**. Pour paint from the can into a bucket so that the level is about 2-3 inches from the bottom. This keeps paint off the ferrule and handle if you dunk the brush in too far. A paint bucket also keeps the outside of the paint can free of messy drips caused by wiping the brush on the edge.

Paint Cup

A paint cup holds small quantities of paint or varnish conveniently and contains a wire to wipe your brush on. Buy a cup about the size of a large coffee mug at a department store. Epoxy or solder a large stiff wire across the cup as shown in **Figure 34**.

If the cup has a handle, you can hold it securely as shown in **Figure 35**. Each time you dip your brush, wipe it gently on the wire. This remove excess paint or varnish, which runs down into the cup instead of down the outside.

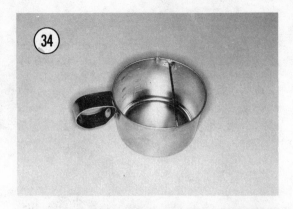

Tack Rag

A tack rag is necessary to remove all traces of dust, grit, and sanding particles from a surface just before painting. No ordinary cloth or painter's duster can clean the surface as well, and no professional finisher would do a job without using one.

Several manufacturers sell tack rags. Any marine chandlery or hardware store should have them. If you wish, you can make your own.

1. Soak a yard square piece of cheesecloth, linen, or cotton cloth in warm water.

2. Wring it out and pour on a small amount of turpentine.

3. Wring it out again and spread it over cardboard or newspaper.

4. Pour a trickle of spar varnish over the whole surface of the cloth. Don't overdo it—about a tablespoon is fine.

5. Wring the cloth out tightly and spread it out again.

6. Hang the cloth to dry for 30-45 minutes before use.

To use, fold the cloth into a square slightly larger than your hand. Lightly wipe the surface to be painted with the cloth. When finished, shake the rag out, roll it up, and store it in a tightly sealed jar. If the rag dries out, add a little water, turpentine, and varnish to restore it. Discard it when it becomes excessively dirty.

Wire Brushes

Wire brushes are invaluable for removing rust, scale, or loose paint. Brushes come in many sizes and shapes. The most useful are block type (see **Figure 36**) and narrow ones with a handle (**Figure 37**).

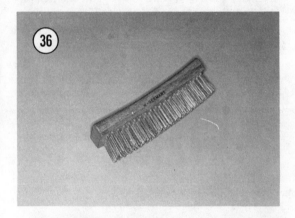

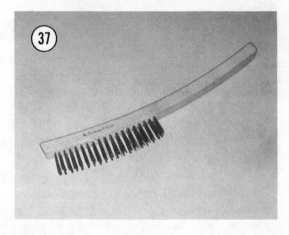

Scrapers

Scrapers can be very handy for removing old paint or varnish. **Figure 38** shows one in general use. Keep the scraper sharp with a fine tooth flat file. Don't change the angle of the cutting edge. Round off the corners to help prevent gouging the underlying material.

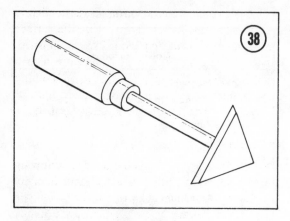

Abrasive Papers (Sandpaper)

Sanding is a very important part of refinishing, whether done to remove old finishes or to smooth between new finishes. Choosing the right sandpaper and sanding method is vital to a professional job.

A very large number of papers are available, but only a few are of interest here. The abrasive material can be garnet, aluminum oxide, or silicon carbide.

Four grades are required for most jobs.

a. Coarse—designated 1(50)
b. Medium—designated 1/0(80)
c. Fine—designated 3/0(120)
d. Very fine—designated 5/0(180) or 6/0(220)

Sandpaper on a paper base must be used dry. Others with a synthetic base and marked "wet or dry" or "waterproof" can be used either wet or dry. Wet sanding enameled or varnished surfaces produces a very fine finish. Soak the sandpaper in water before using and keep it wet while in use. Wipe the sanded surface with a wet cloth or sponge, then wipe with a dry lint-free cloth.

Bronze Wool

Bronze wool comes in many grades from coarse to very fine. Use it as you would sandpaper to remove old finishes.

CAUTION
Do not use steel wool for marine work. Steel wool leaves small shreds of steel imbedded in the surface which rust and discolor the final finish. Use only bronze wool.

Torches

A blow torch or propane torch can be useful for removing large areas of paint. The heat from the torch softens the paint so that it can be scraped away easily. Do not use on section of hull near the fuel tank(s).

WARNING
Be sure to keep a fire extinguisher nearby when using a torch.

When you set the torch down, make sure the flame is not directed toward anything that could burn.

Face Mask

Dust from sanding of spray painting can irritate mucous membranes. Always wear a face mask, which can be purchased at any drugstore or paint supply store. See **Figure 39**. A mask is particularly important when sanding bottom paints which contain mercury, arsenic, or organotin (TBTO) compounds. Also dangerous are primers or other compounds containing lead or zinc chromate pigments.

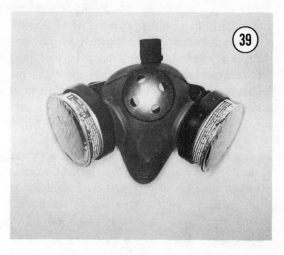

CORROSION

Metals in marine use are subjected to relatively corrosive conditions. Corroding metals either wear away or change chemically—usually for the worse. An understanding of how corrosion occurs can help you select fasteners and fittings of the right metal to minimize damage from corrosion.

There are 2 main corrosive processes in a marine environment:

a. Atmospheric

b. Galvanic

Of the 2, galvanic corrosion can occur faster and more destructively than atmospheric, but is far less understood by many.

Atmospheric corrosion occurs because corrosive elements such as oxygen, carbon dioxide, sulphur compounds, and chlorine compounds are present in the air. When they come in contact with a wet metal surface on a boat, they etch or corrode the metal.

Galvanic corrosion is a simple process, but many boat owners don't really understand it. It is the same electrical process that occurs in your batteries.

Every metal has a specific electrical potential; some higher, some lower. The galvanic series shown in **Table 2** is simply a ranking of metals from those of highest potential to those of lowest potential. Various names are used to describe metals with the highest potential such as least noble, active, and anodic. Metals of lower potential are said to be noble, passive, and cathodic.

When 2 metals are put together in the presence of an electrolyte, an electrical current flows from the most anodic to the most cathodic metal. The most anodic metal corrodes, while the most cathodic metal is actually protected. This is precisely what happens in your batteries—which are nothing more than 2 metals (lead and zinc) immersed in an electrolyte (sulphuric acid and water). The same "battery" is formed when a stainless steel fastener is used on an aluminum hull soaked by a salt water electrolyte. An electric current flows from the aluminum hull to the stainless steel fastener.

The magnitude of the electric current, and therefore, the degree of corrosion, depends on several factors.

a. Distance of metals in galvanic series

b. Strength of electrolyte

c. Relative sizes of the 2 metals

The difference of potential between 2 metals close together in the galvanic series will be small.

Table 2   GALVANIC SERIES

ANODIC (less noble, corrodes)
Magnesium
Magnesium alloys
Zinc
Aluminum 1100
Cadmium
Aluminum 2024-T4
Steel or iron
Cast iron
Chromium iron (active)
Ni-resist
Type 304 stainless (active)
Type 316 stainless (active)
Lead tin solders
Lead
Tin
Nickel (active)
Inconel
Brasses
Copper
Bronzes
Copper-nickel alloys
Monel
Silver solder
Nickel (passive)
Inconel (passive)
Chromium-iron (passive)
Type 304 stainless (passive)
Type 316 stainless (passive)
Silver
Titanium
Graphite
Gold
Platinum
CATHODIC (most noble, protected)

The current flow generated will be small and corrosion will be light. The farther apart the metals are in the series, the larger the difference of potential and the heavier the corrosion.

Electrolyte strength also affects corrosion. Fresh water is a relatively poor electrolyte. Corrosion will be lighter than that occurring between the same 2 metals in salt water, an excellent electrolyte.

The relative size of the 2 different metals affects the amount of corrosion. Corrosion can be quite high when bronze and steel are together in an electrolyte such as salt water. Suppose small steel fasteners are used to join bronze parts and the assembly is submerged in salt water. The steel fasteners will rapidly corrode and the parts can separate. Now suppose small bronze fasteners are used to join steel plates. Corrosion of the steel will be quite small, even negligible, around the bronze fasteners. In fact, the bronze fasteners will receive cathodic protection. For this reason, fasteners should be selected that are equal or lower in potential in the galvanic series than the metal being joined.

Always keep in mind that anti-fouling bottom paints often contain metallic substances. The particular element involved can react with the hull or nearby fittings up or down Table 2 as the case may be. Severe damage can be done by carelessly using the "wrong" type of bottom paint!

Preventing Atmospheric Corrosion

There are some precautions that may be taken against atmospheric corrosion. First, select materials with high resistance to the corrosive atmosphere. Materials such as monel, stainless steel, and bronze are good examples. Next, keep salt from accumulating on the metal. A hose-down after each sail will help considerably.

Preventing Galvanic Corrosion

There are a number of rules to follow when selecting materials to prevent galvanic corrosion.
1. Whenever possible, join metal parts with fasteners made of the same material.
2. Separate dissimilar metals with an insulating (dielectric) material such as paint, phenolic, bakelite, plastic, etc.

3. Make certain the smallest material is the most cathodic.

Galvanic corrosion can be used to protect parts. Magnesium, zinc, and aluminum are most anodic. When connected to any other metal, they become the anode. Therefore, they corrode, sacrificially saving the other metal part.

FASTENER MATERIALS

Boat fasteners are subjected to high stress and corrosive conditions. Therefore, they must be carefully chosen. Most fasteners are metal, but in each case, the right metal must be selected if they are to last in a salt atmosphere.

Many materials are suitable for marine use. Several are discussed in detail in the following sections. In general, boat builders prefer these materials in the following order.

a. Monel
b. T-316 stainless steel
c. Silicon bronze
d. 18-8 stainless steel
e. Chrome-plated brass
f. Naval bronze
g. Brass
h. Aluminum

Bronze and Brass

Bronze and brass are very common materials for marine hardware because of their resistance to rust. Both materials are alloys of copper, tin, and zinc; only the proportions change. Bronze has little or no zinc, while brass has little or no tin. Of the 2, bronze alloys are the most important.

Three bronze alloys are commonly used:

a. Phosphor bronze
b. Naval bronze
c. Silicon bronze

Phosphor bronze is composed of copper, tin, and a small amount of phosphorus. Naval bronze is essentially brass (copper-zinc) to which a small quantity of antimony has been added. Silicon bronze is a general name applied to several copper-silicon alloys. All have good corrosion resistant properties; silicon bronze has the highest strength.

Brass is occasionally used in marine work. However, salt water causes brittleness and deterioration. Brass should not be used where stress is likely.

Copper

Copper is very soft and easily worked. Except as an alloy (bronze, brass), its marine use is limited primarily to copper sheathing the bottoms of wood hulls and as nails for small planked boats.

Monel

Monel, an alloy of about ⅔ nickel and ⅓ copper, is probably the best material available for marine fasteners. It has excellent strength and is extremely corrosion resistant. It is also comparatively expensive. Practically any common marine fastener is available in monel. Monel is usually non-magnetic. However, under some cold-working manufacturing processes, it can develop some magnetic properties.

Stainless Steel

Stainless steel has become increasingly more common as a marine fastener material. Stainless steel alloy 18-8 is usually stronger and more resistant to corrosion than naval bronze. Even more corrosion resistant is T-316 stainless steel, formed by adding 2-3% molybdenum to 18-8 stainless steel.

Titanium

Some fasteners are available made of titanium. This exotic and very expensive metal has excellent corrosion resistance to salt water. Most important, though, it has a very high strength-to-weight ratio, making it useful for spars and hardware on racing sailboats.

Aluminum

Aluminum fasteners are used almost exclusively for jointing aluminum parts such as riveting aluminum hulls. They are also used to join aluminum parts to wood. Aluminum is far too

high (anodic) in the galvanic series, compared to other common marine materials, to be used without careful attention to protecting it from galvanic corrosion.

FASTENER TYPES

In order to better understand and select basic hand tools, a knowledge of various fasteners is important. This knowledge will also aid in selecting replacements when fasteners are damaged or corroded beyond use.

Threads

Nuts, bolts, and screws are manufactured in a wide range of thread patterns. To join a nut and bolt, it is necessary that the diameter of the bolt and the diameter of the hole in the nut be the same. It is equally important that the threads on both be properly matched.

The best way to ensure that threads on 2 fasteners are compatible is to turn the nut on the bolt with fingers only. If much force is required, check the thread condition on both fasteners. If thread condition is good, but the fasteners jam, the threads are not compatible. Take the fasteners to a hardware store or chandlery for proper mates.

Three important specifications describe every thread:

a. Diameter

b. Threads-per-inch

c. Thread pattern

Figure 40 shows the first 2 specifications. Thread pattern is more subtle. Three thread patterns are commonly used: coarse (UNC—Unified National Coarse), fine (UNF—Unified National Fine), and metric (usually used on European and Asian products).

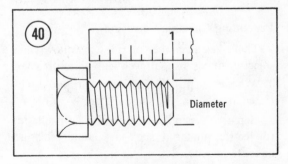
Diameter

Machine Screws

There are many different types of machine screws. **Figure 41** shows a number of screw heads requiring different types of turning tools. Heads are also designed to protrude above the metal (round) or to be slightly recessed in the metal (flat).

When replacing a damaged screw, take it to a hardware store or chandlery. Match the head type, diameter, and threads exactly. In addition, match the type of metal used. For example, if the old screw is bronze, the new one must also be bronze to resist corrosion and rust.

Bolts

Commonly called bolts, the technical name for these fasteners is cap screws. They are normally specified by diameter, threads-per-inch (tpi), and length, e.g., ¼-20 x 1 specifies a bolt ¼ in. diameter with 20 tpi 1 in. long. The measurement across 2 flats on the head indicates the proper wrench size to be used.

When replacing damaged bolts, follow same advice given above for machine screws.

Wood Screws

Wood screws are similar in construction to tapping screws. Wood screws usually have a shallower thread and greater pitch (fewer threads/inch) than tapping screws, however. As discussed below, tapping screws are replacing wood screws in many applications.

Figure 42 shows the parts of a wood screw. When choosing a wood screw, 3 factors should be considered. First, the thickness of the material dictates the length of the screw. The kind of material and strength of the joint required determine the diameter of the screw. Finally, the surface finish appearance determines the screw head type.

Wood screws are normally specified by shank diameter and length. Shank diameters are not in inches; they are coded from No. 0 (about 1/16 in.) to No. 30 (about ½ in.). A No. 10-¾ wood screw has a No. 10 shank and a ¾ in. length.

Sheet Metal (Tapping) Screws

Popularly called sheet metal screws, they are technically tapping screws. See **Figure 43**. They form threads in the materials they join. Their

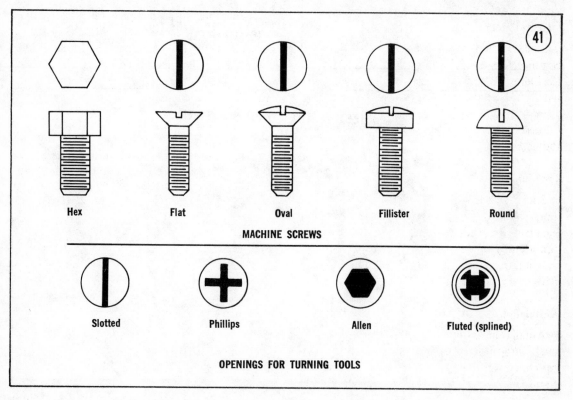

Hex   Flat   Oval   Fillister   Round

MACHINE SCREWS

Slotted   Phillips   Allen   Fluted (splined)

OPENINGS FOR TURNING TOOLS

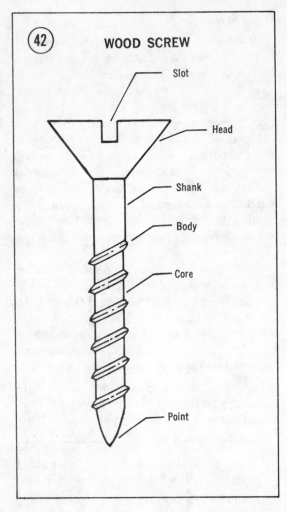

WOOD SCREW

- Slot
- Head
- Shank
- Body
- Core
- Point

popular name derives from their use in joining light sheet metal. However, in nearly every place a wood screw is used, a tapping screw is superior. Tapping screws are usually stronger and easier to drive than wood screws.

Self-tapping screw sizes are specified in the same way as wood screws.

Nuts

Nuts are manufactured in a variety of types and sizes. Most nuts are hexagonal (six-sided) and fit on bolts, screws, and studs with the same diameter and threads-per-inch.

Figure 44 shows several commonly used nuts. The common nut in (A) is normally used with a lockwasher. The nut in (B) has a nylon insert which prevents it from loosening and does not require a locknut. To indicate the size of a nut, manufacturers specify the diameter of the opening and the threads-per-inch (tpi), e.g., ¼-20 indicates a ¼ in. opening and 20 tpi. In addition, the measurement across 2 flats on the nut indicates the proper wrench size to be used.

Figure 44 (C) shows a wing nut. These are designed for fast removal by hand without special tools.

When replacing a damaged nut, take it to a hardware store or chandlery. Match the type, diameter, and threads exactly. In addition, match the type of metal used.

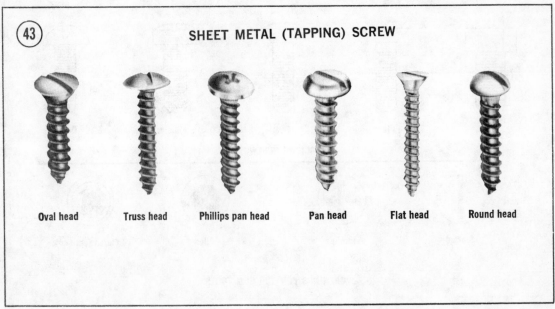

SHEET METAL (TAPPING) SCREW

Oval head   Truss head   Phillips pan head   Pan head   Flat head   Round head

Common nut   Self-locking nut   Wing nut

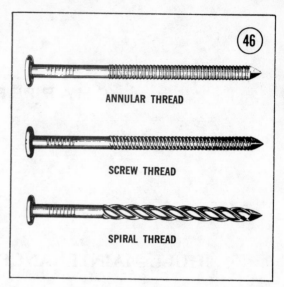

ANNULAR THREAD

SCREW THREAD

SPIRAL THREAD

Washers

There are 2 major types of washers—flat washers and lockwashers. Flat washers are simple discs with a hole to fit a screw or bolt. Lockwashers are designed to prevent a fastener from working loose due to vibration, expansion, and contraction. **Figure 45** shows several washers. Note that flat washers are often used between a lockwasher and a fastener to act as a smooth bearing surface. This permits the fastener to be turned easily with a tool.

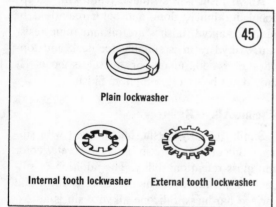

Plain lockwasher

Internal tooth lockwasher   External tooth lockwasher

Threaded Nails

Several threaded nail designs are available. **Figure 46** shows several representative types. These nails are available in monel, 18-8 and T-316 stainless steel, silicon bronze, 80-20 brass, commercial bronze, and copper.

Advantages of threaded nails are numerous. They are less costly than screws, but stronger and easier to drive. They have superior resistance to backing out. In fact, it is impossible to remove one without damaging the wood.

An assortment of these nails should be stowed aboard for emergency repairs.

Rivets

Most rivets require special, expensive equipment to set and are of little use to boat owners. There is one exception. Aluminum pop rivets (see **Figure 47**) can be installed with a very inexpensive handgun.

Many repairs can be made aboard boats with pop rivets. However, keep in mind that aluminum is not very successful as a fastening material except when joining aluminum parts. Aluminum is too anodic in the galvanic series and corrodes rapidly when in contact with nearly any other marine material.

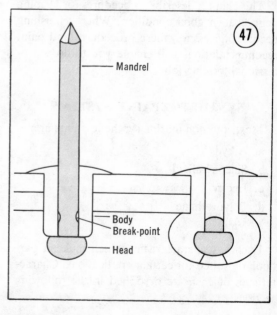

Mandrel

Body
Break-point
Head

CHAPTER THREE

HULL MAINTENANCE AND REFINISHING

There is no such thing as a maintenance-free boat. All boats, whether wood, metal or fiberglass, require periodic attention to keep them beautiful and sound.

When a boat finish is new, simple cleaning and minor touch ups will keep the finish looking good for quite some time. Eventually, though, any exterior finish, including fiberglass gel-coat, will deteriorate to a point where painting will become necessary.

This chapter describes procedures for keeping your boat in good condition. When refinishing becomes necessary, these procedures and paint recommendations will enable you to do a professional looking job.

SYNTHETIC PAINT SYSTEMS

Most common marine synthetic paints are:

a. Alkyd
b. Silicone alkyd
c. Epoxy
d. Polyurethane
e. Vinyl

Each has characteristics which make it particularly suited for certain applications. Characteristics of each are described in the following sections.

Alkyd Resin

Alkyd resin is a synthetic paint with exceptional durability, gloss, and color retention. In addition, alkyd finishes are oil and fume resistant. Alkyd resin is suitable for deck and topsides of wood, metal, or fiberglass boats. It should not be used as a bottom finish.

Silicone Alkyd Resin

Similar to alkyd resin, but fortified with silicone. Silicone alkyd resin has even greater color and gloss retention ability. The addition of silicone also improves moisture resistance and surface hardness. Silicone alkyd resin is an excellent topside and deck finish, but should not be used as a bottom finish.

Epoxy Resin

Epoxy resin is the ultimate marine finish. It has superior surface hardness, abrasion resistance, chemical resistance, and adhesion, as well as long life. As a deck and topside finish, it is unequalled. Epoxy resin also makes an excellent non-antifouling finish for trailerable or beachable boats which are subjected to abrasion.

Epoxy resin can be applied to wood, metal, or fiberglass. Bare wood or metal must be primed first. Use primer specified on label to be certain it is compatible; if not, epoxy may not bond properly. Bare fiberglass can be primed or not. If it is not primed, the epoxy resin will form a chemical as well as mechanical bond with the fiberglass resin.

Epoxy resin can be applied directly over most existing finishes provided the old finish has been on at least 6 months. If in doubt, paint a small test area first.

To insure a good bond, the original finish must be sanded smooth. Epoxy resin will not adhere to vinyl, styrene, or anti-fouling paints; remove these finishes completely first. Epoxy resin cannot be used over rubber, neoprene (synthetic rubber), or vinyl fabrics.

Epoxy paints are normally 2-part systems. The "A" curing agent must be mixed with the "B" pigmented resin exactly as described by the manufacturer. After mixing, the paint has a pot life of 24-48 hours; that is, it must be used in that period or it will harden in the container. Unmixed, epoxy has a nearly unlimited shelf life.

Epoxy paint flows and levels very well. It can be brushed, rolled, or sprayed on. Use natural bristle brushes as the resin can attack synthetic bristles (nylon, etc.). If you spray it on, thin it as directed by the manufacturer.

CAUTION
Use a thinner recommended by the manufacturer.

Epoxy paints are sensitive to temperature and humidity. The temperature should be above 70°F and the humidity below 90%. Most epoxy will cure tack-free in a few hours under these conditions. Curing is faster with higher temperatures. Below 70°F, curing can be very slow. Infra-red lights can be used to speed curing. Full curing may take several days.

Polyurethane Paint

Polyurethane paints produce a durable, high gloss finish. Unlike epoxy paints, polyurethane is non-toxic and requires no catalyst to accelerate curing. Polyurethanes dry by reaction between ingredients and absorption of moisture. In fact, the higher the relative humidity, the faster polyurethane dries tack-free. In addition, the paint has a very long pot life.

Polyurethanes are as good as epoxy at resisting chemical attack. Polyurethane is better than epoxy at resisting abrasion and wear. Many polyurethanes contain ultraviolet screening chemicals to minimize sun deterioration.

Vinyl Paints

Vinyl paints made from poly-vinyl-chloride (PVC) make excellent bottom paints. The finish is hard and slick for maximum boat speed. Vinyl paints make superior anti-fouling finishes when they contain tri-butyl-tin-fluoride (TBTF) or tri-butyl-tin-oxide (TBTO). Since these are organic toxicants, they do not corrode steel and aluminum as much as cuprous oxide. Also, since TBTO and TBTF are colorless, the paint may be tinted any color desired. When using vinyl paint, you must also use a special thinner or solvent.

Varnishes

Varnishes may be:

a. Alkyd resin
b. Phenolic resin
c. Polyurethane resin

Major characteristics of these finishes were described earlier. This section covers special considerations when choosing one of these resins as a clear varnish for brightwork.

Unmodified alkyd resin produces a very pale clear finish. It will not stain or yellow with age as phenolic resin will. Alkyd resin also has superior gloss retention and durability. However, alkyd resin does not have the fullness and lusterous depth of other varnishes. This resin is used where its pale color and non-yellowing characteristics are important such as over blonde or bleached mahogany.

Phenolic resin yields a rich fullness and deep luster to brightwork. This resin darkens and yellows on drying. It has excellent durability and may have ultraviolet screening chemicals in it to minimize sun deterioration. Phenolic resin dries moderately hard and has fair chemical resistance. Phenolic resin is chosen mainly for its durability and appearance.

Polyurethane resin is the best choice for most brightwork. Polyurethane is paler than phenolic resin and shows less age discoloration. When dry, it is unexcelled for hardness and resistance to abrasion. It is also highly resistant to chemical contaminants. Unlike other varnishes, polyurethane can be applied in heavy coats under hot summer sun; other varnishes would wrinkle badly. Polyurethane is the most durable varnish available. It is used wherever a hard, durable, glossy finish is desired. Its abrasion resistance makes it the best choice for decks and cockpits.

Gel-Coat Repair Kits

Gel-coat repairs are usually left to professionals. There are a number of reasons for this, but the main one has been unavailability of gel-coat in small quantities. At least 2 kits are currently offered which make do-it-yourself gel-coat repairs possible.

Seymour, Incorporated, Sycamore, Illinois 60178, markets Spray-Gel. Spray-Gel is a 2-component polyester which duplicates the original finish. Four colors are available to match nearly all shades of white used by most manufacturers. Seymour provides a complete kit (see **Figure 1**), including spray can of tinted polyester, hardener, transfer pump to add hardener to spray can, wet and dry sandpaper, and full instructions. This kit will not fill deep scratches; it is a finish spray only.

Another touch-up kit is offered by Fiberglass Evercoat Company, Cincinnati, Ohio 45242, and Orange, California 92668. This kit contains a color-matched Gel-Stick, plastic spatula, and nylon polishing cloth. See **Figure 2**. The Gel-Stick comes in a dozen colors covering more than 150 manufacturers listed on the back of the package. This product will fill in deep scratches. Prepare the area as described under *Repairing Gel-coat Damage,* Steps 1-4, then follow the simple instructions on the package.

More traditional methods of gel-coat repair are described later.

Thinners, Reducers, and Solvents

Thinners, reducers, and solvents are formulated to work only with a specific paint system. Before adding these chemicals to any paint or marine compound, read the labels carefully to be sure they are compatible.

There are several classes of thinners, reducers, and solvents.

    a. Epoxy

    b. Vinyl

    c. General paint

    d. Marine compound reducer

    e. Fungicidal compound thinner

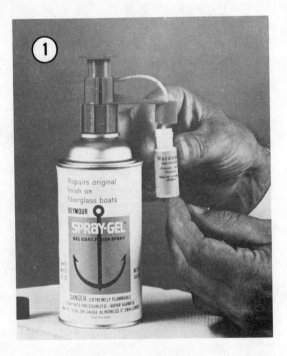

Wood Preservatives

Wood is susceptible to decay caused by mold, fungi, and other microscopic plants. These organisms feed on wood and proliferate when moisture and temperature conditions are right. Though called "wet rot" or "dry rot," the 2 are essentially the same. There is really no such thing as "dry rot" — these organisms need moisture.

Some measures can be taken to minimize rot (described later), but fungicides are the only really effective way to combat decay.

Most fungicides contain either TBTO (tri-butyl-tin-oxide), penta chlorophenol, or copper-napthanate dispersed in a penetrating petroleum solvent. Copper fungicides are green. They can be painted over, although the green may bleed through the first coat. Penta chlorophenol and TBTO fungicides are clear. They are useful for brightwork which will be varnished.

Mixing Paint

Everyone assumes there is nothing special about mixing paint. But most complaints that a paint doesn't cover or dries to different shades stem from improper mixing.

Here is the best way.

1. Pour off the top ⅓ of the paint into another clean can.

2. Stir the remaining paint with a wide paddle.

> NOTE: *If there is any hard settled material on the bottom break it up and blend it in completely.*

3. Continue stirring and gradually add paint that was poured off.

4. When paint is uniform, pour it back and forth between 2 containers.

5. Stir frequently during use.

MAINTAINING WOOD

Wood has been the traditional hull material for thousands of years. Its strength, durability, workability, and beauty are hard to beat even with modern materials. But wood boats have suffered recently in the marketplace. Modern materials are believed to be nearly maintenance free, while wood is believed to be a maintenance

headache. This is simply not true. Some boat-yard operators have estimated that a wood boat requires only about 30% more maintenance than a fiberglass boat.

This section describes a comprehensive inspection procedure which should be done every 2-3 months. In addition, there are instructions for caulking and painting wood hulls and topsides.

Cleaning

As often as necessary, wash the boat with water and mild detergent. Use a sponge or bristle brush to scrub off dirt. Rinse thoroughly with fresh water.

Wood Rot

A large variety of fungal organisms feed on wood. They break down the cellular structure of the wood by eating the cellulose. As structural parts deteriorate, fastenings no longer hold and serious and irreversible damage can occur.

Rot occurs where fresh water accumulates and stands for some time. Salt water inhibits fungus and does not cause fungicidal rot. Fresh water usually comes from condensation, rain water, or leakage from the fresh water system.

Good ventilation and a dry environment are the best ways to prevent rot. There should be some circulation through the entire hull, including hanging lockers and heads with doors. Weather permitting, open all hatches, ports, and cowl ventilators to promote circulation. Keep a light bulb or special damp-chaser heating element on at all times when the boat is dockside to keep air as dry as possible. Fungi cannot survive in a dry, well-ventilated hull.

While adequate ventilation is a good preventive, it is not fool-proof. Every 2-3 months, you should thoroughly inspect the entire hull for signs of rot. Use a flashlight to inspect hard-to-reach areas. Test suspected areas with a pick to make sure that the wood is firm and not punky or soft. Tap wood with a hammer; rotted wood has a dull sound compared to solid wood.

If you find any rot, ascertain the reason. Look for leaks where rain water could enter or condensation collect. Correct problem immediately.

Infected wood should be treated when found. If damage is not extensive, carefully cut away rot with a knife or sharp chisel. Saturate exposed good wood with fungicidal wood preservative. If damage is extensive, the affected wood member should be replaced.

Inspection

Wood boats are susceptible to structural damage caused by a wide variety of marine plant and animal life. Every 2-3 months, the entire boat should be inspected to determine what damage, if any, these organisms have caused.

1. When the boat is hauled, go over the entire exterior very thoroughly. Check planking to be sure fastenings are sound and holding. Corroding fastenings may bleed rust around the fastened area. In addition, rust accumulation may push out the wood plug (bung) covering the fastener so that it protrudes slightly from the planking. If this occurs, the fastener must be replaced or a new fastener installed alongside the old.

2. Inspect all caulked seams for signs of leakage. Recaulk if necessary.

3. Inspect backbone assembly where possible. Check particularly all joints between individual sections of the assembly; the fastenings can work loose.

4. Check tightness of keel bolts at least once a year.

5. Check all floor timbers for rot and looseness.

6. Make sure all limber holes in the bilge are clean and unobstructed. If plugged with debris, rot-inducing water can accumulate in the bilge.

7. Inspect any internal ballast. Internal pigs accumulate a tremendous amount of dirt and grime which promotes fungi growth. If really filthy, remove internal ballast and clean bilge thoroughly. Iron pigs should be sandblasted and dipped in epoxy paint before reinstalling the pigs.

Recaulking

1. Clean out old brittle caulking compound with a scraper.

2. Wire brush the seams to remove remaining compound particles.

3a. If old cotton is clean, tight, and not rotten, leave it in place and go to Step 8.

3b. If old cotton is unsatisfactory, remove it. Make a tool from a piece of large stiff wire to hook the cotton and pull it out.

4. Wire brush the seams to clean them out.

5. Make up ropes from strands of caulking cotton. To do this, lay out 2 strands of cotton and roll them tightly together between your hands. Wind the resulting rope into a ball. Make up similar ropes with 3 or more strands to fit the wider seams.

6. Select a cotton rope that will fill the seam about ⅓ when tightly compacted with a caulking iron. Use a single strand for very narrow seams.

7. Pound cotton tightly into seam with caulking iron and light mallet blows. Do not force cotton completely through hull.

8. Fill seams with elastomeric sealant. Use a putty knife or caulking gun. Make sure no bubbles are trapped.

> NOTE: *Make sure the sealant you choose can be painted over. Polysulfide sealants can be painted, but not all silicone sealants can. Read the manufacturer's label; if it does not specifically state that it can be painted over, don't use it.*

9. When cured, cut the sealant flush with the planking, using a single edge razor blade.

Painting Wood Hulls

Though wood is durable and strong, it must be properly maintained to retain these qualities. A well-painted surface is absolutely essential to protect the wood from weathering. In addition, fungicidal preservatives are available to minimize rot due to living organisms. The following sections describe methods and materials necessary to keep your wood in top condition.

Surface Preparation (Bare Wood)

Bare bottomsides are prepared as follows.

1. Sand to remove surface irregularities.

2a. If anti-fouling paint will be used, no primers, sealers, undercoats, or preservatives should be used on the bottom.

2b. If enamel or racing bronze will be used, apply a wood sealer and let dry overnight.

3. Lightly sand sealer to remove grain fibers that may have raised.

Bare topsides require a slightly different treatment.

1. Sand entire surface to remove surface irregularities.

2. Apply a clear wood sealer and let it dry overnight.

3. Lightly sand sealer to remove grain fibers that may have raised.

4. Apply 1 or 2 coats of undercoat. Let each coat dry overnight and sand lightly between coats with 220 grit paper.

5. After drying overnight, sand final undercoat with 220 grit paper.

Surface Preparation (Previously Painted)

Previously painted surfaces require little preparation if the old paint is in good condition and free of blisters, peeling, or alligatoring.

1. Wash it thoroughly with TSP (tri sodium phosphate) to remove all grease and salt. Rinse with fresh water.

2. Scrape off all marine growth.

3. Sand with 120-220 grit paper.

Bottom Painting (Anti-fouling Protection)

Anti-fouling protection is particularly important on wood hulls. While metal and fiberglass hulls become slow and unsightly from marine growth, wood hulls will sustain structural damage. The different types of anti-fouling paint are described earlier in this chapter.

New coats of anti-fouling paint can be applied over old coats. There is no need to remove old coats if they are not cracked or peeling. Clean the bottom thoroughly, sand with medium grit sandpaper and apply 2 new coats.

CAUTION
The new paint must be the same as, or compatible with, the old coats. If you are not sure, remove all old coats.

Painting an uncoated, bare bottom is easy. Do not use primers, undercoats, or preservatives which will prevent the anti-fouling paint from penetrating the wood. Also, do not use any thinner unless the label clearly states to do so. Apply 2-3 coats to bare wood with a brush or roller. Read label on can to determine proper drying time between coats and drying time (if any) before launching.

Bottom Painting (Hard Enamel)

Many small boats and some one-design racing boats are in the water only when underway. Most of the time, they are on a trailer. These boats do not require anti-fouling protection. Instead, they need a hard scratch resistant surface which will not be damaged during launching and recovery.

Several special bottom coatings are manufactured. Most are based on polyurethane or epoxy. Follow directions on maker's label.

CAUTION
Topside enamels are not recommended for underwater use.

Some of these products, such as epoxy racing bronze, must be applied over bare wood. Most others require that the bare wood be sealed first. Use the sealer recommended on the paint label.

Topside Painting

A top quality, topside finish is possible only when the surface has been carefully prepared. This is described thoroughly in an earlier section.

Nearly any quality deck or topside paint can be applied to wood. Characteristics of different paint systems are described fully at the beginning of this chapter.

Polyurethane and epoxy finishes may be too slippery for decks where sure footing is essential. Add a small amount of non-skid agent to the paint before application. Either coat the entire deck with this specially prepared paint or mask off selected areas for treatment.

MAINTAINING ALUMINUM

Aluminum alloy is becoming increasingly popular as a boat building material. Formerly restricted to small dinghys and runabouts, aluminum alloy is used increasingly for larger sailboats and power cruisers. Aluminum alloys are also popular for engine parts, drive units, spars, and deck fittings.

Though noted for great strength and durability, aluminum must be protected from corrosive salt water. A number of methods are possible. Anodizing and anodizing processes alter the chemical structure of the surface aluminum to make it more resistant to corrosion. This works satisfactorily against atmospheric corrosion, but not against direct salt spray which pits the surface with white deposits. The best protection for aluminum alloys is a quality marine finish. Epoxy and polyurethane are particularly good for spars which take a lot of punishment from slapping halyards and sails. The finest finish of all is epoxy or polyurethane over an already anodized surface.

This section describes maintenance and painting procedures for all aluminum surfaces including hulls, decks, spars, and fittings.

Cleaning and Preventive Maintenance

As often as necessary, wash the boat with water and mild detergent. Use a sponge or bristle brush to scrub dirt off. Rinse thoroughly with fresh water.

Inspect surface for cracks. Repair cracks in sheet aluminum as described later. Touch up any surface damage to the paint finish.

Painting Aluminum

Aluminum should be painted for maximum protection. The surface must be carefully prepared or the paint will not adhere well. Follow procedures in the next sections exactly to obtain best results.

Repairing Dents and Scratches

Aluminum boats are susceptible to scratches and dents above and below the waterline.

Small dents in sheet aluminum can be knocked out with a block of wood and a rubber hammer. Place the block behind the surface as shown in **Figure 3**. Hammer around the edges of the dent, gradually working toward the center. If both sides of the dent are not accessible, filling with epoxy putty is the only answer.

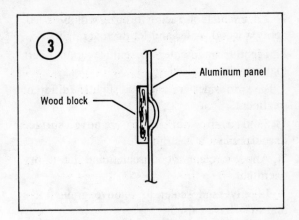

Several epoxy putties are on the market. Typical are Regatta Epoxydur Fairing Compound or Dolfinite Eputty. These products can be trowelled on and sanded or filed after hardening. When the surface is smooth, paint over it as you would aluminum.

Some epoxy putty can be applied over aluminum after washing with a non-petroleum solvent such as Tolinol or lacquer thinner. Others should be applied after the wash primer. Read the manufacturer's label.

Patching Aluminum

Aluminum is simple to patch if the damage is not too extensive. Very small holes can be filled with epoxy putty. Putty a scrap of aluminum behind the hole to keep the putty in place. See **Figure 4**. Fill in the hole and sand flush when cured. Small holes can also be patched by drilling or reaming the hole around and inserting an appropriate size rivet.

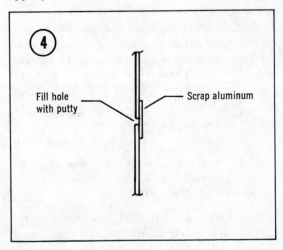

Larger holes are patched more elaborately.

1. Cut a patch from scrap aluminum slightly larger than the damaged area.

2. Shape it to any hull curves by holding it in place and hammering it to fit with a rubber mallet.

3. File edges of hole so that no burrs or raised areas prevent a flush fit.

4. Drill stopping holes at ends of cracks to prevent them from spreading. See **Figure 5**.

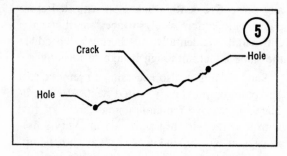

5. Place patch in position, preferably on the inside of the hull.

6. Drill rivet holes every ½-¾ in. around patch and through hull.

7. Spread caulking compound such as life-caulk or other silicone sealant around edges of patch.

8. Rivet patch to hull.

9. If patch is on inside, fill in exposed edges of hull with epoxy putty and fair in with surrounding hull.

Surface Preparation and Painting (Bare Metal)

1. Wash surface thoroughly with clean solvent or brush cleaner to remove grease and oil.

2. Sand lightly with medium grit emery cloth or 100 grit paper to roughen surface.

> NOTE: *If sand blasting equipment is available, use 80 mesh white silica sand.*

3. Clean surface with a clean rag or tack cloth.

CAUTION
Do not wipe with thinner, solvent or gasoline.

4. Apply 1 coat of "wash primer." Do not try to cover the metal completely.

5. Apply 2 coats of anti-corrosive zinc chromate primer to the topsides and 4 coats to the bottomsides.

6. Apply 1-2 finish coats. On bottomsides, use vinyl-based TBTO bottom paint. Above waterline, use any quality topside paint.

Some manufacturers specify using ordinary metallic anti-fouling paints on the bottom. This is possible if several thick barrier coats protect the metal from the anti-fouling paint. If unprotected, galvanic action between the anti-fouling paint metal and the hull will quickly corrode the hull.

Using metallic anti-fouling paints for metal hulls is not good practice. Everytime the hull is scratched, the barrier coats are removed and no longer protect the scratched area. To prevent damage, the hull must be hauled several times a season for touch-ups. The use of TBTO paint eliminates the problem, as it cannot react with bare aluminum to produce corrosion.

Surface Preparation and Painting (Painted Surface)

If old paint is firm, not peeling and otherwise in good condition, little preparation is required.

1. Wash surface thoroughly with TSP (tri sodium phosphate) to remove grease and salt. Rinse with fresh water.

2. Scrape off all marine growth.

3. Sand with 120-220 grit paper.

4. Apply 1-2 finish coats. Make sure that new paint is compatible with old surface. On bottomsides, use vinyl-base TBTO bottom paint. Above waterline, use any quality topside paint.

If old paint is in poor condition, remove paint down to bare metal. Prepare and paint as described in previous section for bare metal.

Painting Aluminum Spars

Painting aluminum spars affords them the best possible protection. New spars can be finished with clear polyurethane to retain natural aluminum color. Any spar, new or old, takes on new beauty when finished with an epoxy color. White is the most popular, but striking results are possible by painting the spars with a color which contrasts or matches the hull.

Aluminum spars should be prepared for painting in the same manner as any other aluminum surface. This includes sanding and etching/priming with a wash primer. New anodized spars do not require this much preparation, though. Simply wash the spar thoroughly with clean solvent.

After preparing the surface, mask around fittings such as sail tracks, cleats, winches, etc. Do not remove these fittings. During removal, the mounting holes become slightly enlarged and it is impossible to fully tighten mounting fasteners.

Paint the spars with a brush or spray gun. Spraying produces a smoother, more glossy surface, but an excellent surface is attainable by flowing epoxy on with a brush; keep back strokes to a minimum.

MAINTAINING STEEL

Steel is the boat building material most vulnerable to corrosion. Besides vulnerability to electro-chemical corrosion (galvanic), it is more susceptible to corrosive effects of salt air. Therefore, considerable thought should go into painting a steel hull.

Most manufacturers have developed products especially for steel. It is wise to select a manufacturer, then use those products throughout the procedure.

This section describes maintenance and painting procedures for all steel surfaces above and below the waterline.

Cleaning and Preventive Maintenance

Steel requires more diligent regular maintenance than any other boat building material. Though very strong, it depends on a well-prepared and well-maintained surface coat for durability; bare steel cannot survive in a marine environment.

As often as necessary, wash the boat with water and mild detergent. Use a sponge or bristle brush to scrub dirt off. Rinse thoroughly with fresh water.

Rust stains cannot be removed by washing. If rust has seeped through the paint, but the surface paint is unbroken, try rubbing compound or wet sanding; touch up with spray paint if necessary. If the paint surface is broken or cracked and rust is bleeding, the rust and surrounding flaky paint must be chipped away to clean bare metal. When repainting the area, follow the procedure for priming and painting covered below.

Surface Preparation

New steel must be carefully prepared even if not rusted. Rolling of sheet steel forms a fine mill-scale which can flake off later. Naturally, any protective coating flakes off with it. Before painting any new steel surface, sandblast the entire hull. Incidentally, weathering will produce the same effect, although it takes a lot longer.

Sandblasting is also necessary to remove rust and paint on previously coated steel. After sandblasting, remove remaining small areas of rust with a heavy wire brush. If you are very ambitious, you can chip flaking rust away with a chipping hammer, then wire brush remaining rust.

Priming and Painting

Steel should be acid-etched, primed with several coats (usually 4) of anti-corrosive primer, then coated with at least 2 finish coats.

Different paint systems require different application procedures too numerous to outline here. The general procedure recommended by most manufacturers is outlined under *Priming and Painting Aluminum*.

On topsides and decks, any quality deck or topside paint is suitable for steel. Refer to the discussion of synthetic paints for characteristics of each type.

If anti-fouling protection is required, select the product carefully. Do not use any product containing flake bronze or mercury compounds; these corrode steel immediately. Cuprous oxide paints can be used if a good barrier coat is applied first, according to the manufacturer's instructions. The best anti-fouling finish for steel is vinyl containing TBTO or TBTF. Read the section on painting aluminum; the same reasons apply here.

MAINTAINING FIBERGLASS

Fiberglass is the most widely used boat building material today. Most boats are molded polyester or epoxy compound reinforced with fiberglass. The polyester resin in contact with the mold usually contains pigment and becomes the smooth outer surface gelt coat. A mold release agent applied to the mold prevents the gel coat from sticking. When the mold is removed, some mold release remains imbedded in the gel coat.

Fiberglass has traditionally been difficult to paint. In most cases, the mold release is the culprit. Designed to prevent adhesion to the mold, it has the same effect on paint.

Another problem is the gel coat itself. The gel coat polyester may vary widely, both chemically and physically, among different boat builders. A paint system which works well on one boat may fail on another. When painting a fiberglass boat, always use a paint system designed specifically for fiberglass and follow manufacturer's directions explicitly.

Cleaning and Preventive Maintenance

Though fiberglass boats require less maintenance than boats of other materials, they are not indestructible. Ultraviolet rays from the sun and abrasion at dockside cause minor cosmetic damage which can detract from the boat's overall appearance.

Maintaining a fiberglass boat finish is similar to maintaining an automobile finish. As often as necessary, wash the boat thoroughly with water and detergent. Use a sponge for loose dirt and a soft-bristle brush for more stubborn areas. Rinse off with fresh water and dry with a clean damp chamois or turkish toweling.

Stains can be difficult to remove. Oil, grease, and tar can be removed with kerosene or paint thinner. As soon as stain is gone, wash area with detergent and water; do not leave solvent of any kind on gel coat for any length of time.

Stains from food or drink are particularly persistant if the surface has not been well waxed. Several liquid fiberglass cleaners are on the market and may work on these stains. You may also try a household cleanser with bleach; but go easy, as most are fairly abrasive.

When the boat is clean and dry, apply a good coat of wax. Automotive waxes are commonly used, but not satisfactory. They are formulated for acrylic or alkyd auto finishes. Fiberglass gel coat is more porous and more likely to fade. For these reasons, special fiberglass waxes are available which fill in the pores to give the surface a hard, high-gloss. In addition, they contain chemicals to screen out harmful ultraviolet rays.

WARNING
Never wax upper surfaces of decks when sure footing is necessary. Waxed gel coat is very slippery, wet or dry.

If the gel coat surface is faded and dull, some measures are possible to restore the original gloss. First try rubbing the surface out with fiberglass paste cleaner. These cleaners are far less abrasive than automotive rubbing compounds, which may remove too much gel coat.

In stubborn cases, the harsher automotive rubbing compound may be necessary. Try it in an inconspicuous area first, this harsh treatment may make things worse.

For really poor finishes, try wet-sanding lightly with 800 grit paper. This method takes off considerable gel coat, so be careful not to sand through to bare glass. The finished surface will be fairly thin. Keep it waxed, because you will not be able to rub it out again. If the resulting surface is not satisfactory, paint it as described elsewhere in this chapter.

Removing Gel-coat Scratches

If scratches are not too deep, they can be sanded out with the following procedure. To repair deep scratches, refer to next procedure, *Repairing Gel-coat Damage.*

Be careful when sanding gel-coat. Some applications are not very thick and you may cut through. If this happens, you will have to spray a gel-coat finish over the area. See *Spraying Gel-coat.*

1. Wipe scratched area with acetone. Saturate cloth so that all loose material is removed.

2. Block-sand scratch with 220 grit paper to remove scratch.

3. Wipe area with water-saturated cloth.

4. Wet-sand area with 400 grit paper.

5. Wet-sand area with 600 grit paper.

6. Buff patched area with rubbing compound to restore gloss.

Repairing Gel-coat Damage

No matter how careful you are, sooner or later the gel-coat will suffer a scratch, nick, or gouge. Trailerable boats seem to get more than their share. Fortunately, gel-coat repairs are not too difficult if you follow the procedure below or use one of the commercially available repair kits described earlier.

1. Clean damaged area thoroughly with acetone.

WARNING
Acetone is very toxic. Avoid breathing fumes or prolonged contact with skin.

2. Form a V-groove along the scratch with a burr or sanding sleeve in the power drill. See **Figure 6**.

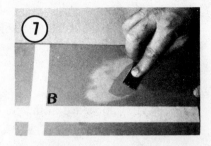

3. Remove flaky edges and feather edges back beyond damaged area. Use 100-220 grit paper.

4. Clean area with dry cloth to remove all dust.

CAUTION
Do not touch repair area with hands.

5. Mix match gel-coat with Cab-o-sil to produce a smooth thick putty. Mix until all lumps and air bubbles are removed.

6. Add catalyst according to manufacturer's instructions. Mix thoroughly or there may be small uncured spots in the patched area.

7. Pack prepared gel-coat into scratch with a putty knife. See **Figure 7**. Force it in tightly to avoid air bubbles. Build up damaged area about 1/16 in. above surface to allow for shrinkage.

8. Spray repaired area with polyvinyl alcohol to prevent entry of air. See **Figure 8**. If PVA is not available, cover patched area with cellophane. Squeeze cellophane down with a single edge razor blade.

9. When putty has cured, remove cellophane or PVA (wash off with water).

10. Block-sand patch with 220 grit paper.

11. If there are pinholes in the patch, fill them with gel-coat and cover again with cellophane or PVA. When cured, remove cellophane or PVA and sand again with 220 grit paper.

12. Wet-sand patched area with 400 grit paper.

13. Wet-sand with 600 grit paper.

14. Buff patched area with rubbing compound to restore gloss.

Spraying Gel-coat

Gel-coat may be sprayed on small areas to hide repairs. There are 2 methods. Seymour markets gel-coat in handy spray cans. See **Figure 9**. At this time, 4 shades of white are available. You can also spray gel-coat with any good quality spray gun, using this procedure.

1. Remove all scratches in surface by wet-sanding with 400, then 600 grit paper.

2. Mask area to be sprayed. Leave at least 2 inches around area. If you spray right up to or over the tape, a thick lap line will form and be difficult to remove.

3. Cover all areas which will be exposed to any overspray.

4. Clean area to be sprayed with acetone.

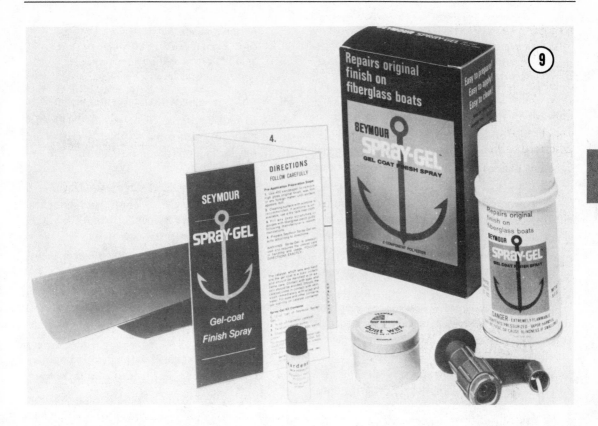

5. Thin prepared gel-coat about 25% with acetone to obtain a good, sprayable consistency.

CAUTION
Do not thin more than 50% or the finish will be dull.

6. Add catalyst to gel-coat. Use exact amount recommended by manufacturer. Mix thoroughly to prevent uneven cure.

7. Spray on about 10-15 mils of gel-coat. This is equivalent to about 2-3 passes with the gun.

8. Spray a very thin film of polyvinyl alcohol (PVA) over gel-coat immediately. This seals off air and speeds the process of curing. It also protects from dust.

9. Remove masking tape.

10. When gel-coat has cured, wet-sand with 400 grit paper to remove all traces of "orange-peel" and lap lines caused by tape.

11. Wet-sand with 600 grit paper.

12. Buff the area with rubbing compound to restore gloss.

Painting Fiberglass

The original gel-coat finish should last for many years if properly cleaned and waxed. But in time, most finishes will begin to chalk and fade. Dark colors such as black, red, and dark blue deteriorate the fastest. If the problem is just fading, rubbing and buffing may restore the finish. However, if the finish is uneven and mottled looking, it must be repainted.

Choice of paint for fiberglass is important. Some boat owners use acrylic and alkyd paints on fiberglass, but these tend to be soft and some don't adhere well. Epoxy and polyurethane finishes are the best choice for fiberglass. They provide excellent adhesion, resistance to chalking, and color retention.

Surface Preparation (Unpainted Gel-coat)

1. Scrub the surface thoroughly with detergent and water.

2. Wash hull thoroughly with fiberglass solvent wash to remove mold release or other waxes from the surface.

CAUTION
*Use plenty of clean rags, discarding
them often, as wax builds up on them.
Otherwise, you will just spread the wax
around. Wipe downward only.*

3. Wash boat again with detergent and water.

4. Sand entire surface to be painted with medium grade production paper (80-120 grit). Sand until the surface has a matte finish with no gloss at all.

5. Above waterline, sand surfaces to be painted with 240-320 grit paper to remove any scratches. This is not necessary below the waterline where anti-fouling paint will be used.

6. Wipe off sanding dust with a clean, solvent-dampened rag.

7. Fill deep scratches and gouges with a special fiberglass filler. Read the label to be sure it is formulated for fiberglass. Mix and apply as directed on label.

8. Sand filled spots flush with surrounding area with 320 grit paper; finish with 600 grit paper.

Surface Preparation (Painted Surface)

1. Scrub surface thoroughly with detergent and water.

WARNING
Wear goggles when scrubbing off metallic anti-fouling paints; some of these are extremely caustic and can cause permanent eye damage.

2a. If old paint is not peeling or cracked, sand surface to be repainted with medium grit paper (80-120 grit). Remove all gloss. Be careful when sanding sharp edges or corners or you may cut through the old paint and gel-coat.

WARNING
Wear a gauze mask or respirator when sanding any anti-fouling paint. Dust from copper, mercury, TBTO and TBTF is very toxic.

2b. If old paint is in poor condition, remove it down to the original gel-coat.

NOTE: *Use a power sander if possible. If this is too slow, try one of the chemical paint removers on the market. Test it on a small, inconspicuous area first*

to make sure it won't damage the gel-coat. Even if it doesn't damage the test area, don't leave it on the surface any longer than necessary.

3. Wash boat again with detergent and water.

4. Sand entire surface to be painted with medium grade production paper (80-120 grit). Sand until the surface has a matte finish with no gloss at all.

5. Above waterline, sand surfaces to be painted with 240-320 grit paper to remove any scratches. This is not necessary below the waterline where anti-fouling paint will be used.

6. Wipe off sanding dust with clean solvent-dampened rag.

7. Fill deep scratches and gouges with a special fiberglass filler. Read the label to be sure it is formulated for fiberglass. Mix and apply as directed on label.

8. Sand filled spots flush with surrounding area with 320 grit paper; finish with 600 grit paper.

Bottom Painting (Anti-fouling Protection)

When fiberglass was first introduced, manufacturers touted the complete freedom from maintenance with the material. Unfortunately, no one told the barnacles and other marine growth found in fouling waters. In many cases, fiberglass gives them a firmer foot-hold. Unlike wood, fiberglass will not be structurally damaged, but growth will slow the boat and is unsightly.

In many cases, anti-fouling paint can be applied over bare gel-coat, if the surface is carefully prepared as described earlier. However, this is not always effective.

Priming the bare gel-coat with a special non-sanding fiberglass primer will provide for better adhesion. Follow the manufacturer's directions exactly. Usually the primer must dry 2 hours, but not more than 8-12, depending on manufacturer. After priming, coat bottom with 2 coats of anti-fouling bottom paint.

CAUTION
Alcohol-solvent paints are not compatible with fiberglass primer.

Stir paint frequently during application to insure even toxicant dispersion. Let each coat dry the recommended time before applying the next. Also let final coat dry as recommended before launching boat.

If painting over a previously painted bottom, priming is not necessary. As long as the old paint is in good condition, prepare surface as described earlier and apply 2 coats of anti-fouling paint. The new paint must be compatible with the old. See earlier section describing compatability of different paint systems.

Bottom Painting (Non Anti-fouling)

If anti-fouling protection is not required, coat the bottom with a racing bronze, polyurethane, or epoxy enamel formulated for underwater use. Many topside enamels are not suitable for use underwater.

The procedure is the same as for anti-fouling painting. In most cases, a primer is not necessary. However, many manufacturers recommend a white undercoat to increase adhesion and hide surface blemishes that would produce an uneven gloss. White undercoat is specially formulated for this purpose. It dries harder than the finish coat, which prevents "checking." Checking occurs when a hard finish is applied over a softer surface.

Topsides

Usually more care is necessary on topsides finishing. Prepare the surface as described in an earlier section. Coat with polyurethane or epoxy topside enamel.

Priming is usually not necessary; follow the manufacturer's recommendation. However, if surface blemishes have been filled or glazed, a coat of white undercoat will even out the surface tone, producing a more uniform final finish.

Polyurethane and epoxy produce very slick finishes which may be too slippery for decks. Add a small amount of non-skid agent such as Woolsey Non-Skid Agent or Regatta Non-Skid Dry Granules to the paint before application. Either coat the entire deck with this specially prepared paint or mask off selected areas for treatment.

3

CHAPTER FOUR

SPARS, RIGGING, AND SAILS

More than anything else, this chapter is unique to sailboats. The sails, supporting spars, and rigging are the sailboat's means of movement. To be able to depend on them, you must inspect everything periodically, and replace or repair questionable parts *before* failure. Quite often, a simple failure such as a turnbuckle break, can cause a chain reaction of failures and considerable damage.

This chapter provides repair or replacement procedures for the spars, standing rigging, running rigging, and winches.

ALUMINUM MASTS

Aluminum masts are relatively troublefree and require little maintenance. Their biggest problem is corrosion, both atmospheric and galvanic (see Chapter Two for a discussion of both).

Masts may be protected from atmospheric corrosion by anodizing or painting. Anodizing is a chemical process which forms a protective surface over the aluminum. Painting works better if the paint is applied exactly as described in Chapter Three.

Galvanic corrosion is more difficult to prevent. All fittings and fasteners should be stainless steel. If brass, bronze, or copper is necessary, they must be insulated from the aluminum mast with wood, teflon, nylon, mica, etc. For example, bronze halyard winches must be mounted on an insulating pad and secured to the mast with stainless steel screws.

The only maintenance required is a yearly check for corrosion, and tightness of all mast fittings. A coat of wax will keep the mast looking good as well as providing added corrosion protection. It is also wise to touch up painted masts where paint has chipped off.

WOOD MASTS

Wood masts require the same maintenance that any painted or varnished surface requires. See Chapter Three. In addition, every year, check tightness of all mast fittings.

MAST FITTINGS

Mast fittings such as the sail track, cleats, and winches are attached to wood masts with wood screws and attached to aluminum masts with self-tapping screws.

Screws should be checked periodically to make sure they are tight. Do not overtighten or you will strip the threads.

CAUTION
Do not remove mast fittings even for painting unless absolutely necessary. Removal and retightening wears the threads; the connection will not be as strong as before.

MAST STEP

The mast step requires very little maintenance whether the mast steps on the keel or on the deck. Occasionally, check the mast step mounting hardware for tightness. Also check the surrounding area for damage caused by stress, and for rot (wood hulls). If the mast step is aluminum, check for galvanic corrosion caused by proximity of keel bolts.

MAST COLLAR

Remove mast collar once every year and check for signs of leakage which may cause rot in wood decks. Also check for signs (e.g., cracks) that indicate the mast may have been working back and forth in the deck hole. This "working" can damage the surrounding deck.

If small wedges hold the mast in place, make sure they are tight. These prevent "working" and transfer the load to the deck. Some boats do not have wedges, depending on the rigging alone for support; all loads are transferred to the keel.

MAST HEAD

Most rigging attaches to the mast head which therefore is subjected to considerable stress. Every year, either go aloft in a bosun's chair or unstep the mast and inspect the mast head. Look for rust and corrosion damage. Make sure welds are good and there are no cracks. Check all fasteners securing rigging (running and standing rigging) to the mast head. All bolts must have lockwashers or self-locking nuts. All clevis pins must be secured with cotters. Check condition of all sheaves mounted on the mast head. Finally, check fasteners securing mast head to mast.

STANDING RIGGING

Wire Rope

The 2 most widely used materials for standing rigging are stainless steel wire rope and galvanized steel wire rope.

Stainless steel is most common on modern yachts. It is stronger, more resistant to rust, and lasts longer than galvanized steel; but it is also more expensive initially.

Galvanized steel is still attractive to some owners. Stainless steel becomes brittle with age and can break without warning. On the other hand, galvanized steel "whiskers" as it nears time to replace it. The inner wires rust first. As they break, the ends spring out to the surface, forming "whiskers" or "meat hooks."

Check condition of wire rope by wrapping with a soft cloth and then wiping up and down. Broken ends will snag the cloth. Presence of these "whiskers" is a warning to replace galvanized wire.

Rod Rigging

Rod rigging is by far the most efficient rigging. It has great strength, less windage because it is smaller, and longer life than wire rope. Since it does not stretch, once it is tuned, it does not usually require retuning. Usually, rod rigging is stainless steel or monel. It is very expensive and found only on specialized racing boats.

Maintenance

Stainless steel rigging is so rust and corrosion resistant that little maintenance is required. Twice a year, check all turnbuckles and mast head fittings for cracks. Replace any cracked fittings immediately, even if the crack is a nearly undetectable hairline. Frequently during the season, clean the rigging with a soapy water solution to remove grime before it soils the sails.

Figure 1 shows one simple way to clean rigging. Wrap a cloth or sponge around shroud or stay and tie it around the middle with a small line. Tie a loop in one end of line. Attach main halyard to loop. Attach another line to shackle so that halyard shackle can be pulled back down again when the rag reaches the top. Saturate the rag or sponge with soapy water. Using the halyard and return line, run the rag up and down the

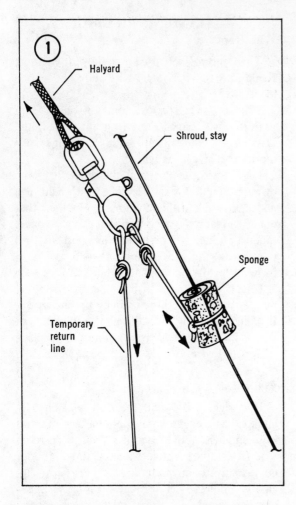

① Halyard

Shroud, stay

Sponge

Temporary
return
line

shroud or stay until clean. Do this for all the standing rigging including the topping lift if made of wire.

Tuning the Rigging

Proper tuning is a matter of considerable experience. The following guidelines will get you close. When in doubt about how tight rigging should be, make it too slack rather than too tight. If too slack, the mast will bend and take up the slack. If too tight, abnormally high compression loading could drive the mast right through the deck or bottom of the boat.

In calm water at dockside, adjust rigging so the mast is perfectly vertical, without sails. Some sailors lie on their back on the deck and sight up the mast to check this, but it is not very accurate. A better way is to tie a line to the main halyard shackle and hoist the end aloft. Use the line to measure the distance from the top of the mast to each main chainplate. See **Figure 2**. If the mast is vertical (side to side), the measurements will be the same. If not, adjust the rigging.

There are some peculiarities to watch for when tuning. Tightening a lower shroud moves the mast head in the *opposite* direction. For example, tightening the port lower shroud moves the mast head to starboard. Tightening an upper shroud moves the mast head *toward* the shroud. That is, tightening the port upper shroud moves the mast head to port.

Rerigging

Both stainless steel and galvanized wire rope require periodic replacement. The job is simple if the mast is unstepped. If the mast is stepped, each section of rigging should be replaced, one at a time, letting the remaining rigging support the mast. Although some relatively short masts stepped to the keel may be self-supporting, you may have a hard time finding someone foolish enough to go aloft on an unrigged mast. The following procedure is best.

1. Remove and replace top rigging such as triatic stays, etc.
2. Remove and replace lower shrouds.
3. Remove and replace upper shrouds.
4. Rig temporary forestay.
5. Remove and replace forestay.
6. Rig temporary backstay.
7. Remove and replace backstay.

This is a tedious procedure, as each piece of rigging must be measured, a new piece made and installed before proceeding to the next. In the end, it may be far less time consuming to have the work done at a boatyard.

Splicing Wire Rope

The 2 most used methods of splicing wire rope to fittings are:

    a. Talurit splice

    b. Swaging

A Talurit splice is shown in **Figure 3**. This splice may be used with galvanized or stainless steel. The ferrule must be chosen to fit the wire

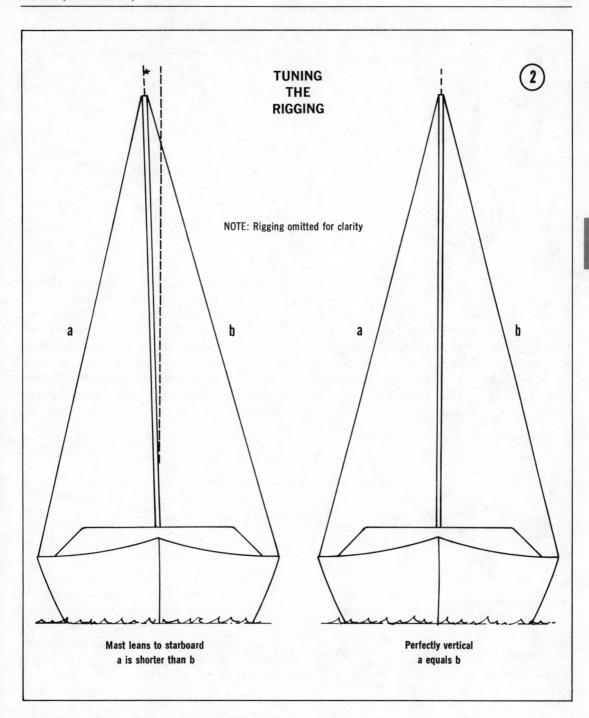

TUNING
THE
RIGGING

2

NOTE: Rigging omitted for clarity

a   b   a   b

Mast leans to starboard
a is shorter than b

Perfectly vertical
a equals b

size. Also, it must be copper for stainless steel wire and alloy for galvanized steel wire.

Swaged splicing (**Figure 4**) is stronger than Talurit splicing and may be used only with stainless steel wire. While the Talurit ferrule may be attached with a relatively inexpensive hand tool, swaging requires a very expensive tool.

Turnbuckles

Turnbuckles permit adjustment of rigging. They are made from several materials.

a. Galvanized

b. Stainless steel

c. Silicon bronze

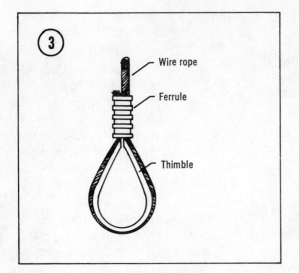

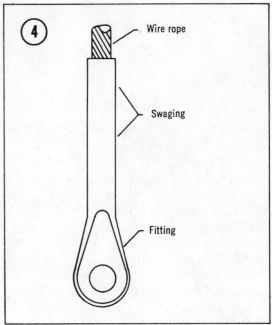

Galvanized turnbuckles may be found on older boats. They are prone to rust and other corrosion from salt water. Modern yachts use bronze or stainless steel. These require no maintenance other than periodic inspection; the material becomes brittle with use and may fail. Check for hairline cracks twice a season.

Turnbuckles are connected to the wire rope in a number of different ways. **Figure 5** shows several.

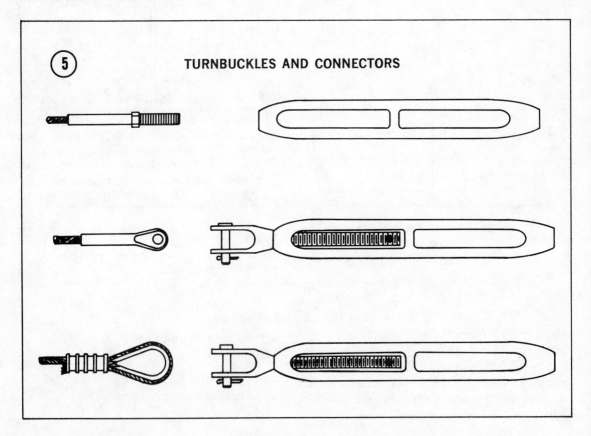

SPREADERS

Spreaders keep the shrouds at an efficient angle to support the mast. Windward spreaders take on considerable stress and can give way if not properly maintained. A broken spreader can cause dismasting.

Once a year, carefully check the fastening securing the spreader to the mast. This requires a trip up the mast in a bosun's chair or unstepping the mast. Don't try to do it from the deck. There are many different fastenings used, but they are all very simple and wear or damage caused by stress or corrosion will be obvious.

Check the outer ends carefully. Look for signs of chafing which can wear away individual strands of the shroud. Also make sure that nothing on the end of the spreader can damage sails. The easiest anti-chafing gear for spreader tips is tape—either vinyl electrical tape or sail tape. In addition, molded plastic or rubber tips are available. See **Figure 6**.

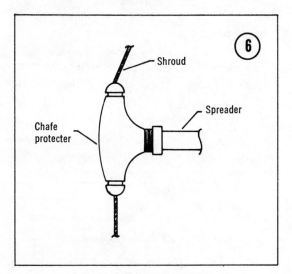

WINCHES

Winches are relatively easy to disassemble and assemble if you take reasonable care. This section includes step-by-step procedures for many popular winches. However, don't hesitate to tackle any similar winch.

Here are some points to keep in mind when disassembling *any* winch.

1. Find a large clean area. Don't try to pull a winch apart on deck. There are too many small

parts which can be mysteriously drawn overboard. Take the winch home or go below and spread newspaper over the dining table.

2. As you take the winch apart, lay the parts out left-to-right and top-to-bottom.

3. Make numerous sketches of parts' orientation as you proceed. Don't think you can remember how everything goes together, because chances are you won't. Interruptions can occur which delay reassembly for hours, days, even weeks after disassembly. Keep your sketches and notes for the next time.

4. Very few winch parts require force for removal. Before using brute strength to separate parts, look carefully for a fastener, C-ring, or snap ring which is holding the parts together.

5. After disassembly, clean each part thoroughly in a petroleum-base solvent such as kerosene or diesel fuel. Scrub parts with a toothbrush to remove stubborn buildups.

WARNING
Never use gasoline for cleaning. It is far too explosive. Metal parts can create sparks and ignite the gasoline.

6. Inspect each part carefully for damage or excessive wear. Look particularly at gear teeth and all aluminum parts.

7. Prior to assembly, lubricate gear teeth and bearings with a *marine* grease made specifically for a salt water environment.

CAUTION
White grease such as Lubriplate, while excellent for many applications, is not suitable for winches. It tends to get gummy when exposed to a salt environment.

8. Lubricate other winch parts such as pawls and springs with light machine oil (SAE 10 or SAE 15), never grease.

CAUTION
Use non-detergent oil; detergent oil will corrode any bronze or brass in the winch.

9. Reel halyard winches with 350°+ friction brakes require additional service. Sand the brake band shoe (the part of the drum on which the brake band grips) lightly with emery paper.

Put a *very thin* coat of light, non-detergent oil on the brake band and shoe to prevent oxidation.

BARIENT WINCHES

Service and Parts Kits

Barient provides two service kits which cover all currently available winches. **Table 1** shows the make-up of each kit. One kit, covering all the winches you have, should be kept aboard during a long cruise. **Table 2** shows tools required to service Barient winches. Be sure that your on-board tool kit includes them.

Table 1   BARIENT SERVICE AND PARTS KITS

KIT A.	For Winches #9, 10, 10H, 16, 20, 21, 22, 26, 3 and 3A Halyard	
1	Set of exploded drawings	
1	Tube of Barlube	
1	Box	
1	00420	Bearing
4	RSN 125S	Snap rings
6	TIM B 00209	Pawl springs
2	TIM B 00330	Pawls
KIT B.	For Winches #9, 10, 10H, 16, 20, 21, 22, 26, 3 and 3A Halyard, 28, 30, 32, 35	
1	Set of exploded drawings	
1	Box	
1	Tube of Barlube	
1	00420	Bearings
4	RSN 125S	Snap rings
6	TIM B 00209	Pawl springs
2	TIM B 00330	Pawls
1	TIM B 11162	Drum nut
2	TIM B 00301	Plunger
2	TIM B 00311	Pawls
2	TIM B 00201	Springs
2	00415	Roller bearings
1	Red cloth	

Disassembly/Assembly
(Barient No. 1, 2, 2A)

Refer to **Figures 7 and 8** for this procedure.

1. Release the brake screw (counterclockwise).

2. Loosen and remove 4 cap screws (27).

3. Lift winch housing straight off. If stuck, pry or tap it off with a soft hammer. Use care while

Table 2   TOOLS REQUIRED—BARIENT WINCHES

Winch	Tool
#3/3A	Screwdriver.
#10 and #10H	Screwdriver or small pointed object.
#16	Screwdriver or small pointed object.
#20	Screwdriver or small pointed object. 3/16 in. pin punch.
#22	Screwdriver or small pointed object.
#26	Screwdriver or small pointed object. ½ in. box wrench.
#28	Screwdriver, universal deck plate key, ¼ in. Allen wrench, and 3/16 in. Allen wrench.
#30 and #32	Screwdriver, universal deck plate key, 5/16 in. Allen wrench, and 3/16 in. Allen wrench.
#35	Screwdriver, universal deck plate key, 5/16 in. Allen wrench, 3/16 in. Allen wrench, 7/16 in. box wrench.

removing the housing; avoid dropping the roller bearings. The bearings could be damaged if allowed to hit a hard deck or floor.

4. Remove the winch drum and the main shaft simultaneously. Do not drop roller bearings from within the drum.

5. Remove brake band assembly, ratchet ring, and anchor pin. Remove brake band screw from the brake band.

> NOTE: *The swivel pin securing brake handle to screw is pressed into place. Do not remove unless replacing brake screw or handle.*

6. Remove gear carrier assembly.

> NOTE: *The following 2 steps are not necessary unless the gear carrier assembly is damaged or corroded.*

7. Remove 2 pawls (11), plungers (9), and springs (8) located near edge of gear carrier.

8. Remove cotter pins securing the other 2 pawls. Remove pawls, plungers, and springs.

CAUTION
a. These 2 pawls are shaped to their respective gears. Mark them and then the gears so that the pawls can be reassembled in their original sockets.

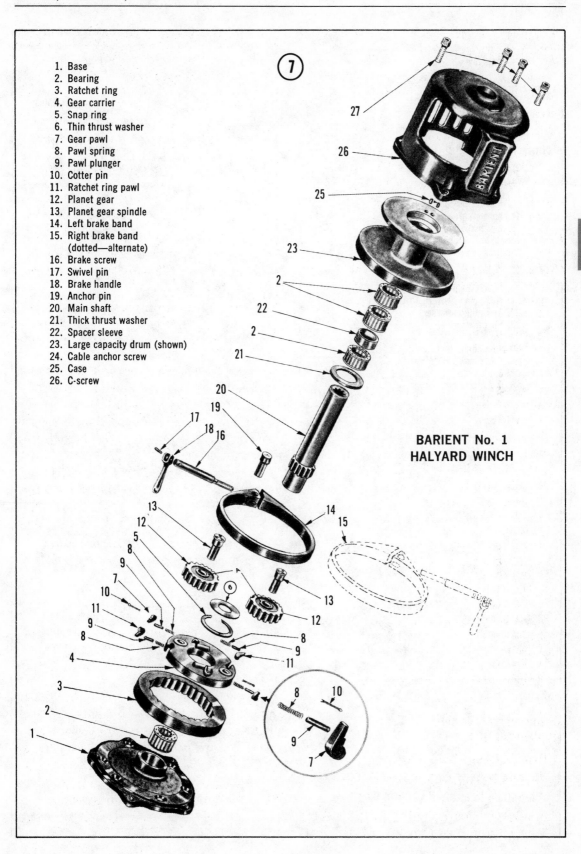

1. Base
2. Bearing
3. Ratchet ring
4. Gear carrier
5. Snap ring
6. Thin thrust washer
7. Gear pawl
8. Pawl spring
9. Pawl plunger
10. Cotter pin
11. Ratchet ring pawl
12. Planet gear
13. Planet gear spindle
14. Left brake band
15. Right brake band
    (dotted—alternate)
16. Brake screw
17. Swivel pin
18. Brake handle
19. Anchor pin
20. Main shaft
21. Thick thrust washer
22. Spacer sleeve
23. Large capacity drum (shown)
24. Cable anchor screw
25. Case
26. C-screw

BARIENT No. 1
HALYARD WINCH

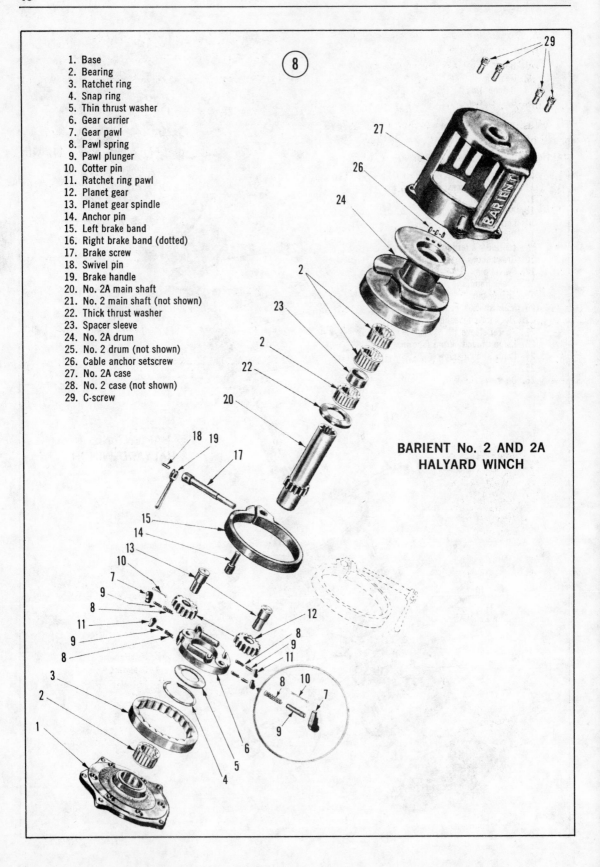

⑧

1. Base
2. Bearing
3. Ratchet ring
4. Snap ring
5. Thin thrust washer
6. Gear carrier
7. Gear pawl
8. Pawl spring
9. Pawl plunger
10. Cotter pin
11. Ratchet ring pawl
12. Planet gear
13. Planet gear spindle
14. Anchor pin
15. Left brake band
16. Right brake band (dotted)
17. Brake screw
18. Swivel pin
19. Brake handle
20. No. 2A main shaft
21. No. 2 main shaft (not shown)
22. Thick thrust washer
23. Spacer sleeve
24. No. 2A drum
25. No. 2 drum (not shown)
26. Cable anchor setscrew
27. No. 2A case
28. No. 2 case (not shown)
29. C-screw

BARIENT No. 2 AND 2A
HALYARD WINCH

b. Do not remove gears and spindles from gear carrier unless they must be replaced. Spindles are pressed into place.

9. Remove roller bearing (2) from winch base.

10. Wash all parts in petroleum solvent. Wire brush off all accumulated foreign matter. Use a stainless steel or bronze brush.

11. Lubricate gear pivots with light machine oil Use an oil can to inject oil through the holes on the gear hubs.

12. Lubricate all the following parts generously with light machine oil: Pawls, plungers, springs, brake band screws, and the raised portion of the winch base that mates with gear carrier. Lubricate the gear teeth of all gears and roller bearings, using "Barient Barlube" or equivalent. *Do not* lubricate the brake band nor its mating ratchet ring.

13. Reassembly is the reverse of these steps.

Disassembly/Assembly (Barient No. 3)

Refer to **Figure 9** for this procedure.

1. Remove screw (15) from the inside top of drum (13).

2. Remove drum (13) from base (1).

3. Remove brake screw assembly (4, 5, and 6).

4. Push anchor pin (7) from base (1) with small pointed object or screwdriver.

5. Remove brake band (3) and ratchet ring (8) from base (1).

6. Inspect 2 pawls (11) and 3 pawl springs (12) on drum (13). Do not remove unless broken.

7. Carefully wash all parts including inside of drum (13) in solvent.

8. Grease inside of drum (13) with Barient Barlube or its equivalent.

9. Oil 2 pawls (11) on drum (13) with light machine oil.

10. Assemble brake band (3) to base (1).

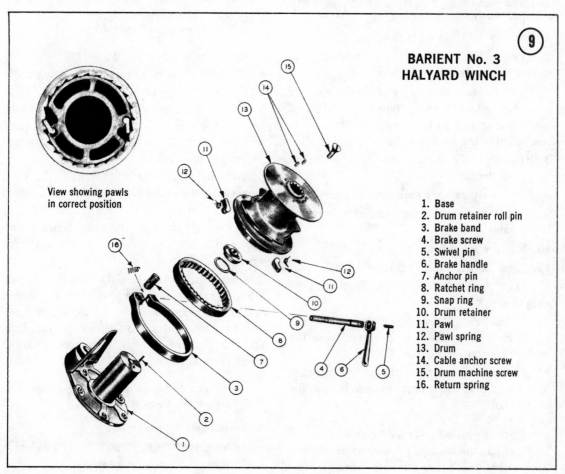

View showing pawls in correct position

BARIENT No. 3 HALYARD WINCH

9

1. Base
2. Drum retainer roll pin
3. Brake band
4. Brake screw
5. Swivel pin
6. Brake handle
7. Anchor pin
8. Ratchet ring
9. Snap ring
10. Drum retainer
11. Pawl
12. Pawl spring
13. Drum
14. Cable anchor screw
15. Drum machine screw
16. Return spring

11. Insert anchor pin (7) through brake band (3) into base (1). Check alignment of anchor pin hole with brake band hole.

12. Install brake screw assembly through brake band. Do not tighten securely until winch assembly is completed.

13. Assemble ratchet ring (8) onto drum (13). Notice correct position of pawls as shown in Figure 9 inset.

14. Assemble drum (13) and ratchet ring assembly (8) to base (1). Ensure that roll pin (2) fits into hole in drum retainer (10).

15. Install screw (15) inside top of drum (13) and tighten.

Disassembly/Assembly (Barient No. 3A)

Refer to **Figure 10** for this procedure.

1. Release the brake screw (counterclockwise).

2. Loosen and remove 4 cap screws (15).

3. Lift winch housing straight off. If stuck, pry it or tap it off with a soft hammer.

4. Remove the main shaft from socket.

5. Remove the drum, brake band assembly, and ratchet ring as an assembly.

6. Place drum assembly on a workbench or other flat surface. Sketch relative orientation of pawls and springs in drum so that they can be reinstalled in the same way.

7. Remove brake band assembly and ratchet ring from drum.

8. Remove 4 pawls and springs from drum.

9. Remove the brake screw assembly from the brake band.

10. Remove roller bearings from base.

11. Clean all parts thoroughly in solvent.

12. Lightly oil pawl sockets in drum with 30 weight oil.

13. Install pawls and springs in drum. The bent leg on each spring rests on the drum, while the straight leg rests in the pawl slot.

14. Install ratchet ring and brake band on drum. Make sure that pawls nest completely into the ratchet notches.

NOTE: *Brake band may be installed to put handle on either side of winch to make it left- or right-handed.*

15. Lightly oil brake screw threads with 30 weight oil and install it in brake band.

16. Pack roller bearings generously with Barient Barlube or equivalent. Install them on base.

17. Install drum assembly on base.

18. Install main shaft. Make sure that pawls engage shaft.

19. Install winch housing. Secure with the 4 cap screws.

Disassembly/Assembly (Barient No. 9)

Refer to **Figure 11** for this procedure.

1. Remove the drum.

CAUTION
Use a large screwdriver with a blade the same width as the screw slot.

2. Lift the drum straight up and off.

CAUTION
Don't let the bearing drop on the deck if it comes off with the drum.

3. Remove the 2 pawls and pawl springs.

4. Wash all parts in petroleum solvent, including the inside of the drum.

5. Assemble the pawls and pawl springs into the base of the winch. The bent leg of the pawl spring must rest against the base and the straight leg against the pawl.

6. With light machine oil, lubricate the pawl sockets in the winch base (15 weight oil). Pawls must move freely.

7. Generously lubricate the drum bearing with Barient Barlube or equivalent and install over winch base.

8. Install the drum over the bearing. Slowly lower the drum into place with the pawl ends displaced toward the center of the winch base. This permits the drum to drop freely into place. Use the blade of a small screwdriver or other small pointed object to deflect pawls outward.

NOTE: *The insert in Figure 11 shows proper pawl orientation.*

9. Install and tighten screw.

10. Check that drum rotates freely clockwise, and not at all counterclockwise.

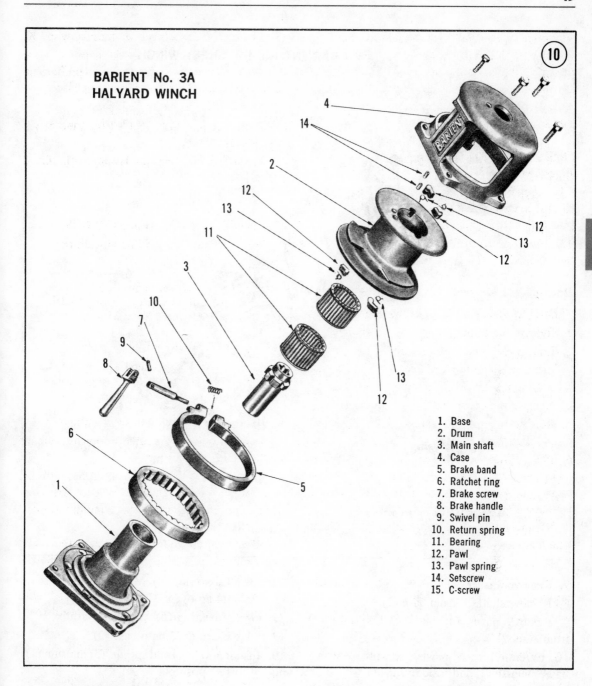

BARIENT No. 3A
HALYARD WINCH

1. Base
2. Drum
3. Main shaft
4. Case
5. Brake band
6. Ratchet ring
7. Brake screw
8. Brake handle
9. Swivel pin
10. Return spring
11. Bearing
12. Pawl
13. Pawl spring
14. Setscrew
15. C-screw

**Disassembly/Assembly
(Barient No. 10H and 10)**

Refer to **Figure 12** for this procedure.

1. Remove snap ring (8) with screwdriver or a small pointed object. Use a spiral motion rather than pulling straight up.

2. Simultaneously lift drum (1) and cover (9) from base (2).

3. Remove cover (9) from drum (1).

4. Remove pawls (4) and pawl springs (5) from the drum (1).

   NOTE: *To proceed further, base (2) must be removed from deck or mast.*

5. Remove bearing (6) from base (2).

6. With a spiral motion, remove snap ring (8) from bottom of base (2).

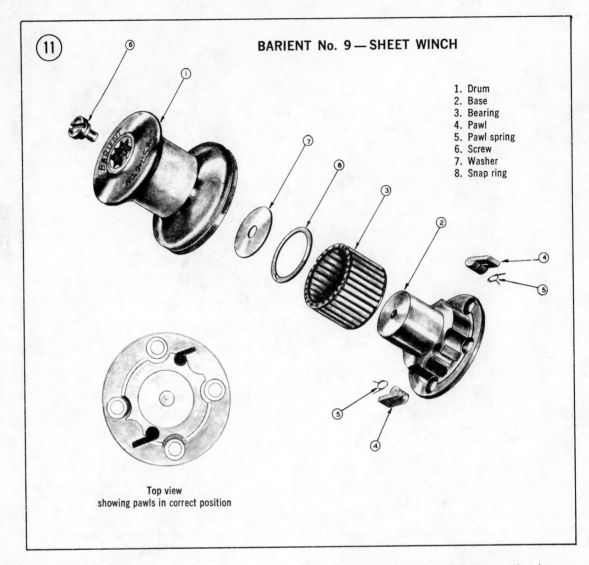

BARIENT No. 9 — SHEET WINCH

1. Drum
2. Base
3. Bearing
4. Pawl
5. Pawl spring
6. Screw
7. Washer
8. Snap ring

Top view
showing pawls in correct position

7. Remove washer (7).

8. Remove shaft (3) from base (2).

9. Remove pawls (4) and pawl springs (5) from base (2).

10. Carefully wash pawls, springs, bearing, base, main shaft, and inside of drum.

11. Lightly grease the inside of base (2) with Barlube or equivalent.

12. Assemble pawls (4) and springs (5) in base (2). Notice correct pawl position. See inset in Figure 12.

13. Oil assembled pawls (4).

14. Install shaft (3) into base (2).

15. Assemble washer (7) onto the bottom of the base (2).

16. Install snap ring (8). Make sure that it seats securely into groove in shaft (3).

17. Grease bearing (6) well with Barlube.

18. Slide bearing (6) onto base (2).

19. Install pawls (4) and springs (5) in drum (1), noting correct position.

20. Assemble drum (1) on base (2).

21. Oil assembled pawls (4) on drum (1).

22. Rotate the drum (1) to check freedom of movement.

23. Assemble cover (9) over top of drum (1).

24. Assemble snap ring (8) over cover (9). Make sure that it seats securely into groove in shaft (3). Use spiral motion as when removed rather than shoving straight down.

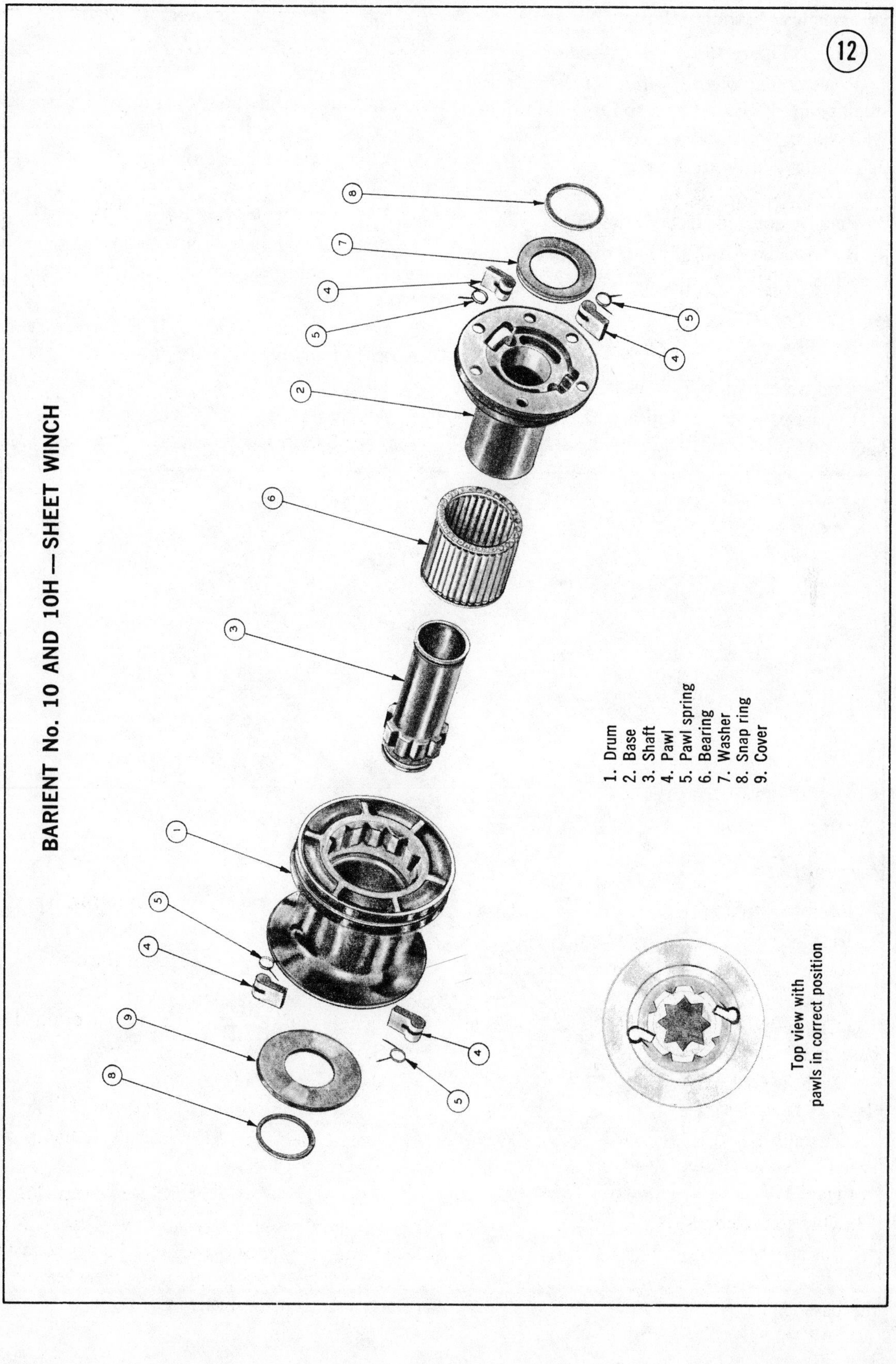

BARIENT No. 10 AND 10H — SHEET WINCH

(12)

1. Drum
2. Base
3. Shaft
4. Pawl
5. Pawl spring
6. Bearing
7. Washer
8. Snap ring
9. Cover

Top view with
pawls in correct position

4

Disassembly/Assembly (Barient No. 16)

Refer to **Figure 13** for this procedure.

1. Remove snap ring (8) with a screwdriver or a small pointed object. Use a spiral motion rather than pulling straight up.

2. Simultaneously lift drum (1) and cover from base (2).

3. Remove cover (3) from drum (1).

4. Remove the pawls (5) and springs (6) from the drum (1).

> NOTE: *To proceed further, base (2) must be removed from deck or mast.*

5. Remove bearings (7) from base (2).

6. Inspect pawls (5) and springs (6) on base (2). Clean and oil. Do not remove unless broken.

7. Using a spiral motion, remove snap ring (8) on bottom of base (2).

8. Remove main shaft (4) from base (2).

9. Carefully wash pawls, springs, bearings, main shaft, base, and inside of drum.

10. Lightly grease inside of base (2) with Barlube or equivalent.

11. Slide main shaft (4) into base (2).

12. Assemble snap ring (8) onto bottom of base (2), seating it securely into main shaft groove. Use spiral motion.

13. Grease bearings (7) with Barlube. Work grease thoroughly into bearings.

14. Slide bearings (7) into base (2).

15. Assemble pawls (5) and springs (6) to drum (1). See correct pawl position (Figure 13).

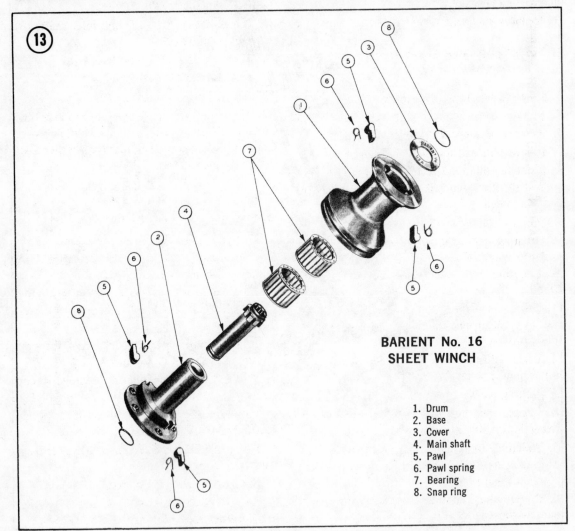

**BARIENT No. 16
SHEET WINCH**

1. Drum
2. Base
3. Cover
4. Main shaft
5. Pawl
6. Pawl spring
7. Bearing
8. Snap ring

16. Install drum (1) on base (2).

17. Oil assembled pawls (5) on drum (1).

18. Rotate the drum (1) to check freedom of movement.

19. Assemble cover (3) over top of drum (1).

20. Assemble snap ring (8) over cover (3). Seat it securely into main shaft groove. Use spiral motion as when removed, rather than shoving straight down.

Disassembly/Assembly (Barient No. 20)

Refer to **Figure 14** for this procedure.

1. Remove snap ring (13) with screwdriver or small pointed object. Use spiral motion rather than pulling straight up.

2. Lift off drum (2) and cover (4) simultaneously from base (1).

3. Remove cover (4) from drum (2).

NOTE: *To proceed further, base must be removed from deck or mast.*

4. Remove bearings (10) from base (1).

5. Remove cotter pins (15) holding retainer (9).

6. Remove retainer (9) covering idler gears (7).

7. Remove idler gears (7) from idler shafts (8).

8. Remove roll pin (14) through collar (16) and main shaft (3) on bottom of base (1) using 3/16 inch pin punch.

9. Remove collar (16).

10. Remove main shaft (3) from base (1), using rotating motion. The ratchet gear (6), pawls (11), pawl springs (12), and gear cover (5) will fall out.

11. Inspect pawls (11) and pawl springs (12) on base (1). Clean and oil them. Do not remove unless broken.

12. Clean all parts including inside of base (1) and drum (2) with solvent.

13. Lightly grease inside of base (1).

14. Grease bearings (2) with Barlube. Work grease thoroughly into bearings.

15. Assemble pawls (11) and pawl springs (12) onto main shaft (3). Note correct pawl position shown in Figure 14.

16. Slide main shaft into base while turning it counterclockwise.

17. Assemble ratchet gear (6) over main shaft from bottom of base. Rotate to check freedom of movement.

NOTE: *Be sure ratchet gear recess faces out.*

18. Oil pawls on main shaft.

19. Assemble the gear cover (5) over the ratchet gear (6).

20. Slide collar (16) over gear cover (5).

21. Install roll pin (14) through collar (16) and main shaft (3) with 3/16 in. punch.

22. Assemble the idler gears (7) over the idler shafts (8).

23. Place retainer (9) over idler gears (7).

24. Oil idler shafts (8).

25. Install cotter pins (15) into idler shafts (8) to secure retainer (9).

26. Slide bearings (10) onto base.

27. Install drum (2) over base.

28. Install cover (4) in drum (2).

29. Place snap ring (13) over cover (4). Make sure that it seats securely into main shaft groove. Use spiral motion as when removing rather than shoving straight down.

Disassembly/Assembly (Barient No. 28)

Refer to **Figure 15** for this procedure.

1. With universal deck plate key, remove drum nut (10) from top of drum (4).

2. Remove drum (4) from rest of assembly. Make sure that the 2 roller bearings (19) do not drop out.

3. Remove roller bearings (19) from the gear housing (2).

4. With ¼ in. Allen wrench, remove 4 cap screws (26) holding gear housing (2) to base (1).

5. Insert lock-in handle into main shaft (9) on gear housing (2) and lock.

6. Using handle, remove gear housing (2) from base, then remove handle.

7. Lay gear housing (2) on its side.

8. Remove 3 cap screws (2, 4, and 25) which hold gear cover (3) to gear housing (2).

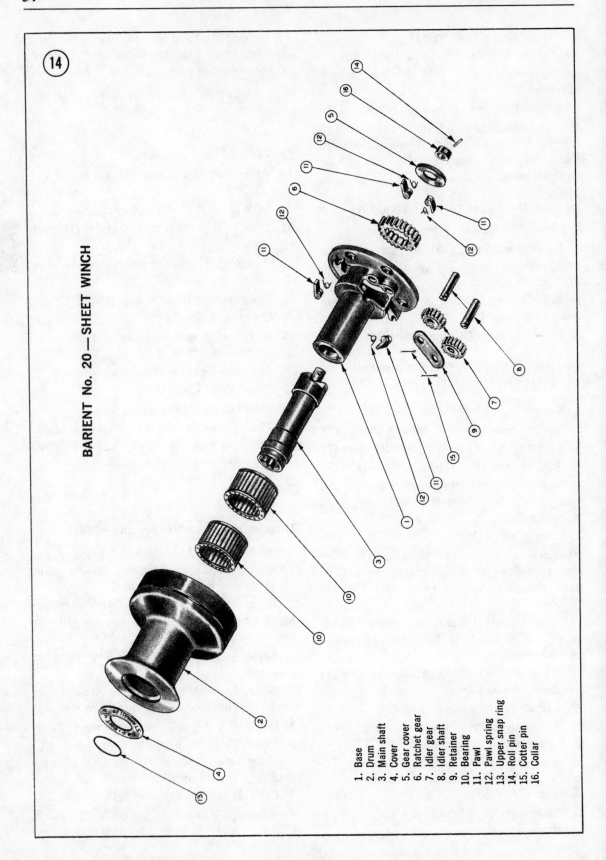

BARIENT No. 20—SHEET WINCH

1. Base
2. Drum
3. Main shaft
4. Cover
5. Gear cover
6. Ratchet gear
7. Idler gear
8. Idler shaft
9. Retainer
10. Bearing
11. Pawl
12. Pawl spring
13. Upper snap ring
14. Roll pin
15. Cotter pin
16. Collar

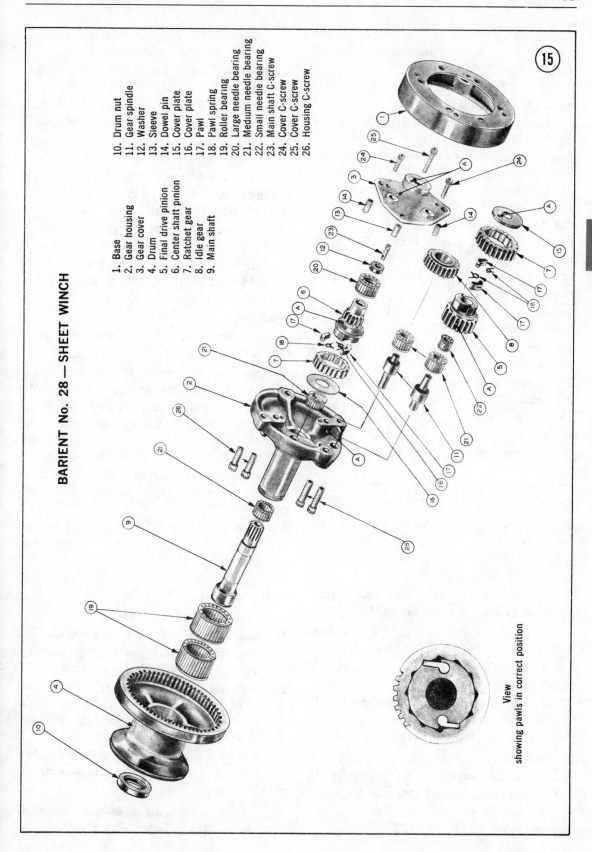

BARIENT No. 28—SHEET WINCH

1. Base
2. Gear housing
3. Gear cover
4. Drum
5. Final drive pinion
6. Center shaft pinion
7. Ratchet gear
8. Idle gear
9. Main shaft
10. Drum nut
11. Gear spindle
12. Washer
13. Sleeve
14. Dowel pin
15. Cover plate
16. Cover plate
17. Pawl
18. Pawl spring
19. Roller bearing
20. Large needle bearing
21. Medium needle bearing
22. Small needle bearing
23. Main shaft C-screw
24. Cover C-screw
25. Cover C-screw
26. Housing C-screw

View
showing pawls in correct position

4

9. Remove cap screw (23) from bottom of main shaft (9). Insert winch handle at other end of shaft to prevent rotation of shaft.

10. Remove washer (12) from center shaft pinion (6).

11. Remove gear cover (3) from gear housing (2). This is a press fit onto dowel pins and should be pried off evenly around the diameter with a screwdriver. Do not use excessive force.

12. Remove sleeve (13) from gear housing (2). The sleeve sits loosely on the gear housing and may have fallen off already.

13. Remove large needle bearing (20) from center shaft pinion (6).

14. Remove cover plate (15) covering final drive pinion (5).

15. Remove final drive pinion (5) and ratchet gear (17) from gear spindle (11).

16. Remove ratchet gear (7) from final drive pinion (5).

17. Remove needle bearings (21 and 22) from gear spindle (11).

18. Remove idler gear (8) from other gear spindle (11).

20. Remove needle bearing (21) from gear spindle (11).

21. Separate center shaft pinion (6), ratchet gear (7), and cover plate (16) from each other.

22. Remove the main shaft (9) from the gear housing (2).

23. Remove 2 needle bearings (21) from gear housing (2).

24. Remove the 2 pawls (17) and 2 pawl springs (18) from final drive pinion (5).

25. Remove the 2 pawls (17) and 2 pawl springs (18) from center shaft pinion (6).

26. Clean all pawls, springs, and bearings in solvent.

27. Grease all bearings with Barlube. Work grease thoroughly into bearings.

28. Slide needle bearings (21) into top of gear housing (2).

29. Install main shaft (9) into gear housing (2).

30. Install needle bearing (21) over bottom of main shaft (9) and seat into recess on gear housing (2).

31. Assemble the 2 pawls (17) and 2 pawl springs (18) to center shaft pinion (6).

32. Assemble the 2 pawls (17) and 2 pawl springs to final drive pinion (5).

33. Oil pawls (17) assembled in Steps 31 and 32.

34. Install cover plate (16) over main shaft (9).

35. Slide ratchet gear (7) onto center shaft pinion (6), noting correct pawl position. Check rotation for freedom of movement.

36. Install center shaft pinion (6) and ratchet gear assembly (7) over main shaft (9).

37. Assemble washer (12) into center shaft pinion (6).

38. Install cap screw (23) through washer (12) and tighten with 3/16 in. Allen wrench.

39. Slide needle bearing (21) over the gear spindle (11).

40. Slide needle bearing (21) over other gear spindle (11).

41. Install needle bearing (22) over gear spindle (11) by cut-away portion of gear housing (2).

42. Assemble ratchet gear (7) over final drive pinion (5), noting pawl position. Rotate to check freedom of movement.

43. Assemble final drive pinion (5) and ratchet gear assembly (7) (with ratchet gear facing out), over gear spindle (11) by cut-away portion of gear housing (2).

44. Install cover plate (15) over ratchet gear (7).

45. Install idler gear (8) over other gear spindle (11).

46. Slide large needle bearing (20) over center shaft pinion (6).

47. Place sleeve (13) into position.

48. Install gear cover (3) onto gear housing (2).

49. Install cap screw (25) through gear cover (3) into sleeve (13). Do not tighten cap screw.

50. Assemble 2 cap screws (24) through gear cover (3) and tighten with 3/16 in. Allen wrench. Now tighten cap screw (25) installed in Step 49.

51. Assemble gear housing (2) to base (1). Insert the lock-in handle in the gear housing to aid assembly.

52. Tighten gear housing (2) to base (1) using 4 cap screws (26) and 1/4 in. Allen wrench.

53. Slide 2 roller bearings (19) on the gear housing (2).

54. Place drum (4) over gear housing (2).

55. Install drum nut (10) over top of drum (4) and tighten with universal deck plate key.

Disassembly/Assembly
(Barient Nos. 30 and 32)

Refer to **Figure 16** for this procedure.

1. With universal deck plate key, remove drum nut (12) from top of drum (2).

2. Remove drum (4) from rest of assembly. Make sure that the 2 roller bearings (21) and bearing spacer sleeve (13) do not drop out.

3. Remove 2 roller bearings (21) and bearing spacer sleeve (13) from gear housing (2).

4. Remove 4 cap screws (28) holding gear housing (2) to base (1).

5. Insert lock-in handle into main shaft (10) on gear housing (2) and lock handle.

6. Using handle, remove gear housing (2) from base (1), then remove handle.

7. Lay gear housing (2) on its side.

8. Remove 3 cap screws (26 and 27) which hold gear cover (3) to gear housing (2).

9. Remove cap screw (25) from bottom of main shaft (10). Insert winch handle at other end of shaft to prevent it from rotating.

10. Remove washer (14) from center pinion (6).

11. Remove gear cover (3) from gear housing (2) using screwdriver. This is a press fit onto dowel pins and should be pried off carefully and evenly around the diameter with a screwdriver. Do not use excessive force.

12. Remove cover spacer sleeve (15).

13. Remove needle bearing (22) from center pinion (6).

14. Remove cover plate (17).

15. Remove final drive pinion (5) and final ratchet gear (7) from gear spindle (11).

16. Remove final ratchet gear (7) from final drive pinion (5).

17. Remove needle bearings (23 and 24) from gear spindle (11).

18. Remove idler gear (9) from other gear spindle (11).

19. Remove needle bearing (23) from gear spindle (11).

20. Remove center pinion (6), center ratchet gear (8), and cover plate (18) from the main shaft (10).

21. Separate center pinion (6), center ratchet gear (8), and cover plate (18).

22. Remove main shaft (10) from the gear housing (2).

23. Remove 2 needle bearings (23) from gear housing (2).

24. Remove 2 pawls (19) and 2 pawl springs (20) from final drive pinion (6).

25. Remove 2 pawls (19) and 2 pawl springs (20) from center pinion.

26. Clean all pawls, springs, bearings, and any other parts that require cleaning in solvent.

27. Grease all bearings with Barlube. Work grease thoroughly into bearings.

28. Insert needle bearing (23) into top of gear housing (2).

29. Install main shaft (10) into gear housing (2).

30. Slide needle bearing (23) over bottom of main shaft (10) and seat into recess on gear housing (2).

31. Assemble 2 pawls (19) and 2 pawl springs (20) to center pinion (6).

32. Assemble 2 pawls (19) and 2 pawl springs (20) to final drive pinion (5).

33. Oil pawls assembled in Steps 31 and 32.

34. Install cover plate (18) over main shaft (10).

35. Install center ratchet gear (8) onto center pinion (6).

36. Install center pinion (6) and center ratchet gear assembly (8) over main shaft (10).

37. Insert washer (14) into center pinion (6).

38. Assemble cap screw (25) through washer (14) and tighten with 3/16 in. Allen wrench.

39. Slide needle bearing (23) over the gear spindle (11).

40. Slide needle bearing (23) over other gear spindle (11).

41. Slide needle bearing (24) over the gear spindle (11) by cut-away portion of the gear housing (2).

4

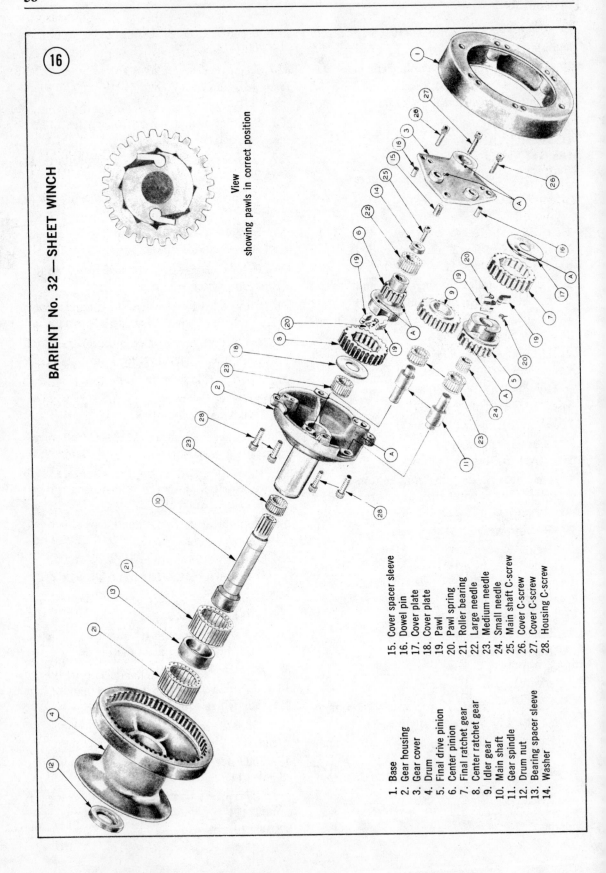

16

BARIENT No. 32 — SHEET WINCH

View
showing pawls in correct position

1. Base
2. Gear housing
3. Gear cover
4. Drum
5. Final drive pinion
6. Center pinion
7. Final ratchet gear
8. Center ratchet gear
9. Idler gear
10. Main shaft
11. Gear spindle
12. Drum nut
13. Bearing spacer sleeve
14. Washer

15. Cover spacer sleeve
16. Dowel pin
17. Cover plate
18. Cover plate
19. Pawl
20. Pawl spring
21. Roller bearing
22. Large needle
23. Medium needle
24. Small needle
25. Main shaft C-screw
26. Cover C-screw
27. Cover C-screw
28. Housing C-screw

42. Install final ratchet gear (7) over final drive pinion (5).

43. Assemble final drive pinion (5) and final ratchet gear assembly (7) (with final ratchet gear facing out) over gear spindle by cut-away portion of gear housing (2).

44. Install cover plate (17) over final ratchet gear (7).

45. Install idler gear (9) over the other gear spindle (11).

46. Slide needle bearing (22) over the center pinion (6).

47. Place cover spacer sleeve (15) into position.

48. Install gear cover (3) onto gear housing (2).

49. Install cap screw (27) through gear cover (3) into cover spacer sleeve (15). Do not tighten.

50. Install 2 cap screws (26) through gear cover (3) and tighten with 3/16 in. Allen wrench. Tighten cap screw (27) installed in Step 49.

51. Assemble gear housing (2) to base (1). Use the lock-in handle for easier assembly.

52. Secure gear housing (2) to base (1) with 4 cap screws (28) and tighten with 5/16 in. Allen wrench.

53. Install roller bearing (21), bearing spacer sleeve (13), and roller bearing (21), in that order, on gear housing (2).

54. Place drum (4) over gear housing (2).

55. Install drum nut (12) over top of drum (4) and tighten with universal deck plate key.

Disassembly/Assembly (Barient No. 35)

Refer to **Figure 17** for this procedure.

1. With universal deck plate key, remove drum nut (17) from top of drum (4).

2. Remove drum (4) from rest of assembly. Make sure that 2 roller bearings (25) and sleeve (15) do not drop out.

3. Remove 2 roller bearings (25) and sleeve (15) from gear housing shaft (25).

4. Remove 6 cap screws (29) from the gear housing (2).

5. Insert lock-in handle into main shaft (13) on gear housing (2) and lock handle.

6. Using lock-in handle, remove gear housing (2) from base (1).

7. Lay gear housing on its side.

8. Remove 2 cap screws (27) and cap screw (28) which holds gear cover (3) to gear housing.

9. Remove gear cover (3) from gear housing (2). This is a press fit onto dowel pins and should be worked off evenly around the diameter with a screwdriver. Do not use excessive force.

10. Remove cap screw (26) from center shaft pinion (12). Insert winch handle at other end of shaft to prevent it from rotating.

11. Remove washer (14) from cap screw (26).

12. Remove main shaft (13) and large needle bearing (24) from center pinion (12).

13. Remove center shaft pinion (12) and other large needle bearing (24) from gear housing (2).

14. Remove all remaining gears together.

15. Remove final drive pinion (10) from low range gear (9).

16. Remove 2 small needle bearings from low range gear (9).

17. Remove ratchet gear (5) from low range pinion (6).

18. Remove 4 pawls (20), 4 pawl springs (18), and 4 plungers (19) from low range gear (9).

19. Remove other ratchet gear (5) from low range pinion (6).

20. Remove 2 pawls (20), 4 pawl springs (18), and 2 plungers (19) from low range pinion (6).

21. Wash all pawls, springs, plungers, bearings, and all other parts that require cleaning in solvent.

22. Oil plunger pockets in low range pinion (6) and low range gear (9).

23. Assemble 4 pawls (20), 4 pawl springs (18), and 4 plungers (19) onto low range gear (9).

24. Assemble 2 pawls (20), 2 pawl springs (18), and 2 plungers (19) onto low range pinion (6).

25. Grease all bearings with Barlube. Work grease thoroughly into bearings.

26. Assemble 2 small needle bearings (23) into low range gear (9).

27. Assemble final drive pinion (10) onto low range gear (9).

⑰ **BARIENT No. 35 — SHEET WINCH**

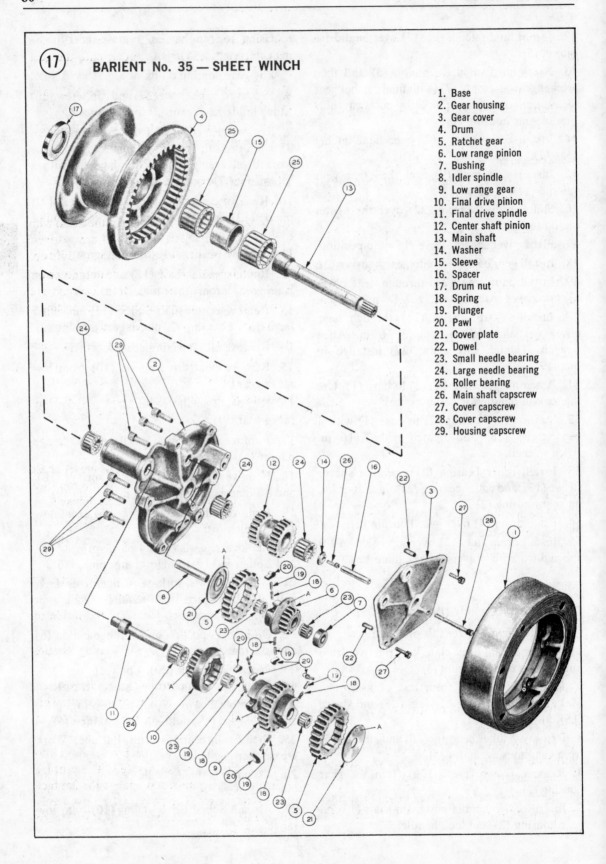

1. Base
2. Gear housing
3. Gear cover
4. Drum
5. Ratchet gear
6. Low range pinion
7. Bushing
8. Idler spindle
9. Low range gear
10. Final drive pinion
11. Final drive spindle
12. Center shaft pinion
13. Main shaft
14. Washer
15. Sleeve
16. Spacer
17. Drum nut
18. Spring
19. Plunger
20. Pawl
21. Cover plate
22. Dowel
23. Small needle bearing
24. Large needle bearing
25. Roller bearing
26. Main shaft capscrew
27. Cover capscrew
28. Cover capscrew
29. Housing capscrew

28. Install ratchet gear (5) onto low range gear (9).

29. Assemble 2 small needle bearings (23) into low range pinion (6).

30. Install ratchet gear (5) onto low range pinion (6).

31. Assemble cover plate (21) to bottom of low range pinion (6) with groove facing pawls.

32. Slide low range pinion (6) onto idler spindle (8) and low range gear (9), and final drive pinion (10) onto final drive spindle (11). Both pinions have to be placed on spindles simultaneously.

33. Assemble cover (21) onto low range gear (9) with groove facing pawls.

34. Install 2 large needle bearings (24) into gear housing (2).

35. Assemble the main shaft (13) into gear housing (2).

36. Assemble center shaft pinion (12) onto gear housing (2).

37. Install main shaft (13) into center shaft pinion (12).

38. Slide washer (14) onto cap screw (26).

39. Insert cap screw (26) into bottom of main shaft (13) and tighten with 3/16 in. Allen wrench.

40. Slide housing (7) onto idler spindle (8).

41. Insert large needle bearing (24) into center shaft pinion (12).

42. Assemble the gear cover (3) onto the gear housing (2).

43. Install 2 cap screws (27) through the gear cover (3) and tighten with 3/16 in. Allen wrench.

44. Assemble spacer (16) and cap screw (2) to gear cover (3). Tighten with 3/16 in. Allen wrench.

45. Insert lock-in handle into the top of main shaft (13) and lock in place.

46. Using lock-in handle, place gear housing (2) onto base (1). Notice that notches on base (1) fit gear housing (2) only one way.

47. Secure gear housing (2) to base (1), using 6 cap screws (29) and tighten with 5/16 in. Allen wrench.

48. Install roller bearing (25), sleeve (15), and roller bearing (25), in this order, onto the gear housing (2).

49. Place drum (4) over gear housing (2) and onto base (1).

50. Install drum nut (17) over top of drum (1) and tighten with universal deck plate key.

Disassembly/Assembly (Barient No. 21)

Refer to **Figure 18** for this procedure.

1. Remove snap ring at the top of the drum with a small pointed object or a small screwdriver. Use spiral motion rather than pulling straight up.

2. Simultaneously remove the drum and cover plate from the gear housing. Drum bearings are heavily greased and can drop out unexpectedly.

3. Remove the cover from the drum.

4. Remove 2 pawls and 2 pawl springs from the drum.

5. Remove 2 bearings from the gear housing.

6. Remove the cluster gear shaft. Lift straight up, using a pointed object or the blade of a screwdriver to pry under the cross pin.

7. Remove the cluster gear group.

8. Remove snap ring at bottom of center shaft in the same manner as the one at the top. See Step 1. Pull center shaft out of gear housing.

> NOTE: *To remove the center shaft, the gear housing must be taken off deck or spar.*

9. Remove the ratchet gear, the pawls, and pawl springs from the pawl carrier gear.

10. Wash all the parts, including the inside of the drum, in petroleum solvent.

11. Install center shaft in gear housing. Secure with snap ring.

12. Inject light machine oil (15 weight) between the gear housing stem and the center shaft. This can be facilitated by lifting the shaft as far as possible.

13. Assemble the 2 pawls and pawl springs into the pawl carrier gear pawl pockets. The bent leg of the pawl spring must rest against the flat face of the gear pocket. The pawls must move freely through the angle of motion required to engage same with ratchet gear.

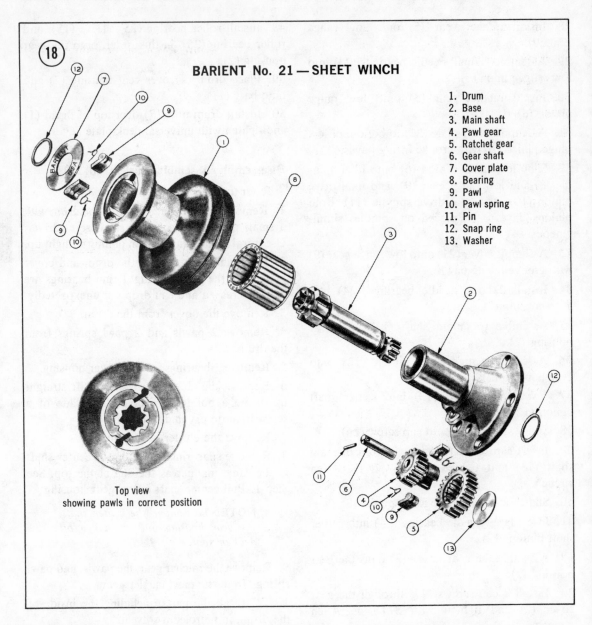

BARIENT No. 21 — SHEET WINCH

1. Drum
2. Base
3. Main shaft
4. Pawl gear
5. Ratchet gear
6. Gear shaft
7. Cover plate
8. Bearing
9. Pawl
10. Pawl spring
11. Pin
12. Snap ring
13. Washer

Top view
showing pawls in correct position

14. Install the ratchet gear. The groove face must be out and the counterbored face next to the pawl carrier.

15. Lubricate the space between the pawls and the gear with light machine oil (15 weight).

16. Lubricate the cluster gear shaft with light machine oil (15 weight) and insert into gear housing and through the gear assembly.

17. Inject light machine oil in the space between the 2 gears.

18. Rotate the 2 gears as a group and also one relative to the other. Gears must move freely.

19. Generously lubricate with Barlube or equivalent the entire circumference of the 2 gears, also 2 drum bearings. Work grease in thoroughly.

20. Install bearings over gear housing stem.

21. Assemble 2 pawls and pawl springs into top of the drum; the bent leg of the spring must rest against the drum, the straight leg must rest against the pawl. The pawls must be oriented as indicated in Figure 18, and must move freely.

22. Install drum over bearings. Hold the pawls away from the center of drum while lowering drum over bearings.

23. Lubricate the space between the pawls and the drum pockets with light machine oil; pawls must move freely.

24. Install drum cover and spiral locking ring. Use spiral motion as when removing same rather than pushing straight down.

25. Manually rotate the drum clockwise. Drum must rotate freely. Insert handle and verify that both speeds work properly.

26. Bend a line around the winch drum. Secure the other end of the line to a cleat and check the winch for proper action.

Disassembly/Assembly (Barient No. 22)

Refer to **Figure 19** for this procedure.

1. Remove snap ring (11), using screwdriver or small pointed object. Use spiral motion rather than pulling straight up.

2. Simultaneously, remove the drum (2) and cover (3) from gear housing (1).

3. Remove cover (3) from drum (2).

4. Remove 2 pawls (8) and 2 pawl springs (9) from drum (2).

5. Remove 2 bearings (10) from the gear housing (1).

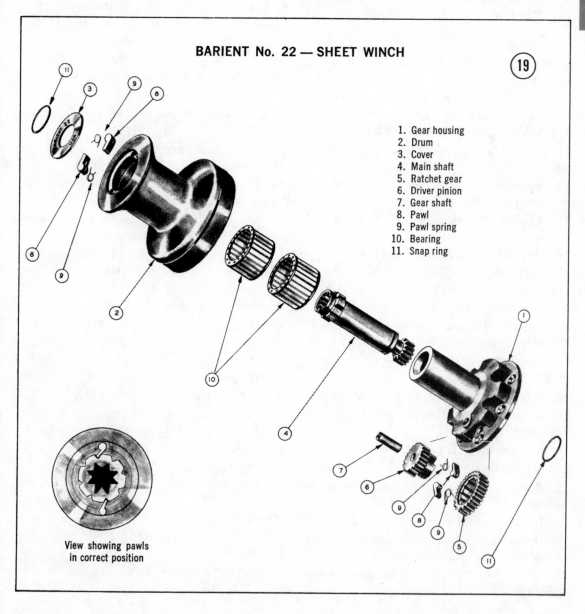

BARIENT No. 22 — SHEET WINCH (19)

1. Gear housing
2. Drum
3. Cover
4. Main shaft
5. Ratchet gear
6. Driver pinion
7. Gear shaft
8. Pawl
9. Pawl spring
10. Bearing
11. Snap ring

View showing pawls
in correct position

NOTE: *To proceed further, gear housing must be removed from deck or mast.*

6. Remove gear shaft (7) from gear housing (1).

7. Remove the ratchet gear (5) from the driver pinion (6).

8. Remove 2 pawls (8) and 2 pawl springs (9) from driver pinion (6).

NOTE: *Removal of center shaft from gear housing is not recommended; the snap ring is very difficult to remove.*

9. Wash all parts including inside of drum in solvent.

10. Inject light machine oil between gear housing stem and center shaft. Lift center shaft as far as possible to make penetration easier.

11. Grease bearings (10) with Barlube or equivalent. Work grease in thoroughly.

12. Assemble 2 pawls (8) and 2 pawl springs (9) to driver pinion (6).

13. Assemble the ratchet gear (5) to the driver pinion (6).

14. Oil pawls (8) on driver pinion (6).

15. Rotate the ratchet gear (5) and the driver pinion (6) together to check freedom of movement and correct rotation.

16. Install ratchet gear (5) with driver pinion (6) assembly on gear housing (1).

17. Install the gear shaft (7) through the driver pinion (6).

18. Slide bearings (10) onto gear housing (1).

19. Assemble 2 pawls (8) and 2 pawl springs (9) onto drum (2).

20. Install drum (2) onto gear housing (1).

21. Oil 2 pawls (8) on drum (2).

22. Rotate drum (2), checking freedom of movement.

23. Install cover (3) over top of drum (2).

24. Install snap ring (11) over cover (3). Seat securely into groove on main shaft (4). Use spiral motion as when removing rather than shoving straight down.

Disassembly/Assembly (Barient No. 26)

Refer to **Figure 20** for this procedure.

1. Remove snap ring (14), using a screwdriver or small pointed object. Remove using spiral motion rather than pulling straight up.

2. Lift off drum (12) and cover (13) from upper gear housing (2).

3. Remove cover (13) from drum (12).

4. Remove 2 pawls (8) and 2 pawl springs (9) from drum (12).

5. Remove 2 follower bearings (11) from upper gear housing (2).

6. Remove 7 cap screws (15) that hold upper gear housing (2) to lower gear housing (1).

7. Using lock-in handle, remove upper gear housing (2) from lower gear housing (1). Do not remove main shaft (10) from upper gear housing (2).

8. Remove the drive pinion (4) from the ratchet gear (7).

9. Remove small needle bearing (6) and large needle bearing (5) from drive pinion (4).

10. Remove 2 pawls (8) and 2 pawl springs (9) from drive pinion (4).

11. Wash pawls, springs, bearings, and inside of drum (12) with petroleum solvent.

12. Grease all bearings with Barlube or equivalent. Work grease in thoroughly.

13. Assemble 2 pawls (8) and 2 pawl springs (9) to drive pinion (4).

14. Oil 2 pawls (8) on drive pinion (4).

15. Assemble the ratchet gear (7) and the drive pinion (4).

16. Install small needle bearing (6) and large needle bearing (5) in drive pinion (4).

17. Install ratchet gear (7) with drive pinion assembly (4) onto lower gear housing (1).

18. Place upper gear housing (2) onto lower gear housing (1), using lock-in handle.

19. Secure upper gear housing (2) to lower gear housing (1) with 7 cap screws (15). Tighten cap screws with ½ in. wrench.

20. Slide 2 roller bearings (11) onto upper gear housing (2).

21. Assemble 2 pawls (8) and 2 pawl springs (9) onto drum (12), noting correct pawl position.

BARIENT No. 26 — SHEET WINCH

⟨20⟩

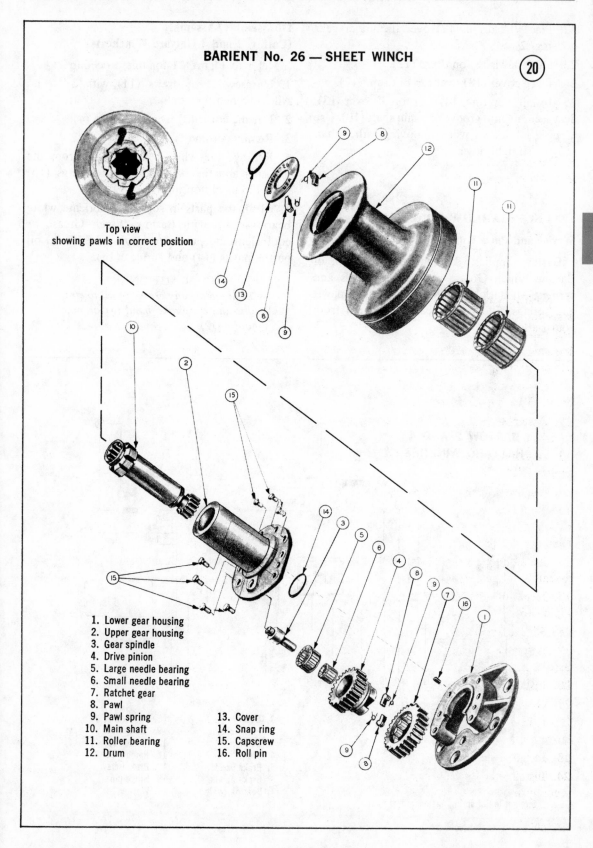

Top view
showing pawls in correct position

1. Lower gear housing
2. Upper gear housing
3. Gear spindle
4. Drive pinion
5. Large needle bearing
6. Small needle bearing
7. Ratchet gear
8. Pawl
9. Pawl spring
10. Main shaft
11. Roller bearing
12. Drum
13. Cover
14. Snap ring
15. Capscrew
16. Roll pin

4

22. Place the drum (12) over the upper gear housing (2).

23. Oil 2 pawls (8) on drum (12).

24. Place cover (13) over top of drum (12).

25. Install snap ring (14) over top of cover (13). Seat securely into groove on main shaft (10). Use a spiral motion as when removing rather than shoving straight down.

BARLOW WINCHES

Service and Parts Kits

Barlow supplies a kit consisting of a tube of Barlow Winch Grease and several pawls and springs. All Barlow winches use the same pawls and springs. Other parts can be ordered from your Barlow dealer.

Disassembly/Assembly
(Barlow 2 and 4 Halyard Winches)

Refer to **Figure 21** for this procedure.

1. Unscrew 3 capscrews (11) with 3/16 in. Allen wrench.

2. Lift the cover (3) from the drum (4).

3. Remove drum (4).

4. Remove the white bearings (10) from the base (1) and the pawls (14) and springs (13) from the pawl housing (2).

5. Clean the parts in solvent. Lubricate white bearings (10) with Barlow Winch Grease or equivalent and put a few drops of SAE 30 oil on the pawls (14) and springs (13).

CAUTION
Do not allow any grease or oil to stray onto the the brake band (5) or pawl housing (2).

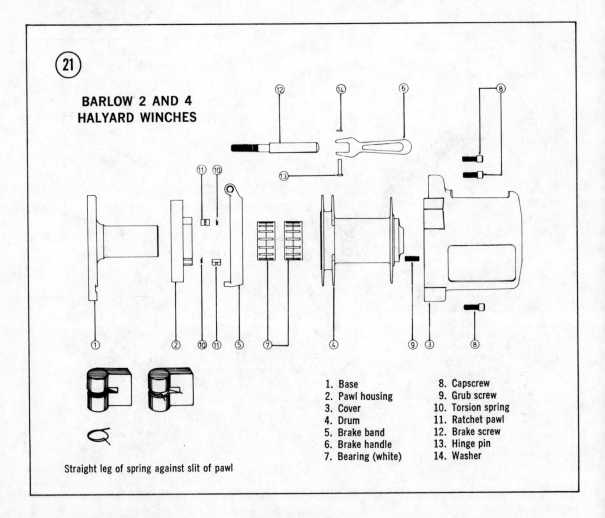

㉑

BARLOW 2 AND 4 HALYARD WINCHES

1. Base
2. Pawl housing
3. Cover
4. Drum
5. Brake band
6. Brake handle
7. Bearing (white)
8. Capscrew
9. Grub screw
10. Torsion spring
11. Ratchet pawl
12. Brake screw
13. Hinge pin
14. Washer

Straight leg of spring against slit of pawl

6. Install the white bearings (10) on the base (1) and the drum (4) on the white bearings (10).

7. Install the cover (3) on the drum (4) and *firmly* tighten 3 capscrews (11) in the cover (3).

Disassembly/Assembly
(Barlow 5 Halyard Winch)

Refer to **Figure 22** for this procedure.

1. Unscrew and remove the brake handle assembly (6).

2. Unscrew the 4 capscrews (11) in the cover (3) with 3/16 in. Allen wrench.

3. Lift the cover (3) and drum (4) from the ratchet carrier (5).

4. Remove the black bearings (9), spring washer (8), pawls (14) and springs (13) from the ratchet carrier (5).

5. Remove the ratchet carrier (5) and gold bearing (10) from the base (2).

6. Clean the parts in solvent and lubricate with Barlow Winch Grease or equivalent. The pawls (14) and springs (13) require a few drops of SAE 30 oil.

CAUTION
Do not allow any grease or oil to stray onto the brake band (1) or ratchet carrier (5).

7. Assembly is the reverse of these steps. Note pawl spring orientation.

Disassembly/Assembly
(Barlow 6 Halyard Winch)

Refer to **Figure 23** for this procedure.

1. Unscrew the 4 capscrews (18) and lift the cover (1) from the drum (4).

2. Remove the drum (4), main shaft (10), grey bearings (16), and bearing spacer (12).

3. Lift gearbox assembly from base (2).

4

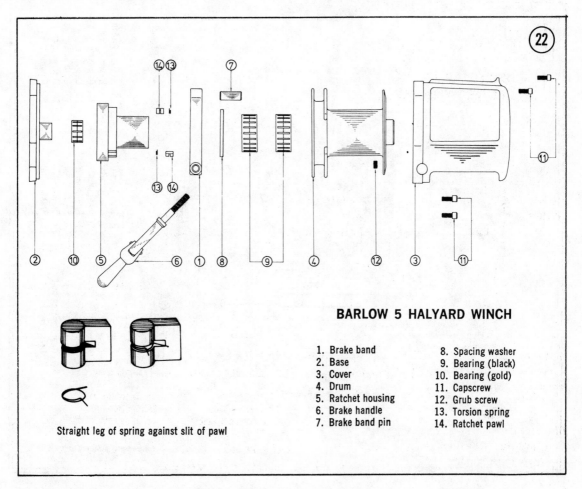

Straight leg of spring against slit of pawl

BARLOW 5 HALYARD WINCH

1. Brake band
2. Base
3. Cover
4. Drum
5. Ratchet housing
6. Brake handle
7. Brake band pin
8. Spacing washer
9. Bearing (black)
10. Bearing (gold)
11. Capscrew
12. Grub screw
13. Torsion spring
14. Ratchet pawl

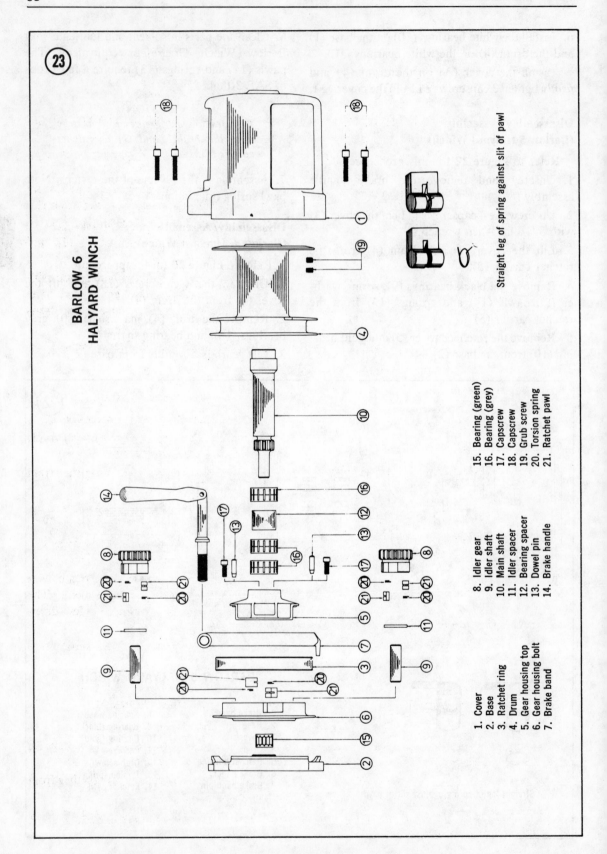

BARLOW 6
HALYARD WINCH

Straight leg of spring against slit of pawl

1. Cover
2. Base
3. Ratchet ring
4. Drum
5. Gear housing top
6. Gear housing bolt
7. Brake band
8. Idler gear
9. Idler shaft
10. Main shaft
11. Idler spacer
12. Bearing spacer
13. Dowel pin
14. Brake handle
15. Bearing (green)
16. Bearing (grey)
17. Capscrew
18. Capscrew
19. Grub screw
20. Torsion spring
21. Ratchet pawl

4. Remove the 2 capscrews (17) and lift off the gear housing top (5).

5. Unscrew brake handle assembly (14) and remove brake band (7).

6. Remove ratchet ring (3), pawls (21), and springs (20) from gear housing bottom (6).

7. Remove the 2 idler gears (8) and their pawls (21) and springs (20) from the gear housing bottom (6).

8. Remove green bearing (15) from base (2).

9. Clean parts in solvent and lubricate with Barlow Winch Grease or equivalent. The ratchet pawls (21) and springs (20) require a few drops of SAE 30 oil.

CAUTION

Do not allow any grease or oil to stray onto the brake band (7) or ratchet ring (3).

10. Assembly is the reverse of these steps.

**Disassembly/Assembly
(Barlow 8 Sheet Winch)**

Refer to **Figure 24** for this procedure.

1. Unscrew the 5 capscrews (20) and lift the cover (10) from the drum (4).

2. Remove the drum (4), main shaft (6), bearings (18), and bearing spacer (11).

3. Lift the gearbox assembly from base (1).

4. Remove the 3 capscrews (19) and lift off the gear housing top (2).

5. Unscrew brake handle assembly (14) and remove brake band (9).

6. Remove ratchet ring (7), pawls (23), and springs (22) from the gear housing bottom (3).

7. Remove 3 idler gears (8), green bearings (16), pawls (23), and springs (22) from the gear housing bottom (3).

8. Remove grey bearing (7) from base (1).

9. Clean all parts in solvent and lubricate with Barlow Winch Grease or equivalent. The ratchet pawls (23) and springs (22) require a few drops of SAE 30 oil.

CAUTION

Do not get any grease or oil on the brake band (9) or ratchet ring (7).

10. Assembly is the reverse of these steps. Note orientation of pawl springs.

**Disassembly/Assembly
(Barlow 15 Sheet Winch)**

Refer to **Figure 25** for this procedure. It is not necessary to remove base.

1. Remove capscrew (8) in top drum with 3/16 in. Allen wrench.

2. Lift top drum (2) from bottom drum (3) and remove pawl (6) and spring (5) in top drum (2).

3. Remove bottom drum (3) from base (1).

4. Remove grey bearings (4), pawls (6), and springs (5) from base.

5. Clean the parts in solvent and grease with Barlow Winch Grease or equivalent. The pawls (6) and springs (5) require a few drops of SAE 30 oil.

6. Assembly is the reverse of these steps.

**Disassembly/Assembly
(Barlow 16 and 20 Sheet Winches)**

Refer to **Figure 26** for this procedure.

1. Remove the capscrew (4) in the top cap (3) with 3/16 in. Allen wrench.

2. Lift drum (2) and top cap (3) together from the drum.

3. Separate drum (2) and top cap (3) and remove pawls (6) and springs (5) from top cap (3).

4. Remove washer (7), pawls (6), springs (5), and black bearings (9) from base (1).

5. Clean parts in solvent and lubricate with Barlow Winch Grease or equivalent. The pawls (6) and springs (5) require a few drops of SAE 30 oil.

6. Assembly is the reverse of these steps.

**Disassembly/Assembly
(Barlow 18 and 22 Sheet Winches)**

Refer to **Figure 27** for this procedure.

1. Remove the capscrew (11) in top cap (4) with 3/16 in. Allen wrench.

2. Lift drum (3) and top cap (4) together from the gearbox (2) and base (1).

3. Remove the black bearings (9 and 15) from the gearbox (2).

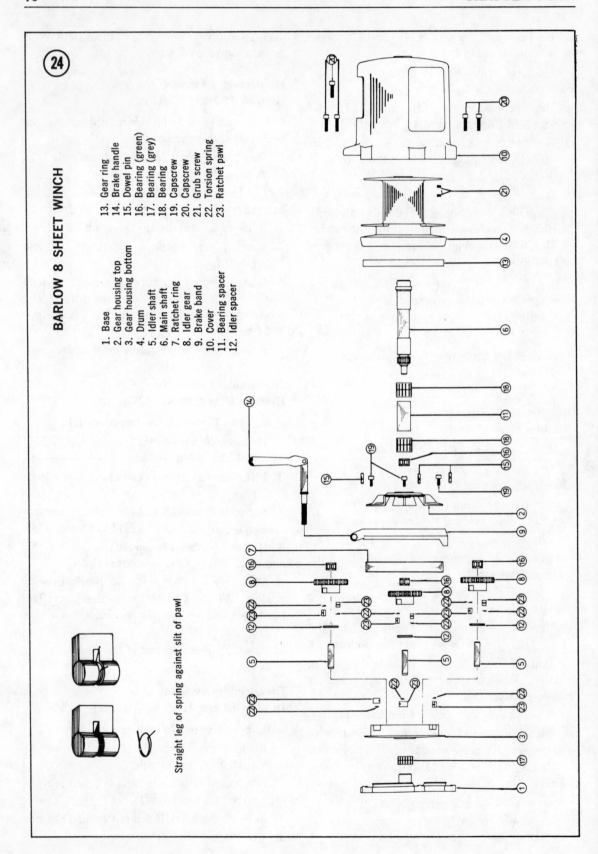

BARLOW 8 SHEET WINCH

1. Base
2. Gear housing top
3. Gear housing bottom
4. Drum
5. Idler shaft
6. Main shaft
7. Ratchet ring
8. Idler gear
9. Brake band
10. Cover
11. Bearing spacer
12. Idler spacer

13. Gear ring
14. Brake handle
15. Dowel pin
16. Bearing (green)
17. Bearing (grey)
18. Bearing
19. Capscrew
20. Capscrew
21. Grub screw
22. Torsion spring
23. Ratchet pawl

Straight leg of spring against slit of pawl

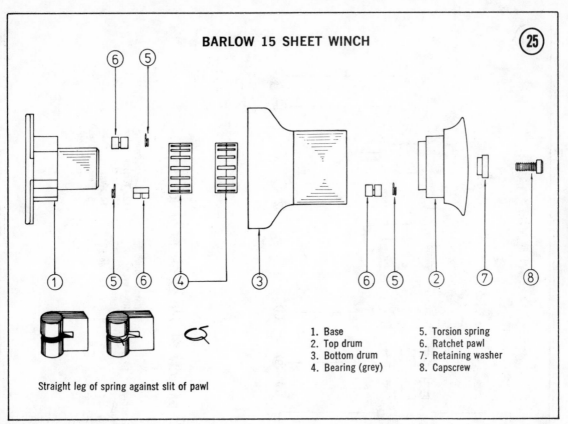

BARLOW 15 SHEET WINCH (25)

Straight leg of spring against slit of pawl

1. Base
2. Top drum
3. Bottom drum
4. Bearing (grey)
5. Torsion spring
6. Ratchet pawl
7. Retaining washer
8. Capscrew

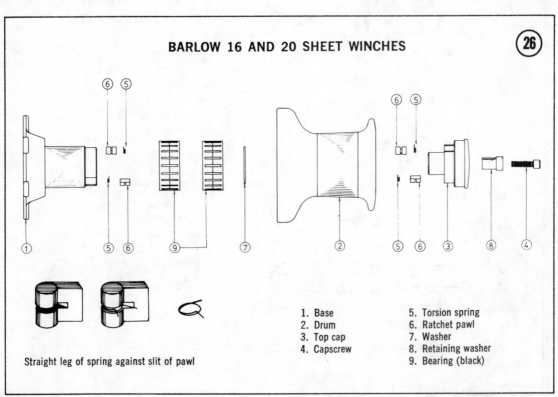

BARLOW 16 AND 20 SHEET WINCHES (26)

Straight leg of spring against slit of pawl

1. Base
2. Drum
3. Top cap
4. Capscrew
5. Torsion spring
6. Ratchet pawl
7. Washer
8. Retaining washer
9. Bearing (black)

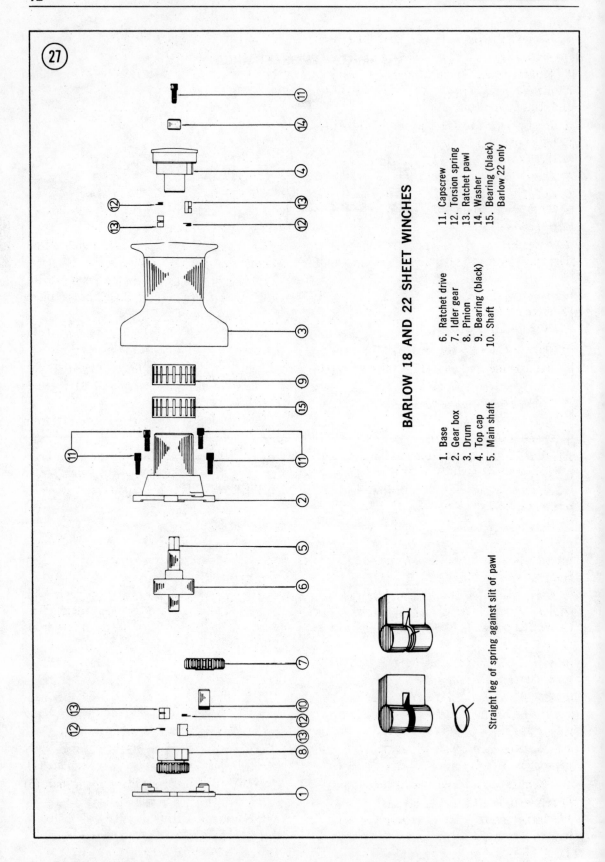

BARLOW 18 AND 22 SHEET WINCHES

1. Base
2. Gear box
3. Drum
4. Top cap
5. Main shaft

6. Ratchet drive
7. Idler gear
8. Pinion
9. Bearing (black)
10. Shaft

11. Capscrew
12. Torsion spring
13. Ratchet pawl
14. Washer
15. Bearing (black)
    Barlow 22 only

Straight leg of spring against slit of pawl

4. Remove 4 capscrews (11) and lift gearbox from base (1).

5. Remove main shaft assembly (5 and 6), pinion (8) and its pawls (13) and springs (12), and remove idler gear (7).

6. Remove top cap (4) from drum (3) and remove its pawls (13), springs (12), and retaining washer (14).

7. Clean parts in solvent and lubricate with Barlow Winch Grease or equivalent. The pawls (13) and springs (12) require a few drops of SAE 30 oil.

8. Assembly is the reverse of these steps. Tighten capscrew (11) firmly.

Disassembly/Assembly
(Barlow 24 Sheet Winch)

Refer to **Figure 28** for this procedure.

1. Remove the capscrew (12) in the top cap (4) with 3/16 in. Allen wrench.

2. Lift drum (3) and top cap (4) together with the gearbox (2).

3. Remove top cap (4) from drum (3), remove pawls (14), springs (13), and retaining washer (16) from top cap (4).

4. Remove washer (15), white bearings (10), and gold bearing (8) from gearbox (2).

5. Remove 3 capscrews (17) from gearbox (2).

6. Lift gearbox (2) from base (1). Remove ratchet pinion (6), pawls (14), and springs (13) from main shaft (5).

7. Clean parts in solvent and lubricate with Barlow Winch Grease or equivalent. The pawls (14) and springs (13) require a few drops of SAE 30 oil.

8. Install pawls (14) and springs (13) in the main shaft (5) and top cap (4).

9. Slip the ratchet pinion (6) over the main shaft (5) until the ratchet pawls (14) are fully engaged in ratchet teeth of this gear.

10. Place ratchet pinion (6) and main shaft (5) in gearbox (2) and rest on base (1).

11. Replace and tighten the 3 capscrews (17) in gearbox (2).

12. Install white bearings (10) and gold bearing (8). Place washer (15) on top of gearbox (2).

13. Install top cap (4) in drum (3) and retaining washer (16) in top cap (4).

15. *Firmly* tighten the capscrew (12) in the top cap (4).

Disassembly/Assembly
(Barlow 26 Sheet Winch)

Refer to **Figure 29** for this procedure.

1. Remove the capscrew (14) in top cap (5) with 3/16 in. Allen wrench.

2. Lift drum (4) and top cap (5) together from gearbox (3).

3. Remove top cap (5) from the drum (4). Remove pawls (16), springs (15), and retaining washer (17) from top cap (5).

4. Remove washer (18), white bearings (11), and gold bearing (9) from gearbox (3).

5. Remove 4 capscrews (19) from gearbox (3).

6. Lift gearbox assembly (1 and 3) together from base (2).

7. Very carefully pry gearbox plate (1) from gearbox (3).

8. Remove the 2 idler gears (8) and green bearings (10) from shafts (12). Do not remove these shafts (12) from gearbox plate (1).

9. Remove main shaft (6) and ratchet pinion (7) from gearbox (3).

10. Remove ratchet pinion (7) from main shaft (6). Remove pawls (16) and springs (15) from main shaft.

11. Clean parts in solvent and lubricate with Barlow Winch Grease or equivalent. The pawls (16) and springs (15) require a few drops of SAE 30 oil.

12. Replace pawls (16) and springs (15) in main shaft (6) and top cap (5).

13. Slip the ratchet pinion (7) over the main shaft (6) until the ratchet pawls (16) are fully engaged in ratchet teeth of this gear.

14. Place 2 green bearings (10) and idler gears (8) on the shafts (12) in gearbox plate (1).

15. Place ratchet pinion (7) and main shaft (6) in gearbox (3).

16. Press the gearbox plate (1) and gearbox (3) together. Place on base (2).

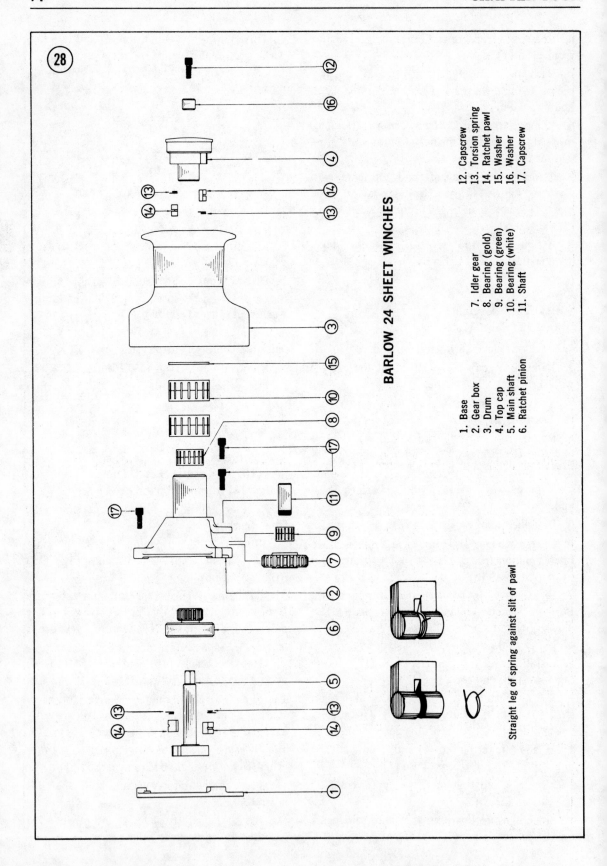

BARLOW 24 SHEET WINCHES

1. Base
2. Gear box
3. Drum
4. Top cap
5. Main shaft
6. Ratchet pinion
7. Idler gear
8. Bearing (gold)
9. Bearing (green)
10. Bearing (white)
11. Shaft
12. Capscrew
13. Torsion spring
14. Ratchet pawl
15. Washer
16. Washer
17. Capscrew

Straight leg of spring against slit of pawl

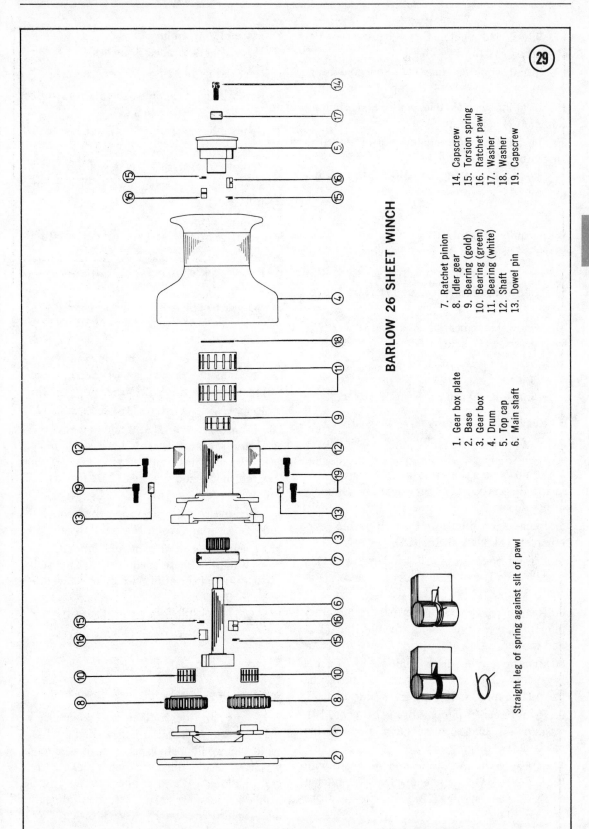

BARLOW 26 SHEET WINCH

1. Gear box plate
2. Base
3. Gear box
4. Drum
5. Top cap
6. Main shaft
7. Ratchet pinion
8. Idler gear
9. Bearing (gold)
10. Bearing (green)
11. Bearing (white)
12. Shaft
13. Dowel pin
14. Capscrew
15. Torsion spring
16. Ratchet pawl
17. Washer
18. Washer
19. Capscrew

Straight leg of spring against slit of pawl

17. Install and tighten the 4 capscrews (19) in gearbox (3).

18. Install white bearings (11) and gold bearing (9). Place washer (18) on top of gearbox (3).

19. Install top cap (5) in drum (4) and retaining washer (17) in top cap (5).

20. Install drum (4) and top cap (5) together on gearbox (3).

21. *Firmly* tighten the capscrew (14) in the top cap (5).

Disassembly/Assembly
(Barlow 28, 30, and 32 Sheet Winches)

Refer to **Figure 30** for this procedure.

1. Remove the retaining nut (7) from top of drum (4) and remove drum (4).

2. Remove black bearings (12) and spacer (27) from gearbox (3).

> NOTE: *The Barlow 28 has only one black bearing above the spacer (27), while the 30 and 32 have 2 bearings.*

3. Remove 4 capscrews (21) in gearbox (3). Keeping the gearbox assembly complete, remove from base (2).

4. Remove main shaft (5) and gold bearing (13) in top of gearbox (3). Turn gearbox assembly upside down.

5. Remove 3 capscrews (19 and 21) from gearbox plate (1). Note spacer (26).

6. Pry gearbox plate (1) off, leaving dowels (16) in gearbox (3) and gear shafts (17 and 18) in gearbox plate (1).

7. Remove grey bearing (15) from center pinion (9), idler gear (6), its green bearing (14), and washer (24).

8. Remove drum drive pinion (8), ratchet gear (11), and separate them. Remove the pawls (23), springs (22), and green bearings (14).

9. Remove center pinion (9), ratchet gear (10), washer (25), and separate them. Remove the pawls (23) and springs (22).

11. Clean parts in solvent and lubricate with Barlow Winch Grease or equivalent. The ratchet pawls (23) and springs (22) require a few drops of SAE 30 oil.

12. Assembly is the reverse of these steps.

Disassembly/Assembly
(Barlow 34 and 36 Sheet Winches)

Refer to **Figure 31** for this procedure.

1. Remove the retaining nut (6) from top of drum (4) and remove drum (4).

2. Remove black bearings (14) and spacer (26) from gearbox (3).

3. Remove 6 capscrews (21) in gearbox (3).

4. Keeping gearbox assembly complete, remove from base (2).

5. Remove main shaft (5) and gold bearing (15) in top of gearbox (3). Turn gearbox assembly upside down.

6. Remove 4 capscrews (20) from gearbox plate (1).

7. Pry gearbox plate (1) off, leaving dowels (17) in gearbox (3) and gear shafts (18 and 19) in gearbox plate (1).

8. Remove spacer (10), then idler drive pinion (12) and idler ratchet gear (9). Separate them and remove their pawls (23) and springs (22).

9. Remove green bearings (16) and washer (24).

10. From gear shaft (18), remove washer (24) and drum cluster gear (13), idler ratchet gear (9), and final ratchet gear (7) together. Separate and remove pawls (23), springs (22) and green bearings (16).

11. Remove gold bearing (15), center pinion (8) and gold bearing (15) in gearbox (3).

12. Clean parts in solvent and lubricate with Barlow Winch Grease or equivalent. The ratchet pawls (23) and springs (22) require a few drops of SAE 30 oil.

13. Assembly is the reverse of these steps.

LEWMAR WINCHES

Service and Parts Kits

Lewmar provides a different maintenance kit for each winch. **Table 3** lists available kits. A typical kit would include pawls, springs, circlips, washers, needle roller bearings, locking caps, etc. In addition, Lewmar offers circlip kits. See **Table 4**. These are easily lost when lubricating and inspecting a winch. Every owner should carry spare circlips for all winches on board.

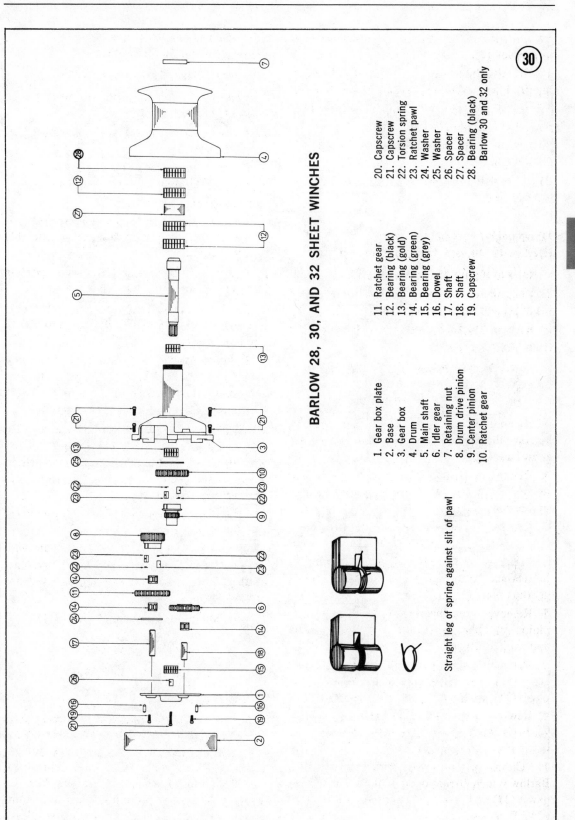

BARLOW 28, 30, AND 32 SHEET WINCHES

1. Gear box plate
2. Base
3. Gear box
4. Drum
5. Main shaft
6. Idler gear
7. Retaining nut
8. Drum drive pinion
9. Center pinion
10. Ratchet gear
11. Ratchet gear
12. Bearing (black)
13. Bearing (gold)
14. Bearing (green)
15. Bearing (grey)
16. Dowel
17. Shaft
18. Shaft
19. Capscrew
20. Capscrew
21. Capscrew
22. Torsion spring
23. Ratchet pawl
24. Washer
25. Washer
26. Spacer
27. Spacer
28. Bearing (black)
    Barlow 30 and 32 only

Straight leg of spring against slit of pawl

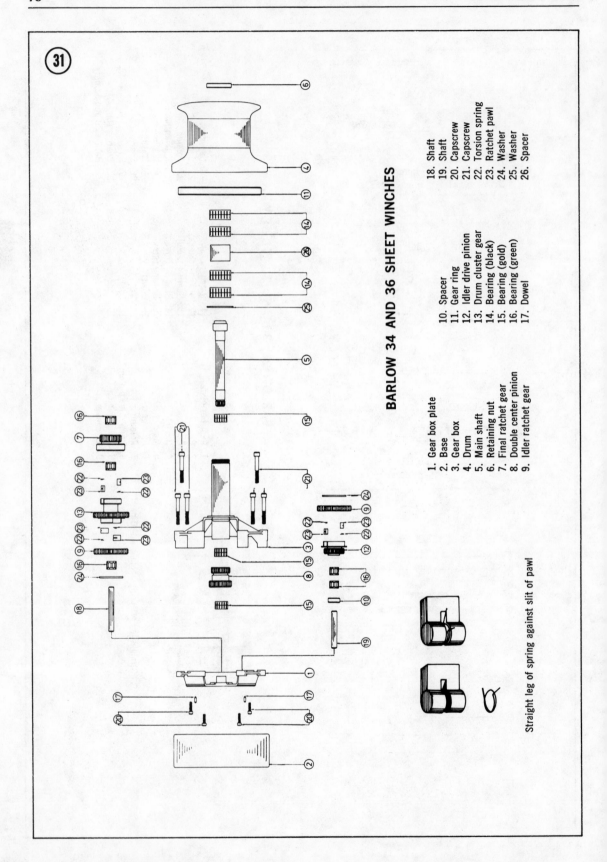

BARLOW 34 AND 36 SHEET WINCHES

1. Gear box plate
2. Base
3. Gear box
4. Drum
5. Main shaft
6. Retaining nut
7. Final ratchet gear
8. Double center pinion
9. Idler ratchet gear

10. Spacer
11. Gear ring
12. Idler drive pinion
13. Drum cluster gear
14. Bearing (black)
15. Bearing (gold)
16. Bearing (green)
17. Dowel

18. Shaft
19. Shaft
20. Capscrew
21. Capscrew
22. Torsion spring
23. Ratchet pawl
24. Washer
25. Washer
26. Spacer

Straight leg of spring against slit of pawl

Table 3   LEWMAR SPARE PARTS KITS

Winch No.	Parts Kit No.
5	1346/5
8	1308/8
16	1309/16
25	1310/25
40	1311/40
43	1312/43
45	1313/45
55	1314/55
65	1315/65
1H	1321/1
2H	1322/3
3H	1323/3
923	1317/923
840	1318/840
924 (60)	1319/924
924 Super (60s)	1320/602
501	1316/507

Table 4   LEWMAR CIRCLIP KITS

Part No.	Winches
1328	8, 16, 1H, and 2H
1329	25, 40, 43
1326	45
1327	55, 65

Disassembly/Assembly (Lewmar No. 5)

1. Remove screw from top of drum.
2. Lift drum off. See **Figure 32**.

3. Remove pawls and springs.
4. Slide bearing off. See **Figure 33**.
5. Wash all parts in petroleum solvent, including the inside of the drum.

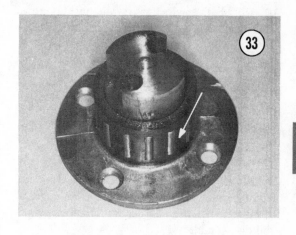

6. Generously lubricate bearing with Lewmar Lube or equivalent, and install over winch base.
7. Install springs in pawls (see **Figure 34**) and fit pawls in winch base. See **Figure 35**.

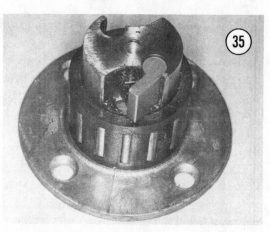

8. Lubricate pawl sockets with light machine oil (SAE 15).

9. Install drum over bearing while holding screw in place in drum.

10. Rotate drum clockwise while pushing down until pawl retracts and drum drops into place.

11. Lift up on the drum slightly and start the center screw.

> NOTE: *A screw starter tool makes this easier.*

12. Tighten center screw.

Disassembly/Assembly (Lewmar No. 8)

Routine cleaning and lubrication does not require removing winch. If there is damage, or complete inspection is desired, remove winch and disassemble.

1. Remove circlip on top of drum with a screwdriver or a small pointed object. See **Figure 36**. Use spiral motion rather than pulling straight up.

2. Lift off the drum. The 2 sets of pawls stay in the drum.

3. Remove winch base from boat.

4. Remove circlip on bottom of winch in same manner as when removing top circlip. See **Figure 37**.

5. Lift off the center shaft. See **Figure 38**.

6. Lift off the bearing. See Figure 38.

7. Clean all parts thoroughly in solvent. Check each part for signs of damage or excessive wear.

8. Lubricate thoroughly with Lewmar Lube or equivalent, and install bearing on winch base.

1. Winch base	4. Keyed thrust washer
2. Center shaft	5. Circlip
3. Phenolic washer	6. Bearing

9. Install center shaft.

10. Install thrust washer over bottom of center shaft and secure with circlip. Make sure key on thrust washer fits in center shaft slot.

11. Install both sets of pawls and springs in the drum. See **Figure 39**.

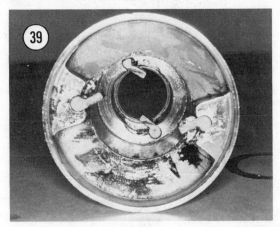

12. Install drum over winch base. Rotate drum clockwise to retract pawls or retract them with a screwdriver until the drum seats firmly.

13. Install circlip on top of drum.

Disassembly/Assembly (Lewmar No. 16)

1. Remove circlip with screwdriver or a small pointed object. Use a spiral motion rather than pulling straight up.

2. Lift off the drum.

3. Remove fiber washer from inside drum. See **Figure 40**.

4. Remove the pawls from inside the drum. See Figure 40.

5. Remove winch base from boat.

6. Remove bottom screw. See **Figure 41**.

7. Lift off center shaft. See **Figure 42**.

8. Remove gear and pawls. See **Figure 43**.

9. Remove side gear by driving out shaft. See **Figure 44**.

CAUTION
One end of the shaft has serrated ridges. See **Figure 45**. *Drive out from end opposite the serrations. On some winches this may be from the top of the winch, on others it may be from*

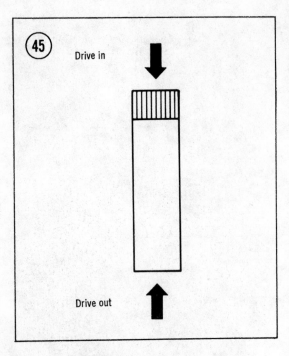

Drive in

Drive out

the bottom. Do not assume that identical winches must be driven from the
same end.

10. Clean all parts thoroughly in solvent.

11. Check parts for damage or excessive wear.

12. Install delrin bearing on center shaft and
insert shaft in winch housing.

CAUTION
Make sure the delrin bearing doesn't
jam up and become damaged.

13. Install pawls and springs in center shaft.

14. Push in pawls and install gear. This gear
has a raised shoulder which must point toward
the bottom of the installed winch.

> NOTE: It is easy to see when the gear
> is correctly installed. The pawls fit per-
> fectly in the gear cutouts. See **Fig-
> ure 46**. If the gear is installed upside-
> down, the pawls do not fit squarely.
> See **Figure 47**.

15. Install washer and screw to secure gear.

16. Install pawls and springs in drum.

17. Install fiber washer in drum to cover pawls.

18. Install drum as far as it will go. Push in
pawls until drum seats firmly in place.

19. Install circlip to secure drum.

Disassembly/Assembly
(Lewmar No. 25, 40, and 43)

These winches are nearly identical except
for size.

1. Remove circlip with screwdriver or small
pointed object. See **Figure 48**. Use a spiral motion rather than pulling straight up.

2. Remove top plate.

3. Lift off drum. The pawls will stay in drum.

4. Drive out side gear shaft from end opposite serrations. See **Figure 49**.

CAUTION
One end of the shaft has serrated ridges. Drive out from end opposite the serrations. On some winches this may be from the top of the winch, on others it may be from the bottom. Do not assume that identical winches must be driven from the same end.

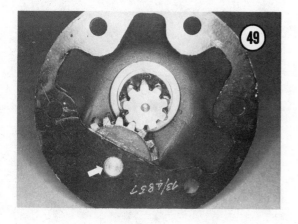

1. Bearing	3. Spacer
2. Bearing	4. Thrust washer

5. Remove side gears.

6. Remove winch base from boat.

7. Remove bottom circlip and keyed washer in the same manner as the top circlip.

8. Lift out the center shaft.

9. Lift off bearings, spacers (Lewmar 40 and 43, only), and bottom washer. See **Figure 50**.

10. Clean all parts thoroughly in solvent.

11. Check each part for damage or wear.

12. Lubricate bearings thoroughly with Lewmar Lube or equivalent.

13. Install bottom washers.

14. Install one bearing, spacer (Lewmar 40 and 43, only), and top bearing. See Figure 50.

15. Install center shaft.

16. Install thrust washer over bottom end of center shaft, making sure key engages in slot. Secure with circlip.

17. Install side gears with phenolic washer on bottom. See **Figure 51**. Apply a light film of grease to both sides of washer.

18. Drive in side gear shaft by tapping on the serrated end.

CAUTION
Do not install shaft backward. Serrated end will not pass through bore inside gears without damaging them.

19. Install pawls and springs in drum. See **Figure 52**.

20. Install drum over winch base as far as it will go. Push in pawls with screwdriver and push down on drum until it seats firmly. See **Figure 53**.

21. Place the top plate in place and secure it with circlip.

Disassembly/Assembly (Lewmar 45)

The Lewmar 45 must be removed from the boat completely to disassemble it.

1. Remove circlip with a screwdriver or a small pointed object. See **Figure 54**.

2. Remove top plate.

3. Remove the first gear drive ring assembly. See **Figure 55**.

4. Lift off drum.

5. Remove winch from boat mounting.

6. Drive out pin in top of center shaft.

7. Remove the center shaft and gears.

8. Drive out side gear shafts. See **Figure 56**.

CAUTION
One end of each shaft has serrated ridges. Drive out from end opposite the serrations. See **Figure 57**. *On some winches this may be from the top of the winch, on others it may be from the bottom. Do not assure that identical winches must be driven from the same end.*

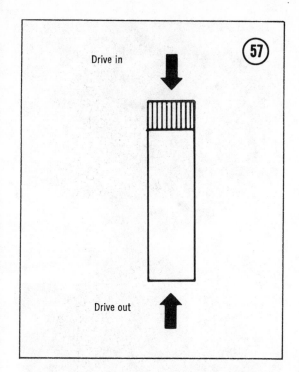

Drive in

Drive out

9. Remove both sets of gears simultaneously.

10. Remove the cap screw, washer, gears, and pawls from center shaft.

11. Disassemble each of the side gear assemblies. Keep the parts for each assembly separate to aid reassembly.

12. Remove small roller bearings from top and bottom of winch base.

13. Clean all parts thoroughly in solvent.

14. Inspect each part for wear or damage.

15. Lubricate all bearings thoroughly with Lewmar Lube or equivalent.

16. Install top and bottom center bearings in winch base.

17. Install pawls and springs in the smaller center gear. Retract pawls and install the larger center gear on the smaller gear.

18. Assemble metal washer, center gear assembly, and plate on center shaft and secure with capscrew.

19. Install center shaft in winch base.

20. Assemble both side gear sets by installing pawls and springs in the smaller gear of the set, retracting the pawls and installing the larger gear on the set. Lubricate pawls with light engine oil.

21. Install phenolic washers against the bottom side gears.

22. Mesh the 2 gear sets together in your hands and install them simultaneously into the winch base. Mesh them with the center gear.

23. Drive side gear shafts through winch base and side gears. Insert in same direction as removed. Tap on serrated end with plastic mallet until fully seated.

24. Mount winch on boat.

25. Slide on thrust washer, 2 bearings, delrin spacer, top bearing, delrin washer, and metal washer over winch base.

26. Lift up on the center shaft and install drive pin in top of center shaft.

27. Install drum over winch base.

28. Install pawls and springs in first gear drive ring assembly. Also install lock pins, spring-end first. See **Figure 58**.

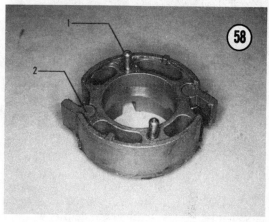

1. Lock pin
2. Pawl

29. Install first gear drive ring in top of drum. Rotate it until it engages the drive pin in the center shaft.

30. Install the top plate. The 2 tabs in the first gear drive ring assembly fit in the cutouts in the top plate.

31. Push down in top plate and install circlip.

Disassembly/Assembly (Lewmar 55 and 65)

1. Remove circlip with a screwdriver or a small pointed object. See Figure 54.

2. Remove top plate.

3. Remove the first gear drive ring assembly. See Figure 55.

4. Lift off drum.

5. Drive out pin in center shaft. See **Figure 59**.

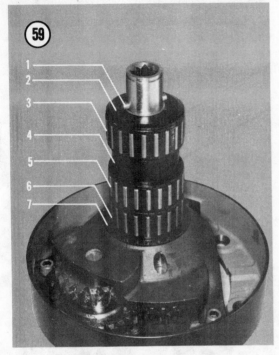

1. Drive pin
2. Metal washer(s) and delrin washer
3. Bearing
4. Delrin spacer
5. Bearing
6. Bearing
7. Thrust washer

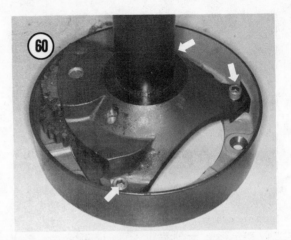

6. Remove metal washer(s), delrin washer, bearings, and delrin spacer and thrust washer. See Figure 59.

7. Remove capscrews securing winch base to mounting plate. See **Figure 60**.

8. Pry off bottom plate with screwdriver in slots. See **Figure 61**. Pry a little bit equally on both sides to work it straight off. If you try to pry it completely off one side, you may break the plate.

9. Remove the center shaft and gears.

10. Lift off both side gear sets simultaneously. Note phenolic washers, if any, on shafts. Count them so the same number will be reinstalled, then remove them.

11. Remove the cap screw, washer, gears, and pawls from center shaft.

12. Disassemble each of the side gear assemblies. Keep the parts for each assembly separate to aid reassembly.

13. Remove small roller bearings from top and bottom of winch base.

14. Clean all parts thoroughly in solvent.

15. Inspect each part for wear or damage.

16. Lubricate all bearings thoroughly with Lewmar Lube or equivalent.

17. Install top and bottom center bearings in winch base.

18. Install pawls and springs in the smaller center gear. Retract the pawls and install the larger center gear on the smaller gear.

19. Assemble metal washer, center gear assembly, and plate on center shaft and secure with a capscrew.

20. Install center shaft in winch base.

21. Assemble both side gear sets by installing pawls and springs in the smaller gear of the set, retracting the pawls and installing the larger gear of the set. Lubricate pawls with light engine oil.

22. Install phenolic washers, if any, removed in Step 10, over the 2 side shafts. Use same number removed.

23. Mesh the 2 gear sets together in your hands and install them simultaneously over the side gear shafts. Mesh them with the center gears and push them down until they seat. Lightly grease the large phenolic washers and install them over the side gears.

24. Place the bottom plate in position over the roll pins and tap it evenly in place with a plastic mallet.

CAUTION
Do not use a steel hammer or you may break the plate.

25. Mount winch base on mounting plate and secure with capscrews.

26. Slide on thrust washer, 2 bearings, delrin spacer, top bearing, delrin washer, and metal washer over winch base. See Figure 59.

27. Lift up on center shaft and install drive pin in top of center shaft.

28. Install drum over winch base.

29. Install pawls and springs in first gear drive ring assembly. Also install lock pins, spring-end first. See Figure 58.

30. Install first gear drive ring in top of drum. Rotate it until it engages the drive pin in the center shaft.

31. Install the top plate. The 2 tabs in the first gear drive ring assembly fit in the cutouts in the top plate.

32. Push down on top plate and install circlip.

Disassembly/Assembly (Lewmar No. 1 Halyard Winch)

It is not necessary to remove the No. 1 halyard winch from the mast for this procedure.

1. Release the brake screw and unreel halyard from drum.

2. Loosen 2 Allen screws securing end of halyard wire and pull wire free of winch.

3. Remove circlip from top of drum with a screwdriver or small pointed object. Use a spiral motion rather than pulling straight up.

4. Lift off the drum.

5. Lift off the brake band. See **Figure 62**.

6. Pull brake shoe from drum. See **Figure 63**.

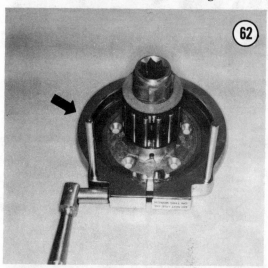

7. Remove winch base from mast.

8. Remove bottom circlip in the same manner as when removing top circlip. See **Figure 64**.

9. Remove center shaft. See **Figure 65**.

10. Lift off bearing. See Figure 65.

11. Clean all parts thoroughly in solvent.

12. Inspect parts for signs of damage or wear.

13. Lubricate bearing thoroughly with Lewmar Lube or equivalent and install bearing on winch base.

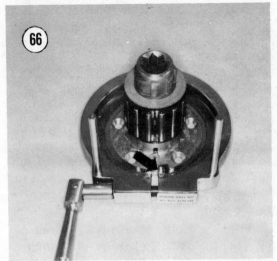

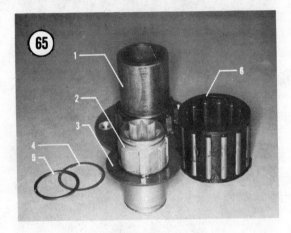

1. Winch base
2. Center shaft
3. Phenolic washer
4. Keyed thrust washer
5. Circlip
6. Bearing

14. Install center shaft and secure at bottom with circlip.

15. Install brake shoe on drum.

> NOTE: *Brake shoe will fit on only in one direction. A shoulder prevents it from being installed backward.*

16. Place brake band over winch base. The tab in the brake band fits in a slot in the base. See **Figure 66**.

17. Install pawls and springs in drum.

18. Install the drum.

19. Secure with circlip.

20. Insert the halyard wire and tighten the Allen screws.

Disassembly/Assembly
(Lewmar 2, 2-2, and 3 Halyard Winches)

These winches must be removed from the mast in order to service them.

1. Unreel halyard wire from drum.

2. Rotate drum as necessary to align clamp screw with hole in base. See **Figure 67**. Loosen clamp screw and pull halyard wire free from drum.

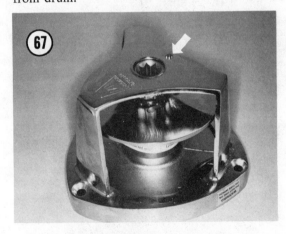

3. Remove 3 screws securing winch to mast.

4. Loosen the brake.

5. Remove 6 base plate screws. Scribe a line on the base plate and the winch housing so the 2 are aligned the same when reassembled. See **Figure 68**.

6. Remove brake screw entirely. See **Figure 69**.

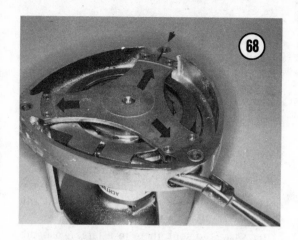

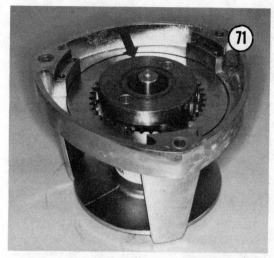

10. Lift out drum. Don't lose the pawls.
11. Lift out the center shaft. See **Figure 72**.

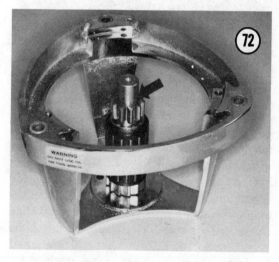

7. Lift off brake band. See Figure 69.
8. Lift off the brake shoe. See **Figure 70.**
9. Lift out planetary gear set on 2-speed halyards. See **Figure 71**.

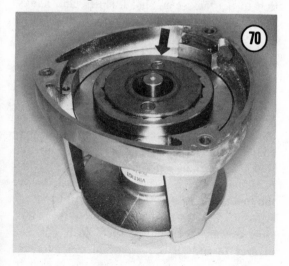

12. Remove the bearings.
13. Clean all parts thoroughly in solvent.
14. Inspect parts for signs of damage or wear.
15. Assembly is the reverse of these steps. Lubricate the bearings with Lewmar Lube or equivalent.

RUNNING RIGGING

Running rigging consists of the halyards and other adjustable lines routinely used to operate the boat. These may be cordage, wire rope, or both. Usually a wire rope line that must be handled has a cordage tail spliced on.

Wire Rope

Unlike standing rigging, running rigging requires flexible wire rope. The most commonly used is 7 x 19 wire—7 strands of 19 wires each, closed around a core. See **Figure 73**.

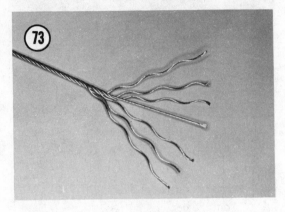

Wire rope for running rigging may be stainless steel or galvanized; stainless steel is the most common.

Running rigging works far more than standing rigging as it bends around blocks and winch drums. High loads on the sides of the wire where it bears on blocks and winches flatten and spread the strands. Repeated straining and relaxing can fatigue stainless wire, leading to failure. Galvanized wire tends to rust.

Check all wire rope used for running rigging several times a season; every 2 months, for example. Look for signs of rust and whiskering (small broken wires which spring out of the strand). Also check for excessive side wear or flattening. Check along the entire length of the rope, not just the ends. While you are at it, check the condition of all blocks through which the rope passes. A worn block can quickly cause rope failure.

Cordage

Nearly all boats today use synthetic ropes rather than natural fiber ropes. Two main materials are used for synthetic rope:

a. Dacron
b. Nylon

Dacron is used mainly for sheets and halyard where its stretch resistance makes sail control under all conditions more positive.

Nylon is used mainly for docking, mooring, anchoring, towing, and other applications where its ability to stretch absorbs surge caused by wind and sea.

Check all lines several times a season. Look for signs of chafe, deterioration, and other damage. Check along the entire length and check all blocks and eyes through which the line passes. Worn blocks can quickly cause new line failure.

When the lines become dirty or in any event when you clean your sails, clean the lines. Some sailors toss them in a washing machine, but any time saved will be used uncoiling the mess. A better way is to soak them in a large wash tub or bathtub. Use a mild detergent and agitate them by hand. Rinse thoroughly and hang to dry.

CAUTION
Do not use bleach. Bleach can discolor and even weaken some synthetics.

SAILS

Care

Sail care is very simple. Keep the sail:

a. Clean
b. Folded
c. Dry
d. Covered
e. Repaired

Sails can accumulate a tremendous amount of dirt and air pollutants. After each sail, hose the sails down with fresh water. Pay particular attention to the tack, clew, head, slides, and hanks. Be sure to let the sails dry thoroughly before putting them away.

Dacron and nylon sails will not be damaged by storing them wet. However, mildew will grow and permanently discolor the sails.

Once dry, fold the sail whenever possible. Most sailors prefer to flake the mainsail down on the boom and protect it with a loose-fitting cover. This lets air in and keeps the sun out. Flaking the main on the boom is not always practical. Trailerable boat sailors must remove the main, fold it, and store it in a sail bag.

As often as practical, but at least at the end of each season, thoroughly inspect each sail. See **Figures 74 and 75**. Spread it out completely on

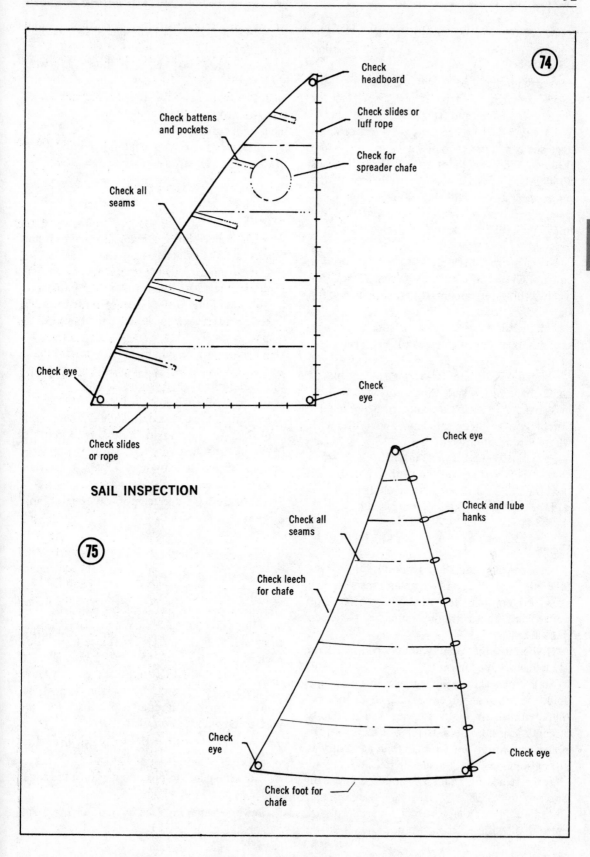

74

Check headboard

Check slides or luff rope

Check battens and pockets

Check for spreader chafe

Check all seams

Check eye

Check eye

Check slides or rope

SAIL INSPECTION

75

Check eye

Check and lube hanks

Check all seams

Check leech for chafe

Check eye

Check eye

Check foot for chafe

a lawn or clean floor. It is difficult to do a thorough job onboard because only a small section is visible at any one time.

Start with the head. Check the headboard for wear caused by the halyard shackle. Check for chafing on cloth and stitching around head. Work down the luff, checking for worn or damaged slides and hanks. Also check eyelets in sail through which the slides attach. If the sail has no slides or hanks, check the cloth around the luff rope. Check all stitching along the luff. Continue along the foot in the same manner as the luff. Check that tack and clew eyes are securely fastened.

Next, inspect the leech. Look for broken stitches. Check both ends of batten pockets for wear. While you are at it, check battens for sharp edges; sand them smooth.

Finally, check every inch of stitching in the sail. A single broken stitch can lead to complete failure under stress.

Synthetic sails are far more susceptible to chafe than canvas sails. Stitching imbeds itself in canvas sails and is protected from chafe. Stitching in synthetic sails lays above the cloth where it is easily broken.

Periodically check rigging, life lines, stanchions, bow pulpit, and any other part of the boat which sails may contact and chafe on. Tape, pad, or replace anything that causes chafe.

Cleaning

Seasonal cleaning should be done by a professional. Many lofts will clean and inspect your sails for a nominal fee—usually about 10 cents per square foot. Minor restitching is often done free.

If you have the room, you may be able to do a satisfactory job yourself.

Stains such as rust can be removed with oxalic acid, available at any well stocked chandlery. Start with a very dilute solution and gradually strength it, if necessary, to remove the stain. Do not use a solution any stronger than necessary as strong solutions can damage the sail.

After removing stains, wash the entire sail. Spread large sails on a lawn or clean surface. Put small sails in a large tub of water. Scrub the entire sail with detergent and a small bristle brush. Don't scrub hard enough to damage the sail surface.

When clean, rinse the sails thoroughly with fresh water and hang to dry. Hang sails by the luff. This will hold the proper shape and let wrinkles drop out. Fold the clean sails and stow them in the sail bag.

Sail bags, winch covers, and other small items can be washed in a washing machine.

Repairs

Every sailor should be able to make minor repairs to sails. Damaged stitching can be replaced by hand or with any zigzag sewing machine. If sewing by hand, follow the pattern of the old stitching with a needle and synthetic thread. Do not draw the stitches tight enough to deform cloth.

When using a sewing machine, thread it with synthetic thread and set controls to produce stitch width and length approximately the same as the original stitches.

Any tear, however small, should be repaired immediately. This should be done by a sail loft. If the sail must be used at all before you can get to a loft, make a temporary repair to prevent further damage.

There are 2 ways to temporarily repair a hole or tear:

a. Darning

b. Patching

A small hole or tear can be darned with a needle and thread.

A tear or hole can also be patched. Self-adhesive vinyl patches come in a variety of sizes to patch small rips and tears. Place a patch on each side of the sail over the damaged area, following the manufacturer's directions. Have sail repaired professionally as soon as possible.

A more permanent repair is possible by sewing on a patch made from sailcloth.

1. Cut a patch so that the weave of the patch will align with the weave of the sail.

2. Hold the patch in position and turn the edges under as shown in **Figure 76**.

3. Sew the patch in place by hand or use a zigzag sewing machine.

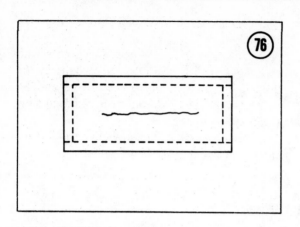

4. Cut out the damaged area of the sail. Leave some material around the edge.

5. Turn the cut edge down and stitch it as well.

BOSUN'S CHAIR

A bosun's chair should be aboard any boat whose mast cannot be quickly unstepped. It is invaluable for periodic inspection of the mast and rigging and makes retrieving or repairing a halyard simple.

A good bosun's chair is far safer than shinnying up the mast. Besides being safer and easier to get aloft, it is also more secure to work from when you get aloft.

For most work, the bosun's chair is hoisted aloft on the main halyard with the halyard winch. If the purpose of going aloft is to replace or retrieve the main halyard, you may not be able to use the bosun's chair. Of course, on a mast head rig, you may use the jib halyard.

4

CHAPTER FIVE

OUTBOARD MOTORS

Nearly all outboard motors used for sailboat auxiliary power are 2-cycle engines under 15 horsepower. These engines are relatively light, portable, and easy to maintain.

Modern outboard motors are smooth, reliable sources of power. Unfortunately, a sailor more interested in the wind as a source of power neglects his outboard until he needs it. When the motor won't start, he curses outboard motors in general. Like any engine, an outboard thrives on use. An occasional running and regular preventive maintenance will pay for itself with a dependable engine when you need it.

The basics of maintaining an outboard are the same as for any engine.

1. Run the engine periodically—even a few minutes every week except during lay-up.

2. Perform regular scheduled maintenance.

3. Fix minor troubles immediately or they will become major ones.

DAILY CARE

Your outboard requires a certain minimum care every time you use it. Besides using the correct fuel/oil mixture and flushing the cooling system after use (older engines), you should quickly inspect the motor before each use.

Inspection

Outboards may sit idle for quite some time between uses. Unless you make a point of inspecting the motor, deterioration can get serious before you notice it. When starting the motor, follow this simple routine.

1. Remove cover.

2. Check condition of starter rope. These fray and deteriorate.

3. Check spark plug wires. Make sure that they are securely connected and in good condition.

4. Check fuel lines. Make certain they are securely clamped and in good condition. A loose or leaky fuel line is a serious fire hazard.

5. Install cover.

6. Start motor and make sure that water emerges from exhaust ports.

Mixing Fuel

The correct ratio of fuel to oil is very important with a 2-cycle engine. The oil in the fuel lubricates the internal engine parts. If there is too much oil, spark plugs foul easily, carbon accumulation is rapid, and the engine runs too hot. If there is not enough oil, engine wear is excessive. Always use the ratio established by the engine manufacturer.

Some common ratios are 50:1, 40:1, 24:1. For example, 50:1 means 50 parts gasoline to 1 part oil. A 6 gallon tank, which is 48 pints of fuel, requires approximately 1 pint of oil. Special measuring cups which permit measuring exact amount of oil required for any ratio and any fuel quantity are on the market. See **Figure 1**. If you can't find one at your local outboard dealer or chandlery, try a motorcycle dealer. An excellent one priced at $1.95 is distributed by Helmet House, Santa Monica, Calif.

Special oils are formulated for use in 2-cycle engines. These oils leave fewer and softer carbon deposits in the engine than automotive engine oil. It is always best to purchase this type rather than use ordinary automotive engine oil. Outboard (2-cycle) oil is packaged in 6-packs of 1 pint cans. If you use less than a pint at a time, pour the excess into a resealable can or jar. Do not leave oil in an open oil can; dirt and moisture will contaminate it.

It is important to mix the oil with the gasoline in a certain way. Never pour the oil into an empty tank. The best way is to fill the tank about ⅓ full, then add all the oil. Install the filler cap and shake the tank well to dissolve the oil. Then add the remaining fuel and shake the tank again. If you are mixing fuel for a motor with integral tank, mix the fuel in a separate 1 gallon can first, then pour mixture into the tank.

Flushing

Modern motors do not require flushing after each use in salt water, as do older motors. The newer ones should be drained at the end of the day's use; a few pulls on the starter cord with the throttle in the OFF position is sufficient. In addition, rinse the exterior of the motor with fresh water to remove salt deposits and wipe dry.

Older motors usually require flushing after each use in salt water. Special flushing attachments to connect a garden hose to the motor are available. If none is handy, direct a high pressure stream from a garden hose into the water inlet. If it works, you will see water emerge from the exhaust outlets. On some motors, this method will not work. In that case, the motor must be run briefly in a fresh water test tank.

TUNE-UP AND LUBRICATION

Every 100 hours, a 2-cycle outboard motor should get an engine tune-up and general lubrication. Usually this consists of:

a. Torquing cylinder head nuts or bolts
b. Replacing and/or adjusting breaker points
c. Replacing or cleaning spark plugs
d. Decarbonizing (every 200 hours usually)
e. Lubricating moving linkage parts
f. Changing drive unit oil

Torquing Cylinder Head

With time, cylinder head fasteners stretch and the head gasket compresses. The fasteners must be retightened to correct torque on some engines. This is a job for your dealer unless you have a service manual for your engine and a torque wrench.

Breaker Points

Breaker points pit and deteriorate with use; they must be replaced and/or adjusted periodically. Usually they are mounted under the flywheel and sealed against moisture; the engine cannot run with wet points.

Replacement and adjustment varies from engine to engine. Take the job to your dealer or follow instructions in a service manual for your particular engine.

5

Spark Plugs

Spark plugs in a 2-cycle outboard tend to "foul" rather easily. This is caused by an accumulation of oil on the plug which prevents it from sparking. In addition, spark plug electrodes erode with use and must be replaced.

You should know how to remove the plugs to clean them periodically, examine them for damage, adjust the electrode gap, and install them.

1. Disconnect spark plug wire(s) by pulling as close to the plug as possible. Otherwise, you will pull the wire right out of the connector.

2. Unscrew plug(s) with a spark plug wrench. See **Figure 2**.

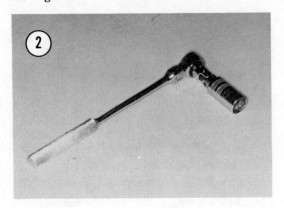

3. Clean off any oil and heavy carbon deposits with solvent.

4. Examine center porcelain cone and electrodes. If damaged or eroded, discard the plug.

5. Check electrode gap with a wire-type feeler gauge. See **Figure 3**. Flat gauges give a false reading. Adjust the gap as necessary to value given in owner's manual or service manual.

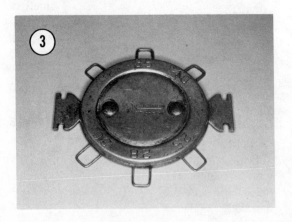

6. Place a drop of clean engine oil on the spark plug threads.

7. Install the plug(s) with a new gasket and tighten *finger-tight*.

8. Tighten plugs ½ turn with a plug wrench. Do not overtighten; this will compress the gasket too tightly and prevent a good seal.

9. Install spark plug wires.

Decarbonizing

All engines suffer somewhat from carbon accumulation on the piston crowns and combustion chambers. Carbon deposits caused by oil in the fuel makes accumulation more rapid in 2-stroke engines.

Carbon deposits effectively raise the compression ratio and make the engine more prone to knock and ping with the normal grade of gasoline. In addition, carbon particles may glow from combustion and preignite the incoming fuel/air mixture before the spark plug can; preignition can cause considerable engine damage.

Every 200 hours or so, the cylinder head must be removed and all carbon deposits cleaned away. This is a job for your dealer unless you have the proper skills and a service manual for your particular engine.

Lubrication

Throttle and choke linkage to the carburetor, and gear shift linkage if equipped, must be lubricated every 100 hours. Follow manufacturer's recommendation for lubricants.

> CAUTION
> *Lubricant substitutions are risky. Some excellent quality white greases on the market are fine for automotive and general use, but get gummy in a salt environment.*

Changing Drive Unit Oil

Oil in the drive unit must be drained and new oil poured in every 100 hours. Most models have a screw-in drain plug at the bottom of the unit. On some, there is a separate filler hole, though others use the drain as a filler with the outboard laying on its side. See owner's manual or service manual for your engine for details.

Use special lubricant recommended by the manufacturer.

SHEAR PIN REPLACEMENT

The output shaft couples to the propeller with a shear pin. A large nut secured with a cotter pin keeps the propeller on the shaft. If the propeller hits an obstruction, the shear pin breaks, preventing any damage to the engine or propeller. When the shear pin breaks, the engine still runs, but the propeller cannot spin until the pin is replaced.

To replace a shear pin:

1. Straighten the ends of the cotter pin and remove it. See **Figure 4**.

2. Unscrew the hub nut.

3. Pull off the propeller.

4. Remove broken halves of shear pin.

5. Install new shear pin in shaft. See **Figure 5**.

CAUTION
Do not substitute anything else. Use a shear pin made specifically for the purpose. Substitutes may be too strong and not shear properly, causing expensive engine damage.

6. Install propeller.

7. Install hub nut finger-tight.

8. Loosen the nut as necessary to align shaft holes with nut and install cotter pin. Bend ends of pin over to secure it.

CAUTION
Do not tighten nut to align holes. Overtightening may prevent shear pin from breaking when necessary to protect engine.

TROUBLESHOOTING

Nearly all modern outboards, if properly maintained, start very easily and run reliably. If the motor doesn't start quickly, especially if it has in the past, don't wear yourself out pulling and pulling on the starter cord. Find out what the problem is and fix it. The following are symptoms and the most likely cause of trouble.

1. Motor won't start.
   a. Check fuel in tank.
   b. Make sure that fuel line is properly connected to engine and remote tank.
   c. Prime carburetor again.
   d. Not enough choke. Pull choke out all the way. Make sure choke is functioning properly.
   e. Flooded engine. Usually strong smell of gas around engine. Push choke off, disconnect fuel line or shut off fuel petcock and crank until flooding is eliminated.

2. Motor won't idle.
   a. Dirty or defective spark plug(s). Remove and clean or replace.
   b. Carburetor adjustment. Adjust low speed adjustment until idle is correct.
   c. Wrong fuel/oil mixture.

3. Motor won't deliver sufficient power.
   a. Restriction in fuel line. Make sure fuel line is not kinked or blocked by dirt.

5

b. Ignition system requires tune-up.

c. Cylinder heads require decarbonizing.

4. Steam coming from exhaust outlets (engine overheating).

a. Water inlet blocked or restricted.

b. Water pump defective.

5. Excessive vibration.

a. Broken or bent propeller.

b. One or more cylinders not firing (except single cylinder engines).

c. Loose flywheel.

d. Internal damage.

ACCIDENTAL IMMERSION

Immersion in water, fresh or salt, can mean the end for an outboard motor. Water finds its way into the motor where it can corrode precision parts beyond repair.

Obviously, the best protection against accidental immersion is prevention. A small chain secured to the transom and a strong area of the outboard will prevent immersion and loss should the clamps loosen or the mounting bracket break.

If the motor was not running when submerged, chances of recovering the engine without damage are fairly good. However, if the motor was running, damage can be extensive. Most serious is the possibility that sand and dirt were drawn into the engine before it stopped.

CAUTION
If there is any sign that dirt or sand could have entered motor, do not use the procedure below or rotate the flywheel. Rinse off the motor with fresh water and take it to a repair shop within 3 hours. If this is not possible, resubmerge motor in fresh water and take it in as soon as possible.

1. Rinse motor with fresh water.

2. Disconnect spark plug leads and remove the plugs.

3. Hold motor horizontally with spark plug holes down. Rotate flywheel with starter cord 25 to 30 times to work out water.

CAUTION
If there is any binding when rotating flywheel, go to Step 8 and do not

attempt to start the motor. Most likely a connecting rod is bent. Have the motor serviced immediately.

4. Remove carburetor and clean it with solvent. Alcohol or kerosene used for the galley stove work well and are relatively safe.

WARNING
Gasoline may be the only solvent on board at the time. If you must use it, keep a fire extinguisher nearby, do not allow smoking or open flames, and be careful not to strike metal parts together.

5. Install carburetor and spark plugs. If you use old plug gaskets, tighten plugs ¼ turn after finger-tight.

6. Start motor in normal manner. Run for ½ hour or more.

7. If motor fails to start, remove spark plugs and look for water between electrodes. Blow dry, reinstall plugs and try to start motor again.

8. If all attempts to start motor fail, or the flywheel binds when turned, take the motor to a repair shop within 3 hours after recovery. If you cannot do this, resubmerge motor in fresh water to avoid exposure to atmosphere. Take it to repair shop as soon as possible thereafter.

LAY-UP AND STORAGE

Because an outboard is such a compact system, preparation for lay-up is very simple.

1. Drain fuel tank.

2. Run motor until all fuel in carburetor is used.

3. Flush the cooling system with fresh water, even if the manufacturer states flushing is unnecessary.

NOTE: *Several adapters are on the market to fit a garden hose to the engine for flushing. If none is available, force water under pressure into the water intake. As an alternative, run the engine briefly at low speed in a fresh water test tank.*

4. Remove spark plug(s). Squirt about ½ teaspoon of oil directly into the spark plug hole(s). Rotate flywheel one revolution.

5. Place a drop of clean engine oil on spark plug threads. Install plugs and tighten finger-tight. Tighten plugs ½ turn with spark plug wrench. Do not overtighten.

6. Change drive unit oil regardless of time since last change. Use oil recommended by manufacturer. Substitutes are risky in precision engines.

7. Clean entire engine with solvent. Remove large grease and dirt deposits with a bristle brush soaked in solvent. Remove all lubricant from moving parts such as gearshifter, throttle linkage, and so forth.

8. Lubricate all moving parts with salt resistant white grease.

9. Spray entire engine with light protective coat of WD-40 or silicone spray.

10. Store motor upright in a clean dry place. Improvise a protective cover that will keep out dust and dirt.

Recommissioning an outboard does not require any special consideration. Fill the fuel tank with the proper fuel/oil mixture and start the engine in the normal manner. There may be some tendency for the plugs to foul from the oil squirted in during lay-up preparation. If the engine is difficult to start or runs roughly, remove the plugs and clean them in solvent. When dry, regap and install them.

5

CHAPTER SIX

INBOARD ENGINES

Marine engines thrive on use. Running the engine circulates oil throughout the engine, preventing build-up of sludge and corrosion. Cooling water also circulates, taking rust inhibitor to all parts of the system. An idle engine is subject to all kinds of corrosion and trouble.

Besides running the engine, you should have an on-going schedule of preventive maintenance. Engines are subject to tremendous stresses and wear from high pressure and friction. Regular maintenance insures that your engine will give good performance, dependability, and safety throughout its normal life. Neglect leads to premature failure, usually when you need the engine most.

Standard Installation

Figure 1 shows the most common inboard engine/drive unit installation. It consists of an engine, final drive unit, a shaft, stuffing box, and propeller.

The engine may be diesel or gasoline. A final drive unit bolts directly to the aft end of the engine block. The final drive may provide a gear reduction between engine and propeller, i.e., the propeller turns slower than the engine. It may instead provide direct drive (1:1) and one or more other gear ratios. In addition, most drive units provide reverse.

The propeller shaft passes through the hull in a stuffing box. The stuffing box is packed with grease to prevent entry of water. The propeller bolts to the end of the shaft and is secured with a castellated nut and a cotter pin.

Some installations have a 2-piece prop shaft joined with a universal coupling. See **Figure 2**. This is sometimes necessary when compromising between available space and desired shaft angle. Some universal couplings require lubrication.

V-drive Installation

Figure 3 shows a V-drive installation. A V-drive works the same way as the standard in-line type. Folding the power transfer back on itself, however, provides additional cabin space by moving engine aft.

V-drive units are available with direct drive, reduction ratios, and reverse. The shifting may be manual or hydraulic.

BASIC ENGINE SYSTEMS

Diesel and gasoline powered engines are alike more than they are different. Gasoline engines use a carburetor to atomize a highly volatile fuel with air. The mixture is compressed by the pistons and ignited by a carefully timed spark

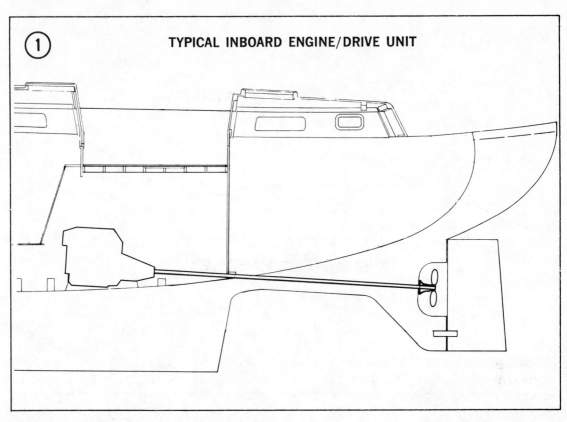

TYPICAL INBOARD ENGINE/DRIVE UNIT

6

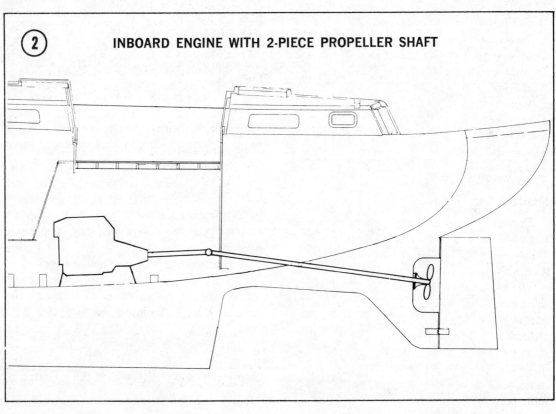

INBOARD ENGINE WITH 2-PIECE PROPELLER SHAFT

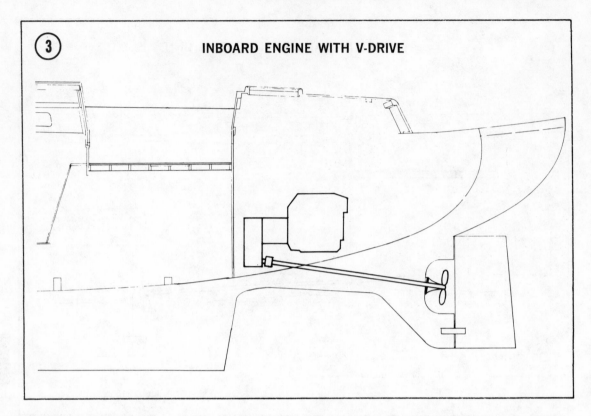

③ INBOARD ENGINE WITH V-DRIVE

to produce power. Diesel engines use a mechanical fuel injection system to inject carefully timed and metered amounts of fuel to each cylinder. The pistons compress the fuel/air mixture. Heat generated by the tremendous compression pressure ignites the mixture rather than having a spark do it. In all other respects, gasoline and diesel engines are virtually identical.

The following sections describe major systems in both types of engines. A knowledge of how each system works will help troubleshooting in case of trouble.

Diesel Fuel Systems

The fuel system for all diesel engines in marine use are similar. **Figure 4** shows a typical system consisting of fuel tank, fuel filters, fuel lift pump, fuel injection pump, and injectors. The fuel lift pump, mechanically driven by the engine, draws fuel from the fuel tank. Some engines, for example, Lehman Ford, have a primary fuel filter between the fuel tank and the fuel lift pump.

The fuel lift pump delivers fuel through another fuel filter to the fuel injection pump. The fuel injection pump, in turn, delivers precisely timed and metered quantities of fuel to the injectors at each cylinder. Overflow lines are provided from the secondary fuel filter, the fuel injection pump, and the injectors back to the fuel tank.

Cleanliness is vital to the proper operation of the fuel system. The fuel injection components are made to precise tolerances and even the smallest particle of dirt in the system will destroy its efficiency.

Gasoline Fuel System

Gasoline fuel systems are similar to diesel fuel systems, but they are usually simpler. See **Figure 5**.

A mechanical fuel pump on the engine draws fuel from the tank. The tank has a filler pipe and a vent which permits air to enter the tank as fuel leaves. Some installations have a fuel filter/water separator between the tank and the fuel pump; if not, you can easily add one. The fuel pump delivers fuel to the carburetor, which atomizes it and delivers it to the cylinders via the intake manifold.

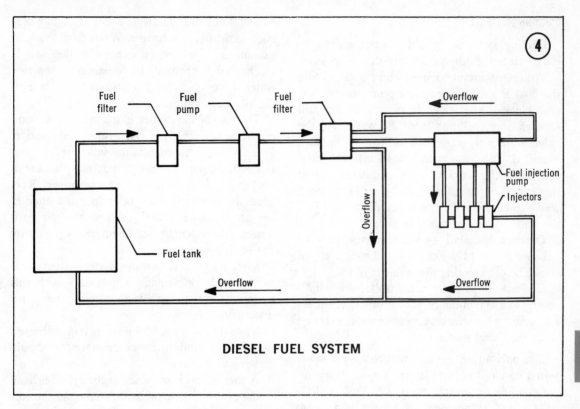

④

Fuel filter · Fuel pump · Fuel filter · Overflow

Fuel injection pump

Injectors

Overflow

Fuel tank

Overflow

Overflow

DIESEL FUEL SYSTEM

6

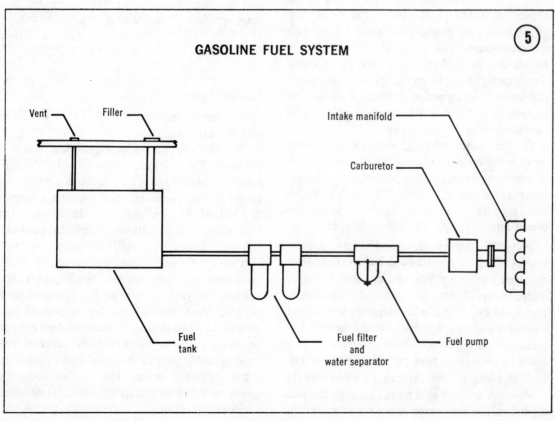

GASOLINE FUEL SYSTEM

⑤

Vent · Filler

Intake manifold

Carburetor

Fuel tank

Fuel filter and water separator

Fuel pump

Cooling Systems

Cooling systems are either open circuit or closed circuit. Both systems are described here.

With open circuit cooling, water from outside the boat is used. A seawater pump on the engine block draws water from outside the hull through a seacock and feeds the water into the exhaust manifold water jacket. From the exhaust manifold, this "raw water" flows into the front of the cylinder block where it circulates around the cylinders and through the cylinder head water jacket. Finally, the water discharges into the exhaust line and out of the boat.

On some installations, water passes from the exhaust manifold water jacket through an oil cooler before entering the cylinder block.

Coolant temperature is controlled by a thermostat to a maximum of 120°F (49°C). A pressure relief valve releases excessive water pressure when the thermostat is closed.

The only advantage of direct cooling is lower initial cost of the installation. Engine temperatures normally remain around 90-100°F (32-38°C), and in no event, are permitted to go above 120°F (49°C). To prevent scale buildup in the water passages, engines should work with a coolent temperature of 150-180°F (65-82°C). Lower than normal coolant temperatures cause considerably heavier engine wear with direct raw water cooling, and increased oil sludge formation. In addition, a cold engine is noisier than one at the correct temperature.

Closed circuit cooling, also called indirect fresh water cooling, consists of a closed circuit of fresh water circulating through the engine block and a heat exchanger. The fresh water, in turn, is cooled by an open circuit raw water system flowing through the heat exchanger.

A typical system is shown in **Figure 6**. A water pump on the engine block draws coolant from the heat exchanger into the exhaust manifold water jacket. From the manifold, the coolant enters the cylinder block, circulates around the cylinders and through the cylinder head water jacket. Finally, coolant discharges from the cylinder head back to heat exchanger for cooling.

Water from outside the hull is used to cool the fresh water coolant as it passes through the heat exchanger. A raw water pump mounted on the engine block draws outside water through a seacock to the heat exchanger. Water from the heat exchanger flows to the exhaust outlet and is discharged overboard. In some cases, the raw water discharge is used for water injection into the silencing system.

The use of keel pipes is a simplified version of the heat exchanger system described above. Fresh water circulation is the same, except that the coolant passes through externally mounted keel pipes instead of a heat exchanger. Keel pipes are normally made of copper and fitted in the angle between the keel and the garboard strake. Their length and diameter depends on the engine size.

Since no open circuit raw water system is required, only one pump is necessary with this system. However, there is no water discharge for a wet silencing system.

Since draining the keel pipes is impossible, an anti-freeze solution, never plain water, should be used as coolant.

A thermostat is mounted at the cylinder head outlet connection to maintain coolant at the correct operating temperature. On pressurized systems, coolant temperatures should be about 190°F (88°C). On unpressurized systems, best coolant temperature is about 170°F (77°C).

Exhaust System

Exhaust systems are classified as dry exhaust and wet exhaust.

The dry type, shown in **Figure 7**, is not very common. Exhaust gases, often as hot as 300°F, heat the pipe. This not only radiates a lot of heat in the engine room, but also presents a serious fire hazard. The end which passes through the hull must be carefully insulated. In addition, this type exhaust is relatively noisy.

The wet exhaust system overcomes the problems inherent in dry systems. See **Figure 8**. The exhaust-carrying inner pipe is enveloped by a water-carrying outer hose. Under normal running conditions, the outer hose stays cool enough to touch. Exhaust fumes from the jacketed line enter a muffler where they mix directly with the water from the jacket. This further cools the gases and silences exhaust noise. Gases and water exit from muffler through a common line.

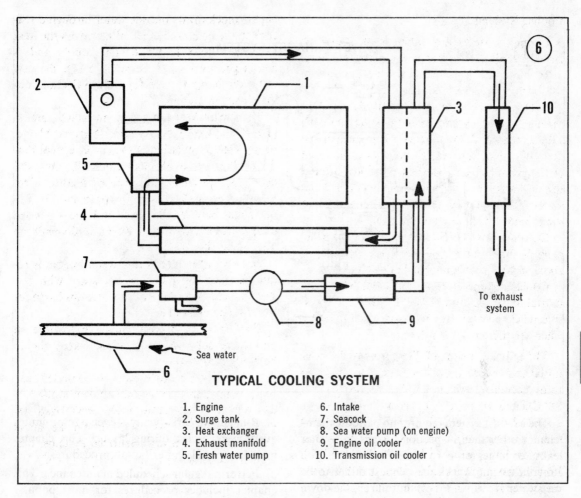

TYPICAL COOLING SYSTEM

1. Engine
2. Surge tank
3. Heat exchanger
4. Exhaust manifold
5. Fresh water pump
6. Intake
7. Seacock
8. Sea water pump (on engine)
9. Engine oil cooler
10. Transmission oil cooler

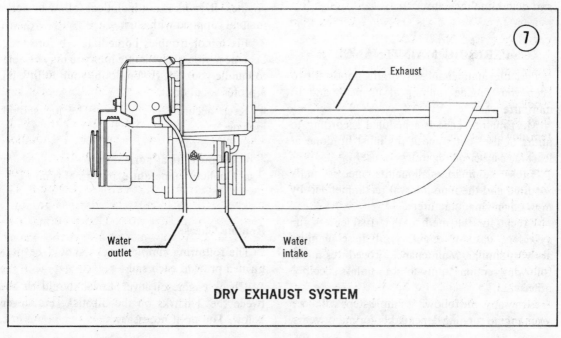

DRY EXHAUST SYSTEM

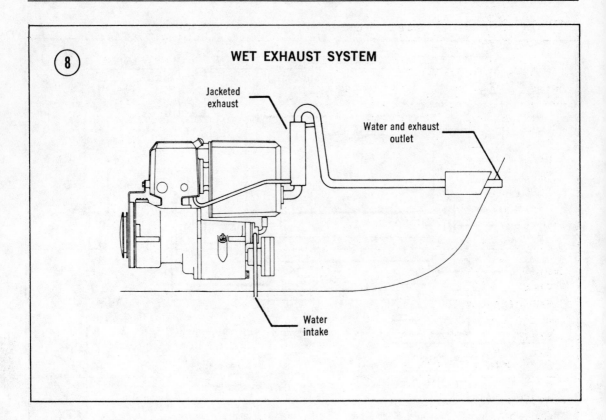

WET EXHAUST SYSTEM

Jacketed exhaust

Water and exhaust outlet

Water intake

The exhaust system requires no periodic maintenance other than inspection for gas and water leaks, damage, or corrosion. Every time you start the engine, check the exhaust outlet to be sure water is exiting. If not, shut the engine down and determine the cause.

PERIODIC MAINTENANCE

Periodic maintenance is vitally important to keep your engine running at its peak and to minimize wear.

Most maintenance is scheduled according to hours of use, but some items must be done at least once a season regardless of use.

Table 1 summarizes all maintenance normally required and the time interval recommended by most engine manufacturers.

Except for the method that fuel enters the cylinders, gasoline engines and diesel engines are very similar. Maintenance procedures in the following sections apply to both unless specified otherwise.

Generally, the following simple steps will keep your engine running dependably for many years.

1. Run engine periodically—even a few minutes every week except during lay-up. This chapter includes special winter lay-up procedures.

2. Perform regular scheduled maintenance. This chapter includes procedures for most popular engines. If yours is not included, follow owner's manual supplied with engine.

3. Fix minor troubles immediately before they become major. Very simple jobs you may be able to handle yourself. If you doubt your ability, let a professional do it.

4. Keep accurate engine log. The log should include:
   a. Hours run
   b. Oil pressure at normal rpm
   c. Coolant temperature at normal rpm

Routine Checks

The following simple checks should be performed prior to each sail.

1. Check engine oil level. Level should be between the 2 marks on the dipstick, but never below. Top up if necessary.

Table 1   ENGINE MAINTENANCE SUMMARY

Interval	Check Fluid Level	Replace	Lubricate	Inspect and/or Clean	Check and/or Adjust	Tighten
Daily						
Coolant	X					
Engine oil	X					
Fuel	X					
Oil pressure					X	
Coolant temperature					X	
Ammeter					X	
Every 50 hours						
V-belt					X	
Battery electrolyte	X					
Every 100 hours						
Engine oil		X				
Oil filter		X				
Every 150 hours						
Engine bolts/nuts						X
Cylinder head nuts						X
Air cleaner				X		
Injector timing (diesel)					X	
Seawater pump				X		
Every 200 hours						
Final drive oil		X				
Every 250 hours						
Primary fuel strainer (diesel)				X		
Carburetor (gas)					X	
Crankcase breathers				X		
Ignition timing (gas)					X	
Final drive breathers				X		
Ignition breaker points (gas)					X	
Spark plugs (gas)		X				
Every 1,000 hours						
Oil cooler				X		
Injectors (diesel)				X		
Valve clearances					X	

6

2. Check battery electrolyte level. Top up with distilled water.

3. Check coolant level.

4. Immediately after starting engine, check oil pressure if gauge is installed.

5. Check level in fuel tank.

6. Check ammeter for battery charging.

7. If the engine has an open cooling system, open the seacocks.

8. Check general engine room condition. Particularly look for signs of coolant, fuel, and engine oil leaks.

9. As soon as engine starts, look for water at the exhaust outlet if engine has heat exchanger cooling system. If water doesn't emerge, stop the engine immediately.

Checking Oil Level

Prior to each day's operation, check oil level with dipstick. Most dipsticks provide 2 marks as shown in **Figure 9**. Check level with warm engine immediately after shutting it off. Level should be between the 2 marks; if level is at or below lower mark, add approximately 1 quart of recommended grade.

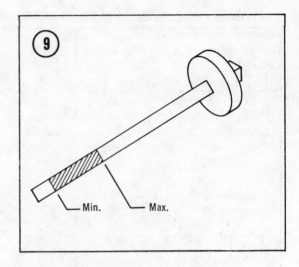

Engine Oil Change

Engine oil should be changed every 50 hours. The drain plug is located at the lowest point on the oil pan under the engine. See **Figure 10**.

To drain oil:

1. Run engine until it reaches normal operating temperature.

> NOTE: *Warm oil drains more quickly and thoroughly than cold oil, taking more impurities with it.*

ENGINE

2a. If there is enough clearance, place a shallow container with sufficient capacity (usually at least 6 quarts) under the drain plug. Remove drain plug and let drain for 10-15 minutes.

2b. If there is no access to the drain plug, suck the oil out through the dipstick opening. Use a siphoning device such as shown in **Figure 11**.

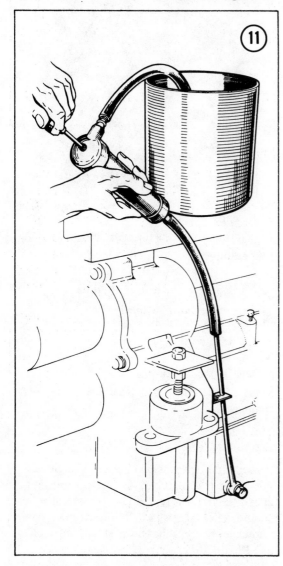

3. Remove oil filter and install new one as described in the next procedure.

4. Install drain plug, if removed.

5. Pour in quantity and type oil recommended in owner's manual.

6. Run engine. Check for leaks around drain plug and base of oil filter.

Engine Oil Filter Replacement (Spin-on Type)

Every 150-200 hours of running time, replace the engine oil filter. This should be done after oil is drained and before new oil is poured in. Lehman Ford, Westerbeke, and Volvo engines use a full-flow, disposable spin-on type frequently found on automobiles and easily available through automotive suppliers.

To remove the filter, unscrew it by hand or use a filter wrench. See **Figure 12**. Wipe the gasket area of the base with a clean, lint-free cloth. Coat the neoprene gasket on the new filter with clean engine oil. Screw the filter on by hand until the gasket just touches the base. Then tighten a half-turn by hand; do not use a filter wrench.

After adding engine oil, start the engine and check for leaks around the filter. Also check the oil level and adjust if necessary.

> WARNING
> *A small amount of oil may be spilled when the filter is removed. Hold a small waste container under the element as it is unscrewed. Oil in the bilges is a serious fire hazard.*

Engine Oil Filter Replacement (Cartridge Type)

This type is used on Perkins engines. The engine oil filter should be replaced every 150 hours or 3 months when the engine oil is changed. This should be done after old oil is drained and before the new oil is poured in.

1. Unscrew the bolt on the filter cover. See **Figure 13**.

2. Remove filter cover and discard oil filter element. See **Figure 14**.

3. Clean inside of cover with solvent.

4. Replace rubber seal in casting.

5. Install new filter element and cover. Tighten the cover bolt just enough to achieve a leakproof seal.

6. After new engine oil has been poured in, run the engine and check for oil leaks around the filter cover.

Final Fuel Filter Replacement

The final fuel filter element should be replaced every 400 hours or every 2 years, whichever comes first.

1. Clean exterior of filter assembly thoroughly.

2. Remove the bolt securing filter bowl. See **Figure 15**.

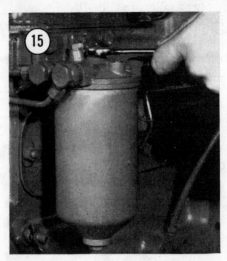

3. Discard fuel in bowl and old filter element.

4. Thoroughly clean the filter bowl in solvent. Clean diesel fuel is excellent for this.

5. Check sealing rings and replace, if necessary.

6. Place a new element in the filter bowl. Fill with fresh, clean fuel and install the filter bowl so that it seats squarely against the filter head.

7. Hold the bowl in position and secure with the bolt. Do not tighten any more than necessary to achieve a good, leak-proof seal.

8. Bleed the fuel system as described in this chapter.

Fan Belt

Since fan belt tension affects the engine cooling and electrical charging, it is important to check it frequently. When correct, the belt should deflect about ⅜ in. (10mm) when pressed midway between the farthest spaced pulleys. See **Figure 16**.

To adjust or replace the belt, loosen all mounting bolts on the generator or alternator, including both ends of the adjustable bracket. Remove the old belt. Install the new belt and adjust belt tension by pulling generator or alternator away from the engine block until correct belt tension is achieved, then tighten all mounting bolts.

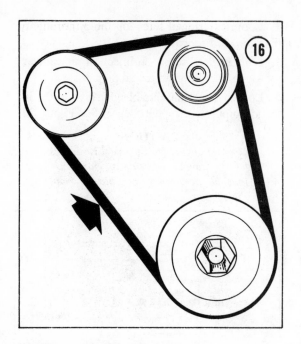

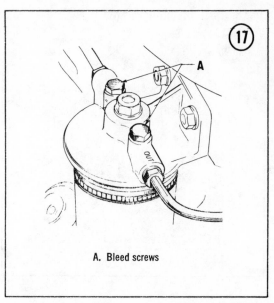

A. Bleed screws

Bleeding Diesel Fuel System

Air can enter the fuel system as a result of running out of fuel, leaks in the system, or changing fuel filters or lines. Air in the system will cause difficult starting, erratic running, or loss of power.

The sections which follow describe the bleeding procedure for several popular auxiliary engines. If your engine is not included, the following general procedure will be helpful.

1. Make sure there is fuel in the fuel tank and the fuel petcock is on.

2. Trace fuel line from tank to engine. The line usually terminates at a fuel pump. Trace the line from the pump to the fuel filter.

3. Open bleed screw (**Figure 17** is typical) on inlet side of filter. Operate prime lever on fuel pump until fuel free of air bubbles issues from around bleed screw. Tighten bleed screw.

4. Open bleed screw on outlet side of filter and repeat Step 3.

5. Trace fuel line to injection pump. Open bleed screw on injection pump and repeat Step 3.

Bleeding Lehman Ford Diesel Engines

This procedure covers the 4-cylinder 242 and 254 engines and the 6-cylinder 363 and 380 engines.

1. Make certain that there is sufficient fuel in the fuel tank and the fuel shut-off valve is turned on.

2. Loosen bleed screws on inlet side of fuel filter (see **Figures 18 and 19**) 2-3 turns.

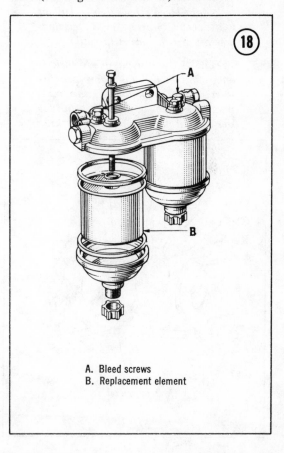

A. Bleed screws
B. Replacement element

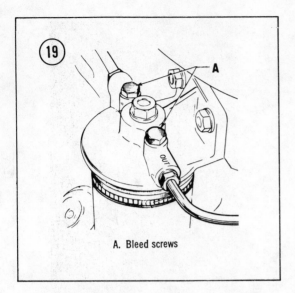

A. Bleed screws

3. Operate the priming lever on the fuel lift pump (see **Figure 20**) until fuel completely free of air is expelled. Tighten the bleed screw.

CAUTION
Slight pressure with the wrench will seal all the bleed screws tightly. Do not use excessive pressure as the castings are soft and threads strip easily.

NOTE: *If the fuel pump eccentric is on maximum lift, the pump priming lever will not operate. In this case, rotate the engine as necessary with the starter until the priming lever works.*

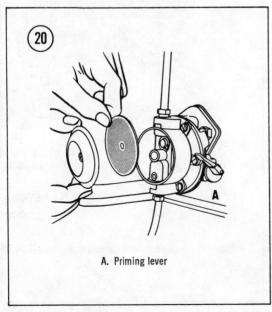

A. Priming lever

4. Loosen the bleed screw on the outlet side of the filter and repeat Step 3.

5. Loosen bleed screw on injection pump nearest to the inlet line and repeat Step 3.

6. Loosen the remaining bleed screw on the injection pump and repeat Step 3. See **Figure 21**.

CAUTION
Operate engine for at least 10 minutes before leaving dockside to make sure that all the air has been purged from the system.

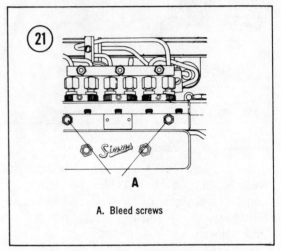

A. Bleed screws

Bleeding Perkins 4-Cylinder Diesel Engines

This procedure covers the following Perkins engines.

a. 4- 99
b. 4-107 } Group A
c. 4-108

d. 4-212
e. 4-236 } Group B
f. 4-248

For convenience in following this procedure, the engines are arranged and referred to in groups. Unless otherwise specified, a particular step applies to both groups.

1. Loosen the vent plug on top of the fuel filter cover 2 or 3 turns. See **Figure 22** for Group A engines and **Figure 23** for Group B.

2. Loosen the vent screw on the side of the fuel injection pump. See **Figure 24** for Group A and **Figure 25** for Group B.

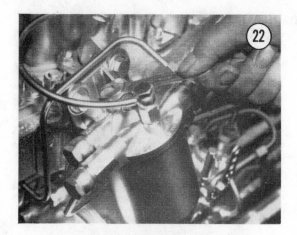

3. Loosen the air vent screw at the top of the fuel injection pump. See **Figure 26** (hydraulic governor) or **Figure 27** (mechanical governor).

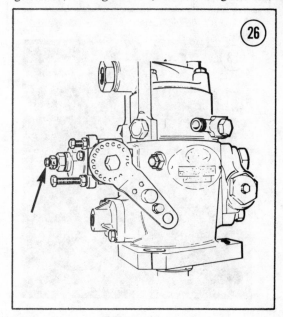

4. Operate the priming lever on the fuel pump (see **Figure 28**) until fuel completely free of air bubbles issues from each vent point.

5. When fuel is bubble-free, tighten the vents in the following order.

    a. Vent plug, Figure 22 (Group A) or
       Figure 23 (Group B)

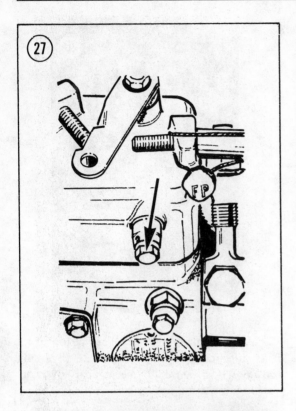

NOTE: *This entire procedure must be carried out until all signs of air bubbles have disappeared. This could take 4 or 5 minutes of hand priming.*

7. Loosen the unions at the injector ends of the high pressure fuel pipes.

8. Open the throttle fully and ensure that the stop control is in the "run" position.

9. Rotate the engine with the starter motor until bubble-free fuel issues from all fuel pipes. If the battery is fully charged, this operation should take 30-60 seconds.

10. Tighten the unions at the fuel pipes.

11. Run the engine and make sure it is running properly.

NOTE: *If, after bleeding the system, the engine runs satisfactorily for a few minutes, then stops, then air must be trapped in the fuel injection pump and the entire bleeding procedure should be repeated.*

Bleeding Perkins 6-Cylinder Diesels

This procedure covers these Perkins engines:

a. 6.354

b. T6.354 (turbocharged)

c. 6.3542

d. T6.3543 (turbocharged)

1. Loosen the vent screw on the hydraulic head locking screw on the fuel pump body. See **Figure 30**.

b. Vent screw, Figure 24 (Group A) or Figure 25 (Group B)

c. Air vent screw, Figure 26 or 27

6. Loosen the union nut at the fuel injection pump inlet. See **Figure 29**. Operate the priming lever on the fuel lift pump until escaping fuel is bubble-free, then retighten the union nut.

2. Loosen the air vent screw at the top of the control gear housing in **Figure 31** (hydraulic governor) or governor control cover in **Figure 32** (mechanical governor).

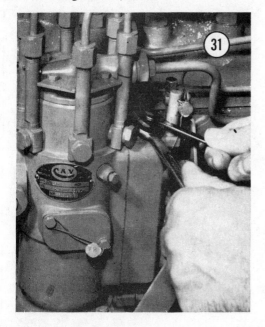

3. Operate the priming lever on the fuel pump (see **Figure 33**) until fuel completely free of air bubbles issues from each vent point.

4. When fuel is bubble-free, tighten the vents in the following order:

    a. Vent screw, Figure 30.

    b. Air vent screw, Figure 31 or 32.

5. Loosen the union nut at the fuel injection pump inlet. See **Figure 34**. Operate the priming lever on the fuel lift pump until escaping fuel is bubble-free, then retighten the union nut.

> NOTE: *This entire procedure must be carried out until all signs of air bubbles have disappeared. This could take 4 or 5 minutes of hand priming.*

6. Loosen the unions at the injector ends of the high pressure fuel pipes.

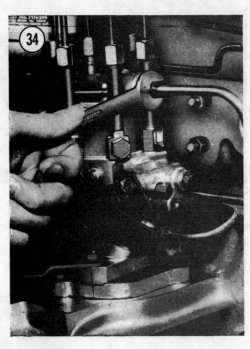

7. Open the throttle fully and ensure that the stop control is in the "run" position.

8. Rotate the engine with the starter motor until bubble-free fuel issues from all fuel pipes. If the battery is fully charged, this operation should take 30-60 seconds.

9. Tighten the unions at the fuel pipes.

10. Run the engine and make sure it is running properly.

> NOTE: *If, after bleeding the system, the engine runs satisfactorily for a few minutes, then stops, then air must be trapped in the fuel injection pump and the entire bleeding procedure should be repeated.*

Bleeding Westerbeke DS Engine

Refer to **Figure 35**. Letters in parentheses refer to specific parts in the figure.

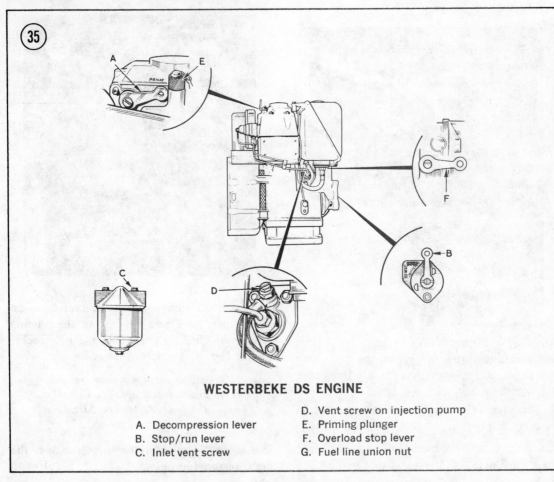

WESTERBEKE DS ENGINE

A. Decompression lever
B. Stop/run lever
C. Inlet vent screw
D. Vent screw on injection pump
E. Priming plunger
F. Overload stop lever
G. Fuel line union nut

1. Put shift lever in neutral.

2. Set throttle control lever to full speed position.

3. Place STOP/RUN lever (B) in RUN position.

4. Loosen inlet vent screw (C) on top of fuel filter, operate the hand priming lever of the fuel lift pump, and when fuel oil free of air bubbles issues from vent screw, tighten screw.

> NOTE: *If the cam on the camshaft driving the fuel lift pump is on maximum lift, it is not possible to operate the priming lever. If such a condition arises, proceed as follows:*

   a. Lift decompression lever (A) to vertical position.

   b. Revolve drive shaft pulley by hand until the fuel lift pump priming lever can be operated.

   c. Position decompression lever (A) in horizontal position.

5. Loosen the outlet vent screw on top of the fuel filter, operate the priming lever as in Step 4 above, and then tighten screw.

6. Loosen the vent screw (D) on injection pump, operate priming lever as in Step 4 above, and then tighten screw.

7. Loosen the fuel line union nut at the fuel injector (fuel line between fuel injection pump and fuel injector). Operate the starter-generator and when fuel oil free of air bubbles issues from union, tighten the union nut.

> NOTE: *Do not crank engine for more than 20 seconds at a time, and leave at rest 2 minutes before attempting to crank engine again.*

8. Run engine until it runs smoothly.

Bleeding Westerbeke 4-60, 4-230, and 6-346 Engines

1. Loosen banjo bolt securing injector fuel return banjo to secondary fuel filter head. See 1, **Figure 36**.

2. Operate prime lever on fuel lift pump until fuel free of bubbles issues from around banjo bolt. Tighten bolt.

> NOTE: *If prime lever on pump does not work, crank starter a few times to change position of camshaft until pump works.*

3. Loosen the air bleed screw on the fuel injection pump, directly above the pump nameplate. See 2, Figure 36. Operate the lift pump priming lever, and when fuel flows from the bleed screw free of air bubbles, tighten the bleed screw.

4. Loosen union nuts at injector end of each of the high pressure pipes. See 3, Figure 36.

5. Put shift lever in neutral.

6. Ensure fuel STOP push-pull control is in full run position. (Push in to run.)

7. Advance throttle to maximum open position (for maximum fuel flow).

8. Turn key switch to START position, and when fuel oil free of air bubbles issues from each injector pipe union, tighten union.

Bleeding Westerbeke 4-91 Engine

1. Loosen the union nut at the filter end of the injection pump feed pipe (A, **Figure 37**). Operate the lift pump and when fuel passing the union is free from air bubbles, tighten the union nut.

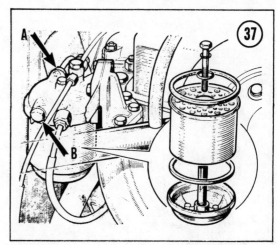

2. Unscrew plug (B, Figure 37) in the unused outlet connection on the filter head 2-3 times. Operate the lift pump and when the fuel issuing from around the plug thread is free from air bubbles, tighten the plug.

3. Loosen the 2 air bleed valves on the fuel injection pump. See **Figure 38**. One bleed valve

6

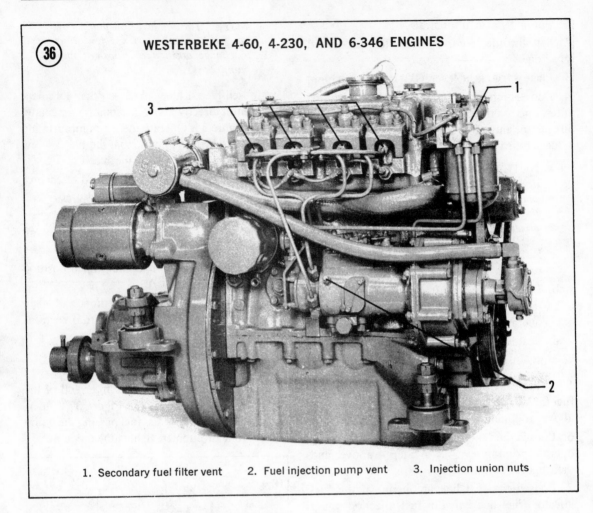

WESTERBEKE 4-60, 4-230, AND 6-346 ENGINES

1. Secondary fuel filter vent   2. Fuel injection pump vent   3. Injection union nuts

is located on the governor housing, while the other is incorporated on one of the hydraulic head locking screws. Operate the lift pump, and when the fuel flowing from both bleed valves is free from air bubbles, tighten the valves.

4. Loosen the union nut at the injector end of any 2 high-pressure pipes. Ensure that the stop control is in the "run" position, and set the accelerator in the fully open position. Crank the engine until the fuel flowing from both pipes is free from air bubbles, then tighten the pipe union nuts.

5. Start the engine and allow it to run until it is firing on all cylinders.

Bleeding Westerbeke 4-107 Engine

Refer to **Figure 39** for this procedure.

1. Loosen vent screw (A, Figure 39) or control gear housing.

2. Loosen one of the 2 hydraulic head locking screws (B) on the side of the pump body.

3. Unscrew the vent plug on top of the secondary fuel filter (C) 2-3 turns.

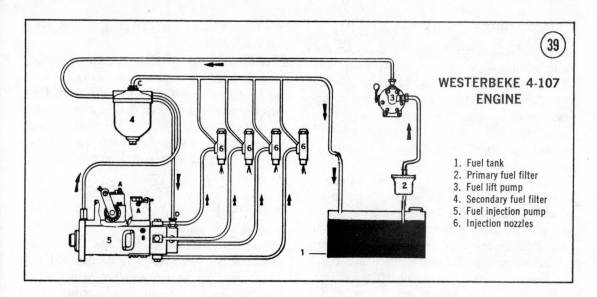

WESTERBEKE 4-107 ENGINE

1. Fuel tank
2. Primary fuel filter
3. Fuel lift pump
4. Secondary fuel filter
5. Fuel injection pump
6. Injection nozzles

4. Operate the priming lever of the fuel lift feed pump until fuel, free from air bubbles, issues from each venting point. Tighten the screws in the following order.

    a. Filter cover vent screw (C)

    b. Head locking screw (B)

    c. Governor vent screw (A)

        NOTE: *If the cam on the camshaft driving the fuel pump is on maximum lift, it is not possible to operate the hand primer. If such a condition arises, crank engine until the hand primer can be operated.*

5. Loosen the pipe union nut (D) at the pump inlet, operate the priming lever and retighten when fuel, free from air bubbles, issues from around the threads.

6. Loosen the unions at the nozzle ends of 2 of the high pressure pipes.

7. Set the throttle at fully open position and make sure that the "stop" control is in the "run" position.

8. Turn the engine until fuel oil, free from air bubbles, issues from both fuel pipes.

9. Tighten the unions on the fuel pipes, and the engine is ready for starting.

Bleeding Westerbeke 4-154 Engine

1. Loosen bolt on top of the secondary fuel filter head casting. Operate the fuel lift pump priming lever. When fuel free of air bubbles issues from bolt threads, tighten bolt.

    NOTE: *If the camshaft driving the fuel lift pump is on maximum lift, it will not be possible to obtain a full pumping stroke with the lift pump priming lever. The engine must be cranked with starter motor one complete revolution.*

2. Loosen bleed screw (A, **Figure 40**). Operate lift pump priming lever. When fuel free of air bubbles issues from bleed screw, tighten screw.

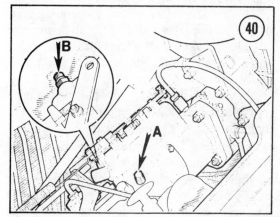

3. Loosen the 4 union nuts at the injector end of the high pressure pipes (pipes going from fuel injection pump to injectors). Operate the starter motor. When fuel free of air bubbles issues from union nuts, tighten union nuts.

GASOLINE ENGINE TUNE-UP

An engine tune-up is a series of mechanical adjustments made to get peak performance from the engine. A tune-up should be performed every 250-300 hours—sooner if the engine becomes hard to start, runs roughly at any power setting, or doesn't seem to have the same power. Running the engine when it needs a tune-up can lead to abnormal wear.

Due to the large number of different engines, it is impossible to provide specific tune-up instructions for each one. This information is contained in the owner's manual available from the manufacturer. Many owner's manuals, however, neglect to mention the order in which parts of the tune-up should be performed. The information in this section applies to all gasoline inboard engines.

Since different systems in an engine interact to affect overall performance, tune-up must be accomplished in the following order.

 a. Valve clearance adjustment
 b. Ignition adjustment and timing
 c. Carburetor adjustment

Valve Clearance

This is a series of simple mechanical adjustments which establish a specified clearance between the valve stems and valve operating gear. If the clearance is too small, valves may be burned or distorted. Too large clearance results in excessive noise. In either case, engine power is reduced.

The owner's manual for your particular engine provides a valve adjustment procedure. In addition, the following hints will help.

1. Determine from owner's manual whether valve clearance should be adjusted with the engine warm or cold. Warm means the engine is at normal operating temperature; run the engine at a fast idle until temperature gauge registers in the normal operating range. If the owner's manual specified a cold engine, let the engine cool overnight and adjust valves the next day before running it.

2. Remove spark plugs. The engine crankshaft must be rotated by hand several times during adjustment. Removing the plugs makes rotation much easier.

3. Determine valve clearances from owner's manual. Often the clearances for exhaust valves and intake valves differ. For example, the Universal Atomic 4 specifies 0.010 in. clearance for exhaust valves and 0.008 in. for intake valves. This is measured with flat feeler gauges; make sure you have the proper sizes on hand.

Spark Plug Wires

Spark plug wires, especially the noise suppressor type, deteriorate with age. Check each wire carefully for cracks in the insulation. If any wire is questionable, replace all of them. Every 2 years, replace them regardless of condition.

Some marine engine suppliers carry pre-cut wire kits. Simply replace old wires with proper length wires from kit. If a kit is not available, or you wish to save some money, purchase the wire and end terminals from any automotive or marine engine parts supplier and cut them yourself. Take a sample of the existing wire to the supplier to be sure that you get the same kind. To avoid mistakes, remove 1 wire at a time, cut a new wire the same length, install end terminals and install new wire on engine.

Ignition Adjustment and Timing

This phase of the tune-up consists of:

 a. Spark plug replacement
 b. Breaker point replacement and adjustment
 c. Distributor cap and rotor inspection
 d. Spark plug wire inspection
 e. Ignition timing adjustment

Once valve clearance is properly adjusted, work on the ignition system. Remove spark plugs and keep them in order or mark each with cylinder number. Examine spark plugs and compare their appearance to **Figure 41**. Electrode appearance is a good indication of performance in each cylinder and permits early recognition of trouble. If in good condition, clean the plugs, regap them and reinstall, using new gaskets.

Next remove the distributor cap and wipe off any dirt or corrosion. Remove the rotor.

41

Normal plug appearance noted by the brown to grayish-tan deposits and slight electrode wear. This plug indicates the correct plug heat range and proper air fuel ratio.

Red, brown, yellow and white coatings caused by fuel and oil additives. These deposits are not harmful if they remain in a powdery form.

Carbon fouling distinguished by dry, fluffy black carbon deposits which may be caused by an over-rich air/fuel mixture, excessive hand choking, clogged air filter or excessive idling.

Shiny yellow glaze on insulator cone is caused when the powdery deposits from fuel and oil additives melt. Melting occurs during hard acceleration after prolonged idling. This glaze conducts electricity and shorts out the plug.

Oil fouling indicated by wet, oily deposits caused by oil pumping past worn rings or down the intake valve guides. A hotter plug temporarily reduces oil deposits, but a plug that is too hot leads to pre-ignition and possible engine damage.

Overheated plug indicated by burned or blistered insulator tip and badly worn electrodes. This condition may be caused by pre-ignition, cooling system defects, lean air/fuel ratios, low octane fuel or over advanced ignition timing.

Spark plug condition photos courtesy of AC Spark Plug Division, General Motors Corporation.

Check breaker points for signs of pitting, discoloration and misalignment. If in doubt about condition, disconnect the primary lead to the distributor and remove the points. Note carefully how they are connected and install new points in exactly the same way. Replace the condenser also. Check that the contacts on the points are properly aligned as shown in **Figure 42**. If not, carefully bend the *fixed* contact to align the contacts.

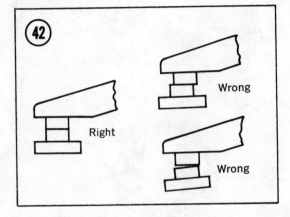

Carefully rotate the distributor body or the crankshaft pulley until a high cam lobe opens the points to the maximum gap. Loosen the screw holding the points, insert a feeler gauge in the gap and adjust to clearance specified in owner's manual. Tighten the retaining screw. More accurate measurement is possible by measuring dwell angle specified by manufacturer. Connect the dwell meter following the meter manufacturer's instructions.

Reconnect the primary wire and install the rotor and distributor cap. Ensure that all wires are connected properly. Tighten the distributor housing clamp screw.

After adjusting breaker gap, set the ignition timing. Normally, this involves rotating the distributor body to establish a certain level of engine performance while underway. Obviously, this requires a man at the helm while you are below making the adjustment.

WARNING
Most engine compartments are very cramped. Be careful not to get fingers, hair, or clothing caught in moving engine parts. In addition, watch out for hot areas such as the exhaust manifold.

ENGINE TROUBLESHOOTING

Any engine requires an uninterrupted fuel supply, air, unfailing ignition (gasoline) and adequate compression. If anyone of these is lacking, the engine will not run. Troubleshooting must first localize the trouble to one of these areas, then concentrate on finding the specific cause. **Tables 2 and 3** will permit you to localize specific troubles with a minimum of effort.

FINAL DRIVE MAINTENANCE

Final drive maintenance is limited to checking the oil level every 25 hours and changing the oil every 100-200 hours or once per season, whichever occurs first.

Checking Oil Level

Check oil level immediately after shutting engine off. Otherwise, oil in the oil cooler and connecting lines will drain back into the drive unit, indicating an abnormally high oil level.

Most final drives have a dipstick somewhere on the case. Some, like the Capitol and Paragon drives, have a pull-out dipstick similar to that on an engine. See **Figures 43 and 44**. Pull out the dipstick, wipe it clean, reinsert it, and observe the level of oil.

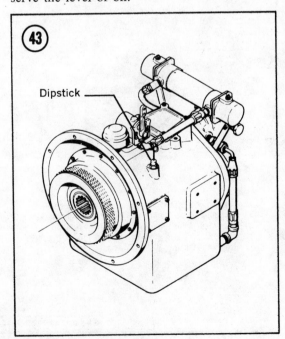

Table 2   TROUBLESHOOTING DIESEL ENGINES

Trouble	Probable Cause
Low cranking speed	1, 2, 3, 4
Will not start	5, 6, 7, 8, 9, 10, 12, 13, 14, 15, 16, 17, 18, 19, 20, 22, 31, 32, 33
Difficult starting	5, 7, 8, 9, 10, 11, 12, 13, 14, 15, 16, 18, 19, 20, 21, 22, 24, 29, 31, 32, 33
Lack of power	8, 9, 10, 11, 12, 13, 14, 18, 19, 20, 21, 22, 23, 24, 25, 26, 27, 31, 32,33
Misfiring	8, 9, 10, 12, 13, 14, 16, 18, 19, 20, 25, 26, 28, 29, 30, 32
Excessive fuel consumption	11, 13, 14, 16, 18, 19, 20, 22, 23, 24, 25, 27, 28, 29, 31, 32, 33
Black exhaust	11, 13, 14, 16, 18, 19, 20, 22, 24, 25, 27, 28, 29, 31, 32, 33
Blue/white exhaust	4, 16, 18, 19, 20, 25, 27, 31, 33, 34, 35, 45, 56
Low oil pressure	4, 36, 37, 38, 39, 40, 42, 43, 44, 58
Knocking	9, 14, 16, 18, 19, 22, 26, 28, 29, 31, 33, 35, 36, 45, 46, 59
Erratic running	7, 8, 9, 10, 11, 12, 13, 14, 16, 20, 21, 23, 26, 28, 29, 30, 33, 35, 45, 59
Vibration	13, 14, 20, 23, 25, 26, 29, 30, 33, 45, 47, 48, 49
High oil pressure	4, 38, 41
Overheating	11, 13, 14, 16, 18, 19, 24, 25, 45, 50, 51, 52, 53, 54, 57
Excessive crankcase pressure	25, 31, 33, 34, 45, 55
Poor compression	11, 19, 25, 28, 29, 31, 32, 33, 34, 46, 59
Starts and stops	10, 11, 12

Key to Troubleshooting Chart

1. Battery capacity low
2. Bad electrical connections
3. Faulty starter motor
4. Incorrect grade of lubricating oil
5. Low cranking speed
6. Fuel tank empty
7. Faulty stop control operation
8. Blocked fuel feed pipe
9. Faulty fuel lift pump
10. Choked fuel filter
11. Restriction in air cleaner
12. Air in fuel system
13. Faulty fuel injection pump
14. Faulty atomisers or incorrect type
15. Incorrect use of cold start equipment
16. Faulty cold starting equipment
17. Broken fuel injection pump drive
18. Incorrect fuel pump timing
19. Incorrect valve timing
20. Poor compression
21. Blocked fuel tank vent
22. Incorrect type or grade of fuel
23. Sticking throttle or restricted movement
24. Exhaust pipe restriction
25. Cylinder head gasket leaking
26. Overheating
27. Cold running
28. Incorrect tappet adjustment
29. Sticking valves
30. Incorrect high pressure pipes
31. Worn cylinder bores
32. Pitted valves and seats
33. Broken, worn, or sticking piston ring(s)
34. Worn valve stems and guides
35. Overfull air cleaner or use of incorrect grade of oil
36. Worn or damaged bearings
37. Insufficient oil in sump
38. Inaccurate gauge
39. Oil pump worn
40. Pressure relief valve sticking open
41. Pressure relief valve sticking closed
42. Broken relief valve spring
43. Faulty suction pipe
44. Choked oil filter
45. Piston seizure/pick up
46. Incorrect piston height
47. Damaged fan
48. Faulty engine mounting (housing)
49. Incorrectly aligned flywheel housing or flywheel
50. Faulty thermostat
51. Restriction in water jacket
52. Loose fan belt
53. Choked radiator
54. Faulty water pump
55. Choked breather pipe
56. Damaged valve stem oil deflectors (if fitted)
57. Coolant level too low
58. Blocked sump strainer
59. Broken valve spring

6

Table 3   TROUBLESHOOTING GASOLINE ENGINES

Trouble	Probable Cause	Correction
Starter will not crank engine	Discharged battery	Charge or replace battery
	Corroded battery terminals	Clean terminals
	Loose connection in starting circuit	Check and tighten all connections
	Defective starting switch	Replace switch
	Starter motor brushes dirty	Clean or replace brushes
	Jammed bendix gear	Loosen starter motor to free gear
	Defective starter motor	Replace motor
Starter motor turns but does not crank engine	Partially discharged battery	Charge or replace battery
	Defective wiring or wiring of too low capacity	Check wiring for worn acid spots.
	Broken bendix drive	Remove starter motor and repair drive
Engine will not start	Empty fuel tank	Fill tank with proper fuel
	Flooded engine	Remove spark plugs and crank engine several times. Replace plugs
	Water in fuel system	If water is found, clean tank, fuel lines, and carburetor. Refill with proper fuel
	Inoperative or sticking choke valve	Check valve, linkage, and choke rod or cable for proper operation
	Improperly adjusted carburetor	Adjust carburetor
	Clogged fuel lines or defective fuel pump	Disconnect fuel line at carburetor. If fuel does not flow freely when engine is cranked, clean fuel line and sediment bowl. If fuel still does not flow freely after cleaning, repair or replace pump
Engine will not start. (Poor compression and other causes)	Air leak around intake manifold	Check for leak by squirting oil around intake connections. If leak is found, tighten manifold and if necessary replace gaskets
	Loose spark plugs	Check oil plugs for proper seating, gasket, and tightness. Replace all damaged plugs and gaskets
	Loosely seating valves	Check for broken or weak valve springs, warped stems, carbon and gum deposits, and insufficient tappet clearance
	Damaged cylinder head gasket	Check for leaks around gasket when engine is cranked. If a leak is found, replace gasket
	Worn or broken piston rings	Replace broken and worn rings. Check cylinders for "out-of-round" and "taper"

(continued)

Table 3   TROUBLESHOOTING GASOLINE ENGINES (continued)

Trouble	Probable Cause	Correction
Engine will not start (ignition system)	Ignition switch "off" or defective	Turn on switch or replace
	Fouled or broken spark plugs	Remove plugs and inspect for cracked porcelain, dirty points, or improper gap
	Improperly set, worn or pitted distributor points. Defective ignition coil	Remove center wire from distributor cap and hold within ⅜ in. of motor block. Crank engine. Clean, sharp spark should jump between wire and block when points open. Clean and adjust points. If spark is weak or yellow after adjustment of points, replace condenser. If spark still is weak or not present, replace ignition coil
	Wet, cracked, or broken distributor	Wipe inside surfaces of distributor dry with clean cloth. Inspect for cracked or broken parts. Replace parts where necessary
	Improperly set, worn, or pitted magneto breaker points (magneto models only)	Remove spark plug wire and hold within ⅜ in. of engine block. Clean, sharp spark should jump between wire and block when engine is cranked. If spark is weak or not present, clean and adjust breaker points
	Improperly set, worn, or pitted timer points. Defective coil or defective condenser	Remove spark plug wire and hold within ⅛ in. of engine block. A clean, sharp spark should jump between wire and block when engine is cranked. Clean and set timer points. If spark still is not present when engine is cranked, replace coil
	Improper timing	Set timing
Excessive coolant temperatures	No water circulation	Check for clogged water lines and restricted inlets and outlets. Check for broken or stuck thermostat. Look for worn or damaged water pump or water pump drive
	Broken or stuck thermostat	Replace thermostat
No oil pressure	Defective gauge or tube	Replace gauge or tube
	No oil in engine	Refill with proper grade oil
	Dirt in pressure relief valve	Clean valve
	Defective oil pump, leak in oil lines, or broken oil pump drive	Check oil pump and oil pump drive for worn or broken parts. Tighten all oil line connections
Low oil pressure	Too light body oil	Replace with proper weight oil
	Oil leak in pressure line	Inspect all oil lines. Tighten all connections
	Weak or broken pressure relief valve spring	Replace spring
	Worn oil pump	Replace pump
	Worn or loose bearings	Replace bearings

(continued)

Table 3   TROUBLESHOOTING GASOLINE ENGINES (continued)

Trouble	Probable Cause	Correction
Oil pressure too high	Too heavy body oil	Drain oil and replace with oil of proper weight
	Stuck pressure relief valve	Clean or replace valve
	Dirt or obstruction in lines	Drain and clean oil system. Check for bent or flattened oil lines and replace where necessary
Loss of rpm	Damaged propeller	Repair propeller
	Bent rudder	Repair
	Misalignment	Realign engine to shaft
	Too tight stuffing box packing gland	Adjust
	Dirty boat bottom	Clean
Vibration	Misfiring or preignition	See correction under preignition
	Loose foundation or foundation bolts	Tighten
	Propeller shaft out of line or bent	Repair
	Propeller bent or pitch out of true	Repair
Preignition	Defective spark plugs	Check all spark plugs for broken porcelain, burned electrodes, or electrodes out of adjustment. Replace all defective plugs or clean and reset
	Improper timing	Retime ignition
	Engine carbon	Remove cylinder head and clean out carbon
	Engine overheating	See correction under "Excessive coolant temperature" portion of this table
Backfiring	Insufficient fuel reaching engine due to dirty lines, strainer, or blocked fuel tank vent. Water in fuel	See correction under "Engine will not start" portion of this table
	Poorly adjusted distributor	See correction under "Engine will not start" portion of this table
Sludge in oil	Infrequent oil changes	Drain and refill with proper weight oil
	Water in oil	Drain and refill. If trouble persists, check for cracked block, defective head gasket, and cracked head
	Dirty oil filter	Replace filter

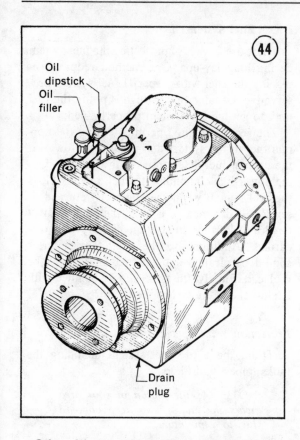

Oil dipstick
Oil filler

Drain plug

clean, then reinsert it until the dipstick plug rests in the hole; do not tighten it. Remove the dipstick and read the level.

Oil Change

Drive unit oil should be changed every 100-200 hours, or once a season, whichever comes first.

The drain plug is located at the lowest point on the case. In some cases, such as Paragon drives, the drain is on the bottom of the case. Others, such as Capitol and Warner, have the drain on the side near the bottom.

To drain the oil:

1. Operate the boat in gear, if possible, to warm oil to operating temperature.

> NOTE: *Warm oil drains more quickly and thoroughly than cold oil, taking more impurities with it.*

2a. If there is enough clearance, place a shallow container with 3 or 4 quart capacity under the drain plug. Remove drain plug and let drain for 10-15 minutes.

2b. If there is no access to drain plug, suck oil out through dipstick opening. Use a siphoning device such as shown previously in Figure 11.

Other drives, such as Warner Gear "Velvet Drives", have a screw-in dipstick. See **Figure 45**. To check these, unscrew the dipstick, wipe it

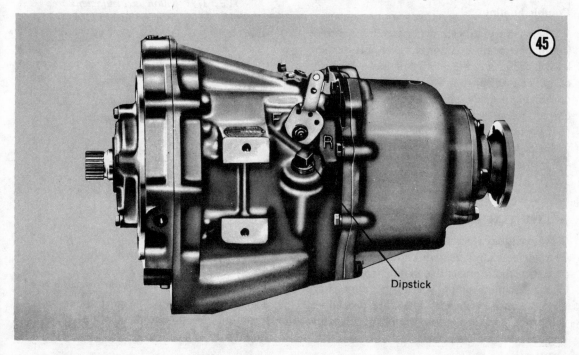

Dipstick

3. Install drain plug, if removed.

4. Measure amount of waste oil removed. This is the amount of fresh oil required in Step 5.

> NOTE: *Oil capacity depends on many variables such as cooler size, connecting line length, installation angle, etc.*

5. Pour in fresh oil. Make sure that it is the proper grade and type. Refer to the owner's manual or call your local distributor; proper oil is very important.

6. Run engine with drive unit in gear to circulate oil. Shut off engine and check oil level with dipstick immediately. If level is too low, add more oil; if level is too high, siphon some out.

Periodic Inspection

Whenever changing oil, inspect entire case for loose bolts, leaks, and loose, deteriorating, or damaged connecting lines. If leakage is around an inspection plate, remove the plate, clean off all traces of old gasket, and reinstall plate with a new gasket. If leakage is from drain plug or connecting line end, tighten just enough to stop leak; overtightening may crack housing. Other leaks must be repaired by qualified mechanic.

Troubleshooting

There is very little an owner can do to correct trouble if it occurs. Major work requires expert knowledge and a wide array of tools. In cases of difficult shifting, noise, or no operation in one or more gears, check the oil level. If it is correct, refer the trouble to a mechanic.

If the trouble is a leak, you may be able to fix it. Refer to *Periodic Inspection*.

WINTER LAY-UP OR STORAGE

As mentioned earlier, engines thrive on use. The engine cannot remain unattended for long periods without preventive maintenance and occasional running unless special precautions are taken to protect it. The following procedures will provide protection for each of the important engine systems.

Diesel Fuel System

There are 2 ways of protecting the fuel system during long lay-ups. One method requires replacing the fuel with a special fuel system preservative. Usually only enough is put in the fuel tank to get the fuel system properly bled.

The second method permits leaving the normal fuel in the system during lay-up. However, the normal fuel deteriorates with time, producing a wax-like contaminant which quickly clogs the fuel system when the engine is returned to service. If this method is used, the old fuel must be drained from the system entirely and discarded. Additionally, the fuel tank interior should be cleaned and all fuel filters must be replaced. Finally, the tanks should be filled with fresh fuel and the system bled.

Protection With Special Preservative

1. Drain the entire fuel system including the tanks, pipes, and filters.

> NOTE: *As the season in your area nears the end, try to keep onboard fuel at a minimum.*

2. Fill fuel tank with about 1 gallon of preservative-type fuel.

> NOTE: *If 1 gallon is insufficient to permit engine to draw fuel, add more preservative.*

3. Bleed fuel system as described elsewhere.

4. Start engine and run for 10-15 minutes at half cruising rpm with no load.

Protection With Normal Fuel Oil

No special steps need to be taken. Simply leave the fuel system primed. Excess fuel in the tanks should be drained to make cleaning easier when the engine is returned to service.

Gasoline Fuel System

1. Drain fuel tank.

2. Run motor until all fuel in carburetor is used.

3. Remove spark plug(s). Squirt about ½ teaspoon of oil directly into the spark plug hole(s). Rotate flywheel 1 revolution.

4. Place a drop of clean engine oil on spark plug threads. Install plugs and tighten finger-tight. Tighten plugs ½ turn with spark plug wrench. Do not overtighten.

Lubrication System

1. Drain engine oil no matter how many hours it has been in use.

2. Remove rocker cover, if any. If sludge build-up is heavy, flush the engine with a flushing oil.

3. Replace the oil filter.

4. Fill the sump with fresh oil. Run engine briefly to circulate the fresh oil.

5. Remove and clean engine breather pipe.

6. Remove injectors and pour 2-4 tablespoons of fresh engine oil into each cylinder. Rotate crankshaft by hand 4 or 5 times to spread oil over cylinder walls.

7. Install injectors with new gaskets.

Cooling System

Drain the entire cooling system as described elsewhere in this chapter. The engine cooling system may remain empty during lay-up. A label or tag should be firmly attached in a conspicuous place. For example, taped over the instrument panel or tied to the throttle lever indicating the system is empty.

Rather than leave the system empty, a better procedure is to refill the system with an ethylene glycol anti-freeze. Be sure it is rated for year-round protection and dilute to protect well below lowest temperature in the area. Ethylene glycol is also an effective rust inhibitor. This same mixture may be left in the system when the engine is returned to service and only replaced prior to each lay-up period.

Electrical System

Prepare battery and electrical system for lay-up as described in Chapter Seven.

Sealing Engine

1. Remove the air cleaner and any air intake pipe that may be installed between air cleaner and air intake. Place a small bag of silica gel just inside the air intake. Carefully seal the air intake with waterproof adhesive tape or duct tape.

2. Disconnect the exhaust pipe from the exhaust manifold and seal the opening in the manifold with tape.

3. Seal the breather pipe opening with tape.

4. Seal the air vent in the fuel tank or filler cap with tape. This will reduce the risk of water condensation.

5. Remove drive belt(s) and store in a cool, dry place.

6

CHAPTER SEVEN

ELECTRICAL SYSTEM

Marine electrical systems vary in complexity. A small trailerable boat may have only one or two interior lamps and the required running lamps. Larger boats may have elaborate 12-volt and 110-volt systems. Even more complex systems include an auxiliary power plant with sufficient capacity to operate air conditioners and high-wattage electrical appliances.

BATTERY SYSTEMS

Most boats depend primarily on 12-, 24-, or 32-volt battery system to power lights, ventilation fans, and water pumps. **Figure 1** is the simplified diagram of a typical system.

On small boats, only one battery is used and the main switch is a simple on-off switch.

On large boats, 2 or more batteries are used. The batteries are separated into banks, each bank consisting of one or more batteries wired in parallel. The main switch selects either bank separately or connects both banks in parallel for greater current capacity.

Very little maintenance is required on battery electrical systems other than checking to be sure that all lights and other electrical accessories operate. Batteries must be checked occasionally for water level and state of charge.

BATTERY SERVICE

Most battery failures can be prevented by systematic battery service.

Electrolyte Level

Check battery electrolyte level frequently. Once a month is recommended; check more frequently during hot weather when many long trips are made. All batteries have some sort of "full" mark indicator under each cell cap. This usually takes the form of a split ring or triangle. Add distilled water as required (**Figure 2**) to bring the electrolyte level up to this indicator. Never overfill a battery; such practice results in loss of electrolyte, terminal corrosion, and short battery life. Never put anything into a battery except pure water. Distilled water, which is available at any supermarket, is best. It is sold for use in steam irons and is inexpensive. In the event distilled water is unavailable, odorless, colorless drinking water may be substituted.

CAUTION
Do not use sea water.

Never allow the liquid level in any cell to drop below the top of the plates. This results in permanent damage to the battery and reduced battery performance.

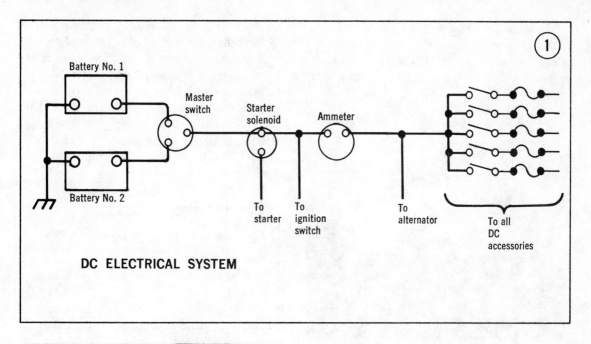

DC ELECTRICAL SYSTEM

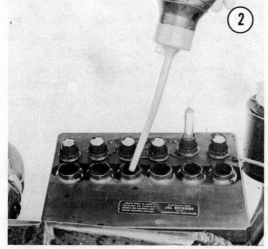

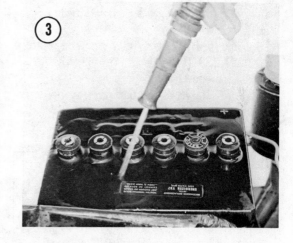

age path between terminals and causes the battery to discharge. Wash the battery with a weak solution of baking soda or ammonia, then rinse completely with clean water (**Figure 3**). Take care to keep all vent plugs tight so that no ammonia or baking soda solution enters the cells.

Excessive battery water usage is an indication of overcharging. Most common causes of overcharging are high battery temperature or high voltage regulator setting. No appreciable usage of water over a period of 2 or 3 months of average vehicle use indicates an undercharged battery condition. Poor cable connections or a voltage regulator set too low are the most common causes for this condition.

Cleaning

It is particularly important to keep batteries clean and free of corrosion. Dirt provides a leak-

Testing State of Charge

Although sophisticated battery testing devices are available, they are not available to the average boat owner and their use is beyond the scope of this book. A hydrometer, however, is an inexpensive tool and will tell much about battery condition.

To use a hydrometer, place the suction tube into the filler opening and draw in just enough electrolyte to lift the float (**Figure 4**). Hold the instrument in a vertical position and take reading at eye level.

Specific gravity of the electrolyte varies with temperature, so it is necessary to apply a temperature correction to the reading you obtain. For each 10 degrees that battery temperature exceeds 80°F, add 0.004 to the indicated specific gravity. Subtract 0.004 from the indicated value for each 10 degrees that battery temperature is below 80°F.

Specific gravity of a fully charged battery is 1.260-1.280. If specific gravity is below 1.220, recharge the battery.

State of charge of the battery may be determined from **Table 1**.

Table 1   BATTERY CONDITION

Specific Gravity	Percent Charged
1.110-1.130	Discharged
1.140-1.160	Almost discharged
1.170-1.190	One-quarter charged
1.200-1.220	One-half charged
1.230-1.250	Three-quarters charged
1.260-1.280	Fully charged

If specific gravity varies more than 0.025 between cells, the battery should be replaced. Don't measure specific gravity immediately after adding water; run the engine for a few minutes to allow thorough mixing of the electrolyte.

It is most important to maintain batteries in a fully charged state during cold weather. Not only do cranking loads increase as engine oil thickens with cold, but battery capacity decreases at the same time. If battery capacity and cranking power required are assumed to be 100% at 80°F, **Table 2** shows what happens at lower temperatures.

Table 2   BATTERY CAPACITY

Temperature	Battery Capacity Available	Cranking Power Required
80°F	100%	100%
32°F	68%	165%
—20°F	30%	350%

At —20 degrees, power required for cranking is 3½ times that required at 80 degrees, but only 30% of battery power is available.

Another reason for keeping batteries fully charged during cold weather is that a fully charged battery freezes at a much lower temperature than does one which is partially discharged. Freezing temperature depends on specific gravity. See **Table 3**.

Table 3   BATTERY FREEZING TEMPERATURES

Specific Gravity	Freezing Temperature
1.100	18°F
1.120	13°F
1.140	8°F
1.160	1°F
1.180	— 6°F
1.200	—17°F
1.220	—31°F
1.240	—50°F
1.260	—75°F
1.280	—92°F

Since freezing may ruin a battery, protect it by keeping it in a charged condition. Remember that many boats are stored outside during cold weather, so be sure to take adequate precautions.

BATTERY CHARGERS

Types

There are 2 basic types of battery chargers.

a. Unregulated

b. Regulated

Unregulated battery chargers or trickle chargers are designed for automobile use. These inexpensive chargers continue to charge the battery at a slow rate even after the battery is fully charged. If left unattended, the battery could be permanently damaged. Unregulated chargers are not suited for boats.

Regulated chargers are more suited to marine use. Two types are available. The automatic charger shown in **Figure 5** is representative. This type will automatically shut off when the battery is fully charged. The constant-voltage charger maintains battery voltage at a constant level regardless of battery condition or shore power voltage variations. See **Figure 6**. Either type can be connected and left indefinitely when the boat is not in use. In fact, the constant-voltage charger is permanently connected. Make sure the charger you buy carries the "UL Marine" label of the Underwriter's Laboratory.

Capacity

Charger capacity is the maximum current the charger can deliver measured in amperes. Your charger should be able to recharge the batteries in a 24-hour period.

To estimate the capacity you need, you must know the current drawn by each electrical accessory on your boat. Multpily the current drawn by each accessory by the time in hours it is normally used in a 24-hour period. This gives you the current drawn from the battery in ampere-hours. Add the ampere-hour figure for each accessory. Divide this figure by 24 (hours) to determine minimum battery charger capacity in amperes. It is best to have a charger with at least 25-50% more capacity than this to compensate for charger inefficiency and future electrical accessory expansion. A charger can be too small, but it cannot be too large.

Current consumption of each electrical accessory can be determined in a number of ways. For radios, radar, electrical appliances, etc., check the owner's manual or contact the manufacturer. For 12-volt lamps, see **Table 4** or consult manufacturer.

To determine the amperage of any appliance or lamp rated only in wattage, use the following formula.

$$\text{Amps} = \frac{\text{Watts}}{\text{Volts}}$$

As a simple example, a 36 watt bulb in a 12-volt system requires 3 amps ($36 \div 12 = 3$). Taking this a step further, note that the same wattage output in a 24-volt system requires

7

Table 4   LAMP CURRENT REQUIREMENTS

Lamp	Current in Amperes
90	0.6
94	1.0
989	1.0
1004	1.0
1006	1.0
1142	1.5
1144	2.0
1416	0.8
9111	1.7

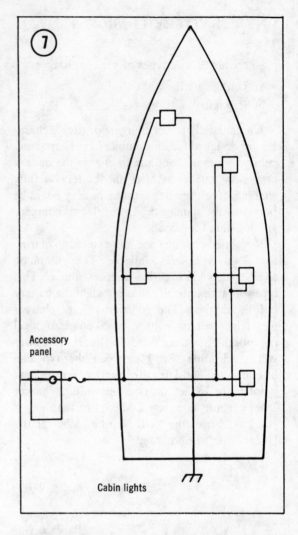

Accessory panel

Cabin lights

only 1.5 amps. Since amperage determines the thickness of wire required, it is obvious that increasing voltage permits the use of lighter conductors—the primary justification for moving up to 12 or 32 volts.

LIGHTING

The majority of boats have the following lighting systems.

  a. Navigation

  b. Cabin

  c. Spreader

A distribution panel supplies battery voltage to each system through a switch and a fuse. See **Figures 7 and 8**.

Lights are simple in that they usually either work or they don't. When a light doesn't work, the problem is most likely a burned-out bulb. Try substituting a bulb known to be good. If that one doesn't work, the following procedure should isolate the trouble. In rare cases where a light is either dim or flickering, look for a loose, damaged, or corroded connection.

1. Check to determine whether only one lamp, or an entire group of related lamps (such as running lamps), is affected. If only one lamp is affected, go on to Step 2. Refer to the paragraph following Step 6 if an entire group is affected.

2. Insert a known good lamp into the socket, then turn on the power switch.

3. Connect one end of a long wire to a good ground. To be absolutely sure of a good ground, it is best to connect this end of the wire to the negative terminal of the battery. Connect the other end of this wire to the outer shell of the affected lamp socket.

4. If the lamp now lights, the problem is a defective ground circuit. Poor grounds are a frequent cause of exterior lamp failure. They may usually be corrected by removing each mounting screw, then replacing it with a star lockwasher under the screw head.

5. If the lamp still does not light, the problem is in the power wiring to the lamp, or possibly in the switch. First, bridge the switch terminals with a small piece of wire. It may be necessary to pierce the insulation on the wires to the switch

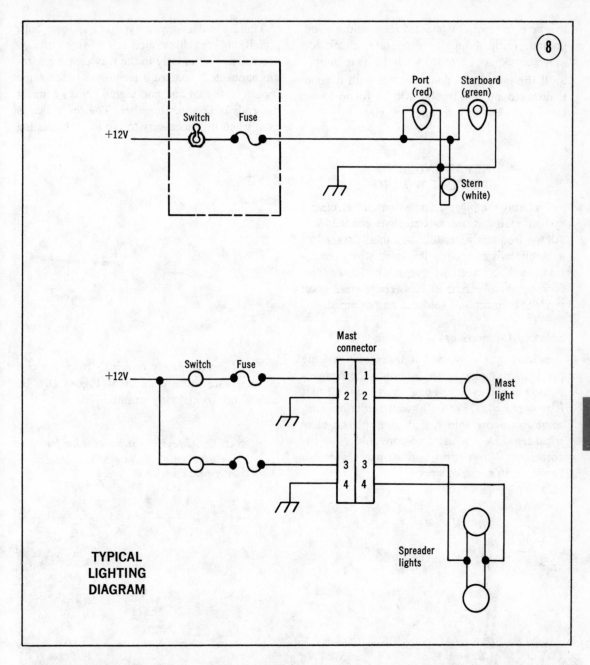

**TYPICAL
LIGHTING
DIAGRAM**

for this operation. If, with the switch bridged, the lamp lights, the switch is defective. Replace the switch.

6. Finally, check the wiring back from the lamp socket. At some point, a loose, broken, or corroded connection will be found.

Sometimes an entire related group, such as running lamps, will go out simultaneously. To find and correct the malfunction, proceed as follows.

1. Check the fuse which protects that circuit. A blown fuse is not necessarily indicative of trouble in the electrical system as sometimes a fuse will blow for no apparent reason. If replacing the fuse corrects the problem, but it blows again shortly afterward, examine all related wiring for chafing or pinched spots, then make any required repairs.

2. If replacing the fuse does not correct the condition, run a temporary ground wire between

the metal base of any affected lamp and a good ground. If the lamps now operate, check for loose, broken, or corroded ground wire to lamps.

3. If the lamps still don't operate with a good known ground, the trouble will be found to be either a broken or disconnected wire.

REPAIRING AND SPLICING WIRING

Probably the biggest single cause of electrical system malfunctions is defective connections. All too frequently, troubles are finally traced to a hastily twisted, poorly insulated wire connection. Such connections eventually loosen and corrode, then become useless. There are 2 good types of connections; soldered and crimped.

Soldered Connections

Soldering is easy, and it takes only a little practice to make perfect, permanent connections. For the average home craftsman, all that is required is a 75- to 100-watt soldering iron, some *rosin-core* solder, and some plastic electrical tape. Do not use acid-core solder as it is corrosive. Wire cutters and strippers are also handy for this type of work.

There are 3 common types of splices: butt, pigtail, and tee, illustrated left to right in **Figure 9**. They differ only in the way that the wires are connected; soldering technique is the same for all. Note that butt and pigtail splices connect the ends of 2 wires together. The tee splice is used when it is necessary to tap into an existing wire.

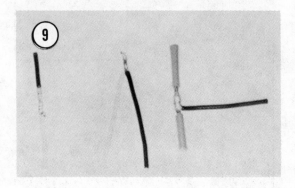

1. Strip approximately one inch from the end of each wire to be connected (**Figure 10**). Be careful not to nick any strands.

NOTE: *Always use stranded wire for all marine wiring. Solid wire will eventually break under vibration.*

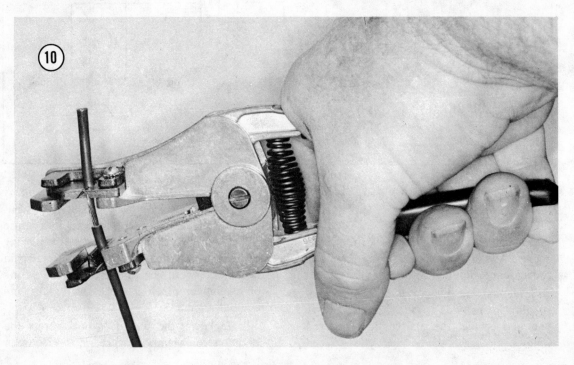

2. Twist the 2 stripped ends together firmly, as shown in **Figure 11**. Mechanical strength of the solder joint depends on this twisting. Be sure that your fingers are clean during this operation, otherwise solder will not adhere to the wire.

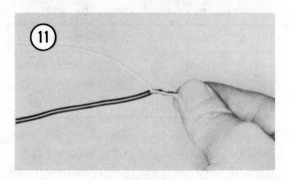

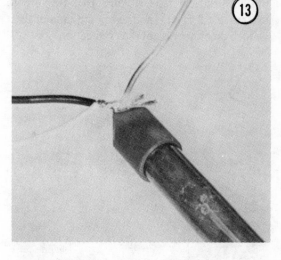

3. Be sure that the soldering iron is well tinned, then hold its tip under the twisted wires to heat the joint (**Figure 12**).

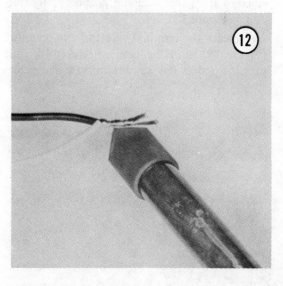

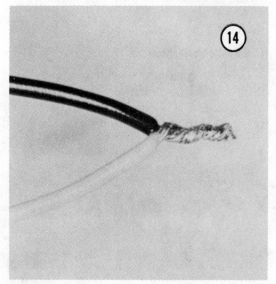

4. When the joint is heated, apply solder slowly to the joint (not the iron itself). Melted solder will flow smoothly throughout the joint (**Figure 13**). Then remove the solder.

5. Remove the soldering iron and allow the joint to cool completely before moving it. A properly soldered connection will be bright and shiny, with shapes of individual wires still visible (**Figure 14**).

6. Cut off any excess wire (**Figure 15**) from the connection.

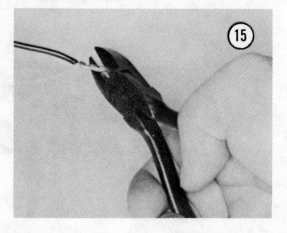

7. Protect and insulate the connection with plastic electrical tape (**Figure 16**). Be sure to use at least 2 layers, and carry the tape at least an inch on either side of the connection.

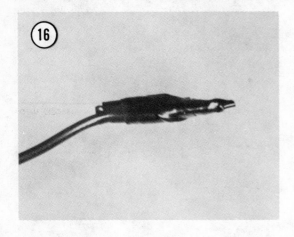

Crimped Connections

Crimped connections are faster and easier than soldered ones, but are also considerably more expensive. **Figure 17** illustrates various types of crimp connectors and the tool required

to make them. Note that crimped connections are small and neat and may be desirable in cramped locations. Crimp connectors are usually color coded to denote wire sizes with which they may be used. See **Table 5**.

Table 5   CRIMP CONNECTOR SIZES

Color	Wire Size
Yellow	10 and 12
Blue	14 and 16
Red	16 and 18

Strip approximately 5/16 in. from the end of the wire to be connected. This distance will vary slightly and can best be determined by experience. The distance is correct when the shoulder formed by the remaining insulation bottoms in the terminal and the stripped end of the wire just emerges from the crimping portion of the terminal (**Figure 18**).

2. Squeeze the terminal with the crimping tool (**Figure 19**) until the jaws are closed. A little practice with a few spare terminals and pieces

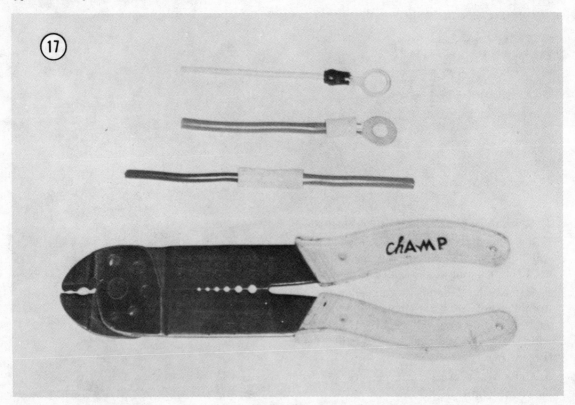

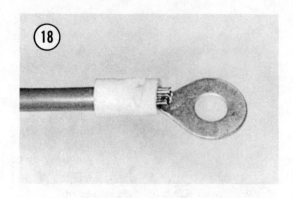

of scrap wire beforehand will ensure good connections every time.

Wiring

It may happen that damaged wiring must be replaced or new wires installed for additional lights or other accessories. Several precautions should be observed when such wiring is done.

1. Be sure that any new circuits are protected by a fuse of appropriate size.

2. Be sure that all wiring is adequately supported and protected against chafing, in particular in areas where it passes over or through metal parts such as engine compartment components. Avoid running wires near hot exhaust manifolds or pipes. As often as possible, attach any additional wiring to existing wire harnesses, using plastic insulation tape.

3. Always use good quality wire designed for automotive application. Such wire is available at any auto parts store, either in bulk or on handy spools. Never use rubber-insulated wire. Automotive wire has plastic insulation which is highly resistant to abrasion.

4. Always use wire of adequate size. **Table 6** lists current carrying capacities of various wire sizes.

Trailer Connectors

Because trailers must be unhitched, all wiring between the 2 passes through a multi-pin connector. These connectors are common sources

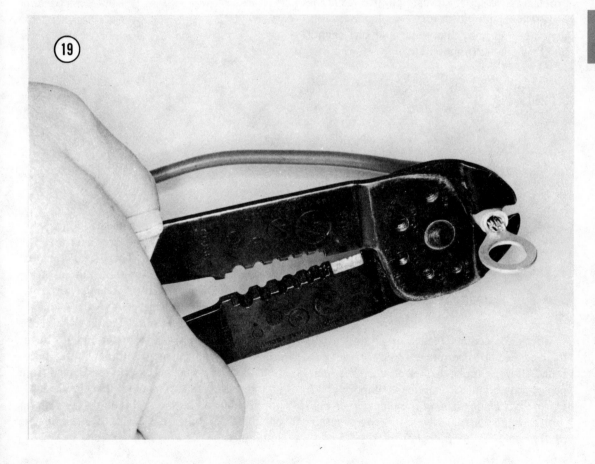

Table 6   WIRE AND FUSES

Wire Size (AWG)	Current Capacity (Amperes)	Fuse Size (Amperes)
10	25	30
12	20	14
14	15	14
16	6	9
18	3	9

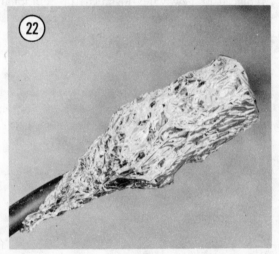

of trouble. Usually the female receptacle is attached to the tow car in a protected location and is equipped with a self-closing cover (**Figure 20**). Such connectors are not so prone to trouble as are the male plugs attached to the trailer (**Figure 21**). When the 2 are uncoupled for an extended period, the owner frequently forgets to protect the plug from exposure. Corrosion sets in, both on the contacts and on the internal connections, resulting in numerous problems. Protect the trailer plug by covering it with heavy plastic sheeting or aluminum foil, then securing it so that water and dirt cannot find their way in (**Figure 22**).

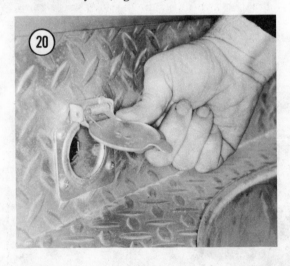

Check the contact blades or prongs on the male connector to be sure that they are not corroded. If your trailer has electric brakes, connector condition is extremely important. *If either the brake or ground terminals in the connector are corroded or damaged, complete loss of trailer braking may result.*

Fuses

Trailer signal lights are connected to the vehicle signal light systems and are therefore protected by the same fuses. The owner's manual for your car or truck gives the location of the fuse panel. On most cars, it is under the dashboard on the driver's side.

Visual examination will determine whether or not a fuse has blown; if so, the inner wire or metal strip will be melted through. But occasionally a fuse wire becomes disconnected from its terminal in such a manner that the defect is not visible, so check any doubtful fuse with an ohmmeter or other device for determining its continuity.

SHORE POWER

Shore power electrical systems **(Figure 23)** consist of 2 parts.

a. External system

b. On-board system

The external system consists of the deck-mounted inlet connection, ship-to-shore cable, and the dockside electrical outlet.

The on-board system consists of the interior wiring, control panel, outlets, switches, circuits, and so forth.

Most shore outlets are rated 110-125 volts. Some are rated 250 volts for large appliances on large boats. Rated load is usually 30 amperes.

The shore power system requires no maintenance other than periodic inspection to ensure that connections are secure. One possible area of concern is the circuit breaker in the dock connection point. Long exposure to moisture and salt could corrode it to the point that moving parts simply fuse together—rendering it a hazard. It is not a bad idea to replace the breaker after 5 years simply as a precaution.

You should have an idea how much shore power current your boat requires. Make a list of all AC-powered appliances on board, along with the current demand of each.

Most appliances list their power requirements on a small tag. In most cases, this is listed in amperes. In some cases, however, it is listed in watts. To convert watts to amperes, divide the wattage requirement by 125 volts.

Add up the current requirement of all appliances. This figure is the current required from the shore power if every appliance is used simultaneously; a very unlikely event. Most manufacturers use 70% of this total current when designing the system.

Here is an example. Suppose all the appliances used on your boat add up to 35 amperes. Seventy percent of 35 amperes equals about 25 amperes. The circuit breaker on your boat and the one dockside must be rated for at least 25 amperes.

MAKING A WIRING DIAGRAM

A good wiring diagram for your boat can save hours, even days, when trying to locate trouble or add electrical accessories. Unfortunately, virtually none of the boat builders supply a diagram.

It is not difficult to make your own wiring diagrams, but it is tedious. You will need a small volt-ohmmeter similar to the one shown in **Figure 24**, extra-long test leads which you can make yourself, and a willing assistant or two.

You may have seen the complex wiring diagrams drawn for automobiles. A similar drawing could be done for a boat. However, it is much easier to make smaller individual diagrams for each of the electrical systems in the boat. This section breaks the electrical systems down into several sub-systems, explains how to draw the diagram, and shows a typical system.

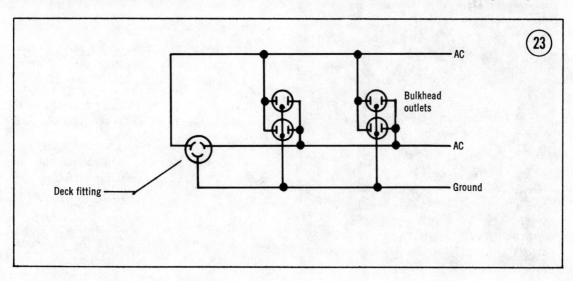

Primary Power

This system consists of the battery (or batteries), engine-mounted alternator/generator, main switch, and connecting wires. Figure 1 is typical.

To draw the schematic, locate the major items shown in the schematic diagram. Start with the battery and trace each wire to its final destination. Note color of insulation and relative size. Keep the following points in mind.

1. Alternators and generators are not wired in the same manner.

2. Some systems use ground busses like the one shown in **Figure 25**. The purpose of a buss is to conveniently connect several wires together. This may be done by connecting them all to one large terminal.

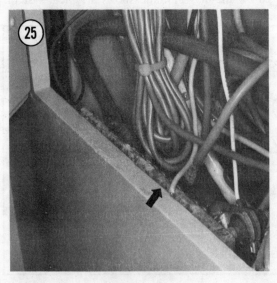

3. Single battery systems will differ slightly. The power switch simply turns power on and off. With multiple batteries, the switch must be able to select each of the batteries or banks separately or both together in addition to turning power on and off.

Cabin Lights

Cabin lights are normally wired in parallel back to the fuse/switch panel. See Figure 7. Usually each light has its own switch.

When making the diagram, trace from the primary power buss, through the main cabin light switch and fuse, to each cabin light. Draw the lights over an outline of the hull to aid trouble location.

Navigation and Spreader Lights

On most boats, navigation lights consists of the bow running lights and a stern light. On sailboats, there is usually a mast light with a separate switch and fuse. Draw both systems on the same diagram. Spreader lights usually connect from mast, through the deck, with the same electrical connector. Therefore, they should also be on this diagram. See Figure 8.

As with other diagrams, trace each system from primary power buss, through each switch and fuse, to the lights. Make note of pin numbers on mast connector. Also note color of insulation.

Fresh Water and Bilge Pumps

If the boat has electric water pumps, make one diagram showing location of each pump and all connecting wires. See **Figure 26**.

Communication Instruments Systems

Make a diagram showing exactly where each communication or navigation instrument such as RDF, VHE, etc., connects to the primary power. Other information such as antenna cable routing could be useful.

A separate diagram should show connections for other instruments such as the knotmeter, depth meter, etc. Trace from instrument back

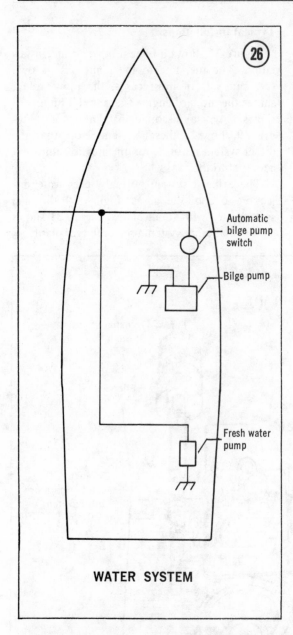

(26)

Automatic
bilge pump
switch

Bilge pump

Fresh water
pump

WATER SYSTEM

to power source. Also trace from instrument to transducer in hull. Show location of each transducer on diagram.

Shore Power

Wiring for shore power is very simple. Alternating current outlets in the cabin are wired in series and terminate at a male 3-prong connector on the deck. In some installations, there may be circuit breakers or fuses installed.

To draw a diagram, trace from the deck connector to each AC outlet. See Figure 23.

WARNING
Make sure the shore power cord is disconnected when tracing the wires. Shore power (110 volts) is lethal.

Large boats with AC generators have a change-over switch to select either shore power or the generator.

BATTERY LAY-UP AND STORAGE

1. Remove batteries and thoroughly clean cases with a baking soda solution.

2. Inspect battery holders and surrounding area for damage caused by spillage of battery acid. Wash the area down with a solution of baking soda and warm water.

CAUTION
Keep cleaning liquid out of the battery cells or the electrolyte will be seriously weakened.

3. Clean battery terminals with stiff wire brush or one of the many tools made for this purpose.

4. Examine battery cases for cracks.

5. Top up cells with distilled water.

6. Recharge the batteries with a battery charger, not the engine charging system.

7. Check specific gravity of each cell as described in the electrical chapter.

CAUTION
Batteries must be disconnected and fully charged prior to lay-up.

8. Lightly smear battery terminals with petroleum jelly.

9. Store the batteries in a cool, dry place. Do not leave the batteries where there is a risk of freezing. Never leave a battery stored on a concrete or dirt floor. The charge will bleed off overnight. Put the battery on wood blocks.

NOTE: *If possible, recharge the batteries once a month.*

10. Disconnect and clean the terminals on the starter and generator or alternator. Reconnect wires and lightly smear with petroleum jelly.

7

AUXILIARY POWER PLANTS

Many large boats are equipped with gasoline or diesel auxiliary power plants which supply enough electrical power to operate almost any appliance found at home. These power plants consist primarily of an internal combustion engine, alternating current generator, and controls.

The following sections describe routine maintenance required for typical gasoline and diesel generating systems. Due to the large number of different systems available, individual power plants are not described. Refer to owner's manual for specifics if necessary.

Typical Installations

Figure 27 shows a typical power plant installation. The fuel line to the plant has its own fuel shut-off. In most cases, the power plant shares the inboard engine fuel supply. Figure 28 shows a typical gasoline installation and Figure 29 shows a diesel system. Note that the diesel system requires return lines to return excess fuel to the tanks.

The exhaust system normally uses water injection to cool the gases. Figure 30 shows a system used with small plants. Figure 31 shows a more elaborate system used on larger plants.

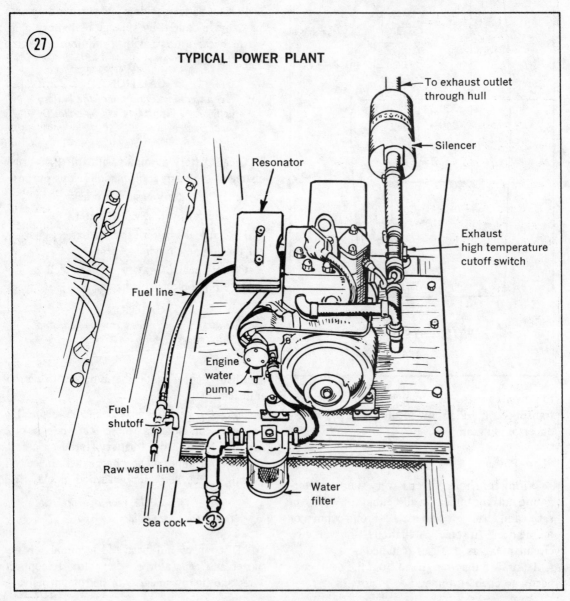

(27)

TYPICAL POWER PLANT

Resonator

To exhaust outlet through hull

Silencer

Exhaust high temperature cutoff switch

Fuel line

Engine water pump

Fuel shutoff

Raw water line

Water filter

Sea cock

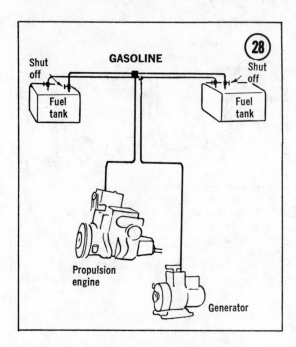

Figure 28 — GASOLINE

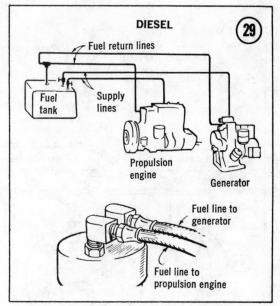

Figure 29 — DIESEL

Water-cooled plans may use:

a. Direct cooling

b. Heat exchanger cooling

c. Keel or skin cooling

Direct cooling systems draw seawater through the hull, pump it through the engine and exhaust it through the muffler system. See **Figure 32**.

Heat exchanger systems use a closed fresh water system containing a rust inhibitor or anti-freeze. Seawater from outside the hull cools the fresh water through a heat exchanger. See **Figure 33**.

Keel cooling is similar to the heat exchanger system. A keel cooler immersed in the sea acts as a heat exchanger. Fresh water is pumped through the keel cooler for cooling (**Figure 34**).

7

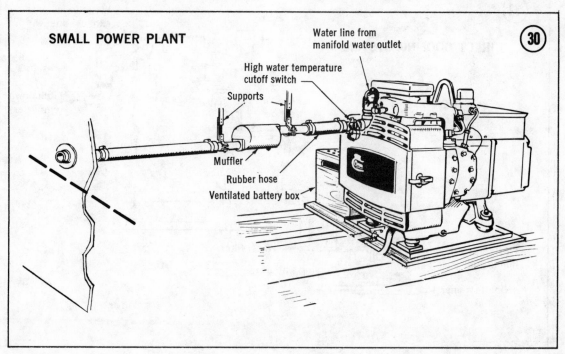

SMALL POWER PLANT

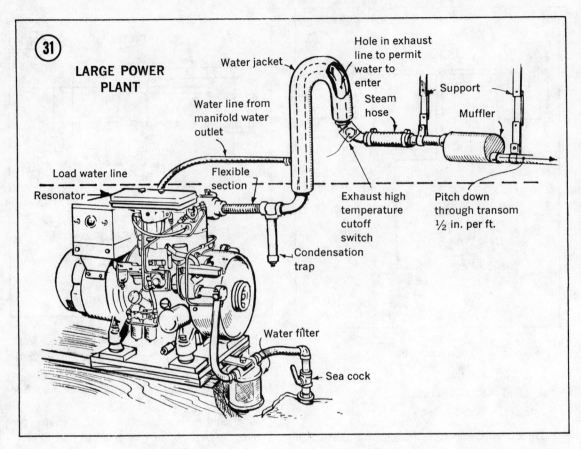

(31)

LARGE POWER PLANT

Water jacket

Hole in exhaust line to permit water to enter

Water line from manifold water outlet

Steam hose

Support

Muffler

Load water line

Flexible section

Resonator

Exhaust high temperature cutoff switch

Pitch down through transom ½ in. per ft.

Condensation trap

Water filter

Sea cock

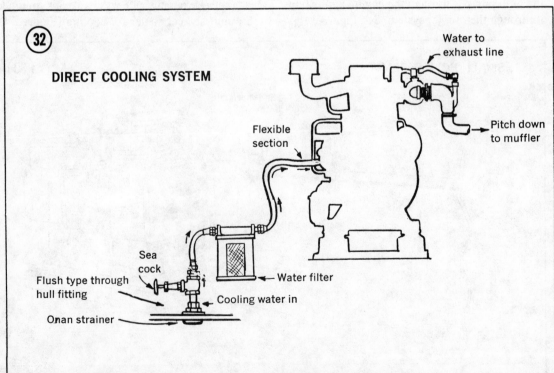

(32)

DIRECT COOLING SYSTEM

Water to exhaust line

Flexible section

Pitch down to muffler

Sea cock

Flush type through hull fitting

Water filter

Cooling water in

Onan strainer

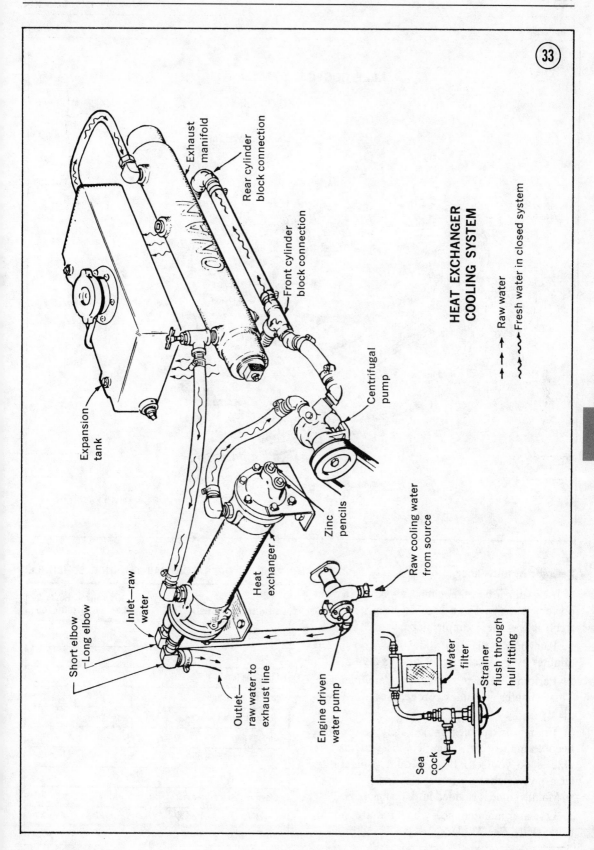

HEAT EXCHANGER COOLING SYSTEM

→ → → Raw water

↝↝↝ Fresh water in closed system

Exhaust manifold

Rear cylinder block connection

Front cylinder block connection

Centrifugal pump

Zinc pencils

Raw cooling water from source

Expansion tank

Heat exchanger

Inlet—raw water

Short elbow

Long elbow

Outlet—raw water to exhaust line

Engine driven water pump

Sea cock

Water filter

Strainer flush through hull fitting

33

7

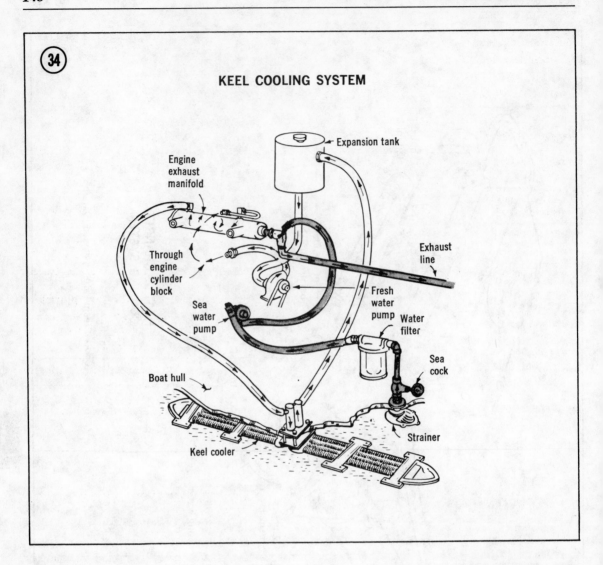

(34)

KEEL COOLING SYSTEM

Expansion tank

Engine exhaust manifold

Exhaust line

Through engine cylinder block

Fresh water pump

Water filter

Sea water pump

Sea cock

Boat hull

Strainer

Keel cooler

Periodic Maintenance

Like your inboard engine, the engine in your power plant thrives on use. To keep it running right, follow these simple steps.

1. Run power plant periodically—even a few minutes every week except during lay-up.

2. Perform regular scheduled maintenance. This chapter includes procedures for most plants.

3. Fix minor troubles immediately before they become major. Very simple jobs you may be able to do yourself. If you doubt your ability, let a professional do it.

Maintenance is divided into 2 categories.

1. Operator maintenance, which requires no unusual skills. See **Table 7**.

Table 7 OPERATOR MAINTENANCE SCHEDULE

Maintenance Items	Operational Hours			
	8	50	100	200
General inspection	X			
Check fuel supply	X			
Check oil level	X			
Service air cleaner		X		
Clean governor linkage		X		
Check spark plugs (gasoline)			X	
Change crankcase oil			X	
Clean fuel filter			X	
Clean crankcase breather				X
Check battery electrolyte				X

2. Critical maintenance, performed by qualified personnel. See **Table 8**.

Table 8 CRITICAL MAINTENANCE SCHEDULE

Maintenance Items	Operational Hours			
	200	500	1,000	5,000
Check breaker points	X			
Check brushes	X			
Clean commutator and collector rings		X		
Remove carbon and lead		X		
Check valve clearance		X		
Clean carburetor (gasoline)		X		
Clean generator			X	
Remove and clean oil base			X	
Grind valves			X	
General overhaul				X

Routine Checks

The following simple checks should be performed prior to each day's use.

1. Check engine oil level. Level should be between 2 marks on dipstick, but never below.

2. Check coolant level.

3. If plant uses direct water cooling, open the seacock.

4. As soon as engine starts, look for water at exhaust outlet. If water doesn't emerge, stop the engine immediately.

Lubricating Oil

Check crankcase oil each day of use. Always maintain the oil level between the "L" and "F" marks on the dipstick (**Figure 35**). Do not operate the power plant with the oil level too high or too low. *In the event of a sudden unexplained loss of oil, discontinue operation of power plant.*

Drain engine oil every 50 hours of operation, or every 6 months, whichever comes first. Run the engine for a few minutes first to warm the oil before draining. For gasoline engines, use only oils meeting API Service MS specifications. Oils meeting this requirement will be plainly marked as such on the can. For diesel engines,

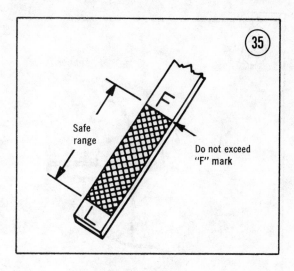

use oil marked specifically for this purpose. Select oil viscosities from **Table 9**.

Table 9 OIL VISCOSITY

Temperature	Oil Viscosity
Above 32°F	SAE 30
0-32°F	SAE 10W-30
Below 0°F	SAE 5W-30

Air Cleaner

Every 50 hours, clean air filter element. Some power plants use a dry element as shown in **Figure 36**. To clean, unscrew wing nut, remove cover, and remove element. Tap element against a flat surface to dislodge loose surface dirt. Do not blow dirt out with air or clean element in any solvent. Replace element every 100 hours.

Some power plants use an oil bath air cleaner similar to **Figure 37**. Every 50 hours, clean screen and cup in solvent such as kerosene or diesel fuel. Fill cup to level indicated with clean oil; use the same type as in the engine crankcase.

Spark Plug(s) (Gasoline Engines Only)

Remove and examine spark plug every 100 hours of operation. A light gray or tan deposit should be visible on the insulator. If the insulator appears dead white, blistered, or burned, overheating of the engine or possibly a lean fuel mixture is the cause. Fluffy black carbon deposits indicate an overrich fuel mixture, caused

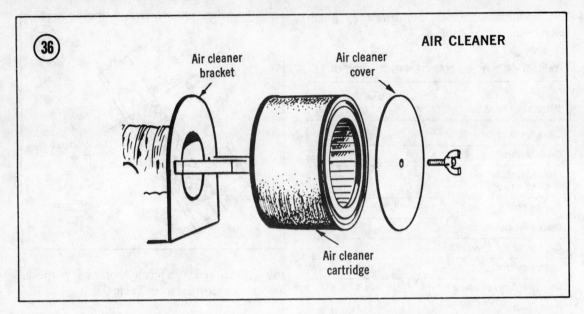

AIR CLEANER

Air cleaner bracket

Air cleaner cover

Air cleaner cartridge

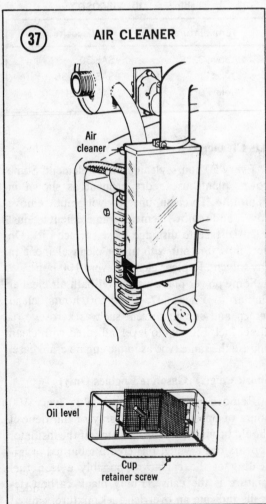

AIR CLEANER

Air cleaner

Oil level

Cup retainer screw

by a clogged air cleaner or misadjusted carburetor. Spark plugs are inexpensive. Do not sandblast, wire brush, or scrape a used plug; replace it with a new one identical to the one removed. Set spark plug gap at 0.025 in. Be sure that spark plug seating surface on the cylinder head is clean, then torque the new plug to 22 ft.-lb.

Air Cooling System

Cooling air is drawn over the generator and through the engine cooling fins by a blower. Be sure that intake louvers, generator cooling openings, cooling fins, and scrollwork are clean and unobstructed at all times. Do not operate the power plant with any cooling system component removed.

Water Cooling System

Before each use, check level in expansion tank if closed cooling system is used. If direct water cooling is used, clean out seawater strainer if equipped.

Every year, have coolant drained and replaced with a 50/50 mixture of water and ethylene glycol anti-freeze or a good rust inhibitor.

Fuel Filter

Refer to **Figure 38**. Every 100 hours or sooner, drain fuel pump and check filter element. Turn hex nut on base of electric fuel pump

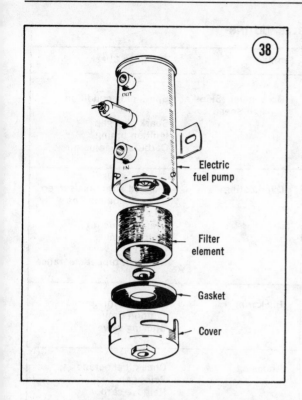

Electric fuel pump

Filter element

Gasket

Cover

to gain access to filter element. If element appears dirty, replace with a new one. Be sure to replace gaskets when reassembling.

Crankcase Breather

Lift off rubber breather cap (**Figure 39**). Carefully pry valve from cap. Otherwise, press hard with both thumbs on top of the cap and fingers below to release valve from rubber cap. Wash this fabric flapper type check valve in a suitable solvent. Dry and install. Position perforated disc toward engine.

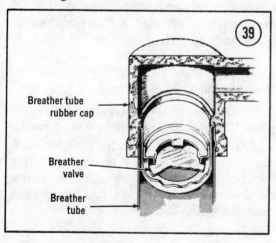

Breather tube rubber cap

Breather valve

Breather tube

Troubleshooting

Table 10 lists possible problems and probable causes for them.

POWER PLANT LAY-UP

When taking a marine generating plant out of service for 30 days or longer, proper storage methods must be used to prevent damage from corrosion, contamination, and temperature extremes.

Fuel System

1. Gasoline only: Drain entire engine fuel system by shutting off fuel supply tank and allow engine to run itself out of fuel.

2. Clean flame arrester or air cleaner thoroughly; do not service air cleaner with oil.

3. Cover or seal exposed flame arrester or air intake openings.

4. Clean throttle linkage (and governor linkage) thoroughly. Lubricate metal ball-joints with light machine oil (do not lubricate plastic ball-joints).

Oil System

1. Change engine lubricating oil while engine is warm regardless of time since last oil change.

2. Remove spark plugs (gasoline only). Remove fuel injectors (diesel only). Pour 2 tablespoons of rust inhibitor oil (SAE 50 substitute) into each cylinder. Crank engine over by hand several revolutions to lubricate cylinder walls, pistons, and rings. Install plugs or injectors (lightly lubricate spark plug threads prior to installation).

3. Remove and service oil filter (if used).

4. Clean crankcase breather valve and breather tube flame arrester (if used).

Cooling System

1. *Air Cooled Only*. Remove access panel and clean all cooling surfaces. Clean air screens and all air ducts.

2. *Water Cooled Only*. Drain entire cooling system including water cooled exhaust manifold and exhaust line. Drain radiator, heat exchanger, or keel cooler components, engine cylinder block, and water pumps.

7

Table 10   TROUBLESHOOTING

Problem	Things to Check	Problem	Things to Check
Hard Starting or Loss of Power	Loose or shorted wire Point gap Point condition Faulty spark plug Defective coil Defective condenser Clogged fuel line Defective fuel pump Dirty carburetor Carburetor adjustment Loose cylinder head Defective head gasket Sticking valves Leaking valves Worn piston rings	Occasional "Skip" at High Speed	Spark plug condition Spark plug gap Ignition timing Carburetor adjustment
		Overheating	Clogged air intake screen Clogged cooling fins Oil supply Lean fuel mixture Ignition timing Overload Incorrect tappet clearance
Erratic Operation	Clogged fuel line Contaminated fuel Gas cap vent plugged Defective fuel pump Carburetor gasket leaking Governor adjustment Carburetor adjustment	Backfiring	Lean fuel mixture Ignition timing Sticking valve
		Knocking	Check fuel octane Point gap Remove carbon Cooling air supply

Generating plants equipped with closed type cooling systems (radiator, heat exchanger, keel cooling) may be filled with a good quality antifreeze if freezing temperatures are expected. Drain only those components not protected from freezing (exhaust lines, water pumps, water intake and outlet lines, etc.).

Electrical System and Batteries

1. Clean generator brushes, commutator, and slip rings by wiping with a clean, dry, lint-free cloth. *Do not lubricate these parts.*

2. Clean static exciter with dry low-pressure air. Remove dust and dirt deposits in control box and junction boxes.

3. Disconnect batteries and remove from vessel. Service batteries by maintaining liquid level and using a trickle charger to maintain voltage.

CAUTION
Discharged batteries are subject to severe damage if exposed to freezing temperatures. Store all batteries in a fully charged condition and maintain charge during storage.

General

1. Cover or seal all exposed openings (exhaust outlet, water parts, etc.).

2. *Tag* and *identify* plant to indicate *service required before attempting to operate.* List all items requiring attention and service prior to operation.

Returning the Plant to Operation

1. Uncover and remove storage seals from entire plant. Remove any dust, dirt, or foreign matter.

2. *Check* fuel supply tanks for moisture accumulations (drain tanks if necessary). *Check* lubricating oil for moisture or contamination (drain if necessary). *Check* fuel line connections, all wiring connections, and exhaust line connections.

3. Completely check exhaust system at least once a season. Disassemble exhaust elbow assembly and exhaust line for complete inspection of all pipe fittings, hoses, gaskets, and exhaust systems. Inspect the exhaust elbow and fittings from the inside out for erosion or corrosion wear. Replace same when wall thickness becomes reduced to ½ original size or noticeable deterioration has started. Onan exhaust elbows have original ¼ inch thickness and pipe fittings original ⅛ inch thickness.

4. Service air cleaner (if used) or clean flame arrester. Clean spark plugs and install. Torque fuel injectors (diesel only) and bleed fuel system (if moisture or contamination are found in fuel—replace secondary filter and clean primary filter).

5a. *Water Cooled Only*. Service cooling system with clean fresh water. Prime water pump and see that all air is bled from cooling system. If anti-freeze was left in closed cooling system, check and service as required.

5b. *Air Cooled Only*. Check to see that all air passages and cooling surfaces are clean. Secure access doors and ducts.

6. Check entire plant for water, fuel, or oil leaks. Correct leakage as required.

7. Install fully charged batteries.

8. Start the plant in normal manner. Check the running plant for leaks, correct voltage output, proper cooling.

7

CHAPTER EIGHT

GALLEY

The galley is often the focal point of the boat. During warm weather, most of the crew shuttles between cockpit and galley for cold drinks and snacks. During cold weather or the dog watch, the galley means hot coffee to get through the night.

To enjoy the comfort and pleasure your galley is intended for, it must be clean and in working order. This chapter describes maintenance required to keep your stove, ice box or refrigerator in good condition.

STOVES

Depending on the size of the boat, the galley stove may be a single one-burner unit or a gimballed multi-burner range with oven. Most popular models are described in this section.

Marine stoves may be fueled by:

a. Alcohol

b. Kerosene

c. Liquid petroleum gas

Each fuel has advantages and disadvantages for marine cooking. Sections which follow describe the characteristics of each fuel. No one fuel is clearly considered best; read each description and decide for yourself.

ALCOHOL/KEROSENE SYSTEMS

Alcohol is by far the most popular stove fuel on boats, mainly because it is generally considered to be the safest. This stems from the fact that it is easily extinguished by water. In addition, alcohol has a less objectionable smell to many people than kerosene.

Despite its popularity, alcohol has a number of serious disadvantages. True, it is easily extinguished by water, but its low flash point makes it 4 times more flammable than kerosene, making the risk of fire greater. Furthermore, when burning, the flame is invisible; if a spill ignites, there is no telltale flame to help locate the fire. Finally, alcohol does not burn as hot as kerosene or propane; alcohol takes twice as long to boil water as kerosene.

Kerosene is replacing alcohol on many boats because of its many advantages. It burns hotter than alcohol, has a higher flash point, and costs nearly half as much as alcohol. Its only serious disadvantage is the smell which many people find objectionable. However, odorless kerosene is available in many areas. Kerosene must be extinguished with a Coast Guard approved fire extinguisher,. but this is standard equipment aboard any boat large enough to have a stove.

When purchasing alcohol for a galley stove, choose carefully. Use a good grade denatured ethyl alcohol. This is available in chandleries marked "marine alcohol stove fuel" or similar words. It is also available in hardware stores for less money as shellac thinner. Read the label carefully, however. Make sure it says *denatured* alcohol. Some shellac thinner is *methyl* alcohol mixed with a petroleum distillate. The petroleum distillate makes this an excellent high heat alcohol cooking fuel, but it cannot be put out with water and may smell bad. Pure *methyl* alcohol (wood alcohol) is also available, but it does not have adequate heat content for cooking.

Typical Systems

The simplest alcohol/kerosene stoves have an integral tank which is pressurized by a small hand pump on the stove. As fuel is consumed, the pump must be operated occasionally to maintain pressure. See **Figure 1**.

More sophisticated systems have a large capacity tank mounted some distance from the stove. The tank must be pressurized with a bicycle tire pump to about 7 psi. See **Figure 2**. A

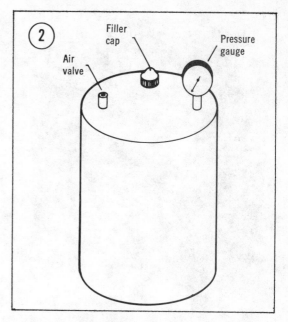

hose connects the fuel under pressure to the stove which may be a simple 2-burner stove or a larger unit with tap burners and an oven. See **Figure 3**.

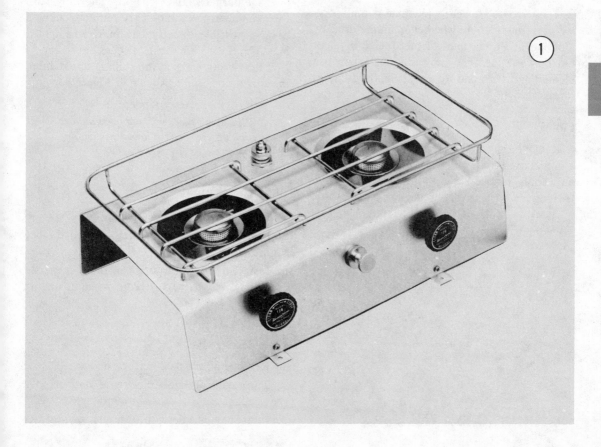

OPTIMUS/PRIMUS ALCOHOL AND KEROSENE STOVES

These stoves are nearly identical and all service procedures apply whether manufactured by Optimus or Primus and whether fueled by alcohol or kerosene. The only difference between alcohol and kerosene stoves is slightly different burner design.

Filling

Remove the safety cap and fill the tank. Use a funnel to prevent spills. See **Figure 4**. Wipe up any spills immediately to prevent fire when igniting the burners. Screw the cap on tight.

Operating the Stove

Refer to **Figure 5**.

1. Make sure that main burner knobs and preheater knobs are closed.

2. Operate pump to pressurize fuel tank. About 30 strokes are necessary with a full tank—more for a partially filled tank.

3. Hold a lighted match at the side of the preheater outlet. See **Figure 6**. Pull the preheater knob out and light the kerosene vapor.

4. Hold knob out and allow to burn for 30-45 seconds. See **Figure 7**.

5. Turn on main control knob and push in preheater knob. Main burner should burn with a blue flame. If a high yellow flame emerges, preheat the burner for another 10 seconds.

6. Regulate flame as desired with main control knob. Operate pump as necessary to maintain pressure in tank.

Cleaning and Maintenance

If the burner smokes or burns unevenly, turn the main control knob quickly counterclockwise as far as possible, then back again. Keep a lighted match handy in case the flame goes out.

If the burner leaks at the stuffing box, tighten the stuffing box nut as shown in **Figure 8**.

WARNING
Wipe up all fuel spills and accumulated cooking grease. If allowed to accumulate a serious fire could occur.

Changing Nipple

1. Remove outer and inner covers. See **Figure 9**.

2. Remove nipple with key provided. See **Figure 10**.

3. Installation is the reverse of these steps. Be careful not to damage needle when installing new nipple.

Changing Needle

1. Remove nipple as described above.

2. Turn control knob clockwise and remove the needle.

3. Insert new needle with tweezers.

Filler cap

⑤

Pump   Preheater knob   Main control knob

⑥

8

NOTE: *If tweezers are not available, stick needle into end of wooden match and insert it.*

4. Turn control knob clockwise until 3 or 4 cogs on the spindle have passed. Keep the needle teeth firmly against spindle. If done correctly, you will hear a click each time a cog passes.

5. Turn control knob counterclockwise as far as possible.

6. Install nipple as described above.

7. When needle is correctly installed the needle will just be visible in the nipple hole when the control knob is opened ⅓ from fully closed. If the control knob must be opened more than this, repeat Steps 3-7.

Changing Stuffing Box Packing

1. Remove nipple and needle, described above.

2. Loosen stuffing box nut and unscrew regulating screw. See Figure 8.

3. Replace packing.

4. Assembly is the reverse of these steps.

Troubleshooting

Optimus/Primus stoves are simple devices and rarely give trouble. If you have a problem, refer to **Table 1** for help.

WILLIS ALCOHOL STOVES

Filling

Unscrew filler cap. Fill tank. Be sure alcohol is clean and free from foreign matter. Do not allow liquid to overflow. Screw filler cap into place. Wipe up any spills.

Operation

1. Be sure burner valves are closed.

2. Operate pump about 20-30 strokes.

3. Open one burner at a time and allow about 2 teaspoons of fuel to run into the preheating tray. Close valve at once. Do not overfill.

4. Repeat priming procedure for each burner to be used.

5. Be sure valves are closed before lighting priming alcohol.

6. Ignite priming alcohol to preheat burners.

7. Allow all the priming alcohol to burn away.

8. When flame in preheating bowl dies out, turn valve on slowly and apply a lighted match to the bottom or the burner.

9. Allow each burner to run for a few minutes with a small flame before turning it fully on.

10. When done, turn valves off. Loosen filler cap (do not remove) to relieve pressure in tank.

Cleaning Burners

Gravity feed and Type K: Refer to **Figure 11**. Shut off valve to tank. Remove capnut (14). Pull out strainer (2), clean with alcohol and tooth-

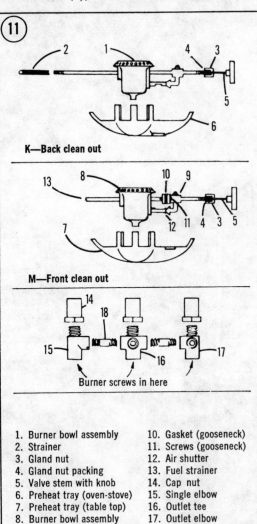

11

K—Back clean out

M—Front clean out

Burner screws in here

1. Burner bowl assembly
2. Strainer
3. Gland nut
4. Gland nut packing
5. Valve stem with knob
6. Preheat tray (oven-stove)
7. Preheat tray (table top)
8. Burner bowl assembly
9. Burner valve (gooseneck)
10. Gasket (gooseneck)
11. Screws (gooseneck)
12. Air shutter
13. Fuel strainer
14. Cap nut
15. Single elbow
16. Outlet tee
17. Outlet elbow
18. Inter connector tube

Table 1   OPTIMUS STOVE TROUBLESHOOTING

Symptom	Problem	Cure
Leakage around tank, lines, preheater	Loose connections	Tighten
	Damaged fittings	Replace fittings
	Holes in tank or solder joints	Replace or repair
	Leakage around burner spindle	Tighten, replace packing, replace spindle
	Leakage at burner connections	Assure that cones are installed and not damaged
	Rubber stoppers on preheater damaged or burned	Replace stoppers. Check that stopper arm swings easily, and fully out of the flame stream
Burner flares up with yellowish flame	Not preheated sufficiently	Repeat preheat procedure
	Burner spindle left open while starting	Close spindle before preheating or pressurizing
	Low air pressure	Pump additionally. See "Low air pressure"
	Loose nipple	Tighten nipple
	Bad or incorrect nipple	Replace or clean
	Carbon caked in burner	Clean or replace
	Bad burner	Replace
	Faulty inner cap	Replace—file down inner tube so it does not protrude above cap
	Center tube too high	File down level with inner cap
	Faulty outer cap	Replace
Burner will not shut off	Cleaning needle maladjusted	Remove and adjust. See **Changing Needle** in text) (Note: If needle is bottoming on the evaporator body, holding the spindle from closing, it can be felt by turning rapidly to the close position. It will stop with a very hard "feel")
	Foreign material in evaporator	Remove nipple needle, open spindle, pressurize tank and flush evaporator. Replace nipple
	Bad spindle	Replace
	Bad burner or evaporator	Replace burner or evaporator
Weak flame	Clogged nipple	Clean or replace nipple and needle
	Maladjusted cleaning needle	Adjust per instructions
	Low pressure	See "Low pressure" symptom
	Clogged wick	Replace wick
	Wrong nipple installed	Replace nipple
Unbalanced flame	Dirty nipple	Clean or replace
	Bad nipple	Clean or replace
	Threads misaligned between burner cup and nipple (No. 88 and No. 99 stoves)	Replace evaporator
	Bent burner cup	Replace
Burner not aligned vertically	Bent out of position	Bend back to proper position with hands

(continued)

8

Table 1   OPTIMUS STOVE TROUBLESHOOTING (continued)

Symptom	Problem	Cure
Erratic flame	Debris in evaporator	Remove nipple, needle, open spindle, pressurize tank and flush evaporator, replace nipple
Low pressure in tank	Bad seal in tank cap	Replace seal or cap
	Cap relief valve leaks	Replace cap
	Tank cap not tight	Tighten
	Pump chatters or provides little resistance when pumped	Change pump leather or O-ring. Change pump check valve
Pressure drops off too fast	Tank too full of fuel (less than ¾ full)	Remove some fuel
	Pressure release screw not tight	Tighten
	Leak	See "Low pressure in tank" above
Preheater blows only air	No fuel in tank	Refuel
Preheater blows little or no mixture	Nipple dirty	Clean
	Bad nipple	Replace
	Clogged lines or strainer at tank end of line	Blow out lines or replace
Preheater shoots stream of fuel instead of mixture fog	Low pressure	Pump tank up
	Dirty or bad nipple	Clean nipple while pressurized or replace
Preheater blows fuel/air mixture but will not light or stay lit if it does light	Low pressure	Pump up
	Dirty or bad nipple	Clean nipple while pressurized or replace
Preheater flame stream impinging on flame tube	Preheater misaligned	Bend bracket to align properly

brush. Remove valve stem (5), blow through. Reassemble.

Pressure feed and Type M: Refer to Figure 11. Relieve pressure in tank. Remove screws (11), take off gooseneck (9). Remove strainer (13). Clean with alcohol and toothbrush. Loosen valve stem (5), blow through. Reassemble.

Troubleshooting

1. *Yellow flame or spitting or sputtering.* To correct, allow burner to run with a low flame for about 2 minutes.

2. *Flame roars.* This is due to too much pressure. To correct, turn burner lower.

3. *Alcohol does not run into preheating tray.* Clean the burners as described above. Never try to force alcohol into the burners by excessive pumping. It should enter readily or burner must be cleaned.

HOMESTRAND ALCOHOL STOVES

Filling

Unscrew filler cap. Fill tank with denatured alcohol using a funnel. Install and tighten cap.

CAUTION
Filler cap has built-in safety valve to prevent excessive pressure in tank. Do not replace with any other type cap.

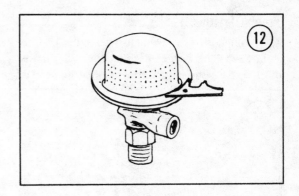

Operation

1. Operate pump 20 or more times to pressurize the tank.

2. Slowly open knob for one burner (counter-clockwise) to allow alcohol to flow into priming cup below burner body. Fill cup about ¾ full, then shut knob off.

3. Ignite priming cup alcohol.

4. When priming alcohol is fully consumed, turn burner on and light it.

WARNING
Burner may flare-up during preheating, particularly if burner is turned on before preheating is complete. If flare-up occurs, turn burner off and restart following the directions above.

5. When stove is shut off, open filler cap to relieve the pressure.

Regulating Flame

There are 2 types of alcohol burners on Homestrand stoves. Prior to about January, 1975, a regulating disc is inside the burner body; the burner must be partially disassembled to regulate the flame. After the date, the burner flange rotates to regulate the flame without disassembly.

To adjust early burners:

1. Light burners as described earlier.

2. If flame is orange, remove inner and outer caps. See **Figure 12**. Turn regulating disc to open holes slightly. See **Figure 13**.

3. If flame is light blue and pulsates, remove inner and outer caps. See Figure 12. Turn regulating disc to close holes slightly. See Figure 13.

4. Install inner and outer caps.

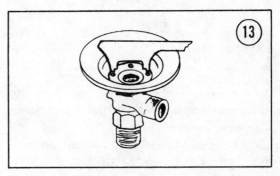

5. Repeat procedure as often as necessary to get a steady blue flame.

To adjust later burners:

1. Light burners as described above.

2. Observe flame. If flame is orange or light blue and pulsating, regulation is necessary.

3. With burners lit, hold burner flange with a pair of pliers and rotate the flange. See **Figure 14**. Adjust until a steady blue flame is achieved. This requires only a few degrees of rotation.

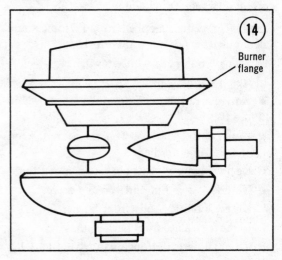

Burner flange

8

Troubleshooting

1. If you find a small flame where the control stem enters the burner, tighten the nut slightly until the flame no longer appears. See **Figure 15**.

2. If you notice alcohol in or around the pump, replace the check valve located in the bottom of the pump barrel.

3. If the pump bounces back when you try to pump, the check valve is stuck and must be replaced.

4. If you pump and get little or no pressure in the tank, the pump leather or U-cup needs to be replaced.

5. If your stove lights but goes out after a while, check for a leaking filler cap.

6. If no alcohol comes through the burner when you attempt to prime, make sure tank is pressurized. Also check the burner filter. This filter rarely clogs, but may be replaced as described later in this section.

Alcohol Burner Disassembly/Assembly

This procedure applies to all Homestrand alcohol burners. Refer to **Figure 16**.

1. Snap off outer cap with screwdriver.

2. Remove inner cap.

3. Unscrew nozzle with special tool shown in **Figure 17**.

4. Turn control knob off (fully clockwise) and lift out cleaning needle.

5. Remove control shaft pin and remove shaft.

6. Unscrew valve nut and remove valve.

7. Unscrew burner body from burner fitting.

8. Remove strainer from burner body.

9. Clean all parts thoroughly in clean fuel.

10. Install strainer in burner body.

11. Screw burner body onto burner fitting. Use copper gasket.

12. Screw valve into burner body. If packing is damaged or needle end of valve is worn, replace the entire valve assembly.

13. Install control shaft.

14. Turn knob fully clockwise.

15. Set cleaning needle in place.

16. Push down firmly on cleaning needle and rotate knob counterclockwise exactly 6 clicks.

17. Install nozzle with special tool.

18. Rotate knob fully clockwise. Rotate ½ turn from fully off; cleaner tip should just appear in nozzle hole. If not, disassemble and repeat Steps 14-18.

19. Install inner and outer caps.

Fuel Tank Disassembly/Assembly

Refer to **Figure 18** for this procedure.

1. Unscrew filler cap to relieve pressure.

2. Drain fuel from tank.

3. Unscrew pump assembly from tank and pull assembly out.

4. Unscrew pump check valve with special tool —the same tool used to remove burner nozzle.

5. Check condition of U-cap on end of pump. If damaged, cracked, or worn, replace it.

6. Install pump check valve with special tool. Do not overtighten.

7. Apply light machine oil to U-cap on end of pump.

8. Insert pump assembly into tank. Do not cut U-cup on tank. Screw assembly tight.

HOMESTRAND KEROSENE STOVES

Homestrand kerosene stoves are identical to the alcohol models except for the burners. Homestrand uses the Optimus kerosene burner described in an earlier section. Fill and operate the kerosene models as described for the alcohol models.

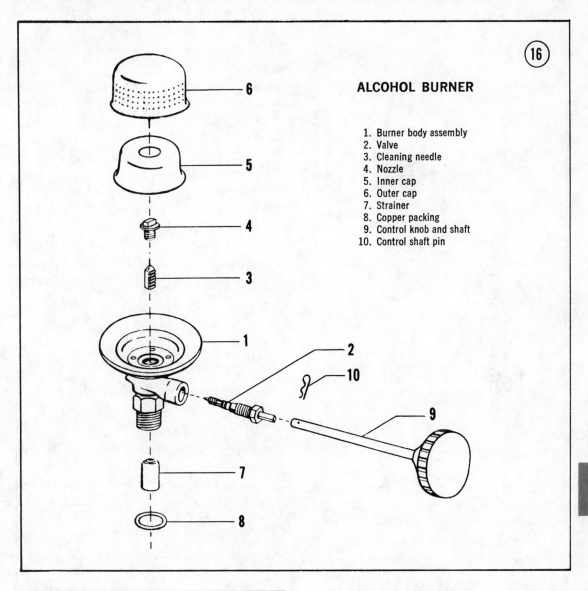

⑯

ALCOHOL BURNER

1. Burner body assembly
2. Valve
3. Cleaning needle
4. Nozzle
5. Inner cap
6. Outer cap
7. Strainer
8. Copper packing
9. Control knob and shaft
10. Control shaft pin

8

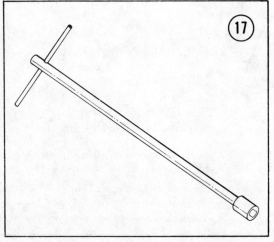

⑰

CONVERTING
GASOLINE STOVES TO ALCOHOL

Most Coleman and Sears gasoline camp stoves can be converted to burn alcohol in a matter of seconds with a kit from Nashcraft Marine Products, San Juan Capistrano, California. The kit costs about $5. Conversion back to gasoline is also simple. The same stove can burn alcohol or gasoline depending on whether you want to use it on your boat or on land.

WARNING
Unconverted gasoline stoves should not be used aboard. Gasoline is far too dangerous.

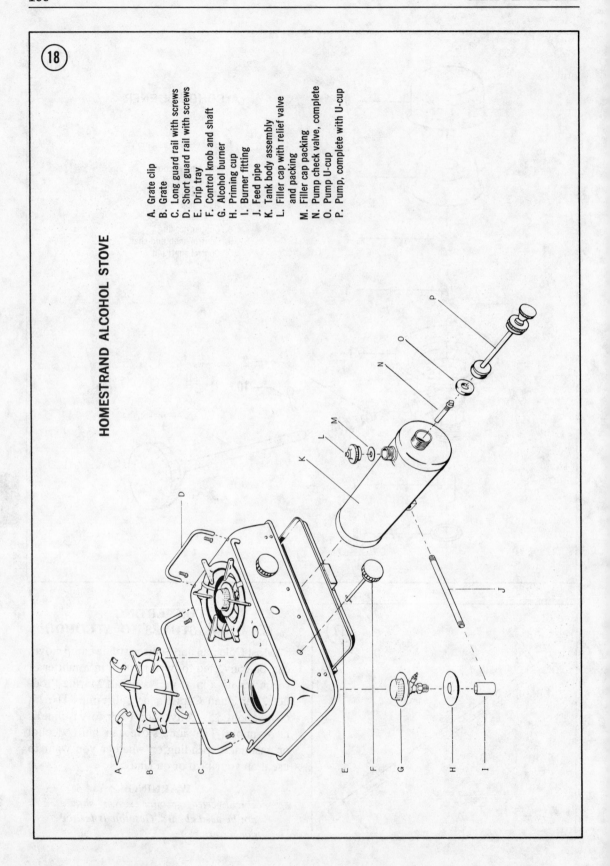

(18)

HOMESTRAND ALCOHOL STOVE

A. Grate clip
B. Grate
C. Long guard rail with screws
D. Short guard rail with screws
E. Drip tray
F. Control knob and shaft
G. Alcohol burner
H. Priming cup
I. Burner fitting
J. Feed pipe
K. Tank body assembly
L. Filler cap with relief valve
    and packing
M. Filler cap packing
N. Pump check valve, complete
O. Pump U-cup
P. Pump, complete with U-cup

Conversion to Alcohol

This kit is used for Coleman 425E and 413G, and Sears 476.72301 and 476.72302 gasoline stoves. All parts are identified in **Figure 19**.

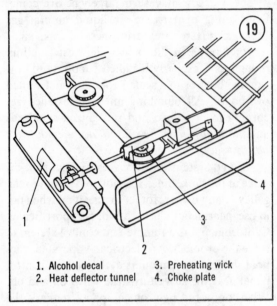

1. Alcohol decal
2. Heat deflector tunnel
3. Preheating wick
4. Choke plate

1. If stove is brand new or if generator (fuel pipe) on stove is brand new, operate main burner of stove using gasoline with fuel valve fully open for 60-90 minutes. Turn burner off and allow to cool for 30 minutes. Drain gasoline from tank.

2. Insert choke plate under mixing chamber (behind main burner) with indented edge of plate closest to burner. Press plate upward until it snaps onto bottom flange of mixing chamber.

3. On small 2-burner stoves, notched corner edges of choke plate should be flush with rear edge of bottom flange on mixing chamber. See **Figure 20** for this procedure.

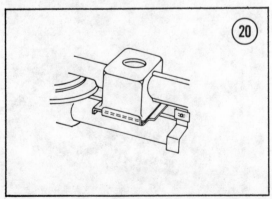

4. On large 2-burner stoves, straight edge between notched corners of choke plate should be flush with rear edge of bottom flange on mixing chamber. See **Figure 21**.

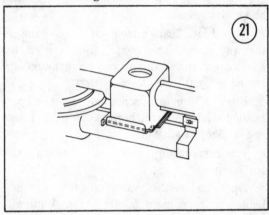

5. With coin or screwdriver, remove mounting screw on cap of main burner and place asbestos preheating wick on screw. Replace screw in burner cap and tighten.

6. Place heat reflector tunnel over main burner so that fuel pipe will pass through it. Slip circular end of tunnel over fuel inlet collar on mixing chamber and press notched legs of tunnel down onto lip of burner bowl. Align tunnel parallel to fuel pipe position.

> NOTE: *On small 2-burner stoves, bend arms of circular end of tunnel slightly together so that they fit snugly around fuel inlet collar.*

7. Apply self-adhesive tank sticker decal to dried surface of fuel tank between fuel filler cap and fuel control valve.

8. Place empty tank and generator assembly in normal position on front panel of stove.

Conversion Back to Gasoline

1. Remove the choke plate from the mixing chamber flange.

2. Remove the heat reflector tunnel from the main burner.

3. Drain alcohol from tank.

> NOTE: *It is not necessary to remove preheating wick from burner — it will not interfere with normal gasoline operation.*

8

Alcohol Operation

1. Fill fuel tank to bottom edge of filler neck with alcohol and install filler cap. Close fuel control valve. Pump pressure in tank with about 40 strokes.

2. Turn brass lighting lever on top of tank all the way down. This control is not used for alcohol operation. Also make sure that auxiliary burner valve is fully closed at start.

3. From a separate container, saturate preheating wick on main burner cap with 1 teaspoon (5cc) of alcohol.

4. Ignite preheating wick and allow to burn for 2 minutes.

5. Open fuel control valve one full turn and ignite flame on main burner. After 1 minute, adjust flame as needed.

6. To light auxiliary burner, first light main burner and open fuel control valve fully. Open auxiliary burner valve fully and ignite flame on burner. Adjust as desired.

7. Maintain pressure in tank as necessary by pumping.

Regulating Flame

Close auxiliary burner valve. Light main burner. Adjust fuel control valve so flame is low (½ open). After burner temperature stabilizes for that flame level (about 5 minutes), blue flame ring should not be separated or detached from corrugated burner openings. If flame blows out or if portions of flame ring extend out detached from burner, move choke plate slightly toward burner, reducing air flow into mixing chamber. To avoid burned fingers, perform this adjustment with flame off and allow burner to cool for awhile.

LPG SYSTEMS

Liquid petroleum gas (LPG) is a clear, odorless, convenient, and instant lighting fuel. Nearly every other marine cooking fuel requires preheating the burners for 30 seconds or more in order to light them, and nearly all have an odor while burning which some consider objectionable.

LPG is not without disadvantages, though. Since it is stored under pressure, leaks can occur. Furthermore, LPG is heavier-than-air and settles in the bilges—a potentially explosive situation.

These disadvantages can largely be overcome. Substituting lighter-than-air liquid natural gas (LNG) can lessen the seriousness of leaks since it won't settle in the bilge. The best solution, though, is a properly installed supply tank outside the boat or in a sealed compartment vented overboard. All plumbing must be installed according to published and recognized standards and *the supply must be shut off at the tank when not in use.*

All LPG systems must have a manual shut-off valve at the tank. Since it is not convenient to the galley, many owners forget to turn it off when not in use. Marinetics Corporation, Newport Beach, California, offers a remote LPG control system to solve the problem. An electrically operated solenoid shut-off valve mounts at the tank. A control panel near the stove turns the valve on and off. When on, a red light on the panel reminds the cook that the gas is on. The valve automatically closes if the electrical supply or pressure regulator fails.

Typical Systems

The simplest LPG system consists of a one- or two-burner stove with integral replaceable cartridges. See **Figure 22**. Replacement cartridges are available at most fuel docks and sporting goods stores.

Large craft usually have a separate refillable storage tank or tanks mounted on deck (see **Figure 23**) or in a sealed, vented compartment, e.g., in the chain locker area. High pressure lines connect the tank to the galley stove. A master shut-off valve mounted at the tank prevents leaks from becoming a disaster.

Filling the Tanks

Filling tanks is a simple operation. First, the man filling the tank shuts off the main valve at the tank outlet, and disconnects the regulator inlet fitting at the same valve. Note that this fitting has a left-hand thread. After connecting the filler hose, he opens a 10-percent valve and the main outlet valve. He then fills the tank until liquid emerges from the 10-percent valve, closes the main tank valve, and closes the 10-percent valve (**Figure 24**). Finally, he disconnects the filler hose and reconnects the regulator.

The 10-percent valve is so designed that liquid will emerge from it before the tank is full. If the tank were filled to capacity, any increase in temperature would cause an enormous increase in pressure, possibly resulting in tank rupture and a possible explosion or fire. By allowing room for expansion, this possibility is prevented.

Tanks are further protected from overpressure by safety valves, which vent any dangerous overpressure.

Maintenance

Maintenance is limited to checking for leaks, checking lines for security or possible chafing, and occasionally painting storage tanks to prevent rust.

Leak Checking

Check every fitting periodically with a small brush and soapsuds (**Figure 25**). Any bubbles indicate a leak. Unless a line has worn through by chafing, leaks that occur will almost always be found at fittings. *Never use a match or any flame for leak checking; to do so may cause an explosion or fire.*

Leaks are almost always caused by a fitting which has loosened under vibration and shock. Tightening should repair it. Always use 2

not smoke, light lanterns or allow any flame until the cause of the leak is discovered and repaired.

Replacing Fittings

Sometimes tightening a fitting does not repair a leak. The flared end of the tube might be split. If so, the tubing must be reflared. For this operation, a tubing cutter and flaring tool (**Figure 27**) are required.

1. Cut off the damaged tube as close as possible to the end, using the tubing cutter (**Figure 28**). Follow the tool manufacturer's instructions.

wrenches to tighten brass fittings; one on the flare nut and the other on the matting fitting (See **Figure 26**).

It is good practice to shut off all gas at the main tank valve when the stove is not in use. LPG is odorized to aid detection in the event of a massive leak. If a strong odor is noticed, shut off the main gas supply at once. Open all hatches and ports to allow the vessel to air out. LPG is heavier-than-air, and will tend to settle in the bilge; run the engine compartment blower. Do

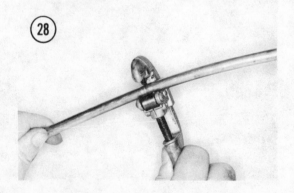

2. Remove and examine the old flare nut. If OK, it may be reused. Replacements are available at most auto parts and hardware stores.

3. Remove any burrs from the cut-off end of the tubing, using the tapered reamer which is part of the tubing cutter (**Figure 29**).

4. Slide the new flare nut onto the tubing. Be sure that the tapered end goes away from the mating fitting.

5. Flare the end of the tubing (**Figure 30**). Follow instructions supplied by the tool manufacturer.

6. Connect and tighten the new fitting.

PRIMUS PROPANE STOVES

Primus propane stoves are simple devices which require virtually no maintenance for years of trouble-free service. If your stove requires disassembly to clean or replace parts, refer to **Figure 31** for a typical stove.

COLEMAN PROPANE STOVES

Coleman makes propane stoves for outdoor camping. While not meant for marine use, the LPG stoves made from aluminum may be used onboard.

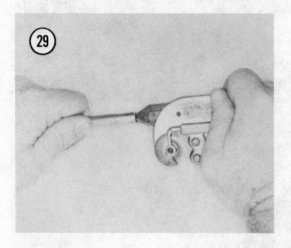

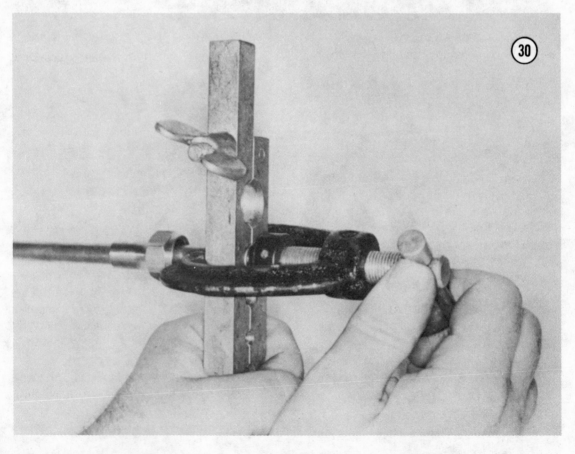

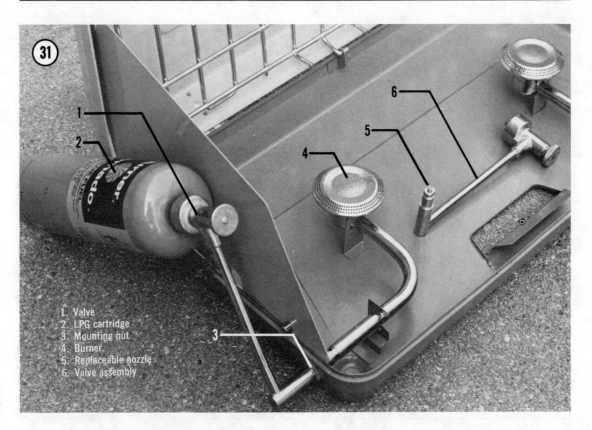

1. Valve
2. LPG cartridge
3. Mounting nut
4. Burner
5. Replaceable nozzle
6. Valve assembly

Propane is very clean burning and the burners will stay clean for long periods. If your stove requires disassembly to clean or replace parts, refer to **Figures 32 to 35** for exploded views of several popular models.

ICE BOX

Most boats big enough to have a galley have a built-in ice box. This is simply an insulated compartment with a drain at the bottom to drain off melted ice.

The ice box requires no maintenance other than frequent cleaning to remove food accumulation. After cleaning, leave lid off to prevent menacing mildew.

REFRIGERATORS

Nearly all refrigerators for marine use are electrically operated, and operate on the same principles as most home appliances. Absorption-type refrigerators, operated from liquid propane gas, are common in land recreation vehicles but these are not as efficient as the electrically operated models.

Basic Principles

Electrically operated refrigerators consist of:

a. Compressor
b. Condenser
c. Dryer
d. Capillary tube
e. Evaporator
f. Thermostat control
g. Thermostat sensing element

Refer to **Figure 36** for the following discussion.

The compressor has 2 functions in the refrigeration cycle. First it removes the refrigerant vapor from the evaporator and reduces the pressure in the evaporator, maintaining the desired evaporating temperature. Second, the compressor raises the pressure of the refrigerant vapor to a level high enough to allow heat rejection to the outdoor ambient air.

The condensor is a finned tube heat exchanger where the heat absorbed by the refrigerant during the evaporating process, and the heat of compression, is rejected to the outdoor ambient air.

8

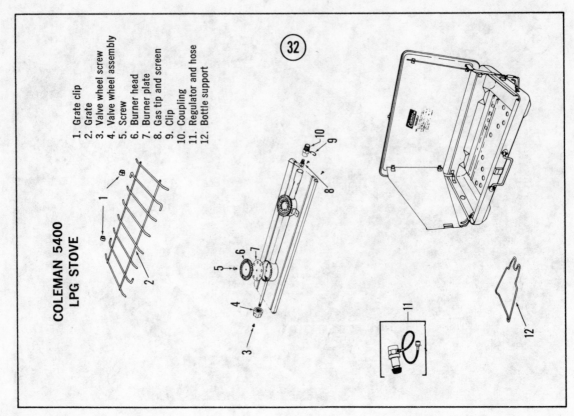

COLEMAN 5400 LPG STOVE

1. Grate clip
2. Grate
3. Valve wheel screw
4. Valve wheel assembly
5. Screw
6. Burner head
7. Burner plate
8. Gas tip and screen
9. Clip
10. Coupling
11. Regulator and hose
12. Bottle support

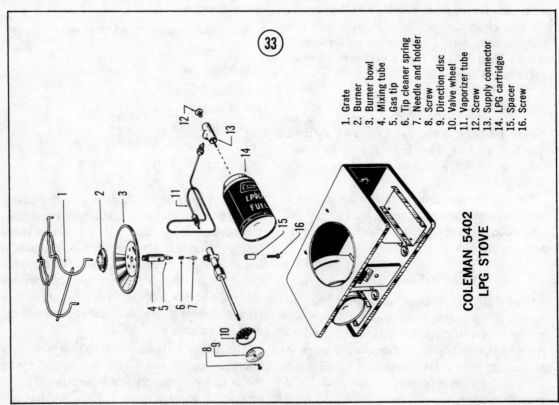

COLEMAN 5402 LPG STOVE

1. Grate
2. Burner
3. Burner bowl
4. Mixing tube
5. Gas tip
6. Tip cleaner spring
7. Needle and holder
8. Screw
9. Direction disc
10. Valve wheel
11. Vaporizer tube
12. Screw
13. Supply connector
14. LPG cartridge
15. Spacer
16. Screw

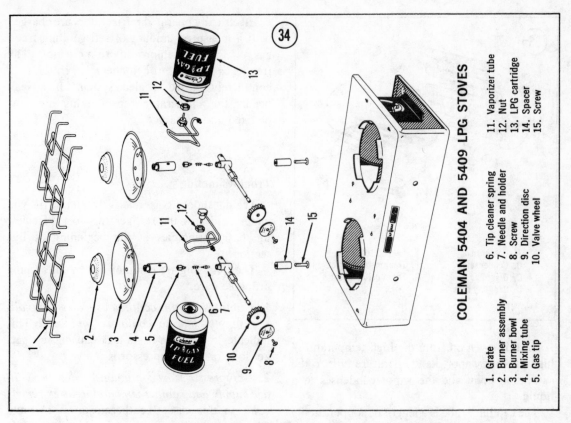

③④

COLEMAN 5404 AND 5409 LPG STOVES

1. Grate
2. Burner assembly
3. Burner bowl
4. Mixing tube
5. Gas tip
6. Tip cleaner spring
7. Needle and holder
8. Screw
9. Direction disc
10. Valve wheel
11. Vaporizer tube
12. Nut
13. LPG cartridge
14. Spacer
15. Screw

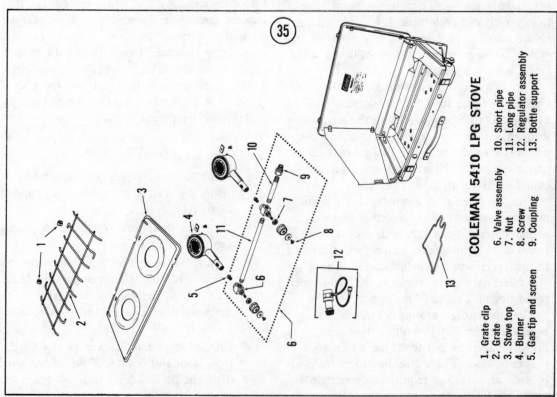

③⑤

COLEMAN 5410 LPG STOVE

1. Grate clip
2. Grate
3. Stove top
4. Burner
5. Gas tip and screen
6. Valve assembly
7. Nut
8. Screw
9. Coupling
10. Short pipe
11. Long pipe
12. Regulator assembly
13. Bottle support

8

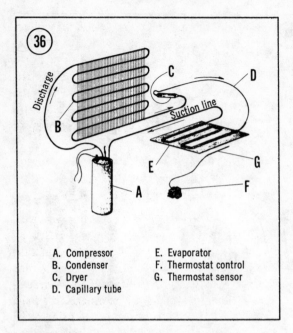

A. Compressor
B. Condenser
C. Dryer
D. Capillary tube
E. Evaporator
F. Thermostat control
G. Thermostat sensor

As heat is given off from the high temperature/ high pressure vapor, its temperature falls to the saturation point and the vapor condenses to a liquid.

The capillary tube is a length of copper tubing of small diameter with its internal diameter held to extremely close tolerance. It is used as a fixed orifice to separate high and low sides of the system and to meter proper feed of liquid refrigerant to the evaporator.

The evaporator is a finned tube heat exchanger in which the liquid refrigerant boils or evaporates, absorbing heat from the air passing through it. Also, the temperature of the evaporator is at a point below the dew point of the air which causes condensation of the water vapor contained in the air.

The dryer performs 2 functions. Its primary purpose is to remove any moisture that may be in the system. If not removed, moisture could freeze in the capillary tube or react with the freon to form corrosive hydrochloric acid. The dryer also filters out small particles in the freon which could clog the capillary tube orifice.

The thermostat sensing element near the evaporator constantly monitors the temperature in the refrigerator and sends the information to the control unit. The control unit turns the compressor on or off as required to maintain the temperature which you select.

Electrically operated refrigerators are charged with a measured amount of refrigerating freon gas — R-12 (dichloro-difloro-methane). The freon gas cycles through the refrigerator in a completely closed, sealed system. If a leak occurs, the refrigerator stops working and must be fixed and recharged.

Troubleshooting

Troubleshooting is relatively simple if you understand how the refrigerator works. Review the basic principles at the beginning of this section.

The following are common symptoms and the probable cure.

1. *Compressor runs continuously on either voltage supply, but no cooling is obtained.* This indicates the system has a leak causing refrigerant loss, or the compressor is faulty.

2. *Compressor runs continuously on either voltage supply and cabinet temperature is extremely cold.* In this case, the thermostat is at fault. Check the capillary bulb of the thermostat. It is located under the evaporator and should be secured directly to the evaporator plate by means of a metal fastener. This tube should have a plastic sleeve and must contact the plate directly. If this capillary tube is intact and the plastic sleeve is in place, then the thermostat is faulty and should be replaced.

3. *Compressor does not operate on either voltage.* Perform the following checks:

    a. Check the voltage supply (AC or DC) to assure the correct voltage is being applied to the refrigerator.

    b. Turn the thermostat knob to the maximum position.

    c. Remove the rubber protective cap from the terminal on top of the compressor. Make sure it is properly connected. Also check the ground wire to see that it is securely fastened.

    d. Check the circuit breaker located at the right front and bottom of the refrigerator. This circuit breaker effects DC operation only.

If steps "a" through "d" are performed and the unit still does not operate, then the thermostat may be defective. Check it as follows.

WARNING

Disconnect AC *cord and operate refrigerator from* DC *supply. Thermostat is energized by 115 volts when* AC *is connected and you could get a lethal shock when performing this procedure.*

Remove the thermostat cover located at the rear or at the inside of the cabinet. Also, remove the gray thermostat lead and bridge the 2 ends of the lead with a suitable strip of metal; such as a paper clip or a hair pin.

If the unit runs after the lead has been shorted, then the thermostat should be replaced.

4. *Compressor runs on* AC *but not* DC. Before assuming that the inverter assembly is defective, check the following.

a. DC connections at the rear of the cabinet to see if polarity is reversed.

b. If connections and polarity are correct, check battery as described in Chapter Eight.

c. Short the thermostat leads. It may be that the thermostat contacts are dirty or pitted, permitting the high potential AC to flow but restricting the low potential DC. Clean the contacts or replace the thermostat.

d. If the above steps do not provide operation, then remove the transformer-inverter assembly from the bottom of the cabinet. Plug the power supply cord into a 115 volt AC outlet. Upon doing so, note the voltage selector relay. When AC is applied to the refrigerator you should hear a discernible "click" of the relay. If "click" is not audible, check the relay movable contact section. When the AC supply is removed, the movable contact armature of the relay should relax, indicating that the DC circuit is closed.

e. If the relay operates normally, then the inverter or transformer is defective.

5. *Compressor runs on* DC *but not* AC. Make the following checks for the malfunction.

a. Check the AC voltage supply.

b. Using an AC voltmeter, check the voltage at the compressor by placing one probe of the voltmeter at the compressor terminal and the other probe to the ground wire. Your voltmeter should read 20-23 volts AC.

c. If you don't get a voltage reading at this check, be sure the voltage selector relay is being energized.

d. If the above steps do not provide operation, then the dual voltage transformer should be replaced.

6. *The compressor operates on* AC *but not on* DC *and unit cycles intermittently regardless of thermostat position.* This is an indication that one or both of the transistors in the inverter are shorted, creating an excessive load on the secondary of the dual voltage transformer. This load causes the bi-metallic element in the primary of the transformer to open and close causing intermittent operation of the unit. Inverter must be repaired by authorized service center.

NORCOLD MODEL MRFT 614

Replacing Refrigeration Unit

1. Disconnect AC cord from power source and DC cord from battery.

2. Remove all food from refrigerator and carefully wipe off all traces of moisture from interior.

3. Remove 9 screws holding the motor cover plate in place. See **Figure 37**.

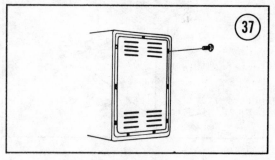

4. Remove the thermostat dial, 2 screws and push the thermostat into the interior of the cabinet. See **Figure 38**.

5. Remove the 2 terminal block screws and push it into the cabinet.

6. Remove the ground terminal nuts and push it into the cabinet.

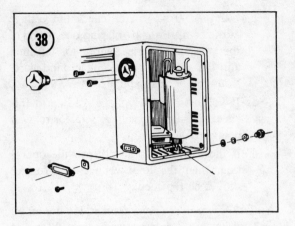

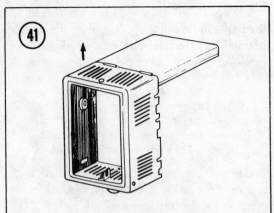

7. Remove fuse holder from the set plate. See **Figure 39**.

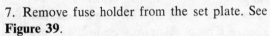
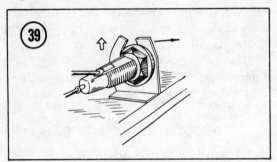

8. Remove 4 condenser cover screws and remove cover. See **Figure 40**.

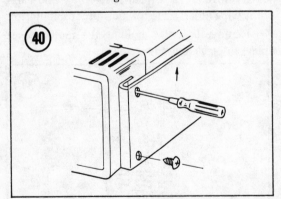

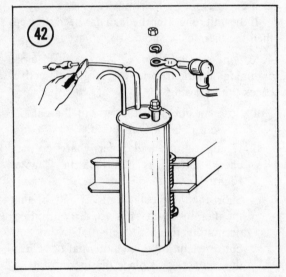

9. Remove the compressor cover screws (3 in front and 1 at the bottom). Loosen the 3 back screws, pull the cover out a little and lift the cover and lid off. See **Figure 41**.

10. Remove the rubber cap, nut, and the lead wire at the swing motor terminal. Cut out the crimp-type connector where the blue and black wires are joined. See **Figure 42**.

11. Remove the 2 blind cover screws and remove cover from the evaporator. See **Figure 43**.

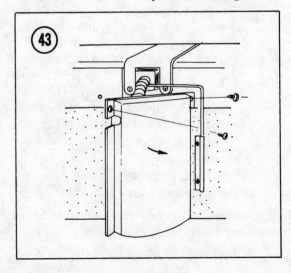

12. Remove both interior and exterior set plate screws and pull the plate up. See Figure 43.

13. Remove the condenser screw at the back and the hanger screw. See **Figure 44**.

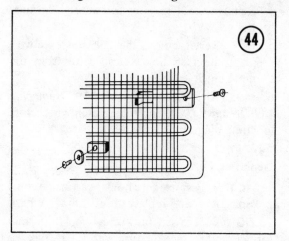

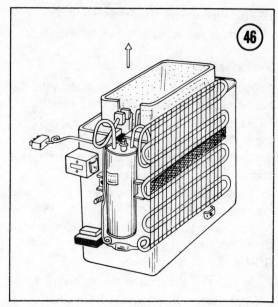

14. Remove the 2 hanger screws on both sides of the swing motor. See **Figure 45**.

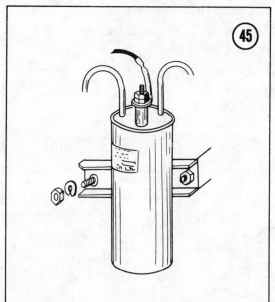

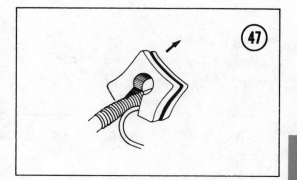

15. Pull hanger forward until it is free of the bolts. Pull the evaporator gently out of the cabinet, and at the same time pull the cooling unit out of the cabinet. See **Figure 46**.

16. Remove the rubber bushing. See **Figure 47**.

17. Loosen the 2 thermostat holder screws and remove the capillary tube from the evaporator. See **Figure 48**.

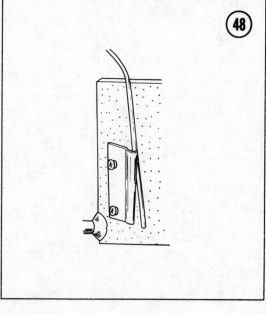

18. Remove sponge covering suction pipe.

19. Installation is the reverse of these steps.

Replacing the Thermostat

1. Remove the compressor cover and lid case. See Steps 1-9, *Replacing Refrigeration Unit.*

2. Remove the 2 blind cover screws and take the cover out of the evaporator.

3. Remove the 2 interior and 2 exterior set plate screws and pull the plate up.

4. Loosen the 2 thermostat holder screws and take the capillary tube out of the evaporator.

5. Pull the rubber bushing up and separate the thermostat from it.

6. Remove the lead wire.

7. Install new thermostat by reversing Steps 1-10, *Replacing Refrigeration Unit.*

Replacing Inverter

1. Remove the terminal block and ground terminal as described in Steps 1-7, *Replacing Refrigeration Unit.*

2. Remove the compressor rubber cap and the nut, and cut the lead wires from the pipe.

3. Remove the thermostat cover screws and remove the thermostat lead wires.

4. Remove the 4 inverter screws and 4 transformer screws.

5. Pull inverter out of the compressor cover, separate the fuse holder lead wire from the terminal block lead wire.

6. Install by reversing Steps 1-10, *Replacing Refrigeration Unit.* Carefully match wire colors to wiring diagram, **Figure 49**.

Replacing Fuses

1. *AC fuse:* Remove fuse holder cap inside compressor cover, and replace fuse with a 1A fuse.

2. *DC fuse:* Loosen fuse screws on the transformer, and replace the fuse with a 10A fuse.

NORCOLD MODEL DE-250

Replacing Refrigeration Unit

1. Disconnect AC cord from power source and DC cord from battery.

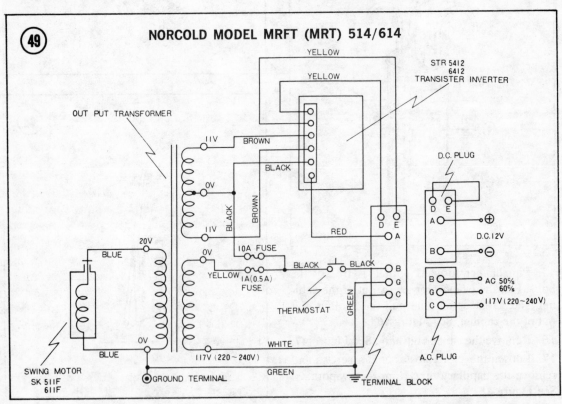

49 NORCOLD MODEL MRFT (MRT) 514/614

2. Remove food and wipe off interior of cabinet.

3. Open door, pull out thermostat dial and remove the screws on both sides of shaft. Remove the thermostat and lay it on the evaporator. See **Figures 50 and 51**.

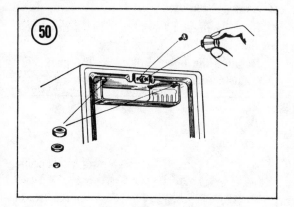

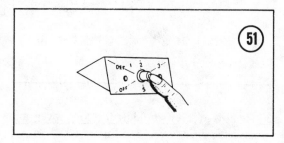

4. Remove 2 nuts located on the front of the evaporator. Lower only the front part of the evaporator. When it disengages, slowly pull it toward you and remove it from the rubber cushions. See **Figure 52**.

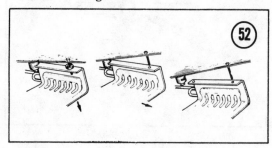

5. Remove the 2 condenser holders at the rear. See **Figure 53**.

6. Remove the 8 clamping screws on the blind cover plate and the cord holder on the left side. See Figure 53.

7. Remove the 2 nuts on the motor hanger. See Figure 53.

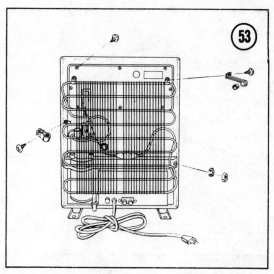

8. Slowly pull out the refrigeration unit holding both sides of the hanger. Do not catch the evaporator on the inner case window. Refer to **Figure 54** for this procedure.

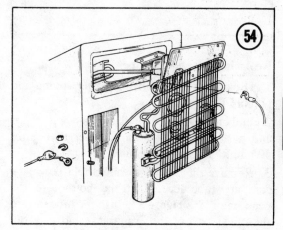

9. When the refrigeration unit is pulled half way out, remove the cord from the swing motor terminal. The ground lead must also be removed. See Figure 54.

10. Lay the refrigeration unit on one side, and remove the 2 screws on the blind cover. Move the blind cover in the direction indicated by the arrow and remove the blind cover, the heat insulator and the blind cover plate. See **Figures 55 and 56**.

11. Remove the bushing.

12. Replace the old unit with a new one by reversing these steps.

8

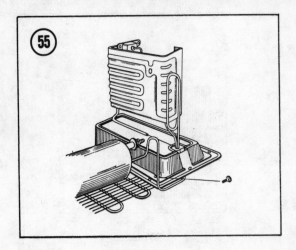

Replacing the Thermostat

1. Disconnect AC cord from power source and DC cord from battery.

2. Pull off the thermostat dial. Remove 2 screws and push thermostat inward. Refer to Figures 50 and 51 for this procedure.

3. Remove the 2 screws which hold down the capillary tube located at the bottom of the evaporator. See **Figure 57**. Push the tube toward the upper part of the evaporator and take out the thermostat toward you.

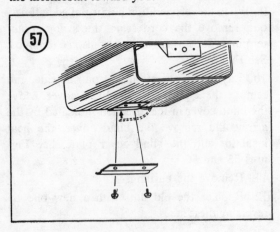

4. Disconnect the push-on connectors from the thermostat.

5. Install new thermostat by reversing this procedure.

Replacing Inverter

1. Remove the refrigeration unit as described previously.

2. Remove the cover holder at the back and take out the cord cover B. See **Figure 58**.

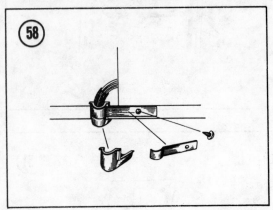

3. Remove 6 screws holding the cord cover and remove the cord cover. See **Figure 59**.

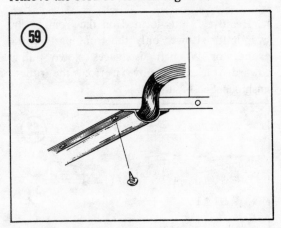

4. Remove the 3 switch cover screws and remove cover as shown in **Figure 60**. Remove 2 switch holder mounting screws (Figure 60).

5. Remove 4 inverter cover screws and place the inverter cover as shown in **Figure 61**. Remove the transformer screws, the inverter and the cord holders.

6. Install transformer and inverter.

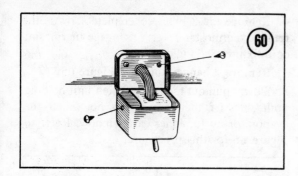

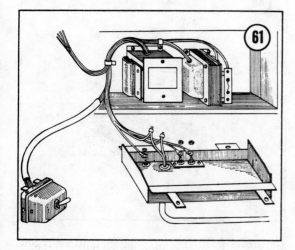

7. When connecting the wires, carefully match the colors of the cords with those indicated on the wiring diagram. See **Figure 62**.

Replacing the Toggle Switch

1. Remove the cover holder at the back and remove cord cover B. See Figure 58.

2. Remove the cord cover. See Figure 59.

3. Remove the 3 switch cover screws, pull the switch cover out as shown in Figure 60 and remove the switch insulator.

4. Loosen the switch locknut and remove the switch cover.

5. Mark all wires with terminal numbers and unsolder them.

6. Install switch by reversing these steps.

NORCOLD MODEL DE-250A

Replacing the Refrigeration Unit

1. Disconnect AC cord from power source and DC cord from battery.

2. Remove food and wipe off interior of cabinet.

3. Remove the thermostat dial. See **Figure 63**.

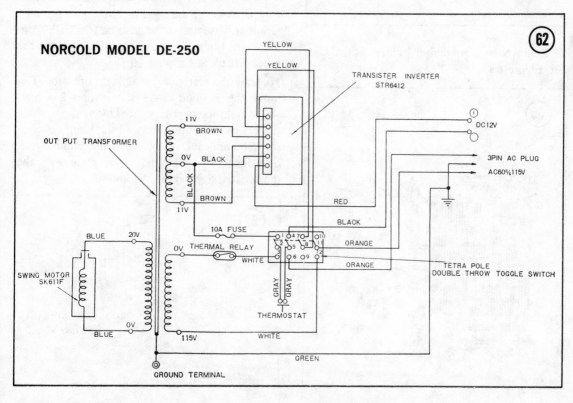

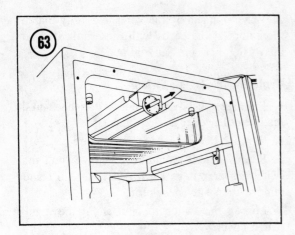

4. Remove the 2 evaporator nuts located on the front. Lower the front of the evaporator. When it disengages, slowly pull it toward you until it comes out of the rubber cushions. See **Figure 64**.

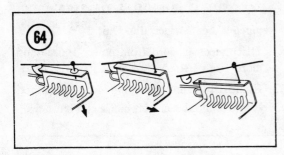

5. Remove the 2 condenser holders at the rear. See **Figure 65**.

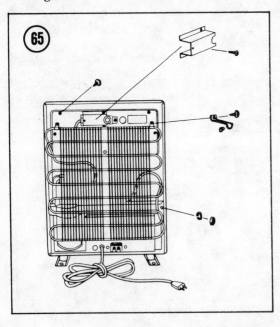

6. Remove the 8 blind cover plate screws and remove thermostat cover. Disengage thermostat cord fixture. See Figure 65.

7. Remove 2 hanger nuts. See Figure 65.

8. Slowly pull out the refrigeration unit holding both sides of the hanger. Do not catch the evaporator on the inner case window. Refer to **Figure 66** for this procedure.

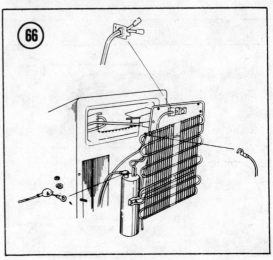

9. When the refrigeration unit is pulled out half way, disconnect the cord from the swing motor terminal. Disconnect the push-on terminals from the thermostat terminals. Also disconnect the ground lead. See Figure·66.

10. Lay the refrigeration unit on one side. Remove the 2 blind cover screws and 2 screws which hold the capillary tube. Move the bushing (inner) with suction pipe and the blind cover in the direction shown. Remove the blind cover, heat insulator and blind cover plate with the thermostat. See **Figures 67 and 68**.

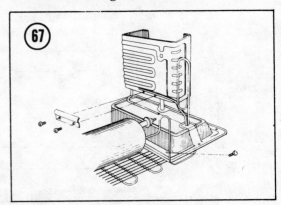

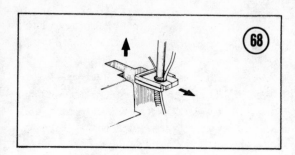

11. Remove the bushings.

12. Install by reversing these steps.

Replacing the Thermostat

1. Remove the refrigeration unit as described earlier.

2. Remove the 2 screws which secure the thermostat to the blind cover plate and pull out the thermostat. See **Figure 69**.

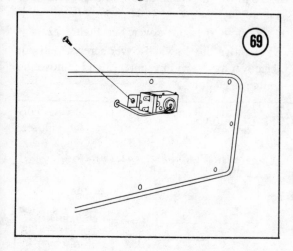

3. Pull out the split pin and detach the thermostat rod. See **Figure 70**.

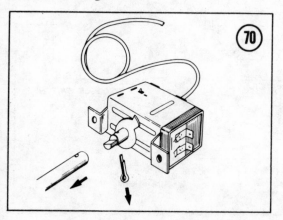

4. Installation for new thermostat is the reverse of these steps.

Replacing the Inverter

1. Remove the cover shown in **Figure 71**.

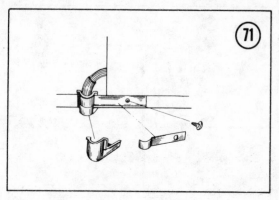

2. Remove the 6 screws holding the cord cover and remove the cord cover. See **Figure 72**.

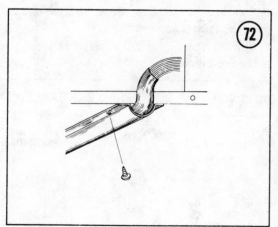

3. Remove the 3 switch cover screws, and pull it out as shown in **Figure 73**. Remove the 2 switch holder screws.

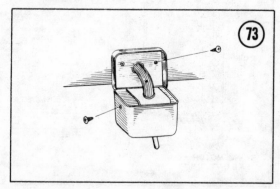

8

4. Remove the 3 inverter cover screws through the condenser.

5. Remove the 2 hanger nuts. Pull the refrigeration unit out a little and take out the inverter cover in the direction indicated in **Figure 74**.

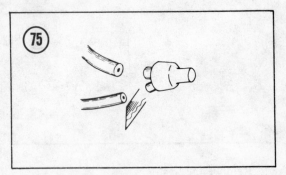

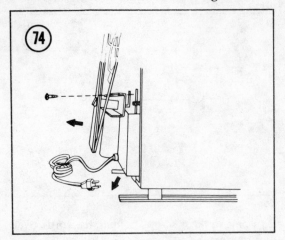

6. Remove the transformer and inverter screws and take these components out.

7. Cut off the lead wires at each connection point. See **Figure 75**.

8. Install transformer and inverter by reversing these steps.

CAUTION
Carefully match wire colors to wiring diagram. See **Figure 76**.

Replacing the Toggle Switch

1. Remove the cover holder and cover **B**. See Figure 71.

2. Remove the cord cover. See Figure 72.

3. Remove the 3 switch cover screws, pull out the cover as shown in Figure 73 and remove the switch insulator.

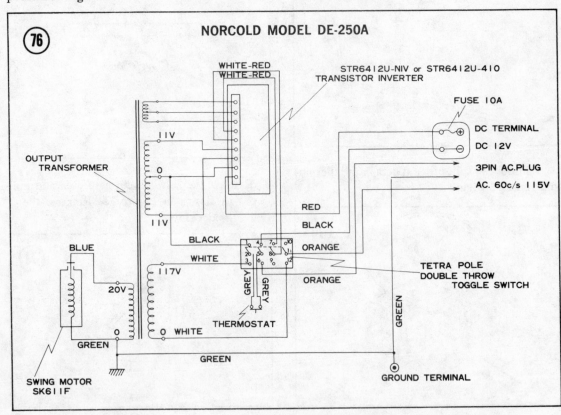

4. Loosen the switch locknut and remove the switch cover.

5. Mark wires with terminal numbers and un-solder them.

6. Install new switch by reversing these steps.

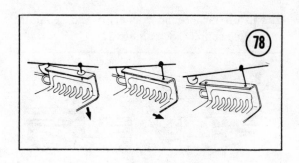

NORCOLD
MODELS DE-250C AND DE-251A

Replacing Refrigeration Unit (DE-250C)

1. Disconnect AC cord from power source and DC cord from battery.

2. Remove food and wipe out the interior of the cabinet.

3. Remove 3 screws which secure the thermostat assembly to the cabinet. See **Figure 77**.

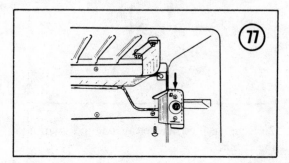

4. Remove 2 nuts securing evaporator and lower the front part. When it disengages, slowly pull it toward you until it is free of the rubber cushions. See **Figure 78**.

5. Remove 8 screws from the blind cover plate at the rear of the refrigerator. Remove 2 nuts from the unit hanger bar and let refrigeration unit hang free. See **Figure 79**.

6. Remove wire protector plate and pull cords from motor and thermostat. See **Figure 80**.

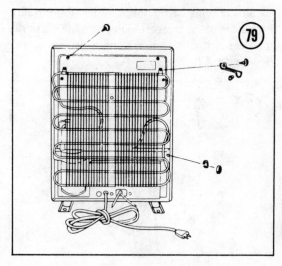

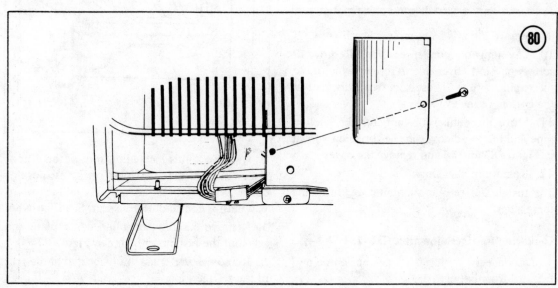

7. Cut off the ground connector and separate the 4-pole coupler. See **Figure 81**.

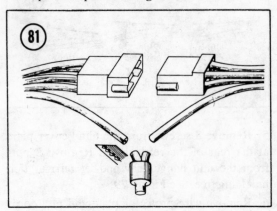

8. Slowly pull refrigeration unit out holding both sides of the hanger. Make sure the evaporator does not catch on the inner case window. See **Figure 82**.

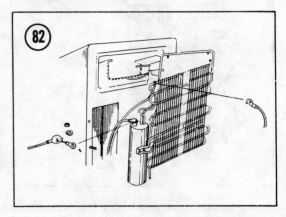

9. Remove 2 cords from motor. See Figure 82.

10. Lay unit on condenser side. Remove 2 screws on bind cover and 2 screws which hold the capillary tube. These screws are located at the bottom of the evaporator.

11. Move the rubber bushing for the suction pipe and the blind cover in the direction shown in **Figures 83 and 84** and remove the cover.

12. Remove the bushings.

13. Install the refrigeration unit by reversing these steps.

Replacing Refrigeration Unit (DE-251A)

1. Disconnect AC plug from power source and DC cord from battery.

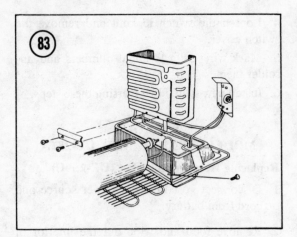

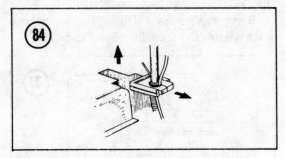

2. Remove food and clean out the interior of the cabinet.

3. Remove 3 screws which secure the thermostat assembly to the cabinet. See **Figure 85**.

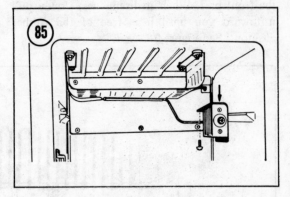

4. Remove 2 nuts located in front of the evaporator and pull the front part of the evaporator down. When it disengages, slowly pull it toward you until it comes out of its seat. See **Figure 86**

5. Remove 6 screws on blind cover plate and take out the insulation pad. See **Figure 87**.

6. Remove inverter assembly located at the rear of the refrigerator.

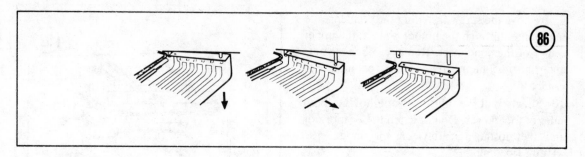

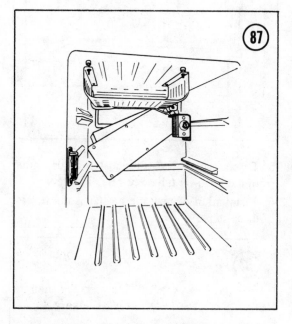

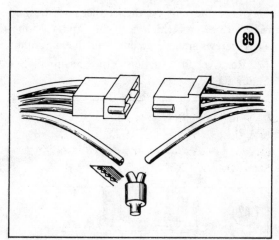

7. Cut off the thermostat ground cord at the connecting points and separate the 4-pole coupler which connects the thermostat cord assembly and inverter assembly. Refer to **Figures 88 and 89**.

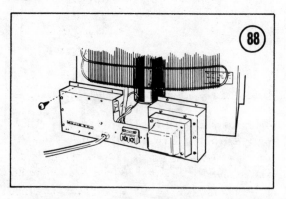

8

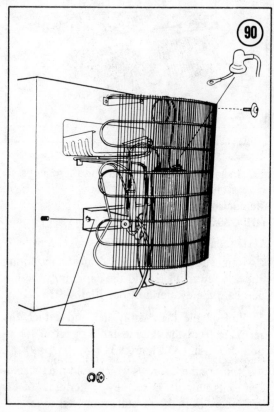

8. Disconnect the lead wire from the motor terminal. Do not turn the lowest nut. Remove the ground lead wire. See **Figure 90**.

9. Remove the screw fastening the condenser to the cabinet through the holder plate at the upper center of the condenser. Remove 2 hanger nuts and let unit hang free of the cabinet. See Figure 90.

10. Slowly pull the unit out while holding both sides of the hanger. Do not catch the evaporator and thermostat assembly on the inner case window opening.

11. Place the unit on the condenser side and remove 2 screws which hold the capillary tube. These screws are located underneath evaporator.

12. Remove the suction pipe bushing. See **Figure 91**.

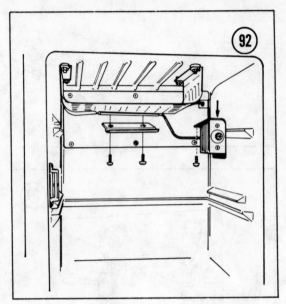

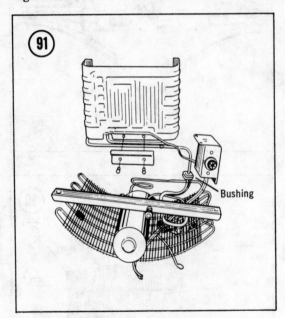

Bushing

13. Install new unit by reversing these steps.

Replacing Thermostat
(DE-250C and DE-251A)

1. Disconnect AC cord from power source.

2. Remove 3 screws on the thermostat mounting and 2 screws which hold the capillary tube underneath the evaporator. See **Figure 92**.

3. Pull off the thermostat dial and detach the set plate from the thermostat support in direction shown in (A) **Figure 93**.

4. Remove the 2 screws which hold the thermostat to its support. Detach eyelet terminal of the green cord from thermostat ground terminal.

5. Disconnect the 2 thermostat cords (gray) from the push-on tabs. See (B), Figure 93.

6. Installation of new thermostat is the reverse of these steps.

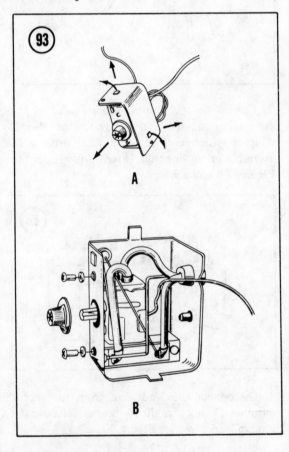

A

B

Replacing Inverter (DE-250C)

1. Disconnect AC cord from power source and DC cord from battery.

2. Remove 4 inverter cover screws accessible through the condenser openings.

3. Remove 2 unit hanger bar nuts.

4. Pull unit out far enough to allow the inverter cover to be removed. See **Figure 94**.

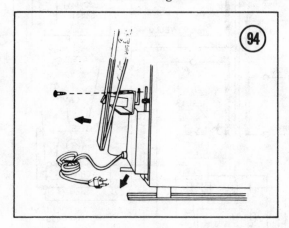

5. Remove all mounting screws from the transformer, inverter, and relay. Remove these components.

6. Cut ground wire (see Figure 81) and separate the 4-pole coupling which connect the thermostat cord to the inverter assembly.

7. Separate the 2-pole coupling which connects inverter assembly to transformer. See **Figure 95**.

8. Reconnect the transformer and inverter and reconnect the 2 green ground wires. Securely fasten couplings.

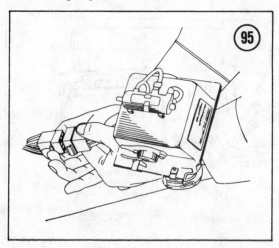

CAUTION
Carefully match wire colors to the wiring diagram, **Figure 96**.

Replacing Inverter (DE-251A)

1. Disconnect AC cord from power source and DC cord from battery.

2. Remove the inverter assembly by removing all the mounting screws.

3. Cut off the thermostat ground cord at the connecting points and separate the 4-pole coupler which connects the thermostat to the inverter. See Figures 88 and 89.

4. Detach the inverter harness from the inverter cover by loosening the inverter, transformer, and relay screws. Cut off the AC supply cord at the connection points and also detach the strain relief which secures the DC cord. See **Figure 97**.

5. Separate the 9-pole coupler which connects inverter and transformer as shown in **Figure 98**.

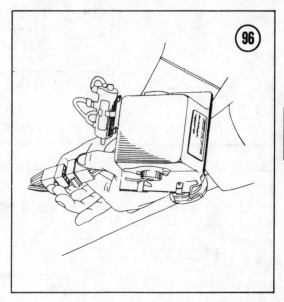

6. Reconnect the transformer and inverter and install the inverter by reversing these steps.

CAUTION
Carefully match wire colors to the wiring diagram, Figure 96.

Replacing Relay

1. Disconnect AC cord from power source and DC cord from battery.

96

NORCOLD MODELS DE-250C AND DE-251A

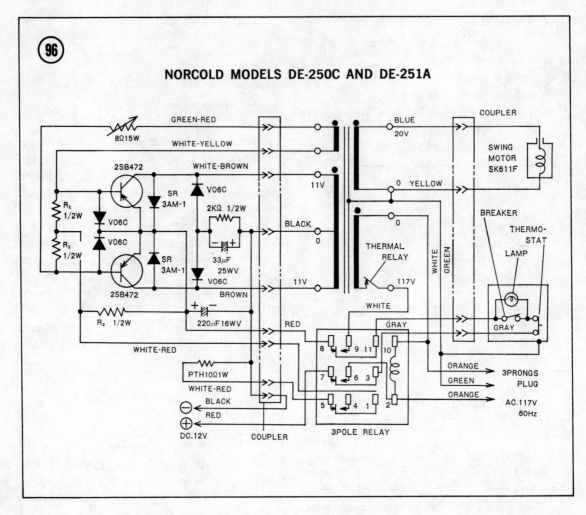

97

NORCOLD MODEL DE-251A

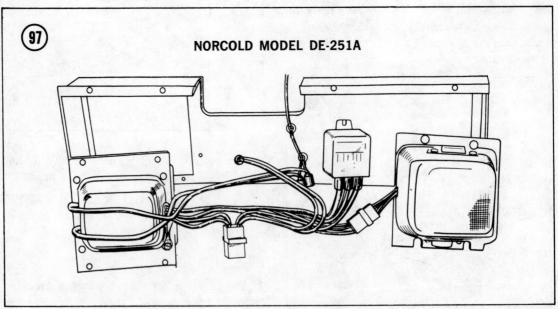

2. Remove the inverter assembly and inverter harness as described earlier.

3. Unsolder the lead wires from relay. See **Figure 99**.

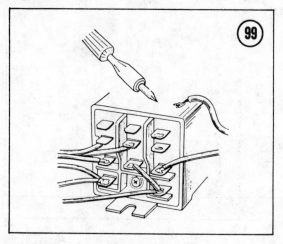

4. Install new relay.

CAUTION

Make sure the wire colors match the wiring diagram, Figure 96.

5. Complete the relay replacement by reversing these steps.

NORCOLD MODEL (DE-400)

Replacing Refrigeration Unit

1. Disconnect AC cord from power source and DC cord from battery.

2. Remove food and wipe out the interior of the cabinet.

3. Open evaporator door and remove evaporator hinge. See **Figure 100**.

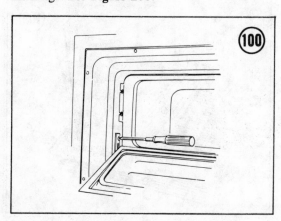

4. Pull off thermostat dial and remove evaporator frame. See **Figures 101 and 102**.

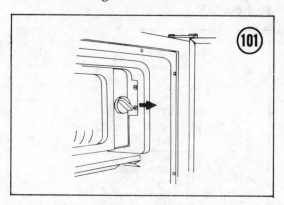

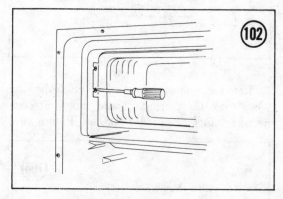

5. Remove 2 evaporator nuts located on the front of the evaporator. When it disengages, pull it slowly toward you and remove it from spacer (B). See **Figures 103 and 104**.

8

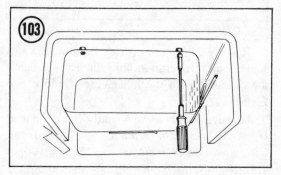

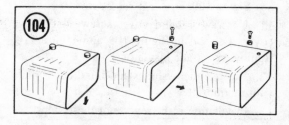

6. Remove 2 condenser holders and then un-screw 10 screws from blind cover plate. See **Figure 105**.

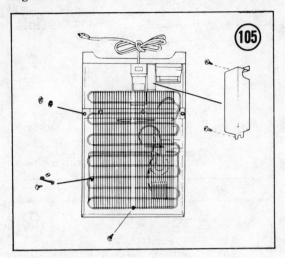

7. Remove connector cover and cut off the lead wires from the thermostat and motor at con-necting points. See Figure 105 and **Figure 106**.

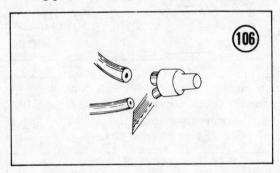

8. Remove 2 hanger nuts (see Figure 105) and slowly pull refrigeration unit out. Do not catch the evaporator on the inner case window. See **Figure 107**.

9. Remove cord holder (A) and detach the lead wire from the motor terminal. The ground lead wire must also be removed. See **Figure 108**.

10. Remove the 2 thermostat holder screws. See **Figure 109**.

11. Unscrew 4 blind cover screws and move cover as shown in Figure 109 and **Figure 110**. Remove cover and insulator.

12. Remove the bushings and blind cover plate with thermostat.

13. Installation is the reverse of these steps.

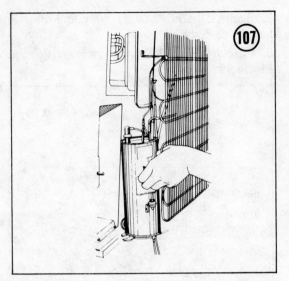

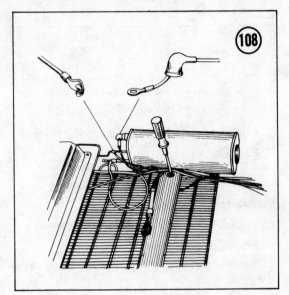

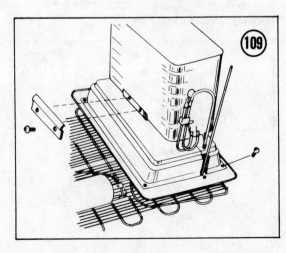

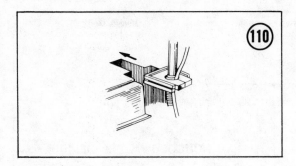

(110)

Replacing Thermostat

1. Remove the refrigeration unit as described earlier.·

2. Remove the thermostat cover and take out thermostat cord fixture with AC and DC thermostat cords. See **Figure 111**.

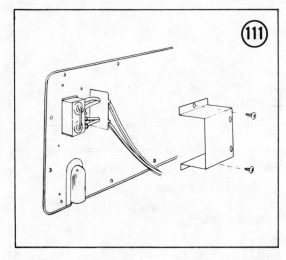

(111)

3. Pull out the split pin which locks thermostat rod to thermostat shaft and remove thermostat rod. See **Figure 112**.

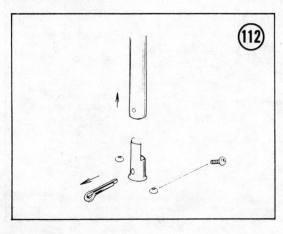

(112)

4. Installation of new thermostat is the reverse of these steps.

5. When connecting the thermostat rod to the shaft, make sure they are aligned properly. When correct, the guide marks will match.

Replacing Inverter

1. Remove the connector cover and cut off the lead wires from the thermostat and motor at connecting points. See Figures 105 and 106.

2. Remove the transformer and inverter screws and take these components out.

3. Install transformer and inverter by reversing these steps.

CAUTION
Carefully match wire colors with wiring diagram, **Figures 113 and 114**.

Replacing Relay

1. Remove inverter assembly, described above.

2. Remove 5 screws and detach the inverter cover. See **Figures 115 and 116**.

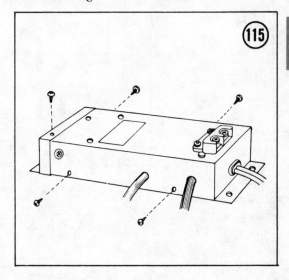

(115)

8

3. Remove set screw(s) from the relay and remove the relay. See Figure 116.

4. Unsolder the lead wires from the relay. See **Figure 117**.

5. Install new relay. Make sure wire colors match wiring diagram, Figures 113 and 114.

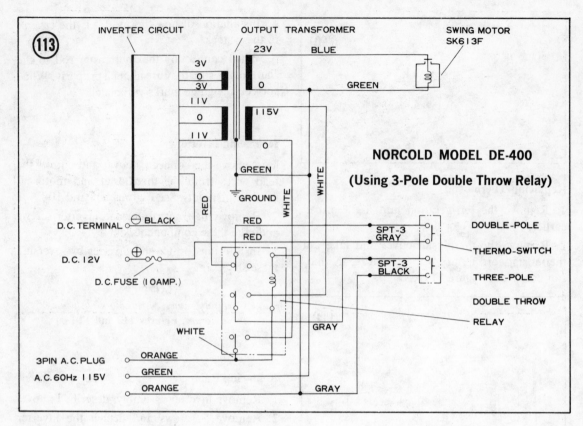

NORCOLD MODEL DE-400

(Using 3-Pole Double Throw Relay)

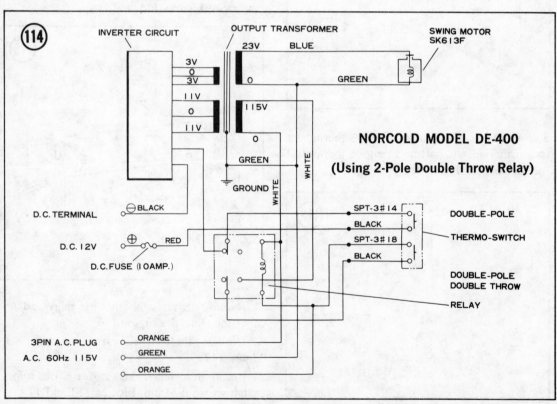

NORCOLD MODEL DE-400

(Using 2-Pole Double Throw Relay)

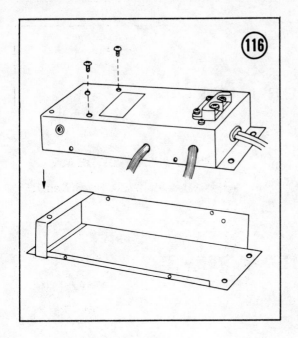

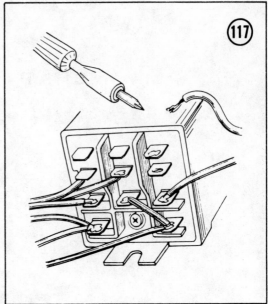

8

CHAPTER NINE

FRESH WATER SYSTEMS

Water systems range from a couple of jerry cans and a bowl to elaborate pressurized hot and cold water systems with multiple sinks and heads.

SIMPLE WATER SYSTEMS

The jerry can system is the simplest and requires no explanation. Next comes the system with a water tank and one or more faucets with hand or electric pumps. See **Figures 1 and 2**. These systems are not pressurized and are for cold water only. On some boats an additional faucet pumps sea water from a through-hull fitting.

Figure 3 shows a Par 37000 series pump. In case of power loss, a faucet with a hand pump will draw water from the tank through the pump. Other pumps, such as the Jabsco 14940 series, require a bypass circuit. See Figure 2. A hand pump faucet cannot draw water through the electric pump. The check valve permits water to flow only from input to output side of the pump, not vice versa.

PRESSURIZED WATER SYSTEMS

Pressurized systems aboard boats operate on a demand principle. **Figure 4** is typical. When all faucets in the system are closed the pump motor

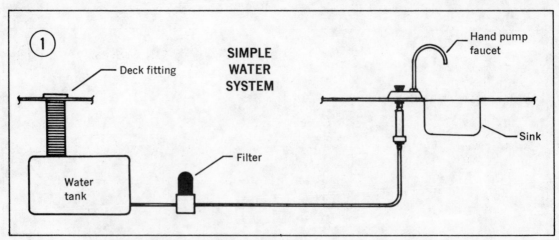

① SIMPLE WATER SYSTEM

Deck fitting

Hand pump faucet

Sink

Filter

Water tank

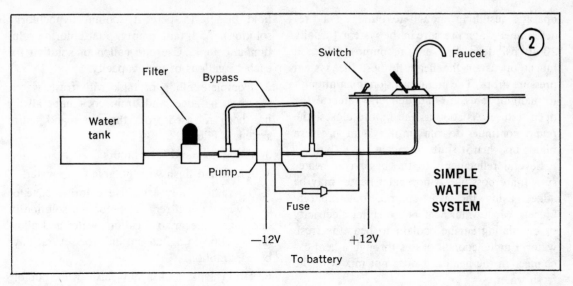

Filter · Bypass · Switch · Faucet · Water tank · Pump · Fuse · —12V · +12V · To battery

SIMPLE WATER SYSTEM ②

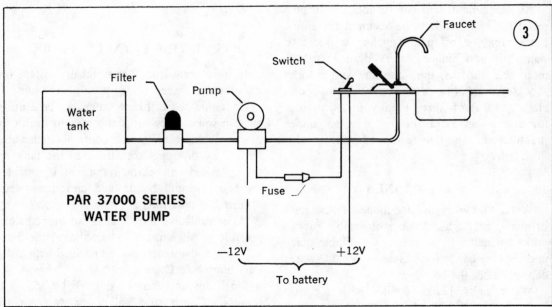

Filter · Pump · Switch · Faucet · Water tank · Fuse · —12V · +12V · To battery

PAR 37000 SERIES WATER PUMP ③

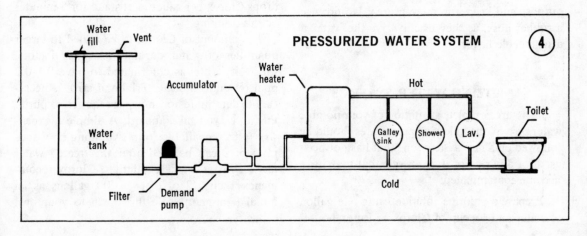

PRESSURIZED WATER SYSTEM ④

Water fill · Vent · Accumulator · Water heater · Hot · Toilet · Water tank · Galley sink · Shower · Lav. · Filter · Demand pump · Cold

9

operates just long enough to build up a pre-determined water pressure in the system, (usually 20-40 psi depending on the pump). When a faucet opens or the head flushes, the system pressure drops. The pump turns on in an attempt to maintain pressure and delivers water to the open fixture. As soon as the fixture closes, the pump continues to run until system pressure builds up, then it shuts off again.

Several refinements to the basic cold water system are possible. A hot water heater may be added using the same pump, but separate faucets. Most water heaters use either electricity or circulating engine coolant to heat the fresh water. Engine coolant passes through a heat exchanger in the heater; it does not mix with the fresh water.

An accumulator tank can be added to further refine the system. First, the accumulator eliminates rapid on/off pump cycling to increase pump life and reduce battery drain. Furthermore, this smoothes the water flow and absorbs shock pressures (water hammer) due to sudden closure of water fixtures. Finally, the accumulator assures an extra reserve of water under pressure, an important feature of systems with flush toilets.

WATER TANKS

Water tanks are usually made of fiberglass or metal, although a number of flexible rubber tanks are made. These fit in any available space and are very handy for increasing potable water capacity after the boat is built.

Water tanks should be filled with a plastic hose reserved for this purpose. Mark it for this purpose and keep it in a clean area. Do not use a rubber hose, as they usually give the water a disagreeable flavor.

SANITIZING WATER SYSTEMS

To assure complete sanitation of your potable water system, the following procedures should be followed on a new system, one that has not been used for a period of time, or one that may have become contaminated:

1. Prepare a chlorine solution using one gallon of water and ¼ cup of Clorox or Purex house-hold bleach (5 percent sodium hypochlorite solution). With tank empty, pour chlorine solution into tank. Use one gallon of solution for each 15 gallons of tank capacity.

2. Complete filling of tank with fresh water. Open each faucet and drain cock until all air has been released from the pipes and entire system is filled.

3. Allow to stand for 3 hours.

4. Drain and flush with potable fresh water.

5. To remove any excessive chlorine taste or odor which might remain, prepare a solution of one quart vinegar to 5 gallons water and allow this solution to agitate in tank for several days by boat motion.

6. Drain tank and again flush with potable water.

PURIFYING POTABLE WATER

In some areas it may be necessary to take on questionable water.

Contaminated drinking water can be a nuisance in some cases and dangerous to health in others. Water can become contaminated while aboard by dropping something in the tank or taking on bad water through the vent. If possible, the water should be drained and the system sanitized as described earlier.

When replacing the water is not immediately possible, or when forced to take aboard questionable water, the water may be purified with ordinary household Clorox.

Small amounts may be purified by adding 1 teaspoon Clorox to 5 gallons of water or 16 drops Clorox per gallon. Let stand for 5 minutes before drinking.

The amount of Clorox to be added to larger quantities of water depends on many factors. Most city water is chlorinated to have 0.1-0.2 ppm residual chlorine. Trial and error is necessary to determine how much is required to purify the water you take aboard. A simple inexpensive test kit available from swimming pool supply stores can be used after the treated water has set for at least 10 minutes. Clorox recommends 1 cup (8 oz.) per 1,000 gallons as an initial treatment; scale this down to your own capacity.

To avoid the trial and error method altogether, simply treat small amounts of contaminated water from the system as it is needed. Use the proportions given earlier.

Within reason a high residual chlorine content will flavor the water but it will not be harmful. To remove the taste, boil the water after treating it with Clorox.

WARNING

Boiling is not recommended for purifying water; use it to remove residual chlorine only. Some germs can survive boiling temperature at sea level, but cannot survive in a Clorox solution.

WATER PUMPS (DEMAND)

Demand water pumps operate whenever pressure drops in the output line from the pump, e.g., when any faucet is open. When pressure drops an internal switch turns on the pump motor. When the faucet is closed, pressure again builds up in the outlet line, causing a pressure switch to open, which then turns off the pump.

Figure 5 illustrates a typical demand type water pump. This pump is permanently lubricated, and requires no periodic service.

PAR PUMPS

Repair

Replacement parts are available for the Par pumps. Most commonly required parts are included in a service kit. Order by pump model number from your Jabsco dealer.

> NOTE: *Service kits for each pump should be carried aboard for extended cruises.*

Figure 6 shows exploded views of Par pumps. Refer to it when performing the following procedures and to help in identifying parts for replacement.

Replacing Valve Assemblies

Valve assemblies are part of the factory service kit.

1. Turn off power to pump.

2. If system is filled with water, open a faucet to relieve pressure. Close intake and discharge lines near pump.

3. Remove 4 motor mounting screws.

4. Lift motor and diaphragm assembly from the pump base.

5. Lift valve assemblies from seats and clean all foreign material from valve and seat.

6. Install new valve assemblies into seats, being sure rubber valve with small hole is UP on intake and rubber valve without the small hole is DOWN on discharge.

CAUTION

Do not use small holed valve on discharge side of pump.

Diaphragm and Connecting Rod Assembly Replacement

The diaphragm and connecting rod assembly are included in the factory service kit.

1. Turn off power to pump.

2. If system is filled with water, open a faucet to relieve pressure. Close intake and discharge lines near pump.

3. Remove 4 motor mounting screws.

4. Lift motor and diaphragm assembly from the pump base.

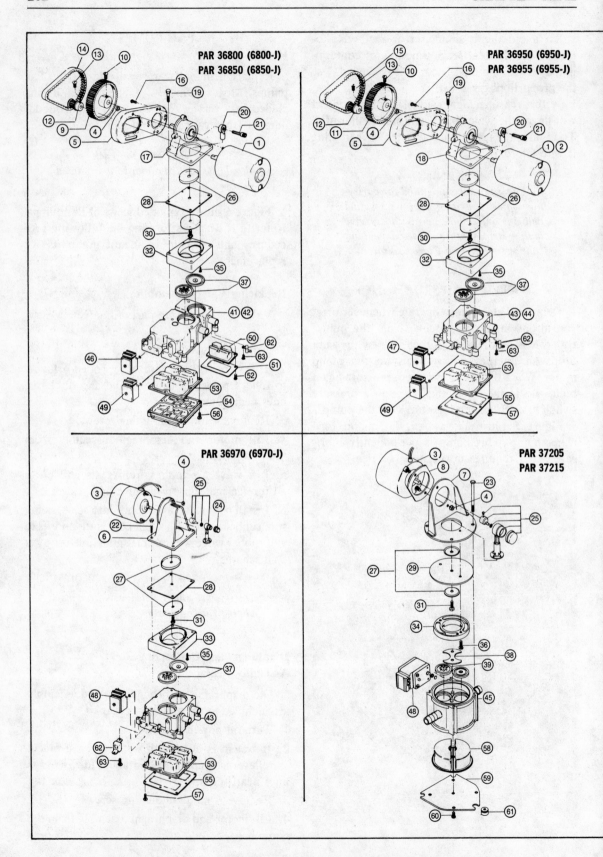

PAR 36800 (6800-J)
PAR 36850 (6850-J)

PAR 36950 (6950-J)
PAR 36955 (6955-J)

PAR 36970 (6970-J)

PAR 37205
PAR 37215

PAR PUMPS

1. Motor
2. Motor
3. Motor
4. Motor nut
5. Motor mount
6. Motor mount
7. Motor mount
8. Motor gasket
9. Large pulley
10. Setscrew
11. Large pulley
12. Small pulley
13. Setscrew
14. Belt
15. Belt
16. Jack shaft screw
17. Jack shaft
18. Jack shaft
19. Tie down screw
20. Connecting rod
21. Eccentric screw
22. Tie down screw
23. Tie down screw
25. Connecting rod kit (contains eccentric rod and screw)
26. Diaphragm plate
27. Diaphragm plate
28. Diaphragm
29. Diaphragm
30. Diaphragm screw
31. Diaphragm screw
32. Diaphragm ring
33. Diaphragm ring
34. Diaphragm ring
35. Diaphragm ring screw
26. Diaphragm ring screw
37. Valve set
38. Valve retaining plate
39. Valve set
41. Base
42. Base
43. Base
44. Base
45. Base
46. Pressure switch
47. Pressure switch
48. Pressure switch
49. Dry tank switch
50. Pulsation dampener
51. Bottom plate
52. Screw
53. Pulsation dampener
54. Bottom cap
55. Bottom plate
56. Screw
57. Screw
58. Pulsation dampener
59. Base plate
60. Screw
61. Grommet
62. Vibration dampener
63. Screw

5. Remove 2 diaphragm ring screws and detach diaphragm ring.

6. Loosen eccentric retainer screw and pull connecting rod assembly away from motor shaft.

7. Remove diaphragm screw to separate diaphragm from connecting rod assembly.

8. Inspect entire rubber diaphragm for cuts and cracks.

9. Check connecting rod assembly for breaks, cracks or excessive wear on eccentric rod and bearing. If connecting rod is to be reused, open cover and relubricate by packing built-in reservoir with automotive chassis lube. Original lubricant normally lasts the lifetime of the pump.

10. Reassembly is the reverse of these steps. When reassembling connecting rod to diaphragm, be sure to align. Proper alignment is achieved when rod slips straight onto motor shaft and the diaphragm rests squarely on motor mount pad. Misalignment will create a strain on diaphragm and significantly shorten its life.

Pulsation Damper Replacement

1. Turn off power to pump.

2. If system is filled with water, open a faucet to relieve pressure and close both intake and discharge lines near the pump.

3. Remove pump from installation.

4. Remove 9 screws and the bottom plate from the base.

5. Pull out rubber pulsation damper.

6. Inspect damper for excessive deformation, ruptures and leaks.

7. Reassembly is the reverse of these steps. Make sure damper flange is correctly seated.

Pressure Switch Replacement

1. Turn power off to pump and open a faucet to relieve pressure from the system.

2. Disconnect all wires from pressure switch.

3. Remove switch front cover and 2 screws located at bottom corners inside switch case.

4. When installing the new switch, be sure the O-ring is seated properly. Care must be taken to avoid thread damage.

5. Reconnect electrical wires. See **Figure 7**.

9

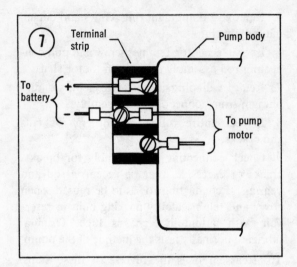

4. Remove 2 motor nuts and pull motor away from motor mount, while holding back eccentric/connecting rod assembly.

5. When installing new motor, make sure flat on shaft is well secured by the eccentric/connecting rod screw.

6. Rewire motor leads to center and right terminals on pressure switch. See Figure 7.

JABSCO PUMPS

Repair

Replacement parts are available for Jabsco pumps. Most commonly required parts are included in a service kit available from your Jabsco dealer.

Disassembly/Assembly

Figures 8 and 9 show exploded views of the 17840 automatic multi-fixture pump and the 14940 single fixture pump, respectively. Refer to these figures for disassembly and assembly of Jabsco pumps.

Motor Replacement

1. Turn off power to pump.

2. Disconnect motor wires from pressure switch terminal.

3. Loosen eccentric/connecting rod screw holding motor shaft.

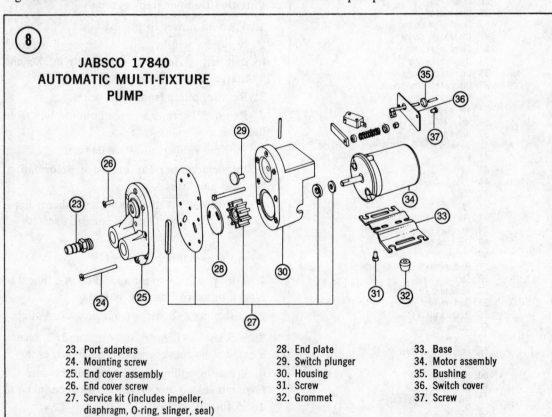

JABSCO 17840 AUTOMATIC MULTI-FIXTURE PUMP

23. Port adapters
24. Mounting screw
25. End cover assembly
26. End cover screw
27. Service kit (includes impeller, diaphragm, O-ring, slinger, seal)
28. End plate
29. Switch plunger
30. Housing
31. Screw
32. Grommet
33. Base
34. Motor assembly
35. Bushing
36. Switch cover
37. Screw

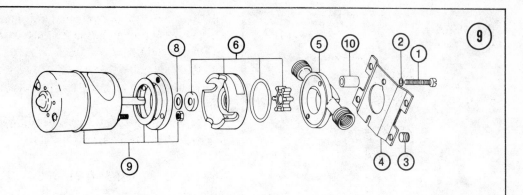

JABSCO 14940 SINGLE FIXTURE PUMP

1. Screw
2. Lockwasher
3. Grommet
4. Base
5. Body
6. Impeller service kit (includes seal, O-ring, ring, and impeller)
7. Seal housing
8. Slinger
9. Motor assembly
10. Stand off

WATER FAUCETS

After prolonged use, water faucets tend to leak. Such leakage is particularly troublesome in boats, not only because of a limited water supply, but also because water leaks may result in water pump failure.

Two Handle Faucets

To replace leaky faucet washers:

1. Turn off the water pump, or shut off the water supply.

2. Remove knob retaining screw (**Figure 10**).

3. Pull the knob from the valve stem (**Figure 11**). There may be some corrosion holding the knob to the valve stem; if so pry off gently, taking care not to mar any finished surfaces.

4. Loosen the valve stem assembly by turning it counterclockwise (**Figure 12**), then unscrew it completely from the faucet (**Figure 13**).

5. Remove the washer retaining screw (**Figure 14**).

6. Pry out the old washer (**Figure 15**), using any convenient tool. An ice pick or scratch awl is ideal for this purpose.

7. Select a new faucet washer of correct size and press it into position (**Figure 16**). Note that

replacement washers are frequently marked on the bottom side with size numbers, as "OO".

8. Assembly is the reverse of these steps.

> NOTE: *Be sure that the valve stem is turned fully counterclockwise (faucet open position) before tightening the valve stem assembly.*

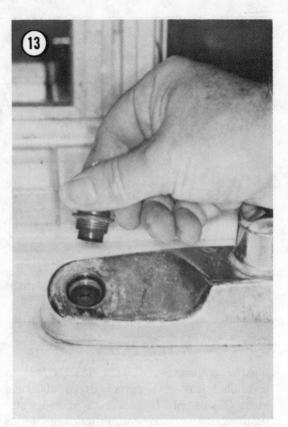

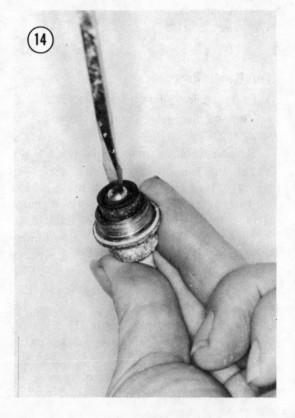

Single Handle Faucets

To stop leaks from single handle faucets, replace the ball assembly as follows:

1. Turn off the water pump or shut off water supply to faucet.

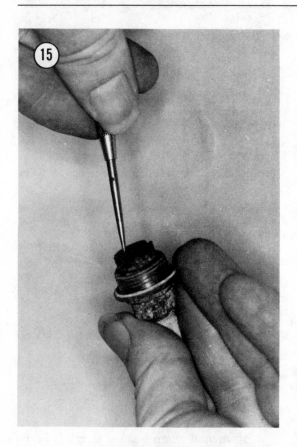

2. Loosen setscrew and lift off handle. See **Figure 17**.

3. Unscrew cap assembly and lift off. See **Figure 18**.

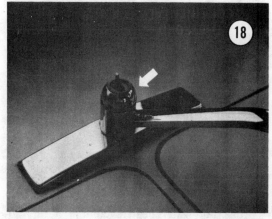

4. Remove cam assembly and ball. See **Figure 19**.

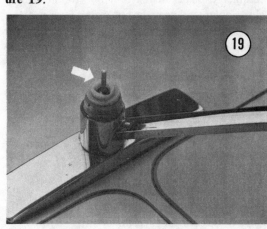

9

5. Install new ball into body over seats.

6. Install cam assembly over ball stem, and engage it with slot in body. Push down firmly until it seats.

7. Partially unscrew adjusting ring (see **Figure 20**).

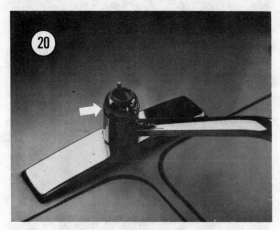

8. Place cap assembly over stem and screw down tight.

9. Turn on pump or water supply.

10. Tighten adjusting ring until no water leaks around stem when faucet is on and pressure is exerted on handle to force ball into socket.

11. Install handle and tighten setscrew.

WATER HEATER

Most hot water heaters contain a thermostatically controlled emersion element to heat the water at dockside. An optional heat exchanger extracts heat from the circulating engine coolant to provide hot water underway.

There is no preventive maintenance to the water heater itself. When preparing for lay-up follow the system procedure in this chapter.

TROUBLESHOOTING

Non-Pressurized System

1. Pump does not prime—no water at faucet.
   a. Check water level in tank.
   b. Check hoses for kinks.
   c. Check hoses for leaks.
   d. Check for clogged tank vent.

2. Electric pump fails to turn on.
   a. Check pump fuse—use SLO-BLO type only.
   b. Check electrical connections to battery, switch and pump.
   c. Check for defective pump by replacement.

3. Electric pump fails to turn off.
   Check for shorted switch.

Pressurized Demand System

1. Low or no water pressure
   a. Check water level in tank.
   b. Check power supply, fuse, and all electrical circuit connections to ensure full voltage on the pump.
   c. Check inlet filter at water tank.
   d. Check for clogged tank vent.
   e. Dismantle and service pump.

2. Pump cycles—open faucets
   a. Check all faucets for leaks.
   b. Check toilet for leak.
   c. Check all connections for leaks.
   d. If internal pump leakage seems to be the only explanation, dismantle and service pump.

3. Pump noisy and erratic
   a. Check inlet filter at water tank.
   b. Check all plumbing for restrictions.
   c. Clean aerator screen in all faucets. (Permanently removing aerator screens will provide better flow.)
   d. Check for clogged tank vent.
   e. Check plumbing near pump to ensure that it is not amplifying normal pump vibrations.
   f. Dismantle and service pump if necessary.

4. Pump does not operate
   a. Check fuse.
   b. Check for restrictions in system.
   c. Check and replace pressure switch if necessary.

5. Motor blows fuses
   Under normal operating conditions the drive motor will barely get warm. If the unit is re-

quired to pump a significant volume of water at severly reduced voltage, the drive motor will overheat, melt the insulation, short out the windings, and blow the fuse.

It is not feasible to repair the motor under these conditions, and the only cure is to replace the drive motor. The entire circuit should be checked to establish the reason for the low voltage problem to ensure that the replacement motor does not meet the same fate.

LAY-UP

Whenever the boat will be idle or stored for a long period, particularly when freezing temperatures are expected, the system should be winterized. There are 2 methods. One requires draining the system completely and leaving it dry. The other system uses a special non-toxic potable water anti-freeze solution such as Winter-Pruf available from recreational vehicle equipment suppliers.

WARNING
Do not use automotive type radiator anti-freeze under any circumstances. It is poisonous.

Winter-Pruf protects the system to −50°F and colors the water green to indicate its presence. Although it is non-toxic, do not drink the solution. The system must be thoroughly drained and flushed to remove all traces of green when the boat is recommissioned.

Non-Pressurized System

1. Drain the water tank.
2. Operate pump on all faucets until no water comes out (1 to 2 minutes).

   NOTE: *The following steps apply only if special non-toxic anti-freeze is to be added.*

3. Remove filter element (if installed).
4. Fill tank with fresh water and amount of anti-freeze recommended by manufacturer.

WARNING
Do not use automotive type radiator anti-freeze under any circumstances. It is poisonous.

5. Operate pump on all faucets starting from the one furthest from the tank until colored water emerges.
6. If no anti-freeze has been used, simply add fresh water to tank when recommissioning.
7. If anti-freeze has been added, drain tank.
8. Operate all faucets until emerging water is clear.
9. Fill tanks with fresh water and operate all faucets until water emerges.
10. Let fresh water set in tank for 10-15 minutes.
11. Drain and flush tank until water is no longer colored.
12. Add fresh water when system is clear. Install new filter element.

Pressurized Systems

1. Open all faucets and allow pump to empty water tank and intake lines. Run the pump dry for 1 to 2 minutes before turning off.
2. Open all drains, including the one on the water heater (if any).
3. Disconnect discharge and intake hoses from the pump. Start the pump and allow to run until all water is expelled from unit. Running dry will not harm the pump.
4. Reconnect the hoses, close the drains, and leave faucets open.
5. Remove the pump fuse if anti-freeze will not be used.

   NOTE: *The following steps apply only if special non-toxic anti-freeze is to be added.*

6. Remove filter element (if installed).
7. Fill tank with fresh water and amount of anti-freeze recommended by manufacturer.

WARNING
Do not use automotive type radiator anti-freeze under any circumstances. It is poisonous.

8. Open all faucets, one at a time, starting with the furthest from the water pump. Be sure that

you open hot water faucets as well to fill water heater with anti-freeze.

9. When colored water flows from each faucet, close it and leave it closed.

10. Remove the pump fuse to prevent cycling during lay-up.

Recommissioning

If anti-freeze has not been used, simply install pump fuse, fill system with water and open each faucet (starting with furthest from pump) until all air is removed from system. If anti-freeze was used:

1. Drain system following Steps 1-4 of lay-up procedure.

2. Fill with fresh water and let it set in tank for 10-15 minutes.

3. Drain and flush tank until water is no longer colored.

4. Add fresh water when system is clear. Install new filter element.

5. Bleed air from system as described above.

CHAPTER TEN

HEADS

There are few calamities at sea to match a defective head. This chapter describes most of the popular portable and permanent systems in use. Each section deals with a specific model, providing preventive maintenance, trouble-shooting, repair, and lay-up procedures. By properly maintaining the head at dockside, you can prevent the embarrassment of a defective head at sea.

THETFORD SEAFARER

The Seafarer is a portable, self-contained unit. It is divided internally into 2 sections, a 2-gallon fresh water chamber and a 4-gallon waste chamber. Up to 50 fresh water flushes are possible. The unit is easily emptied at any permanent toilet facility.

Maintenance

Minimum maintenance is required. Clean the Seafarer with a high quality non-abrasive cleaner. Do not use abrasive, highly concentrated, or acid content household cleaners. They may damage the rubber seals.

The seat and seat cover are easily removed for cleaning. Lift the seat and cover to open position. Flex sides of cover outward at hinge and lift cover off. Flex sides of seat inward at hinge and lift off. See **Figure 1**.

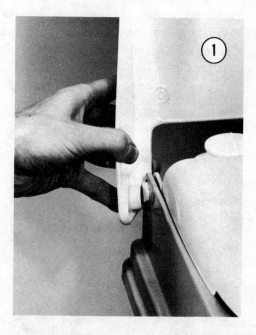

If the bowl sealing blade does not operate freely, apply a light film of silicone spray to the blade.

Winterizing

For cold season use, where temperatures are likely to drop to freezing or below, fill fresh water tank with one gallon of anti-freeze suitable for plastic then top to normal level with fresh water.

Lay-up

Completely drain fresh water tank and holding tank. Clean holding tank thoroughly. Clean bowl and exterior surfaces and spray with a disinfectant.

Troubleshooting

The Seafarer is so simple that little can go wrong.

1. *Bellows pump leaks or fails to operate*—Replace as described under *Maintenance*.

2. *Valve operates harder than normal or sticks*—Apply a light film of silicone spray lubricant to the valve blade.

3. *Holding tank leaks when unit is carried*—Disassemble and check condition of seals.

Pump Assembly Replacement

The pump receives the most wear and after extended use may deteriorate. To replace pump:

1. Cut open old pump with scissors from top to bottom. See **Figure 2**.

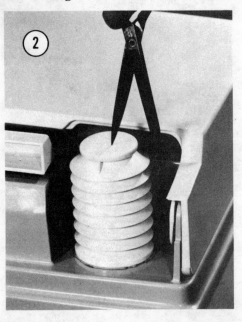

2. Fold the bellows inward and remove the pump assembly.

3. Remove bellows and inlet tube assembly from flush tube.

4. Connect a new bellows assembly to the flush tube.

5. Align the inlet (short) tube on the bellows with the back of the toilet and press down until it snaps into place.

Disassembly/Assembly

Refer to **Figure 3** for this procedure.

1. Clean unit inside and out.

2. Remove seat cover and seat as described under *Maintenance*.

3. Remove valve handle.

4. Turn unit upside down. Remove the screws holding tank perimeter.

5. Separate the holding tank, diaphragm, and water tank.

6. Remove screws securing bowl to water tank.

7. Inspect all seals and valve blade for deterioration or damage. Replace if necessary.

8. Clean away any caked or foreign material.

CAUTION
Do not use an abrasive cleaner.

9. Assembly is the reverse of these steps.

THETFORD PORTA POTTI CONTINENTAL

The Porta Potti is a portable self-contained unit providing fresh water flushes and a removable holding tank which can be emptied at any permanent toilet facility.

Maintenance

Minimum maintenance is required. Clean the Porta Potti with a high quality, non-abrasive cleaner. Do not use abrasive, highly concentrated or high acid content household cleaners. They may damage the rubber seals.

If the bowl sealing blade does not operate freely, apply a light film of silicone spray to the blade.

Winterizing

For cold season use, where temperatures are likely to drop to freezing or below, fill fresh water tank with one gallon of anti-freeze suitable for plastic then top to normal level with fresh water.

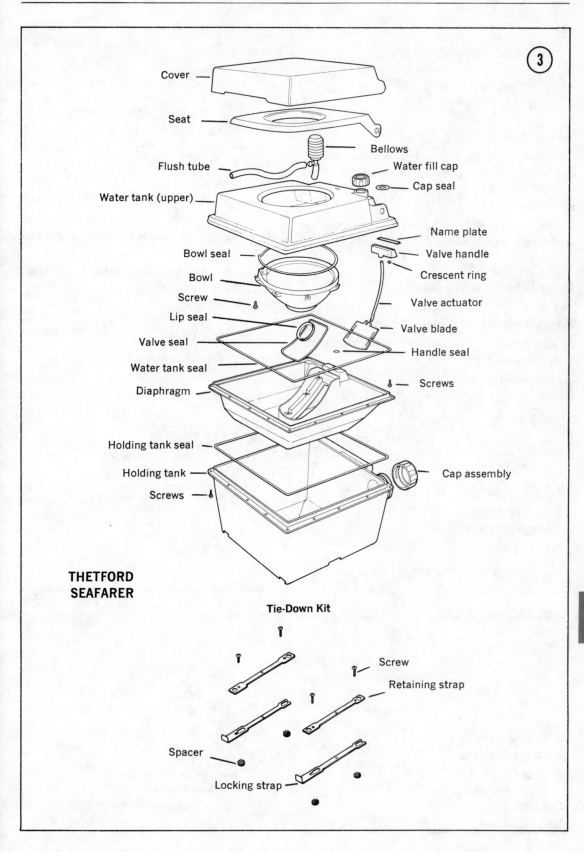

③

Cover

Seat

Bellows

Flush tube

Water fill cap

Cap seal

Water tank (upper)

Name plate

Valve handle

Bowl seal

Crescent ring

Bowl

Screw

Valve actuator

Lip seal

Valve blade

Valve seal

Handle seal

Water tank seal

Diaphragm

Screws

Holding tank seal

Holding tank

Cap assembly

Screws

**THETFORD
SEAFARER**

Tie-Down Kit

Screw

Retaining strap

Spacer

Locking strap

10

Lay-up

Completely drain fresh water tank and holding tank. Clean holding tank thoroughly. Clean bowl and exterior surfaces and spray with a disinfectant.

Troubleshooting

1. *Holding tank blade does not seal completely* —Check blade groove for foreign matter. Clean out with end of coat hanger wire. Do not damage rubber seal.

2. *Foot pedal operates harder than normal*— Apply light film of silicone spray to blade.

Pump Assembly Replacement

The pump receives the most wear and after extended use may deteriorate. To replace pump:

1. Cut open old pump with a scissors from top to bottom. See **Figure 4**.

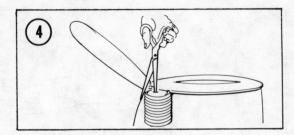

2. Fold the bellows inward and remove the pump assembly.

3. Remove bellows and inlet tube assembly from flush tube.

4. Connect a new bellows assembly to the flush tube.

5. Align the inlet (short) tube on the bellows with the back of the toilet and press down until it snaps into place.

Disassembly/Assembly

Refer to **Figures 5, 6, and 7** for this procedure.

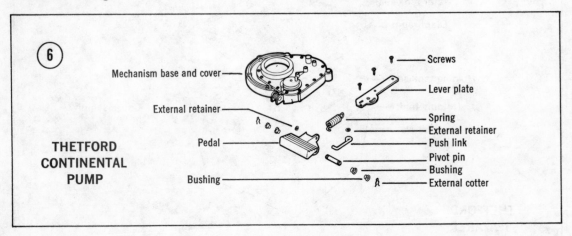

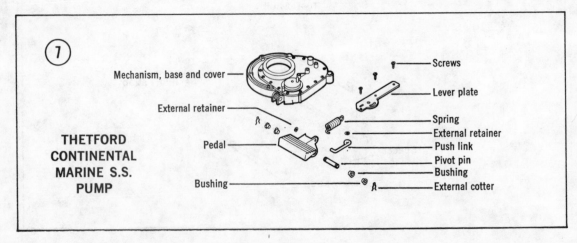

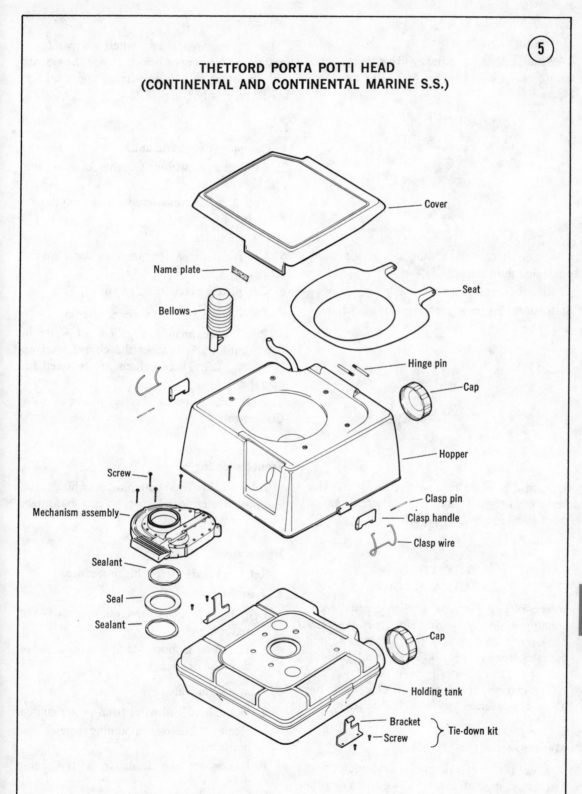

⑤

THETFORD PORTA POTTI HEAD
(CONTINENTAL AND CONTINENTAL MARINE S.S.)

Cover

Name plate

Bellows

Seat

Hinge pin

Cap

Hopper

Screw

Clasp pin

Clasp handle

Mechanism assembly

Clasp wire

Sealant

Seal

Sealant

Cap

Holding tank

Bracket

Screw

Tie-down kit

1. Detach holding tank.

2. Clean unit inside and out.

3. With seat cover closed, drive hinge pin toward center with pin punch or large nail. See **Figure 8**.

4. Lift cover on bellows side and push toward other side until free.

5. Remove seat in the same manner.

6. Remove 5 screws securing sealing mechanism to holding tank. See **Figure 9**.

7. Assembly is the reverse of these steps. Use new sealant rings and seal between sealing mechanism and holding tank.

THETFORD
ELECTRA MAGIC

The Electra Magic is a self-contained recirculating system requiring no separate water hook-up or holding tank installation. The unit operates from 12 volts DC and has a level indicator to indicate water level in tank.

The marine version of the Electra Magic has a sump connection for dockside discharge.

Maintenance

There is no periodic maintenance other than evacuating the tank when full and cleaning the unit. Use a high quality, non-abrasive cleaner such as Aqua Bowl Cleaner.

Winterizing

For cold season usage, where temperatures may fall to freezing or below, charge the system with ½ water and ½ anti-freeze approved for plastic pipe only.

Lay-up

1. Completely evacuate unit.

2. Refill unit to within 3 inches of bowl top with fresh water.

3. Add 2 inches (measured on the bottle) of Aqua Bowl Cleaner.

4. Cycle 3 times.

5. Let stand for a few minutes for cleaning action.

6. Completely evacuate unit again.

When returning unit to service after lay-up:

1. Pour approximately 3 gallons of water in bowl (until water reaches the charge level on indicator lens). Three gallons are required for operation.

2. Add one 8 ounce bottle of Aqua Kem Concentrate.

Troubleshooting

Table 1 below lists symptoms, possible causes, and probable remedies for problems that might be encountered.

Disassembly

Refer to **Figure 10** for this procedure.

1. Fuse Replacement

    a. Remove 2 cover mounting screws and motor cover.

    b. The fuse is now readily accessible for checking or changing.

2. Timer Removal

    a. Disconnect lead wires from power source.

    b. Remove 2 cover mounting screws and motor cover.

    c. Disconnect the leads from the pump assembly motor.

    d. Remove 2 timer bracket mounting screws and timer assembly.

Table 1   THETFORD ELECTRA MAGIC TROUBLESHOOTING

Symptom	Probable Cause	Remedy
Toilet wobbles	a. Closet bolt nuts not tight. b. Mounting brackets not seated to floor (see Figure 3). c. Closet flange too high or mounting surface uneven.	a. Tighten nuts. b. Tighten nuts. c. Check closet flange height by laying straight edge across flange and measuring gap between straight edge at four leg locations (¼ to 7/16 inch is recommended).
Toilet cycles when seat cover is raised	Actuator button protrudes too far from motor cover.	Alternately press one side of the button, then the other, to work button back further into housing. If button still protrudes too far, replace timer assembly.
Toilet does not cycle properly (5-9 seconds)	a. Reversed wiring polarity. b. Battery run down. c. Wiring too small. d. Defective timer.	a. Wire correctly. b. Charge battery. c. Install heavier wiring. d. Replace timer.
Flushing weak or noisy	a. Pump is running backwards (reversed wiring polarity). b. Cycling unit without enough charge water. c. Pump damaged by continuous dry operation.	a. Wire correctly. b. Charge to capacity. c. Replace pump.
Lack of capacity (less than normal number of flushes)	Too much water.	Use only 3 gallons to charge.

3. Pump Removal

a. Complete Steps 2a-2c above.

b. Completely evacuate unit.

c. Remove cover and bowl assembly screws (2 in rear from top side and 2 in front from bottom side) and remove the cover and bowl assembly.

d. Remove 4 pump mounting screws.

e. Disconnect flush tube from pump outlet.

f. Remove pump assembly.

4. Slide Valve Removal

a. Disconnect lead wires from power source.

b. Completely evacuate unit.

c. Remove 2 molding mounting screws and remove 2 base moldings.

d. Remove 2 nuts and washers from closet studs (one each side underneath unit).

e. Lift Electra Magic from closet flange and invert unit.

f. Remove 4 screws and remove valve.

5. Sump Removal

a. Complete Steps 4a-4d, above.

b. Remove flexible hose from sump and invert unit.

c. Remove 4 screws and remove the sump (**Figure 11**).

THETFORD AQUA MAGIC

The Aqua Magic is a permanent toilet developed specifically for marine use. Each flush, controlled by a foot pedal, is accomplished with fresh water. Models C and G have separate water rinse and flush pedals.

10

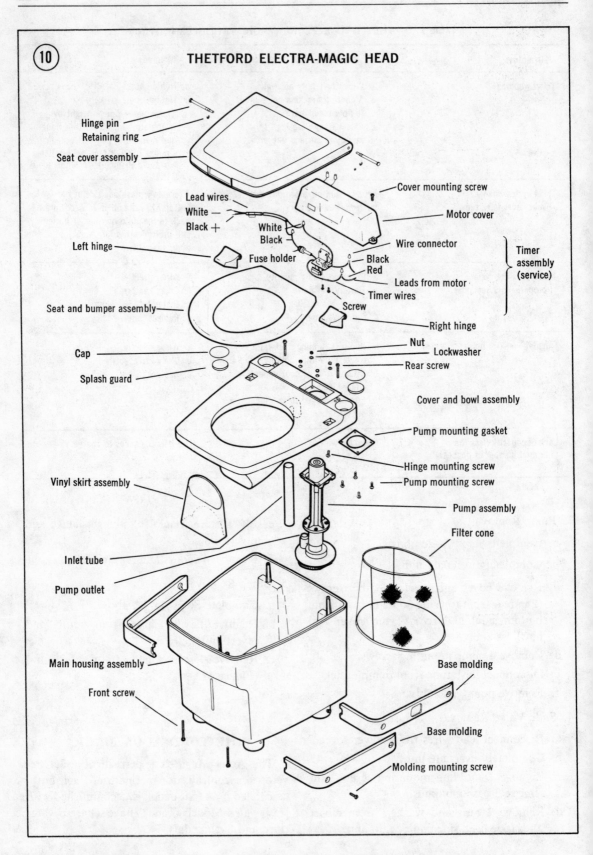

⑩ THETFORD ELECTRA-MAGIC HEAD

Hinge pin
Retaining ring

Seat cover assembly

Cover mounting screw

Lead wires
White
Black +

Motor cover

White
Black

Wire connector

Left hinge

Fuse holder

Black
Red

Timer assembly (service)

Leads from motor

Timer wires

Seat and bumper assembly

Screw

Right hinge

Cap

Nut
Lockwasher

Splash guard

Rear screw

Cover and bowl assembly

Pump mounting gasket

Vinyl skirt assembly

Hinge mounting screw
Pump mounting screw

Pump assembly

Filter cone

Inlet tube

Pump outlet

Main housing assembly

Base molding

Front screw

Base molding

Molding mounting screw

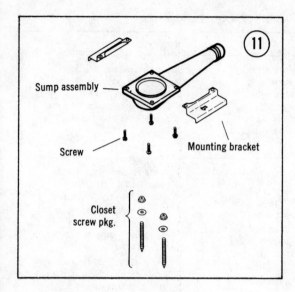

Maintenance

There is no periodic maintenance other than evacuating the tank when full and cleaning the unit. Use a high quality, non-abrasive cleaner such as Aqua Bowl Cleaner.

Winterizing

Since fresh water comes from the boat's fresh water supply, no anti-freeze can be used.

Lay-up

1. Drain or pump out boat's fresh water tanks.

2. Leave water supply valve to toilet open.

3. Depress foot pedal and insert soft drink bottle into outlet at bottom of bowl. Release foot pedal slowly until blade holds bottle in place. This holds valve open, preventing residual water from collecting and freezing.

4. Empty and flush holding tank thoroughly.

Troubleshooting

Table 2 below lists likely troubles, causes, and cures.

Disassembly

Thetford Aqua Magic toilets disassemble into 4 main subassemblies.

    a. Seat and cover assembly.

    b. Vacuum breaker.

    c. Mechanism assembly.

    d. Hopper assembly.

Refer to **Figures 12-14** for this procedure.

1. Remove the seat and cover assembly—turn the toilet upside down. The seat and cover are attached to the bowl with a standard hinge and bolt assembly. Remove the nuts from the hinge bolts and lift the cover and seat from the bowl.

2. Remove the vacuum breaker—turn the toilet upside down. To remove water lines from the vacuum breaker base, pinch hose clamps with a pair of pliers and slide them up the water line. Water lines may be pulled off. Remove the 4 vacuum breaker attachment screws.

3. Remove the mechanism assembly—turn the toilet upside down. Remove the 6 screws that are now visible. Lift up mechanism to gain access

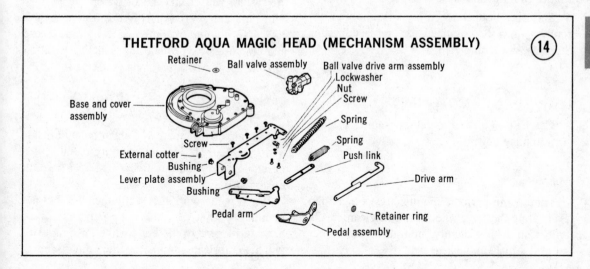

10

THETFORD AQUA MAGIC HEAD (MECHANISM ASSEMBLY)

Table 2   THETFORD AQUA MAGIC TROUBLESHOOTING

Symptom	Probable Cause	Remedy
Water keeps running into the bowl	The blade in the bottom of the bowl is not closing completely, which in turn keeps the water control valve partially open. The groove into which the blade seats when completely closed is clogged with foreign material.	Insert the end of a coat hanger or similar object into the sealing groove and remove the foreign material. Avoid damaging the rubber seal while celaning.
Toilet leaks. There is water on the deck.	Determine if water is leaking from: a. The vacuum breaker b. The water control valve. c. Bowl-to-mechanism seal (if this is the problem, water will not stay in bowl).	a. If the vacuum breaker leaks when flushing the toilet, replace the vacuum breaker. b. If the vacuum breaker leaks when the toilet is not in operation, replace the water control valve. c. Leaks at the bowl-to-mechanism seal—remove mechanism and replace mechanism seal. d. Leaks at closet flange area—check front and rear closet flange nuts for tightness. If leak continues, remove the toilet, check closet flange height. The height should be between $\frac{1}{4}$ and 7/16 in. above the floor. Adjust closet flange height accordingly and replace closet flange seal.
Foot pedal operates harder than normal or the blade sticks.		Apply a light film of silicone spray to blade.

to water line hose clamps. Pinch hose clamps with a pair of pliers and slide them up the water line. Pull water lines off mechanism. See Figure 14 for available service parts.

4. Servicing hopper assembly—the hopper assembly may be serviced or replaced after Steps 1-3 are completed.

CRAFT-TOILET

The Craft-Toilet is a self-contained electric recirculating unit.

Maintenance

There is no periodic maintenance other than evacuating the tank when full and cleaning the unit. Use a high quality, non-abrasive cleaner such as Aqua Bowl Cleaner.

Winterizing

If head is used during cold season when temperatures may fall to freezing or below, charge the system with a mixture of water and permanent-type automotive anti-freeze (ethylene glycol). Use amount recommended by anti-freeze manufacturer to protect the toilet's 9 gallon capacity to temperature range expected.

Lay-up

Completely evacuate and clean the unit inside and out. Pour in a small quantity of undiluted permanent-type automotive anti-freeze in unit during storage.

When recharging, it is recommended, but not mandatory, that you add 1 cup permanent-type auto anti-freeze to the bowl while flushing. This will help lubricate pump, impeller, and discharge

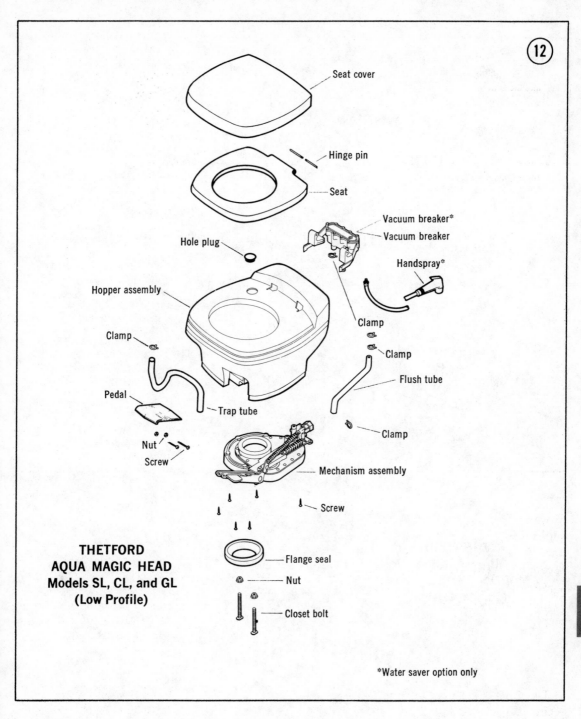

(12)

Seat cover

Hinge pin

Seat

Vacuum breaker*
Vacuum breaker

Hole plug

Handspray*

Hopper assembly

Clamp

Clamp
Clamp

Clamp
Flush tube

Pedal

Trap tube

Clamp

Nut
Screw

Mechanism assembly

Screw

**THETFORD
AQUA MAGIC HEAD
Models SL, CL, and GL
(Low Profile)**

Flange seal

Nut

Closet bolt

10

*Water saver option only

valve. This is especially recommended if your toilet will be idle for long periods.

Troubleshooting

Table 3 below lists likely troubles, probable causes, and methods of correction.

Recharging

1. Move discharge control level (see **Figure 15**) to FLUSH.

2. Pour approximately 3 gallons of water into unit. This is accomplished by filling and draining the bowl 3 times into base tank. If permanent

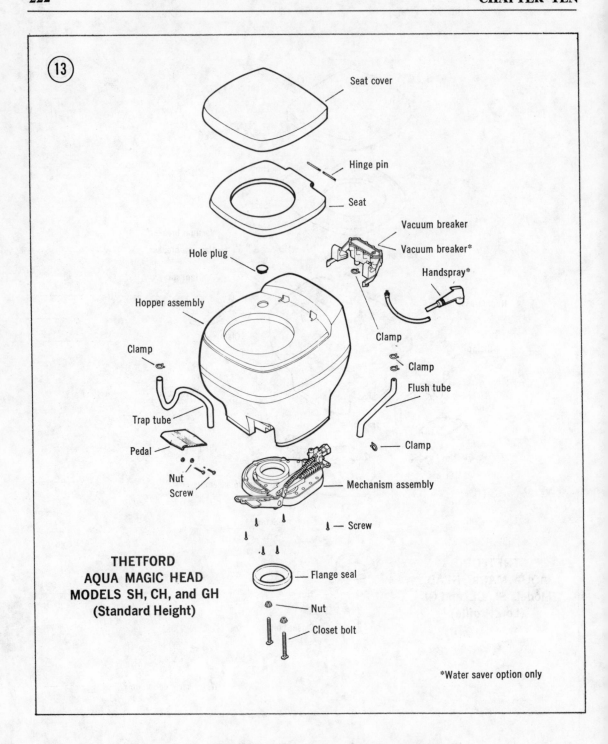

⑬

Seat cover

Hinge pin

Seat

Vacuum breaker

Vacuum breaker*

Handspray*

Hole plug

Hopper assembly

Clamp

Clamp

Clamp

Flush tube

Trap tube

Pedal

Nut

Screw

Mechanism assembly

— Screw

**THETFORD
AQUA MAGIC HEAD
MODELS SH, CH, and GH
(Standard Height)**

Flange seal

Nut

Closet bolt

*Water saver option only

refill connection is made to fresh water system, pull activator handle and run water until level reaches macerator blade.

3. Pour in 1 package of Craft-Chem Neutralizer or other toilet chemical while flushing. Continue flushing 10-30 seconds.

Evacuating and Rinsing

The unit is full and requires emptying when the waste level reaches within one inch of the bowl. Pull the activator handle (Figure 15) forward to observe the level through the opening at the rear of the bowl.

Table 3   CRAFT-TOILET TROUBLESHOOTING

Symptoms	Probable Cause	Check	Correct
Motor runs but poor or no flushing action	Flush tube kinked or clogged	Tube	Straighten or clean
	Unit empty	Level	Fill with 3 gallons of water and CRAFT-CHEM
	Clogged inlet pipe	For seeds	Remove and clean
	Clogged pump	Pump	Remove top cover, clean and lubricate
	Loose connection between suction tube and pump	Coupling nut	Tighten
	No prime (rarely happens, initially only)		Turn handle to empty, add water to forward opening port, press switch
	Low voltage		Check power source
Motor fails to operate when switch is depressed	Electrical failure	Fuse	Check and replace
		Loose connections	Correct
		Power source	Correct
	Motor failure	Motor burned out	Replace
		Defective switch or connection	Replace or correct
	Pump clogged	Foreign matter binding impeller or improper chemical has deformed	Clean, lubricate, or replace impeller if defective
Excessive vibration	Foreign matter enmeshed in screen or macerator blade	Remove top of toilet and inspect	Clean with stiff brush
Liquid level backs into bowl	Unit full	Level	Empty, rinse, and recharge
	Louvers clogged	Check basket	Remove top and clean out louvers with brush
Bad odor	Overextended use	Color	Add CRAFT-CHEM or pump out, rinse with water, recharge
	Improper or no rinsing of unit		Remove top, rinse out thoroughly with pressure if possible
Unit flushes, but when valve is put in empty position will not pump out	Evacuation tube clogged or kinked	Tube	Remove top and clean or straighten
	Valve clogged	Valve	Rotate valve from flush to empty while depressing switch. Remove valve and put pressure through it or replace
Will not pump out or flush	Directional control valve	Position of valve	Push valve down to original position

10

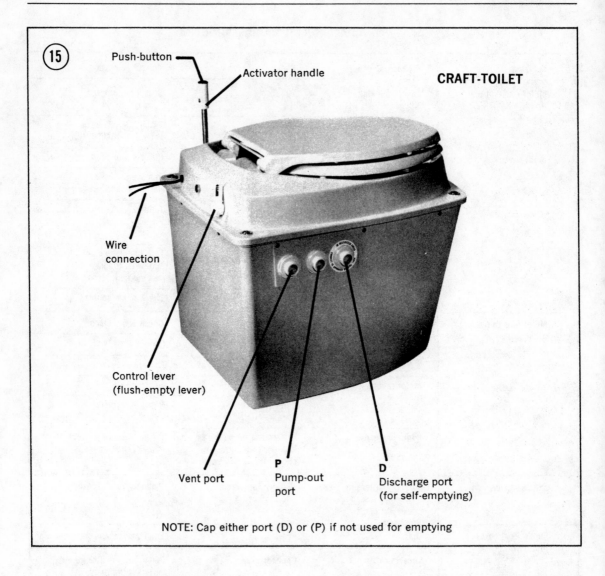

⑮ Push-button

Activator handle

CRAFT-TOILET

Wire connection

Control lever (flush-empty lever)

Vent port

P Pump-out port

D Discharge port (for self-emptying)

NOTE: Cap either port (D) or (P) if not used for emptying

NOTE: *Regardless of level, it is best to empty, rinse, and recharge unit every 2 weeks.*

Automatic Emptying

1. Move discharge control lever (see Figure 15) to EMPTY. Connect garden hose to discharge part D, Figure 15. Cap part P.

2. Put other end of hose into regular toilet or waste storage tank.

WARNING
Permanently mark the hose in some way to indicate it is for use only for waste and not for drinking water.

3. Depress push-button on activator handle. Hold until tank is empty.

4. Fill bowl with clean water and a small amount of non-abrasive toilet cleaner. Pull activator handle forward to drain bowl into the base tank.

5. Depress push-button again to empty tank of cleaning solution.

6. Repeat Steps 4 and 5 as often as necessary to rinse tank.

7. Move discharge control lever back to FLUSH and recharge or prepare for lay-up.

Dockside Pump-out

1. Leave discharge control handle on FLUSH.

2. Connect dockside pump hose to deck fitting.

> NOTE: *Obviously, the installation must include a hose from pump-out port to a standard waste deck fitting. The discharge port must also be capped.*

3. Rinse and recharge as described in Steps 4-7 under *Automatic Emptying*.

Disassembly/Assembly

Figures 16 and 17 provide exploded views of the complete toilet and pump/motor assembly.

MONOGRAM HANDIHEAD II

The Handihead II is a self-contained recirculating toilet. The integral holding tank may be emptied through a deck-mounted fitting or pumped overboard out a through-hull fitting above or below the waterline.

Typical Installations

Figures 18-20 show typical installations. Dockside discharge is via a 1½ inch monoflex tubing. Overboard discharge requires a Hand-O-Pump. The through-hull fitting may be above or below the waterline. If any portion of the Handihead is below the waterline at any angle of heel, a 1½ inch vented loop (Wilcox-Crittenden or equivalent) must be installed between Handihead and seacock.

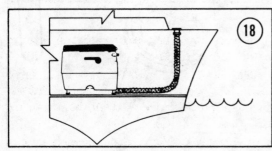

Top of vent loop must be at least 4 inches above waterline at greatest angle of heel.

> **CAUTION**
> *The vented loop is not a substitute for a seacock. The loop prevents back filling or siphoning of water into head when seacock is open. Keep seacock closed when head is not in use.*

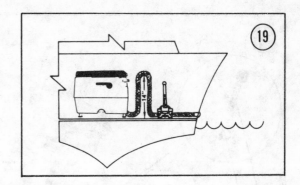

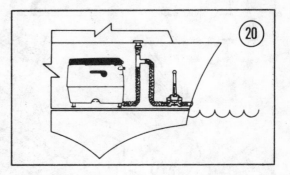

Recharging

1. Depress lever on side of toilet to open the bowl seal.

2. Pour ½ gallon of water into toilet.

3. Close bowl seal and add one quart of water to the bowl.

4. Add one package of Monochem PTC Chemical or equivalent to bowl.

5. Open bowl seal to empty bowl.

6. Flush several times to circulate chemicals. If flushing action is weak or water splatters, add up to one more quart of water.

Emptying

When fluid level is level with bottom of bowl opening, toilet must be emptied.

Dockside Discharge

1. Connect dockside pump to deck fittings and start pump.

2. When empty, rinse base tank with fresh water through bowl opening.

3. When unit is completely empty of rinse water, turn off dockside pump and remove hose.

4. Recharge or prepare for lay-up.

10

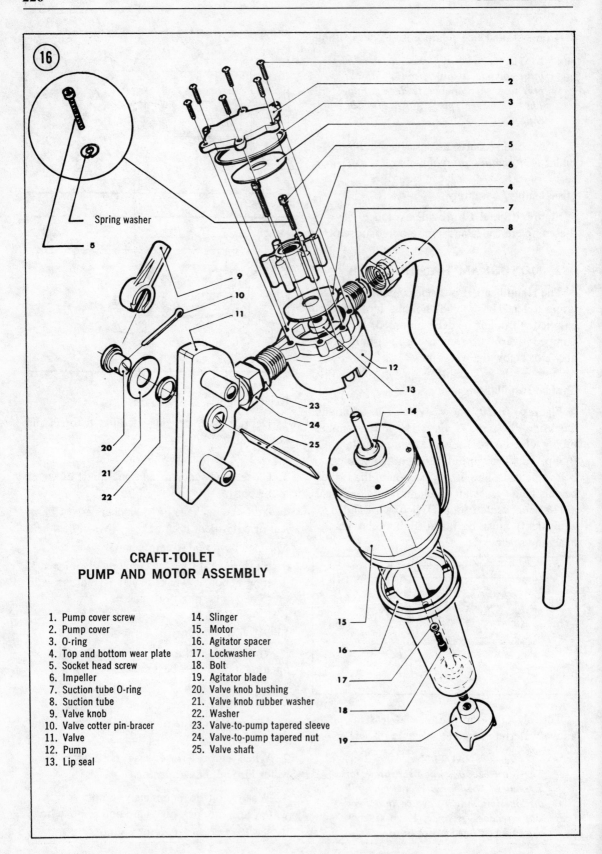

Spring washer

**CRAFT-TOILET
PUMP AND MOTOR ASSEMBLY**

1. Pump cover screw
2. Pump cover
3. O-ring
4. Top and bottom wear plate
5. Socket head screw
6. Impeller
7. Suction tube O-ring
8. Suction tube
9. Valve knob
10. Valve cotter pin-bracer
11. Valve
12. Pump
13. Lip seal
14. Slinger
15. Motor
16. Agitator spacer
17. Lockwasher
18. Bolt
19. Agitator blade
20. Valve knob bushing
21. Valve knob rubber washer
22. Washer
23. Valve-to-pump tapered sleeve
24. Valve-to-pump tapered nut
25. Valve shaft

CRAFT-TOILET
(See Next Page for Legend)

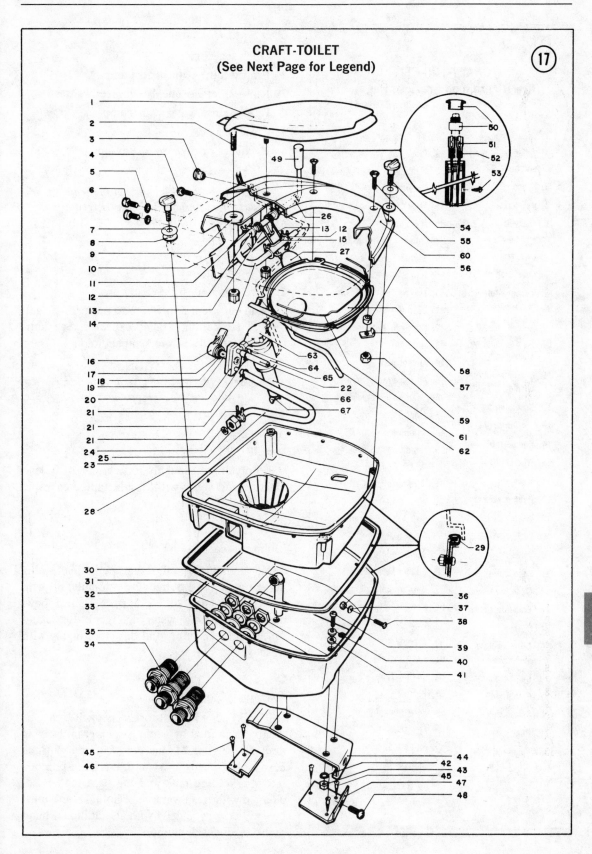

CRAFT-TOILET
(See Diagram on Previous Page)

1. Toilet seat	31. Bushing nut
2. Toilet seat hinge and bolt	32. Fiber washer
	33. Rubber washer
3. Heyco bushing	34. Outlet bushing
4. Hex screw	35. Tank
5. Lockwasher	36. Hex nut
6. Socket head capscrew	37. Internal tooth washer
	38. Bolt
7. Cover bolt washer	39. Bolt
8. Rubber white bolt washer	40. Flat washer
	41. Lead flat washer
9. Rubber washer	42. Spring lockwasher
10. Motor mounting bracket	43. Nut
	44. Anchor plate
11. Handle mounting bushing	45. Anchor bracket screw
	46. Rear anchor bracket
12. Hose clamp	47. Front anchor bracket
13. Torsion spring	48. Cad plated screw
14. Handle tube	49. Handle switch housing
15. Wire clip	50. Switch
16. Valve knob	51. Wire terminal
17. Rubber washer	52. Wire insulator
18. Washer	53. Switch housing screw
19. Valve shaft	54. Cover bolt
20. Valve	55. Bowl mounting screw
21. Hose clamp	56. Rubber bowl washer
22. Flush tube	57. Bowl mounting bracket
23. Evacuation tube	58. Bowl complete with gasket
24. O-ring	59. Nut
25. Coupling nuts and sleeve	60. Top cover
	61. Bowl gasket
26. Handle grommet	62. Suction tube
27. Gate plate	63. Pump
28. Splash tray	64. Valve coupling nut
29. Body gasket	65. Electric motor
30. Pump out pipe with elbow	66. Agitator spacer
	67. Agitator blade

Overboard Discharge

1. Open seacock.
2. Empty toilet with hand pump.
3. Rinse toilet thoroughly with fresh water.
4. Empty rinse water with pump.
5. Close seacock.
6. Recharge or prepare for lay-up.

NOTE: *For health and environmental reasons, dockside discharge is recommended whenever possible.*

Winterizing

1. Clean the unit inside and out.

2. Add sufficient anti-freeze to protect 3½ gallons at temperature range expected. See anti-freeze manufacturer's recommendation.

CAUTION
Use only ethylene glycol anti-freeze Do not use alcohol products.

Lay-up

Empty and thoroughly rinse base tank. Clean exterior and spray with disinfectant. Leave the unit dry.

Maintenance

No maintenance other than periodic cleaning and emptying is required. Occasionally, fill with fresh water and add ½ cup of Vanish bowl cleaner or a cold water detergent. Let stand for 30 minutes, empty and rinse thoroughly with fresh water.

Extending Capacity

The system waste storage capacity can be greatly expanded by adding an external holding tank. See **Figure 21**. Instead of discharging the base tank contents overboard, it is hand-pumped into the holding tank and the base tank is recharged with fresh water. The holding tank must be emptied periodically with an additional hand pump or dockside pump.

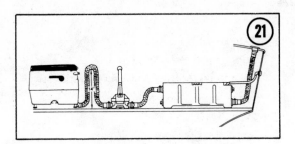

Disassembly/Assembly

Figure 22 shows an exploded view of the Handihead II.

MONOGRAM MONOMATIC II

The Monomatic II is a self-contained recirculating flush unit with a 7 gallon capacity (3 gallons fresh water/4 gallons waste).

Typical Installations

Figures 18-20 show typical installations. Dockside discharge is via a 1½ inch monoflex tubing. Overboard discharge requires a Hand-O-Pump. The through-hull fitting may be above or below the waterline. If any portion of the Handihead is below the waterline at any angle of heel, a 1½ inch vented loop (Wilcox-Crittenden or equivalent) must be installed between Handihead and seacock.

Top of vent loop must be at least 4 inches above waterline at greatest angle of heel.

CAUTION
The vented loop is not a substitute for a seacock. The loop prevents back filling or siphoning of water into head when seacock is open. Keep seacock closed when head is not in use.

Recharging

1a. If the fill connection is made to the boat's pressurized water system, turn on water valve. When the sound of the water entering the tank changes significantly, the water has reached the 3 gallon level. Turn the water off.

1b. If the unit is not connected to pressurized water system, pour 3 gallons of fresh water directly through the open bowl.

2. Operate foot pedal several times to prime the pump.

3. While flushing, pour one package of Monochem T-5 or equivalent into the bowl.

4. Flush several times to dissolve and circulate the chemical.

Emptying

The tank must be emptied when the waste level becomes visible at the bottom of the bowl.

Dockside Discharge

1. Connect dockside pump to deck fitting and start pump.

2. When tank is empty, run fresh water into system while continuing to pump for about one minute to rinse tank.

3. Shut off fresh water.

4. When tank is empty, turn off dockside pump.

5. Recharge or prepare for lay-up.

Overboard Discharge

1. Open seacock.

2. Operate hand pump.

3. When empty, run fresh water into system for about one minute while operating pump.

4. Shut off rinse water.

5. When tank is drained, depress foot pedal several times to completely empty pump.

6. Close seacock.

7. Recharge or prepare for lay-up.

NOTE: *For health and environmental reasons, dockside discharge is recommended whenever possible.*

Winterizing

1. Empty and rinse system as described above.

2. Pour in enough anti-freeze to protect 7 gallons at temperature range expected according to anti-freeze manufacturer's directions.

3. Add fresh water to the system to make total charge 3 gallons.

CAUTION
Use ethylene glycol base anti-freeze. Do not use alcohol products.

10

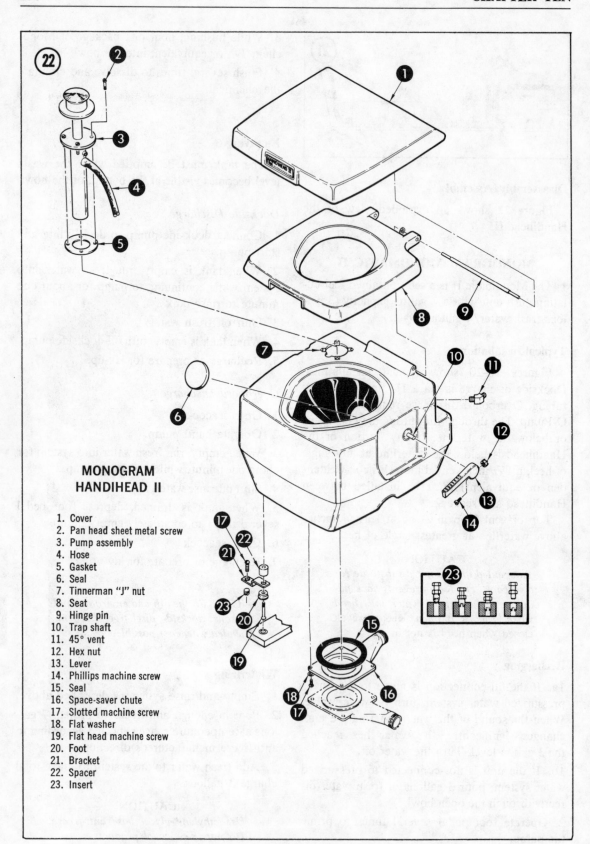

**MONOGRAM
HANDIHEAD II**

1. Cover
2. Pan head sheet metal screw
3. Pump assembly
4. Hose
5. Gasket
6. Seal
7. Tinnerman "J" nut
8. Seat
9. Hinge pin
10. Trap shaft
11. 45° vent
12. Hex nut
13. Lever
14. Phillips machine screw
15. Seal
16. Space-saver chute
17. Slotted machine screw
18. Flat washer
19. Flat head machine screw
20. Foot
21. Bracket
22. Spacer
23. Insert

Lay-up

1. Empty and rinse base tank thoroughly as described earlier. Use Vanish bowl cleaner. See *Maintenance*.

2. When unit is completely drained, depress foot pump several times to completely empty pump.

Disassembly/Assembly

Refer to **Figure 23** for this procedure.

1. Remove service port cover. See **Figure 24**.

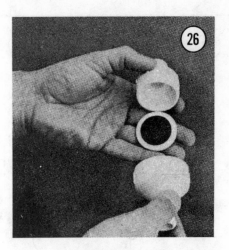

2. Disconnect hoses from anti-siphon valve and lift valve out. See **Figure 25**.

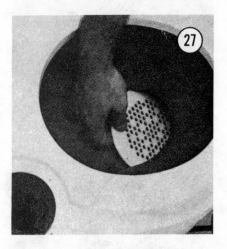

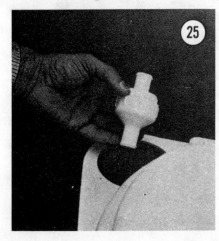

3. Unscrew anti-siphon valve and inspect parts. See **Figure 26**.

4. Remove pin filter mounting screws through service port.

5. Remove pin filter parts through bowl. See **Figures 27 and 28**.

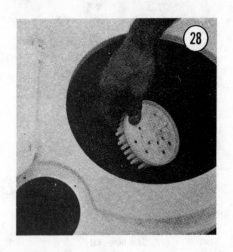

6. Remove base skirt. Remove closet bolts with 7/16 inch wrench. Lift toilet off.

7. Turn toilet upside down.

10

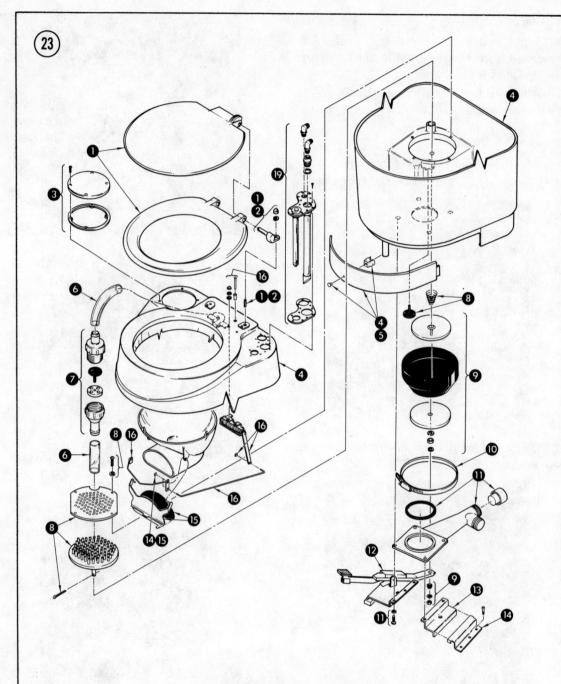

MONOGRAM MONOMATIC II

1. Seat assembly
2. Seat hinge set
3. Access cover
4. Shell assembly
5. Removable skirt
6. Hose
7. Check valve assembly
8. Grid and valve assembly
9. Diaphragm assembly
10. Band clamp
11. Drain fitting and plug
12. Foot pedal assembly
13. Bracket mounting
14. Bracket mounting
15. Flapper assembly
16. Actuator assembly
17. Rinse-vent and level assembly

8. Remove screws securing slide valve and lift valve off.

9. Remove locknut from bottom of diaphragm. Remove foot pedal assembly.

10. Unscrew bank clamp and lift off rubber diaphragm.

MANSFIELD VACU-FLUSH

The Vacu-flush system is unique in that waste is positively drawn from the toilet into the holding tank by a strong vacuum.

Each system consists of at least one toilet, one tank, and one pump. **Figure 29** shows a typical installation. The vacuum pump draws air from the tank and discharges it through the vent. A strong vacuum (10" Hg) builds up in the holding tank. When the unit is flushed, the ball valve in the bottom of the bowl opens and waste is drawn into the holding tank.

Waste in the holding tank can be pumped out at dockside by an external pump or discharged overboard with the system pump.

Emptying and Rinsing

Figure 29 shows a typical installation. It is wise to trace out your installation and compare to figure. Correct the figure to conform to your system.

Dockside Pump-out

Basically, the dockside pump draws waste from the holding tank at the deck fitting. The path from tank to toilet is opened to permit air to replace waste in the tank and prevent any vacuum buildup.

1. Close fresh water valve.

2. Open Valve No. 1 (between tank and toilet).

3. Prop toilet ball valve open.

4. Turn on dockside pump. Operate until tank is empty.

5. Turn dockside pump off.

6. Turn fresh water valve on and fill tank with fresh water to rinse, then close valve.

7. Turn dockside pump on to empty tank.

8. Repeat Steps 5-7 as often as necessary.

9. When tank is empty, leave Valve No. 1 open and cap deck fitting. Remove prop holding toilet ball valve open and turn fresh water valve on.

Overboard Pump-out

For this method, the vacuum pump is used to pressurize the holding tank and force its contents out of the below-water seacock. The valve between the tank and toilet must be closed or waste will be forced out the toilet as well.

1. Close Valve No. 1.

2. Open seacock (Valve No. 2).

3. Turn 4-way valve to "pump-out."

4. Push "Start" button on toilet.

5. When tank is empty, turn 4-way valve to NORMAL. Leave seacock *open* and Valve No. 1 *closed*. The vacuum pump will draw seawater through seacock and fill tank for rinsing.

6. Turn 4-way valve back to PUMP-OUT and push "Start" button on toilet to empty tank of rinse water.

7. Repeat Steps 5 and 6 as often as necessary.

8. Close seacock.

9. Return 4-way valve to NORMAL.

10. Open Valve No. 1. Pump will operate until (10" Hg) vacuum builds up in tank, then will automatically turn off.

> NOTE: *For health and environmental reasons, dockside discharge is recommended whenever possible.*

Winterizing

Since the system uses the boat's fresh water supply, no winterizing is possible.

Lay-up

1. Completely rinse and empty the system of all waste.

2. Drain boat's fresh water tanks.

3. Leave fresh water valve open.

4. Prop toilet ball valve open.

Disassembly/Assembly

Figures 30-33 provide exploded views of all major components of the Vacu-flush system.

10

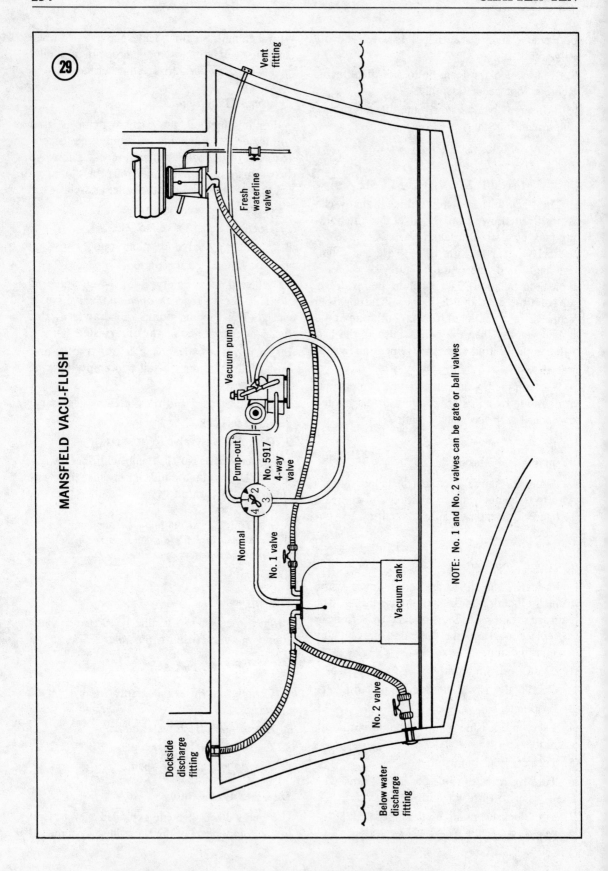

MANSFIELD VACU-FLUSH

Vent fitting

Fresh waterline valve

Vacuum pump

Pump-out

No. 5917 4-way valve

Normal

No. 1 valve

Vacuum tank

NOTE: No. 1 and No. 2 valves can be gate or ball valves

Dockside discharge fitting

No. 2 valve

Below water discharge fitting

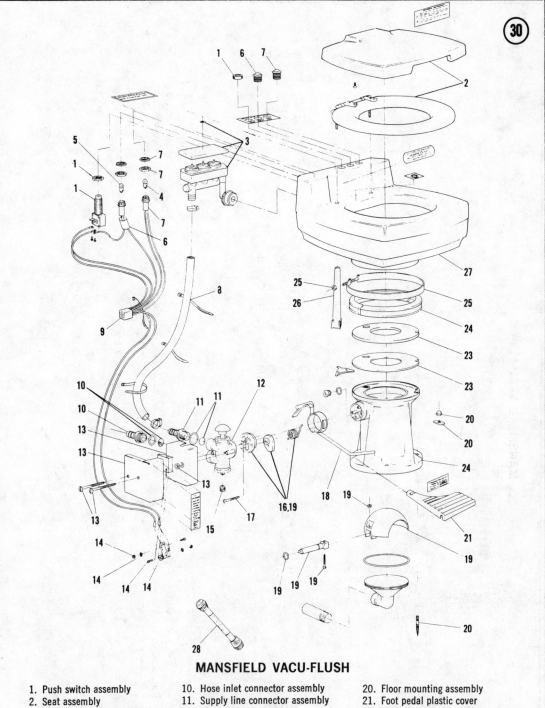

MANSFIELD VACU-FLUSH

1. Push switch assembly
2. Seat assembly
3. Vacuum breaker assembly
4. Light bulb (red)
5. Light bulb (green)
6. Light assembly (green)
7. Light assembly (red)
8. Supply hose
9. Electrical plug

10. Hose inlet connector assembly
11. Supply line connector assembly
12. Water valve assembly
13. Valve cover assembly
14. Micro switch assembly
15. Drain cap
16. Cartridge
17. Valve spacer screw
18. Flush lever
19. Ball rotor shaft assembly

20. Floor mounting assembly
21. Foot pedal plastic cover
22. Base assembly less water valve
23. Seal assembly
24. Half clamp
25. Clamp ring and nut
26. Seat assembly to bowl nut
27. China bowl
28. Pedal holder

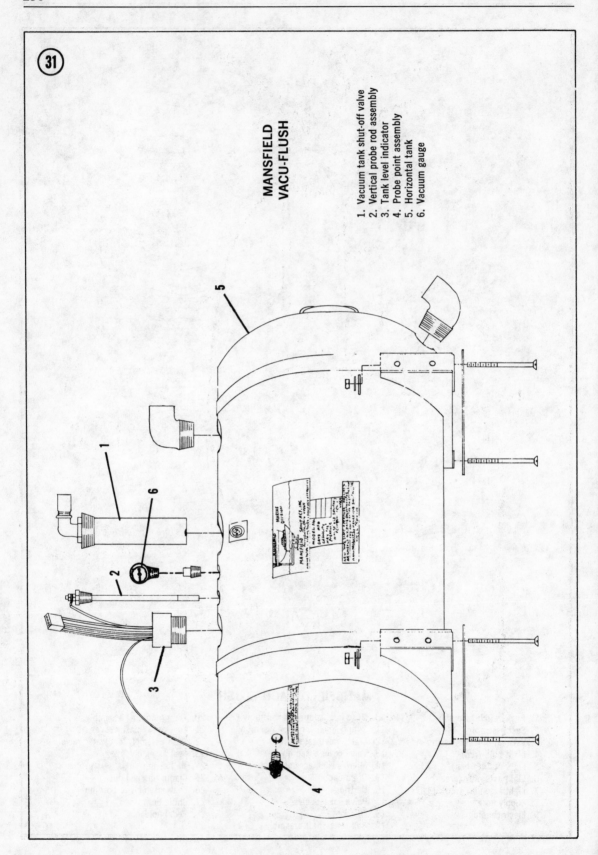

㉛

MANSFIELD
VACU-FLUSH

1. Vacuum tank shut-off valve
2. Vertical probe rod assembly
3. Tank level indicator
4. Probe point assembly
5. Horizontal tank
6. Vacuum gauge

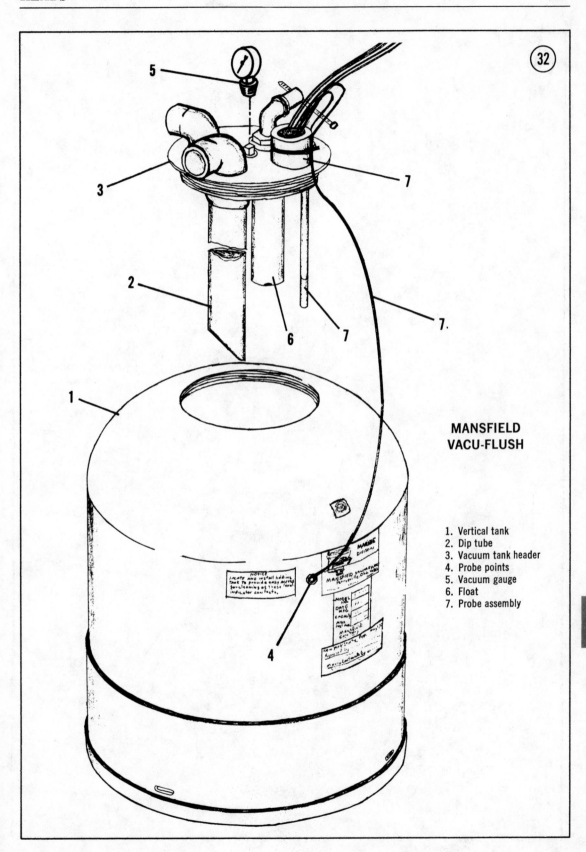

MANSFIELD
VACU-FLUSH

1. Vertical tank
2. Dip tube
3. Vacuum tank header
4. Probe points
5. Vacuum gauge
6. Float
7. Probe assembly

10

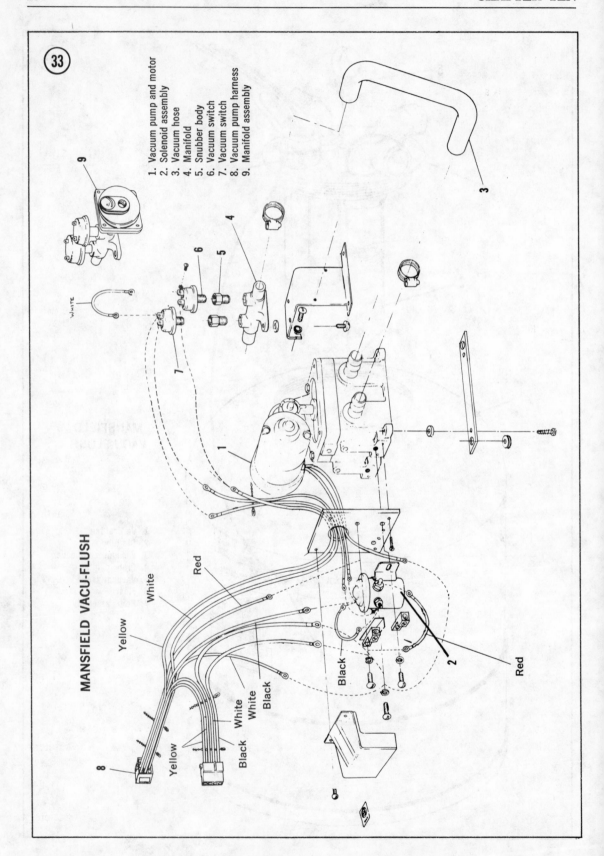

(33)

MANSFIELD VACU-FLUSH

1. Vacuum pump and motor
2. Solenoid assembly
3. Vacuum hose
4. Manifold
5. Snubber body
6. Vacuum switch
7. Vacuum switch
8. Vacuum pump harness
9. Manifold assembly

MANSFIELD 911/912 — M28

This toilet with top discharge holding tank offers a simple method to conform to new anti-pollution legislation. Model 911 — M28 is for use with pressurized water systems. Fresh flushing water comes from boat's water supply. Model 912 — M28 is for use in boats without a pressurized system. A hand-operated pump draws sea or lake water from outside hull. See **Figure 34**. The 912 — M28 should not be connected to the onboard water supply. Both models can be pumped out at dockside pumping stations. See Figure 34 and **Figure 35** for typical installation of systems.

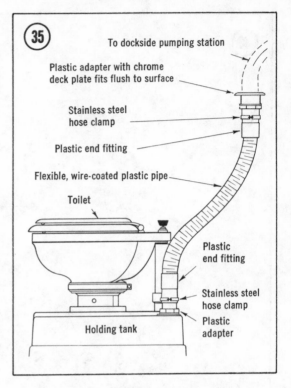

To dockside pumping station
Plastic adapter with chrome deck plate fits flush to surface
Stainless steel hose clamp
Plastic end fitting
Flexible, wire-coated plastic pipe
Toilet
Plastic end fitting
Stainless steel hose clamp
Plastic adapter
Holding tank

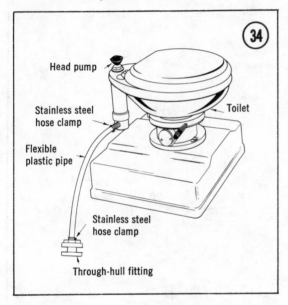

Head pump
Stainless steel hose clamp
Flexible plastic pipe
Toilet
Stainless steel hose clamp
Through-hull fitting

Lay-up

Completely rinse and empty holding tank. On systems with pressurized water, drain onboard water supply and leave fresh water valve to toilet open. Prop toilet ball valve open.

On 912 — M28 models without pressurized water connection, rinse and empty holding tank. When boat is hauled out, operate pump several times to purge residual water in pump and line. Prop toilet ball valve open.

Emptying and Rinsing

1. Connect dockside pump directly to holding tank or through deck fitting if equipped.

2. Turn pump on and empty tank.

3. Fill holding tank with fresh water.

4. Pump tank out.

5. Repeat Steps 3 and 4 as often as necessary.

Maintenance

There is no maintenance other than a thorough cleaning inside and out periodically.

Disassembly/Assembly

Figure 36 shows exploded view of 911/912—M28 toilets.

JENSEN 770E, M

The Jensen 770 is a self-contained, "wet flush," recirculating toilet. Both manual and electric versions are available.

Recharging

1. Lift flush handle and move out of rear detent.

2. Pour one package of Jensen Chemkare, or equivalent, into toilet bowl. Slowly add 3½ gallons of water directly into bowl.

3. Flush toilet until chemical is completely dissolved.

10

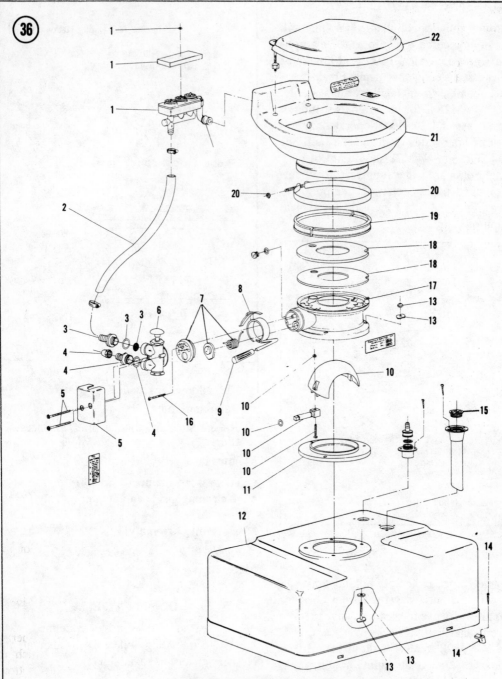

MANSFIELD 911/912 — M28 HEAD

1. Vacuum breaker assembly
2. Supply line
3. Push on hose adaptor assembly
4. Flare nut assembly
5. Valve cover and attaching hardware
6. Water valve
7. Cartridge
8. Flush lever
9. Pedal cover
10. Shaft and ball assembly
11. Base-to-flange seal
12. Tank
13. Floor flange bolt, washer, and nut
14. Hold down clip and screw
15. Plug
16. Valve spacer screw
17. Base assembly
18. Seal assembly
19. Half clamp
20. S.S. clamp ring and nut
21. China bowl
22. Bemis seat and lid assembly

Emptying

Overboard, dockside, or holding tank discharge is possible with the Jensen 770, depending on installation. After emptying, fill tank with fresh water and pump out again to rinse. Recharge unit or prepare for lay-up.

Winterizing

1. Empty and rinse holding tank thoroughly.

2. Recharge in normal manner, except use enough anti-freeze in place of water to protect 8 gallons to temperature range expected. See anti-freeze manufacturer's recommendation.

CAUTION

Use only ethylene glycol base anti-freeze. Do not use alcohol base products.

Lay-up

Empty and thoroughly rinse holding tank. Clean exterior and spray with a disinfectant. Leave unit dry.

Maintenance

No periodic maintenance is necessary other than emptying and cleaning. Occasionally, flush system with a fresh water charge and one cup of Vanish bowl cleaner or cold water detergent. Let stand in tank for 15-30 minutes, then pump out. Rinse tank thoroughly with fresh water.

Disassembly/Assembly—770 Electric

Refer to Figures 37-42. Numbers in parentheses refer to key numbers in figures.

1. Flush Handle (**Figure 37**)

   a. Unscrew and remove retaining screws (1).

   b. Lift off handle (2).

2. Access Cover (Figure 37)

   a. Remove flush handle (Step 1).

   b. Unscrew 6 screws (3) holding access cover (4).

   c. Carefully remove access cover to avoid damaging gasket (5).

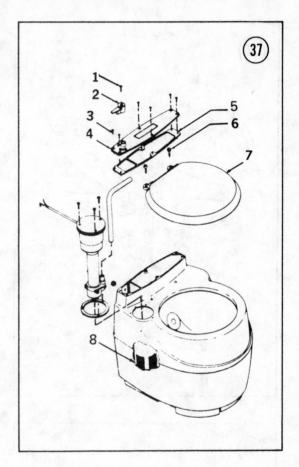

3. Electric Switch (**Figure 38**)

   a. Disconnect toilet from power supply.

   b. Remove flush handle (Step 1).

   c. Remove access cover (Step 2).

   d. Carefully unscrew nut (3) on top of the switch (4).

   e. Lift switch up and off pins.

   f. Slide off cable terminals (5 and 6). It is not necessary to unscrew wire nut (7).

   g. When reinstalling switch, depress operating button located on side of switch to clean cam as switch approaches bottom of pins.

4. Electric Pump Assembly (**Figure 39**)

   a. Disconnect toilet from power supply.

   b. Remove flush handle (Step 1).

   c. Remove access cover (Step 2).

   d. Remove 3 screws (1) securing motor and pump assembly to top of toilet.

10

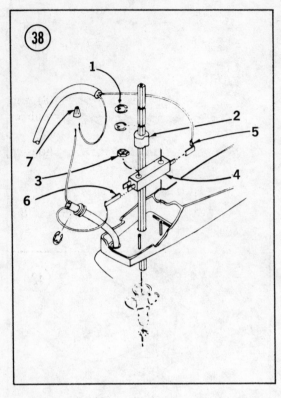

e. Lift motor cover (2) and remove wire nuts (3) from motor leads (4) and cable (5).

f. Pull cable (5) from inside toilet switch housing (Figure 38) until the cable slips through hole inside of motor housing (6).

g. Lift motor housing (6) out far enough to disconnect pump assembly from hose (7) in toilet. Remove gasket (8).

5. Disassembly Procedures for Pump and Motor Assembly (Figure 39)

a. Remove 4 screws (9) from bottom of pump housing (10).

b. Remove the impeller blade (11) from the pump shaft (12).

NOTE: *Pump shaft (12) may separate from motor (4) while impeller blade is being removed. Do not attempt to remove pump shaft (12) before removing motor mounting nuts (13) and motor (4).*

c. Remove motor mounting nuts (13) and motor (4). If pump shaft (12) separates from motor (4), slide it out through motor housing (6).

6. Assembly Procedures for Pump and Motor Assembly (Figure 39)

a. Install coupling (14) midway onto motor shaft and install knurled end of pump shaft (12) into coupling (14).

b. Install motor (4) and pump shaft (12) into housing (6) and secure with washers and motor mounting nuts (13).

NOTE: *If difficulty is experienced in attempting to guide the pump shaft (12) through the pump base (10), a length of string may be put through the base (10) and tied to the shaft (12).*

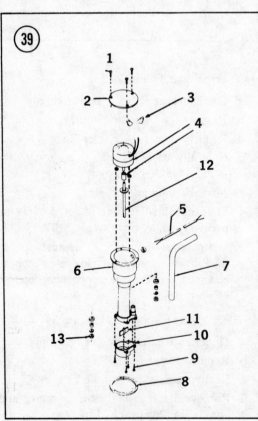

c. Install the impeller blade (11) on the pump shaft (12).

d. Install bottom of pump housing (10). *Don't overtighten screws (9).*

7. Pump Filter (Figure 37)

Remove pump assembly (Figure 39) as per Step 4 and lift out filter (8).

8. Stopper Arm Assembly (**Figure 40**)

   a. Remove E-ring (15) holding stopper arm link (16) to stopper arm shaft (17).

   b. Remove one E-ring (18) holding stopper arm pivot shaft (19) and slide shaft out of assembly (20).

   c. Remove assembly from tank.

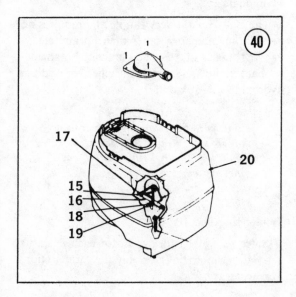

9. Operating Shaft (**Figure 41**)

   a. Remove flush handle (Step 1), access cover (Step 2). It is not necessary to remove E-rings or cam (Figure 38) to remove the shaft.

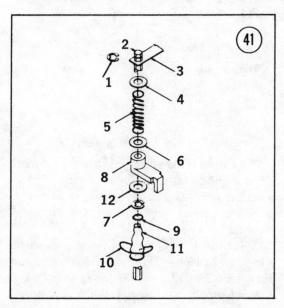

   b. Remove E-ring (1) from shaft (2).

   c. Lift off link (3).

   d. Lift off washer (4), spring (5), and second washer (6).

   e. Remove E-ring (7).

   f. Push shaft (2) through bearing (8) and washer (12), remove O-ring (9), rubber band (10), and cot (11).

   g. Push the shaft through the toilet housing and remove.

10. Toilet Seat (**Figure 42**)

   Remove 2 screws (6) from the rear of the seat assembly (7).

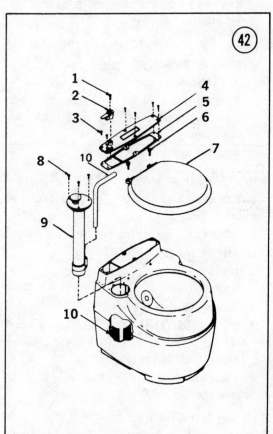

Disassembly/Assembly—770 Manual

   Refer to Figures 37-42. Numbers in parthentheses refer to key numbers in figures.

1. Flush Handle (Figure 42)

   a. Unscrew and remove retaining screws (1).

   b. Lift off handle (2).

10

2. Access Cover (Figure 42)

 a. Remove flush handle (Step 1).

 b. Unscrew the 6 screws (3) holding the access cover (4).

 c. Carefully remove access cover (4) to avoid damaging gasket (10).

3. Manual Pump Assembly (Figure 42)

 a. Remove 3 screws (7) securing pump assembly (8) to top of toilet.

 b. Lift pump assembly (8) out far enough to disconnect pump.

4. Pump Filter (Figure 42)

 Remove pump assembly (Step 3) and lift out filter (9).

5. Stopper Arm Assembly (Figure 40)

 a. Remove E-ring (15) holding stopper arm link (16) to stopper arm shaft (17).

 b. Remove one E-ring (18) holding stopper arm pivot shaft (19) and slide shaft out of assembly (20).

 c. Remove assembly from tank.

6. Operating Shaft (Figure 41)

 a. Remove flush handle (Step 1), access cover (Step 2).

 b. Remove E-ring (1) from shaft (2).

 c. Lift off link (3).

 d. Lift off washer (4), spring (5), second washer (6).

 e. Remove E-ring (7).

 f. Push shaft (2) through bearing (8) and washer (12), remove O-ring (9), rubber band (10) and cot (11).

 g. Push the shaft through the toilet housing and remove.

7. Toilet Seat (Figure 37)

 a. Remove 2 screws (6) from rear of seat assembly (7).

BALL-HEAD

The unit operates by the variation of air pressure in the bowl for flushing and refilling. Pressure variations are created by the ball-like diaphragm mounted on the cover. A vented handle breaks the vacuum for easy opening. The hinged cover is secured by a stainless steel lock and an airtight seal with the bowl. A spring-loaded valve maintains water in the bowl and prevents flooding when heeled.

Maintenance

The Ball-Head is very simple and requires no periodic maintenance other than normal cleaning. It is made of ABS (acrylonitrile-butadiene-styrene) resin; detergents, bleaches, or sodium hydroxide will do no harm.

CAUTION
Do not use the following chemicals as they are solvents of ABS resin: ethylene dichloride, methyl-ethyl-ketone, acetone, and ethyl acetate.

Winterizing and Lay-up

Since seawater is drawn in for each flush, no separate winterizing or lay-up preparations are necessary.

Typical Installations

The Ball-Head can discharge straight down through a hole in the hull, through an existing seacock or through-hull fitting into a holding tank, or into a chlorinator such as the Raritan. See **Figure 43**.

Disassembly/Assembly

Figure 44 is an exploded view of the Ball-Head.

RARITAN CROWN HEAD

The Crown Head comes in a Standard Model for mounting above or up to one foot below waterline (measured from outlet connection). A Deep Draft model may be mounted as much as 5 feet below the waterline.

A built-in macerator chops waste products into a fluid which is easily decontaminated and discharged. Fluid from a decontaminant tank is metered into the bowl along with the flush water.

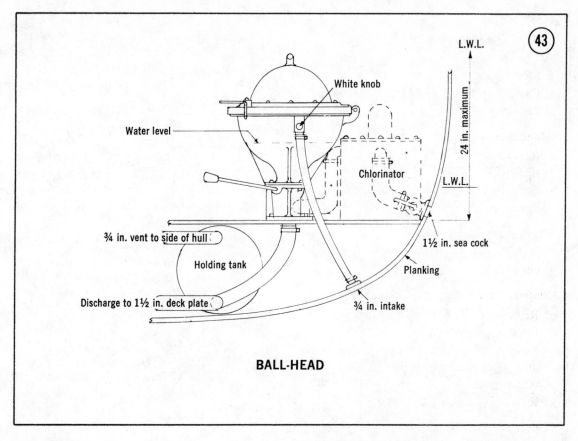

43

L.W.L.

White knob

Water level

24 in. maximum

Chlorinator

L.W.L.

¾ in. vent to side of hull

1½ in. sea cock

Holding tank

Planking

Discharge to 1½ in. deck plate

¾ in. intake

BALL-HEAD

Charging

1. Pour 2 ounces of Raritan Concentrate (decontaminant) into decontaminant tank.

2. Fill tank with fresh water.

Maintenance

No periodic maintenance is required other than replenishing the decontaminant tank as necessary and periodic cleaning of the unit.

Lay-up

1. Drain decontaminant tank completely by inverting it and rinsing it out.

2. Rinse the "syphon" assembly (CH-136, **Figure 45**) and drain.

3. Close inlet seacock. Remove inlet hose from pump assembly.

4. Temporarily attach a short length of hose to the inlet pump where the permanent hose was removed. Pour about 1 quart of permanent type anti-freeze (ethyl glycol) into a coffee can or other container. Let the motor run until the color of the fluid running down from the rim of the bowl indicates the anti-freeze has circulated and is being discharged through the outlet seacock. *Do not use anti-leak anti-freeze.*

5. Close the outlet seacock.

6. Let the anti-freeze remain in the Crown Head until the boat is recommissioned.

7. When danger of freezing is past, reconnect the inlet hose and open both seacocks.

8. Replenish the decontaminant tank, replace the "syphon." Start the motor and flush out the anti-freeze. The head is now recommissioned.

Troubleshooting

Refer to Figure 45, the exploded view, for part numbers, e.g., CH-16.

1. *Poor water flow, especially at the front of the bowl. Water does not accumulate appreciably in the bowl itself.*—An empty decontaminant tank or low voltage. Check the tank first to see

10

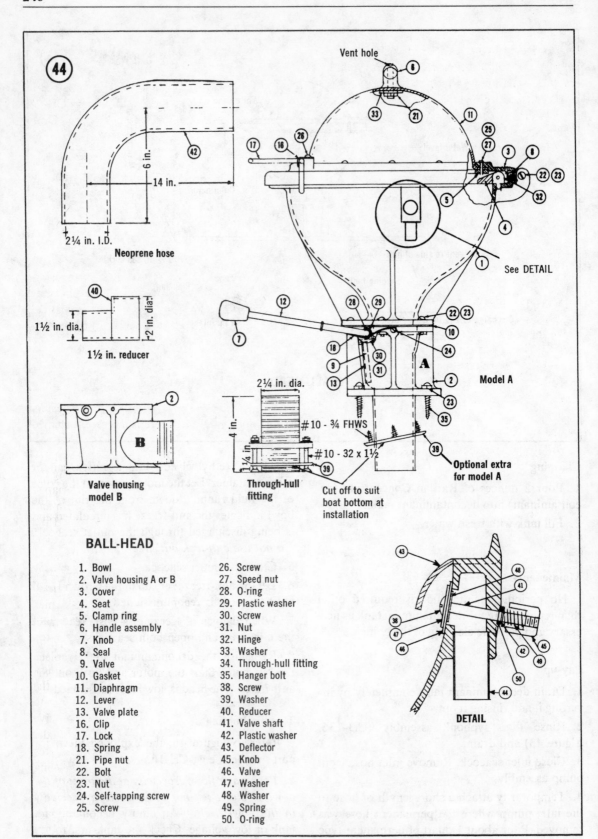

Neoprene hose

1½ in. reducer

Valve housing
model B

Through-hull
fitting

Cut off to suit
boat bottom at
installation

Optional extra
for model A

Model A

See DETAIL

DETAIL

BALL-HEAD

1. Bowl
2. Valve housing A or B
3. Cover
4. Seat
5. Clamp ring
6. Handle assembly
7. Knob
8. Seal
9. Valve
10. Gasket
11. Diaphragm
12. Lever
13. Valve plate
16. Clip
17. Lock
18. Spring
21. Pipe nut
22. Bolt
23. Nut
24. Self-tapping screw
25. Screw

26. Screw
27. Speed nut
28. O-ring
29. Plastic washer
30. Screw
31. Nut
32. Hinge
33. Washer
34. Through-hull fitting
35. Hanger bolt
38. Screw
39. Washer
40. Reducer
41. Valve shaft
42. Plastic washer
43. Deflector
45. Knob
46. Valve
47. Washer
48. Washer
49. Spring
50. O-ring

if it is full. Low voltage will cause trouble if out-let CH-16 is *above* the water line. Check voltage *only at the motor terminals while the motor is running*. Minimum voltage should be 11.5, 23, or 30 volts respectively, for a 12-, 24-, or 32-volt installation. If the values are below minimum figures, check battery condition. Look for resist-ance in the circuit breakers or fuses. Check wire sizes all the way back to the batteries. Make sure there is no voltage drop at the switch. Look for loose or corroded electrical connections.

2. *A persistant and obnoxious odor that is ema-nating from the bowl*—Clogging of the toilet in-let seacock by eel grass that has worked its way through the pump, lodged in the passageway on the inside of the rim of the bowl, and is decaying there. You may see little black specks of this eel grass, looking like bits of tobacco, flowing down the sides of the bowl from the wash holes under the rim. The immediate cure is to connect a pressure hose to the elbow CH-50 and thoroughly flush it out. Another method is to flush with a cleaning solution. Disconnect the inlet hose, connect another short hose to the pump, and allow the pump to suck up a solution of Drāno or equivalent from a bucket. To pre-vent recurrence, install a strainer on the inlet line. Be sure *in advance* that strong chemicals will not damage internal parts or lines.

3. *The decontaminant tank empties even when no one has used the head*—The ball check valve CH-12 is not holding. Clean out as described for eel grass, etc., under Step 1.

4. *Water leaks from under the end bell CH-15* —This can only come from five possible sources.

a. A leak at the joint between the china bowl and the bronze casting. Gently tighten the nuts CH-41.

b. A leak at the seal between front cover CH-18 and end bell CH-15. Inspect the O-ring CH-25 for damage. Replace with new O-ring, using grease to help re-assemble.

c. Water comes from a small hole under the end bell near the motor or under the pump CH-101. Inspection reveals seals CH-24 and/or CH-11 must be replaced. It is not recommended that these seals be replaced

in the field. However, if there is no alterna-tive, follow carefully the procedure out-lined under Step 7.

d. Water comes from under the outlet con-nection CH-16. Tighten the screws CH-28 *very gently*. If CH-16D (Deep Draft Model), tighten the screws snugly.

If you prefer, the entire base unit can be ex-changed for a factory remanufactured unit at low cost. See your Raritan Service Center or write the factory for details.

5. *The unit makes a very loud metallic noise like metal striking metal*—The pivoted arms of the macerator may be striking the notched housing. Or something hard, such as a bobby pin, may have fallen into the bowl and lodged against the macerator. Remove front cover CH-18 and in-spect cavity for foreign objects. Use a ½ in. open end wrench to rotate macerator plate. Slip the wrench over one of the pivoted arms and turn the plate counterclockwise. Note if either of the pivoted arms touches the notched housing. If one does, note that there is a crescent shaped boss on the face of the macerator plate that acts as a stop to keep the pivoted arms from flying out too far. Determine which arm is striking the housing and then spread the crescent shaped boss by striking it lightly with a centerpunch and a hammer. Clearance between the arm and the housing should be about .010-.020 in.

6. *Sometimes motor starts, sometimes it doesn't. Or motor runs sluggishly although voltage meas-ured at the motor is normal*. A motor brush may be hanging up and not contacting the commuta-tor correctly. Remove the name plate on the top of the motor. If the motor does not start, tap the motor housing CH-101 lightly with a ham-mer while the operating switch is on. If the motor then starts, the trouble is most likely to be a stuck brush. It is also likely that excessive arcing of the commutator will be seen. If the motor does not start, disconnect one of the wires to the motor terminals. Holding the operating switch down, note if a slight spark appears when the removed wire is lightly touched to its motor terminal. If there is no spark, one of the brushes is not making contact or the wire is not "hot".

10

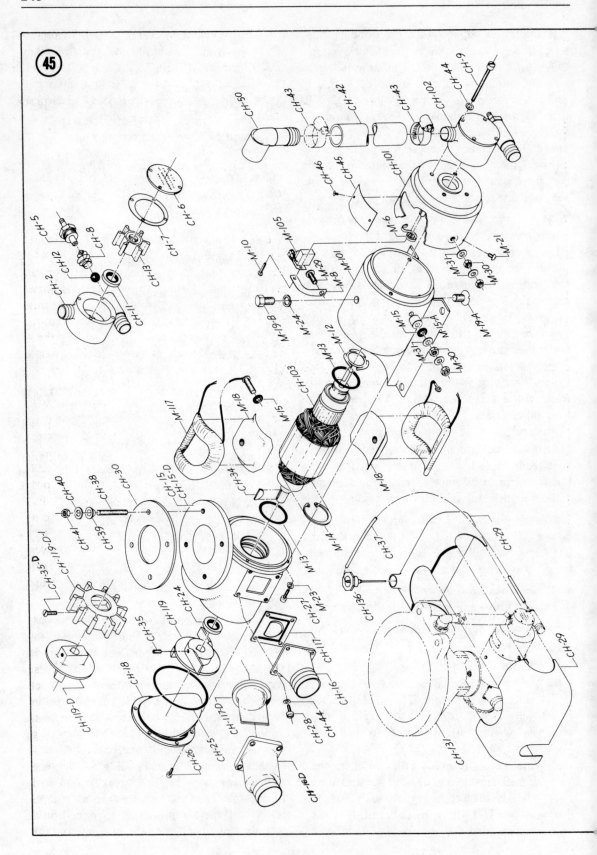

45

RARITAN CROWN HEAD

CH-101	Assembly
CH-2	Pump body
CH-102	Assembly
CH-103	Assembly
CH-5	Metering plug
CH-6	Pump cover plate
CH-7	Pump gasket
CH-8	Check valve spring
CH-9	Pump screw
CH-11	Pump shaft seal
CH-12	Check ball
CH-13	Impeller
CH-15	End bell
CH-15D	End bell
CH-16	Outlet connection
CH-16D	Outlet connection
CH-117	Assembly
CH-117D	Joker valve
CH-18	Front cover
CH-119	Assembly
CH-119D	Macerater plate
CH-119D1	Macerater impeller
CH-24	Macerater shaft seal
CH-25	Front cover O-ring
CH-26	Front cover screws
CH-27	End bell screws
CH-28	Outlet connection screws
CH-29	Shroud
CH-30	Bowl gasket
CH-131	Assembly
CH-32	Standard bowl and seat
CH-32H	Household size bowl and seat
CH-32HC	Household size bowl and seat—color
CH-34	Woodruff key
CH-35	Allen setscrew
CH-35D	Impeller screw
CH-136	Assembly
CH-37	Siphon tube
CH-38	Bowl studs
CH-39	Bowl rubber washer
CH-40	Bowl washer
CH-41	Bowl stud nuts
CH-42	Hose
CH-43	Hose clamps
CH-44	Fiber washer
CH-45	Name plate
CH-46	Name plate screws
CH-50	Bowl elbow
M-101	Housing assembly
M-105	Assembly
M-6	Brush spring
M-8	Ground strap
M-10	Brush plate screw
M-12	Ball bearing thrust spring
M-13	Ball bearing O-ring
M-14	Ball bearing snap ring
M-15	Fiber flat washer
M-15A	Fiber sleeve
M-117	Assembly
M-18	Pole shoes
M-19A	Pole shoe screw
M-19B	Pole shoe capscrew
M-21	Dome screw
M-23	Lockwasher
M-24	Lockwasher
M-29	Terminal screw
M-30	Terminal nut
M-31	Terminal washer

To check out the latter, lightly and very momentarily touch the loose wire against the other motor terminal. If very bright sparking occurs, the wire is "hot" and the trouble is within the motor. If no sparking occurs, look elsewhere for broken continuity in the circuit.

CAUTION

This method for determining whether a wire is "hot" or not is NOT recommended for higher voltages. A meter should be used by a competent electrician.

The top brush is accessible through the name plate hole and can be checked to see if it slides freely and makes proper contact. If the problem persists, it will be necessary to remove the armature to check out the lower brush. To do this, remove the whole head to a workbench. Remove the pump assembly CH-102 by removing the 4 screws CH-9. Remove 4 screws CH-27. Insert a knife blade between motor housing M-101 and the flange of the end bell CH-15. Separate the two and the armature will come out intact with the end bell. One of the leads from the field coils will be attached to the lower brush by a screw which must be removed. Remove 4 screws M-21. Separate assembly CH-101 from motor housing. Complete inspection of both brushes is now possible. If either brush is sticking, remove it. Put sandpaper on a flat surface and rub the side of the brush (that area which is approximately ⅞ x ⅞ in.) until enough thickness is removed to allow the brush to slide freely in its slot. Check condition of the brush springs and armature commutator.

If it is necessary to turn down the commutator, it must be done by holding the *ball bearing* in a "steady rest" in a lathe. DO NOT attempt to do it by turning the armature between lathe centers. Reassemble CH-101 and M-101. Do not forget to replace the field lead to the brush plate. Again check if the brushes still slide freely in their slots. Push the upper brush up so high that its spring can be pushed down *beside* the brush thus locking it in the up position. Take a stiff wire about 8 in. long (such as a coat hanger) and bend one end into a right angle about 3 in. from the end. Bend the other end about 45° about 1 in. from the end. Insert the 45° end through the

10

oval brush hole which the name plate covers and push the lower brush down.

The armature can now be slid in so that the commutator is past the lower brush. Remove the bent wire and push the armature in all the way. Replace screws CH-27. Move the top brush spring so that its end is in its proper position, i.e., bearing down on top of the brush. The motor should now operate properly. Replace the name plate.

When replacing the pump, carefully check the 5/16 in. armature shaft for burrs, especially where the flat blends in the round portion. With a slight twisting motion, carefully replace the pump housing so as not to damage the seal. Replace the impeller with the chamfered side of the brass insert bushing toward the motor. A small amount of grease on the shaft and inside of the pump housing is helpful. Use silicone grease if the unit will not be put into service immediately.

Put a dab of grease on the cover plate CH-6. Replace the screws, CH-9. It is not necessary to over torque them, remembering that the female threads in CH-101 are plastic and easily stripped by overtightening. If by chance they are stripped, fill the hole with epoxy ("Devcon 5-minute epoxy" does a good job). Let set thoroughly and re-tap 10x32. Make sure that the tap goes in deep enough to accommodate the full length of each screw.

7. *Inspection reveals that either seals CH-24 or CH-11 must be replaced* — The factory recommends exchanging the unit. However, if it is decided to replace seal CH-24 in the field, the following hints and precautions should be observed. To remove the armature from the end bell CH-15, remove snap ring M-14 and set screw CH-35. Access to the latter can be gained through the discharge port where CH-16 attaches. After the seal has been replaced, it is important that great care be taken in reassembling the armature that the key CH-34 is not allowed to damage the seal. Therefore, it is best to insert the key into the armature shaft *after* the shaft has been passed through the seal. This can be done through the discharge port. The macerator plate can be replaced only by lining up the wings with the wide slots top and

bottom in the end bell. In Deep Draft models this is not applicable.

Disassembly/Assembly

Figure 45 shows an exploded view of the Crown Head.

RARITAN COMPACT, PH AND PHE

"COMPACT" and "PH" and "PHE" heads can be mounted above or below the water line. They are equally suitable for use with a holding tank, recirculating system or a flow-through sewage treatment device such as a chlorinator. The use of a vented loop or "swan's neck" on the discharge is common practice with this system, especially in sailboats.

The PHE is an electric version of the PH. In fact, holes are pre-drilled at the factory in PH models to accept electric parts. Conversion is described later in this section.

Conversion To Electric Operation

Raritan PH hand toilets are designed for easy conversion to electric operation, using the Raritan Electric Conversion Kit. The conversion can be made in fifteen minutes by the average person, using basic tools. Fasten the electric drive unit to the drilled pad using the bolts and washers provided. Move the pump handle until the top of the arm aligns with the hole in the handle socket. Insert the arm bolt and tighten the nut. Remove the handle. Back off the arm bolt if it binds. Lubricate moving parts with a few drops of oil.

Maintenance

Very little maintenance is required. Ordinary scouring powders such as Ajax will keep the bowl clean. If for any reason a deodorizer is indicated, use Clorox rather than solvents such as Pine Oil or Lysol. A little Vaseline applied to the piston rod, especially to the "PHE" will prolong the lift of "U" cup seals and gland. A few drops of oil on both ends of the connecting rod of the PHE in fall and spring are recommended. It should never be necessary to add grease to the PHE gear box.

Lay-up and Commissioning

Improper winter lay-up is the major cause of all marine toilet failures.

1. Close inlet seacock. Remove inlet hose from pump housing and temporarily attach a short length of hose to the inlet.

2. Pour about 1 quart of permanent type anti-freeze (do not use anti-leak types) into a coffee can or other container. With the open end of the temporary hose in the container, pump the head until the color of the fluid running down from the rim of the bowl indicates the anti-freeze has circulated and is being discharged through the outlet seacock.

3. Close the outlet seacock.

4. Let the anti-freeze remain in the toilet until it is recommissioned. This method of winterizing protects both the inlet side of the pump and the discharge areas. Simply pouring anti-freeze into the bowl protects only the discharge side. This is why so many marine toilets give trouble in the springtime.

5. When danger of freezing is past, reconnect the inlet hose and open both seacocks.

6. Apply a little Vaseline to the piston rod.

Troubleshooting

NOTE: *It is wise to carry on board a Raritan head repair kit for the model you have. These kits provide all the parts you are apt to use for normal servicing.*

1. *Water accumulates in the bowl faster than it pumps out*—Trash lodged under the outlet flapper. The trash can be cleared by partially or completely closing the inlet valve and continuing to pump. A degree of resistance will be noted in pumping which is normal. After the bowl is cleared of all debris, open the valve again and flush a few strokes to clear the discharge lines.

If the problem persists, the flapper valve in discharge is not seating. It could be squeezed too tight, stretching the hinge, or it could be swollen due to use of certain deodorants. Replace flapper valve. Tighten screws only enough to preclude leaking; overtightening will stretch hinge and prevent proper seating.

2. *Water rises in bowl when boat is dockside. Rim of bowl is below waterline of boat*—Either outlet joker valve is leaking or inlet check valve is leaking. Close first one seacock, then the other, to determine whether water comes in outlet or inlet. If outlet leaks, replace joker valve.

NOTE: *It is a wise precaution to install a vented loop or "swan's neck" in the discharge. This will prevent back syphoning through the discharge if either the joker valve or flapper valve leak.*

If the water comes from the inlet, make sure there is no trash under the inlet check valve. In the "PH" models, an additional stainless steel spring, obtainable from Raritan at no charge, is available for installations considerably below the waterline. It is wise to close the inlet valves when the boat is left unattended.

3. *Water fills up the bowl when the boat is underway*—This is more likely to happen when the head is located far forward. Water pressure due to the speed of the boat unseats the ball check on the inlet (PH model). Raritan provides, on special order, a spring designed to eliminate this problem. As an alternative, a water scoop can be installed backwards on the outside of the hull over the inlet seacock. This will deflect the water pressure. On the "Compact" model, the water scoop will cure the trouble. In any case, it is wise to close the inlet valves when underway, especially in rough water.

4. *Inlet water flow is poor and/or water builds up in bowl. Handle seems to work harder than it should. Trouble does not seem to be due to causes described previously*—In certain areas such as Florida, concrete-like deposits build up in both the inlet and outlet connections and adversely affect all types of marine toilets. This appears to be a type of coral. The only cure is periodic cleaning.

5. *A. persistant and obnoxious odor emanates from the bowl of the head*—Eel grass or other marine vegetation has worked its way through the pump and is lodged in the passageway that is molded in the rim of the bowl. Here it decays and gives off a "rotten egg" smell. Perhaps you will note little black specks that look like tobacco crumbs flowing down the sides of the bowl from

10

the wash holes under the rim. The immediate cure is to connect a garden hose to the spud at the back of the bowl and flush it thoroughly under pressure. Another method is to disconnect the inlet hose and temporarily attach another short hose so that the toilet can suck a strong solution of Drāno from a bucket. Be sure *in advance* that strong chemicals will not damage internal parts or lines. To prevent recurrence, we advise installing a strainer on the inlet line.

Another remote possibility for this odor is that the inlet connection is on the same side of the boat as the discharge and so near it that some of the effluent is actually being drawn back into the inlet. In systems that, due to stringent anti-pollution laws, use recirculating water, a deodorant as recommended by the manufacturer of the recirculating device *must* be used.

6. *On the "PHE" when operated electrically, the pump works very slowly and the motor labors—* This is due almost always to low voltage, especially in 12-volt models. Check voltage with a meter by baring wire close to motor (2 in.). Voltage should not be less than 11.5 volts when the motor is running. Other voltages should not show more than a 10% drop. If voltage drop is excessive, check if wiring and fuses conform to those recommended in the table. Check operating switch for adequate capacity. For 12-volt models, switch should be rated for 30 amps or more; 32-volt and 115-volt models require a switch rated for 10 amps. Look for corroded connections, especially at fuse clips. See that piston rod is lubricated. Disconnect connecting rod and check if pump operates freely when hand pumped.

7. *Water squirts up piston rod when pumped—* Seal is leaking. Replace seal, make sure retaining washer is replaced evenly and just snug, not tight.

8. *Changing the water height in the bowl—* Some people prefer to have the bowl retain some water after flushing. Others prefer that practically all the water be pumped out so that it will not slop and splash when heeled over in a seaway. As shipped from the factory, very little

water will remain in the bowl under normal conditions. To retain water in the bowl, have your boatyard install a vented loop in discharge hose.

Disassembly/Assembly

Figures 46-48 show exploded views of the Raritan PH and PHE toilets.

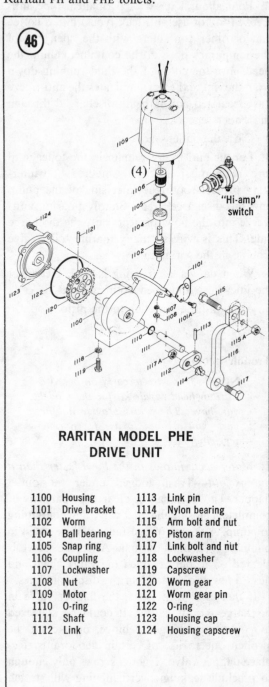

RARITAN MODEL PHE DRIVE UNIT

1100	Housing	1113	Link pin
1101	Drive bracket	1114	Nylon bearing
1102	Worm	1115	Arm bolt and nut
1104	Ball bearing	1116	Piston arm
1105	Snap ring	1117	Link bolt and nut
1106	Coupling	1118	Lockwasher
1107	Lockwasher	1119	Capscrew
1108	Nut	1120	Worm gear
1109	Motor	1121	Worm gear pin
1110	O-ring	1122	O-ring
1111	Shaft	1123	Housing cap
1112	Link	1124	Housing capscrew

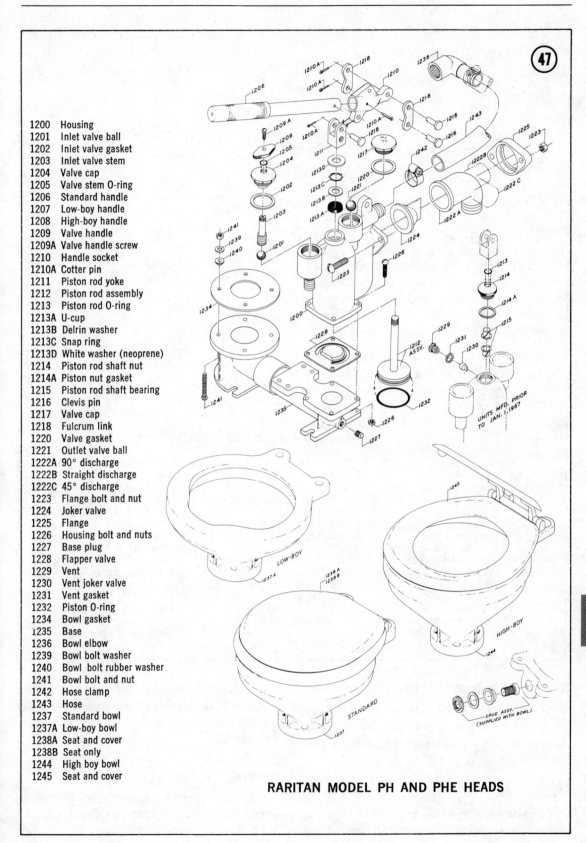

1200　Housing
1201　Inlet valve ball
1202　Inlet valve gasket
1203　Inlet valve stem
1204　Valve cap
1205　Valve stem O-ring
1206　Standard handle
1207　Low-boy handle
1208　High-boy handle
1209　Valve handle
1209A　Valve handle screw
1210　Handle socket
1210A　Cotter pin
1211　Piston rod yoke
1212　Piston rod assembly
1213　Piston rod O-ring
1213A　U-cup
1213B　Delrin washer
1213C　Snap ring
1213D　White washer (neoprene)
1214　Piston rod shaft nut
1214A　Piston nut gasket
1215　Piston rod shaft bearing
1216　Clevis pin
1217　Valve cap
1218　Fulcrum link
1220　Valve gasket
1221　Outlet valve ball
1222A　90° discharge
1222B　Straight discharge
1222C　45° discharge
1223　Flange bolt and nut
1224　Joker valve
1225　Flange
1226　Housing bolt and nuts
1227　Base plug
1228　Flapper valve
1229　Vent
1230　Vent joker valve
1231　Vent gasket
1232　Piston O-ring
1234　Bowl gasket
1235　Base
1236　Bowl elbow
1239　Bowl bolt washer
1240　Bowl bolt rubber washer
1241　Bowl bolt and nut
1242　Hose clamp
1243　Hose
1237　Standard bowl
1237A　Low-boy bowl
1238A　Seat and cover
1238B　Seat only
1244　High boy bowl
1245　Seat and cover

RARITAN MODEL PH AND PHE HEADS

10

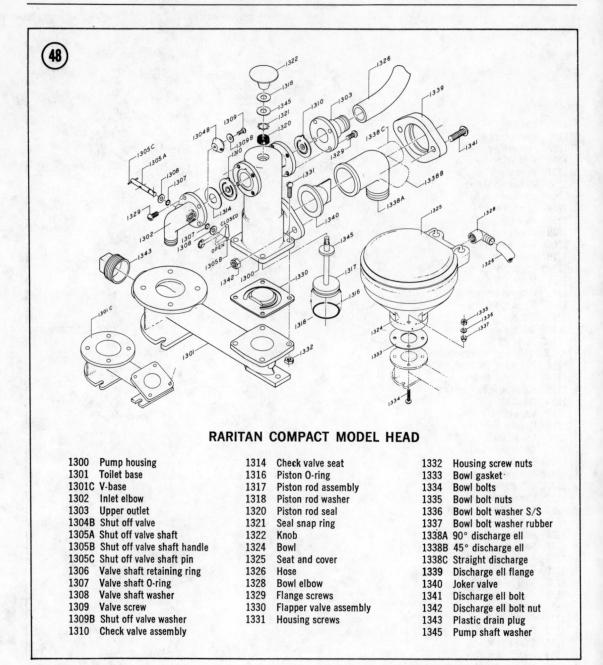

RARITAN COMPACT MODEL HEAD

1300	Pump housing	1314	Check valve seat	1332	Housing screw nuts
1301	Toilet base	1316	Piston O-ring	1333	Bowl gasket
1301C	V-base	1317	Piston rod assembly	1334	Bowl bolts
1302	Inlet elbow	1318	Piston rod washer	1335	Bowl bolt nuts
1303	Upper outlet	1320	Piston rod seal	1336	Bowl bolt washer S/S
1304B	Shut off valve	1321	Seal snap ring	1337	Bowl bolt washer rubber
1305A	Shut off valve shaft	1322	Knob	1338A	90° discharge ell
1305B	Shut off valve shaft handle	1324	Bowl	1338B	45° discharge ell
1305C	Shut off valve shaft pin	1325	Seat and cover	1338C	Straight discharge
1306	Valve shaft retaining ring	1326	Hose	1339	Discharge ell flange
1307	Valve shaft O-ring	1328	Bowl elbow	1341	Discharge ell bolt
1308	Valve shaft washer	1329	Flange screws	1342	Discharge ell bolt nut
1309	Valve screw	1330	Flapper valve assembly	1343	Plastic drain plug
1309B	Shut off valve washer	1331	Housing screws	1345	Pump shaft washer
1310	Check valve assembly				

HOLDING TANKS

Holding tanks are usually made from fiberglass and range greatly in capacity—a few gallons to 30 or more in large cruising boats with multiple heads.

Maintenance

No maintenance is required on holding tanks other than flushing after emptying and occasional checks to be sure that all fastenings are secure. Various chemicals are available at trailer supply stores to control odors and help break down solids.

Emptying

The method of emptying depends on the rest of the system. See sections on toilets for emptying and rinsing procedures.

Flexible Holding Tanks

A number of flexible holding tanks are available. See **Figure 49**. These may be added to existing systems with through-hull discharge to comply with new legislation. They may also be used to extend capacity. The main advantage in them is the ability to put them in nearly any available space without major alterations to the boat.

RARITAN CHLORINATOR

The chlorinator is a miniature sewage treatment plant for use aboard small pleasure craft. See **Figure 50**. A macerator finely chops solid waste so that chlorine in the system can immediately attack and decompose it.

The chlorinator uses readily available household, 5¾ % sodium hypoclorite solution ("Clorox") to destroy bacteria and decompose waste.

Maintenance

Very little maintenance is required. The most important care needed is to replenish the "Clorox" supply as depleted. Always carry a spare bottle on board.

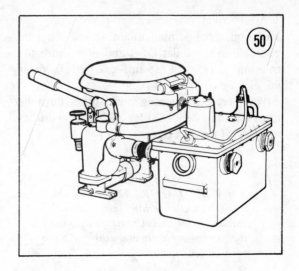

Properly used, the chlorinator will never require cleaning out. The primary cause of clogging is too short maceration time and consequent inability of chlorine to decompose solids.

Lay-up and Recommissioning

Prepare toilet for lay-up as described in previous sections. If your toilet is not listed, follow manufacturer's instructions or pick a toilet in this book which works on the same principles as yours.

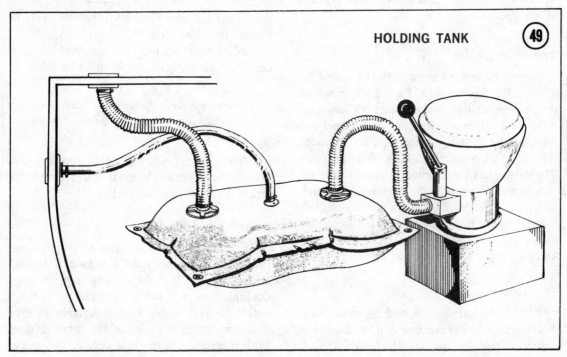

HOLDING TANK

10

After toilet has been prepared, pour at least 3 quarts of permanent anti-freeze (ethylene glycol) into the toilet bowl and pump into the chlorinator. (Do not use anti-leak types.) *Never use alcohol or kerosene.*

When recommissioning in the spring, flush the toilet the equivalent of at least 10 normal flushes to expel *all* the anti-freeze.

> ### WARNING
> *It is VERY IMPORTANT to do this BEFORE connecting the "Clorox" bottle. The chemical reaction between sodium hypochlorite and ethylene glycol can generate heat.*

Disassembly/Assembly

Figure 51 is an exploded view of chlorinator.

LER RECIRCULATOR

The recirculator is a specially designed holding tank which filters solids and feeds decontaminated liquid waste back to the toilet for flushing. An initial charge of 3 gallons fresh water provides 70-100 flushes and a total tank capacity of 8.5 gallons.

Typical Installation

Figures 52 and 53 show typical installations of the LER Recirculator. Figure 52 shows the simplest installation, while Figure 53 shows addition of 2 valves for convenience. Valve 1 permits normal flushing action to draw seawater through toilet into tank for convenient charging. The valve must be returned to recirculate position to prevent overfilling and consequent backup of waste. Valve 2 permits selection of dockside pump-out or through-hull discharge. Variations are possible by omitting either of the valves.

Maintenance

Since the recirculator is nothing more than a holding tank, no preventive maintenance is required except for rinsing. The unit should be

rinsed each time it is emptied. Occasionally, back-flushing can be used to clean interior screen. To do this, disconnect hoses between recirculator and toilet. Connect shore water source to intake fitting on brass plate and collect outflow from top connection in large container. See **Figure 54**. Dump contents into permanent toilet, not overboard.

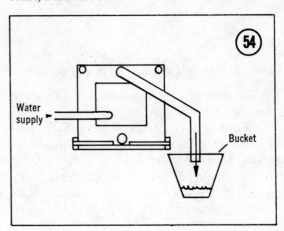

Charging

Charge recirculator with 3 gallons of water after emptying and rinsing. There are 3 methods.
1. Add to toilet and bowl and flush into tank.
2. Fill through discharge deck fitting.
3. If installed as in Figure 53, the valve may be turned to admit seawater when the toilet is flushed. The valve must be returned to recirculate position when tank is about 1/3 full.

> ### CAUTION
> *Never fill tank through vent line. The unrelieved pressure could possibly burst the tank.*

After charging, add one package or bottle of deodorizer specifically made for recirculating toilets. Flush it into the tank.

Emptying and Rinsing

The LER Recirculator can be emptied and rinsed like any other holding tank and depends on installation. If a deck fitting is provided, a dockside pumping station can pump the waste out. Add fresh water as if recharging to rinse tank and pump that out in the same manner. With a separate pump installed, the waste can

RARITAN CHLORINATOR

2001	Tank	2022	Flange nuts	2027	Strap screws
2002	Cover	2023	Flange bolts	2028	Hi-amp switch
2003	Neoprene seal	2024	Air vent	2029	Plugs
2004	Cover screws	2025	Air vent valve	2030	Inlet-outlet
2005	Cover nuts	2026	Bottle strap	2031	Seal
2006	Cover washers				
2007	Motor				
2009	Motor screws				
2010	Motor washers				
2011	Motor lockwashers				
2012	Bearing				
2013	Bearing screws				
2014	Blade				
2015	Blade lockwasher				
2016	Blade screw				
2017	Chlorine syphon				
2018	Tubing				
2019	Connector				
2020	Joker valve				
2021	Housing and flange				

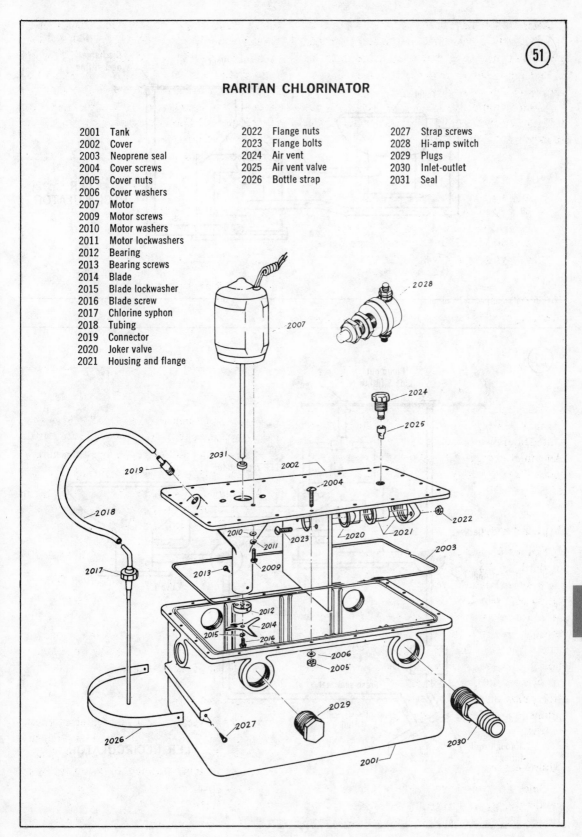

10

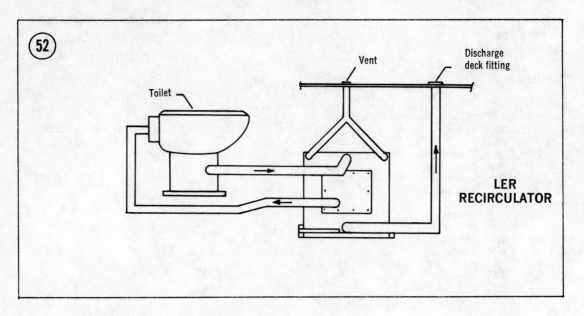

LER RECIRCULATOR

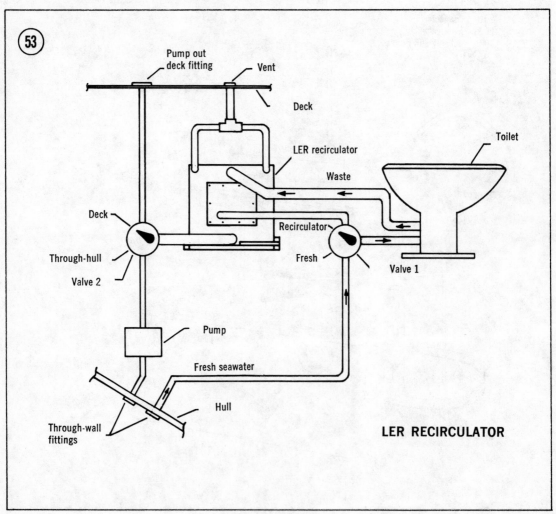

LER RECIRCULATOR

be pumped overboard out a through-hull fitting (if legal).

Winterizing

Empty and rinse as described previously. Add sufficient anti-freeze instead of water to protect 8.5 gallons to temperature range expected. Follow anti-freeze manufacturer's intructions.

CAUTION

Use ethylene glycol base anti-freeze only. Do not use alcohol or anti-leak products.

Lay-up

Empty and thoroughly rinse recirculator. Leave unit dry.

10

CHAPTER ELEVEN

MARINE ELECTRONICS

Marine communications gear is impossible to repair without specialized training and skills. In fact, it is illegal to do anything to a transmitter which could affect its operation.

What goes on inside the "black box" must, therefore, remain a mystery. But external connections to the power source and the antenna are accessible to the owner. He can and should acquaint himself with the installation so that he can keep at least that much of the system in good working order.

This chapter shows typical installations for VHF, SSB communication equipment, and navigation equipment such as RDF's, radar, and omni. The chapter describes a simple preventive maintenance routine for all this gear. In addition, some troubleshooting hints are described to help find common troubles external to the unit itself. Finally, simple repairs are described including how to make proper solder connections.

TYPICAL INSTALLATION

Each installation varies in detail but each consists of a transceiver (VHF or SSB), RG-8/U transmission line, antenna, and power cord. See **Figure 1**.

The power cord usually contains an in-line fuse holder. Fuse size depends on the unit and

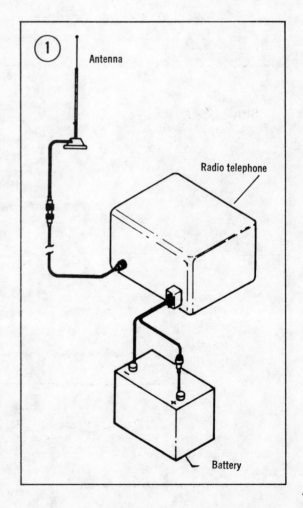

must be determined from the manufacturer's literature.

The VHF antenna is mounted as high as possible and clear of metal objects. Effective range of a VHF transmitter depends on the height of the transmitting and receiving antennas. The higher your antenna, the farther you can communicate. Most antennas have a small length of coaxial cable permanently attached and terminated with a male connector. Since the coaxial transmission line also uses a male connector, a special coupler must be used. See **Figure 2**. This connection should be securely taped with several layers of waterproof vinyl tape or covered thoroughly with silicone sealant. Otherwise, exposure to salt atmosphere will corrode the connections and permit water to seep under the outer vinyl jacket.

A single side band antenna may also be a whip mounted near the mast head like the VHF antenna. Some installations, however, use a wire antenna. Often the backstay is insulated from the mast and hull and used as an antenna. See **Figure 3**.

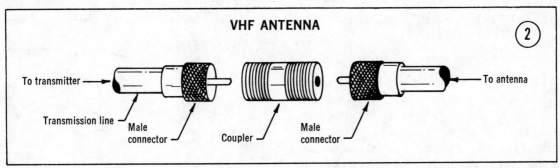

VHF ANTENNA

2

To transmitter — Transmission line — Male connector — Coupler — Male connector — To antenna

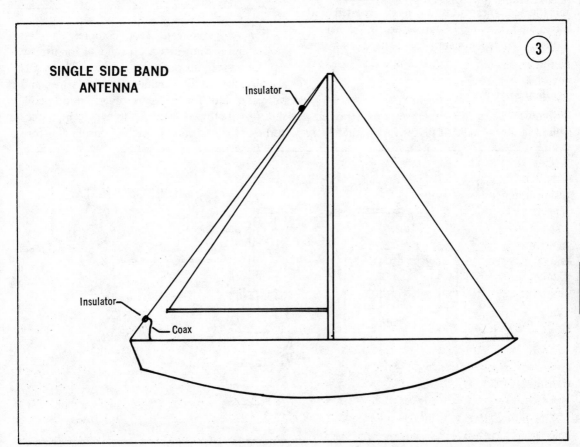

SINGLE SIDE BAND ANTENNA

3

Insulator

Insulator — Coax

11

Almost without exception, RG-8/U antenna lead is recommended over the smaller diameter RG-58/U. The reason is simple. All coaxial lines attenuate the transmitted signal to some extent, i.e., not all the power leaving the transmitter reaches the antenna. However, at marine frequencies, RG-58/U wastes more than twice as much power as RG-8/U. This loss also occurs when receiving; less of the signal gathered by the antenna reaches the receiver, making reception more difficult with RG-58/U.

For short runs, less than 20 feet, either RG-58/U or RG-8/U may be used, as losses are small. For longer runs, use only RG-8/U.

NOISE SUPPRESSION IN RECEIVING EQUIPMENT

Man-made interference may be generated in gasoline engine ignition systems, voltage generating systems, and other electrical devices. This will be heard from the radio telephone speaker as popping, whining, hissing, or crackling. In most cases, these noises can be isolated and eliminated. Common sources are listed below, along with recommendations for curing the trouble.

Ignition System

Ignition noise usually appears as a popping sound in the speaker. It disappears immediately when the engine is shut off. This type interference can be reduced by installing resistor-type spark plugs and a suppressor between the coil and distributor. Also, install a 0.1 μfd coaxial capacitor (see **Figure 4**) in series with primary lead to coil from ignition switch. These are available from any marine or automotive parts distributor. Do not put it in series with secondary lead between coil and distributor. See **Figure 5**. Finally, make sure the ignition coil is mounted directly to the engine. Clean away paint so that there is a good electrical connection between both of them.

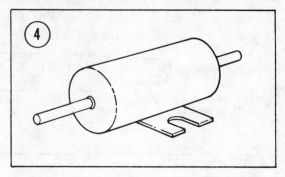

For very stubborn cases, complete ignition noise suppression kits are available for use on both inboard and outboard engines. These kits usually consist of shielded ignition wires and special shields for the spark plugs, ignition coil, and distributor. However, the engine manufacturer or boat dealer must be consulted before

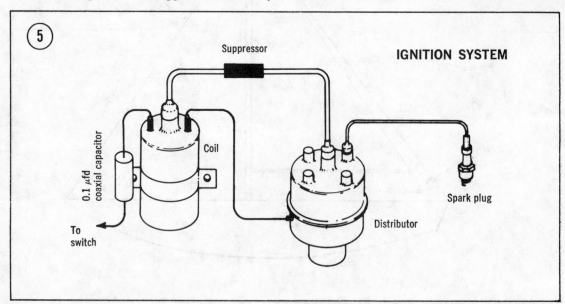

using these kits. Other specialized kits available for inboard engines contain a copper or bronze screen that is used to line the entire engine compartment or special pan-type metal shields that bolt directly to the engine.

Charging System

Noise from the alternator or generator is usually a high-pitched whine. When the ignition switch is turned off, the noise persists for a short time until the engine actually stops turning. A 0.5 μfd coaxial capacitor in series with the armature lead usually cures the trouble. See **Figure 6**. Make sure that contact areas between capacitor and alternator/generator frame are clean, and the capacitor is firmly mounted. If more suppression is required, install copper braided shield over field and armature leads between alternator/generator and voltage regulator. Securely ground both ends of braid.

Voltage regulator noise may be a ragged, rasping sound. Like alternator/generator noise, it persists for a short time after ignition is switched off. Install a 0.1-0.25 μfd coaxial capacitor in series with battery lead to voltage regulator. See Figure 6. Since alternator/generator whine is usually present also, install the other parts shown in Figure 6. Do not install a capacitor in series with the field lead.

If capacitors do not eliminate voltage regulator noise, replace the regulator with a solid state regulator.

Tachometers

Some electronic tachometers cause interference. To identify this source, disconnect tachometer from distributor. If the noise stops, the tachometer is causing it. Replace wire between tachometer and distributor with a shielded lead. Connect distributor end of the shield to ground.

Instrumentation

Noise generated by engine instruments is usually a hissing or crackling sound. Gauges employing rheostats are most likely to produce trouble. A low-pitched clicking sound is generally caused by the oil pressure sender. The clicking rate will vary as the oil pressure varies with engine speed. The offending gauge or gauges can be isolated by disconnecting the hot leads from the gauges and then reconnecting the leads, one at a time, to their respective gauge. After the lead is reconnected, jar the gauge. If noise is observed, connect a 0.25-0.50 μfd capacitor between the hot lead and ground. See **Figure 7**.

All sensitive electronic equipment is subject to interference from ignition systems, motors, and faulty connections. Depth indicators show interference in the form of erratic flashes around the dial. Reduction of interference is accomplished by bonding all electrical grounds with metal fittings that are in contact with the water.

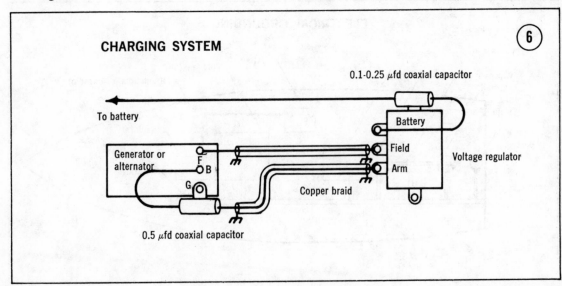

CHARGING SYSTEM ⑥

0.1-0.25 μfd coaxial capacitor

To battery

Battery

Field

Generator or alternator

F
B
G

Arm

Voltage regulator

Copper braid

0.5 μfd coaxial capacitor

11

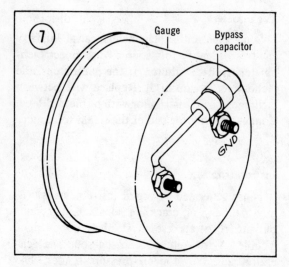

See **Figure 8**. Bonding straps are made of one inch wide No. 20 gauge copper. These straps interconnect all metal fittings and ignition grounds. Secure the bonding straps under a screw of the fitting, making sure that the metal under the screw is brightened for a good electrical connection and coated with grease to prevent future corrosion.

PREVENTIVE MAINTENANCE

Marine equipment is operated in a comparatively hostile environment. Not only must it operate in extremes of hot and cold, it must also contend with a humid, corrosive (salt) atmosphere. Furthermore, engine vibration and sea conditions subject the equipment to vibration and mechanical shock. That they work at all is cause for wonder.

To help minimize troubles caused by the environment, the following procedure should be performed periodically (once a month during the season, for example). Also, use it to prepare for any cruise in which proper equipment operation is vital.

1. Check that all connectors, plugs, and terminals are securely fastened to the instrument. Check for fraying or broken wires.

2. Check power connections at battery. Make sure that they are clean and tight. Service the battery as described in Chapter Seven.

3. Unscrew coaxial connector from instrument. Check both connectors for corrosion; clean if necessary.

4. Check resistance between center conductor and outer conductor. It should measure infinity.

5. Make certain that antenna mounting hardware is tight.

6. Tighten all equipment mounting screws.

7. Perform operational check of equipment as described later.

On a less regular basis, e.g., prior to yearly recommissioning, the following maintenance should be performed.

1. Have qualified FCC licensed electronic technician check the following.

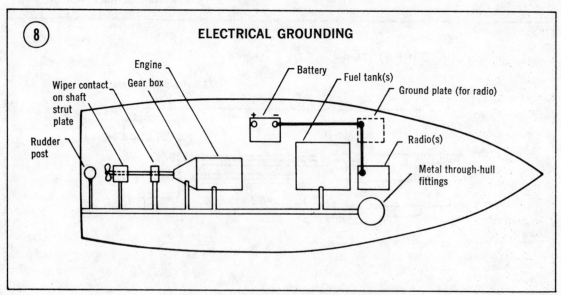

ELECTRICAL GROUNDING

a. Interior of equipment for loose connections and corrosion.

b. Performance of receiver (sensitivity) and transmitter (power output).

c. Condition of antenna relay.

d. Antenna "reflected" power.

e. Transmitter frequency and deviation.

2. Have electrical charging system checked. Excessive voltage output can damage electrical equipment.

Operational Check (Radiotelephone)

1. Turn equipment on following manufacturer's instructions.

2. Select any inactive channel.

3. Turn volume control to comfortable level.

4. Turn squelch control until noise from the speaker stops.

5. Select weather channel or any other active channel. Make sure reception is clear and undistorted.

6. Select local public correspondence channel. See **Figure 9** for closest one.

7. Call operator and ask for radio check. This service is available to anyone. Registration with telephone company is not necessary. The procedure is described below.

Radio Check Calling Procedure

It is not necessary to be registered with the telephone company to request a simple radio check and no charge is made. Of course, you must have a valid station license and operator's permit to operate the transmitter.

1. Select local public correspondence channel. See Figure 9 for closest one.

2. Ensure that the channel is not in use.

3. When clear, operate transmitter and say "Marine operator. This is (call sign and name of vessel)."

4. Wait for reply. If there is no reply, call again after 2 minutes.

5. When marine operator answers, say "This is (call sign and name of vessel). Please give me a radio check." If everything is OK, the operator will say something like "loud and clear." If there

is any problem such as weak signal, distortion, etc., the operator will say so; have it checked by a licensed technician.

6. After radio check, say "This is (call sign and name of vessel). Out."

SOLDERING

Several repairs to marine electronic systems require soldering. Good solder joints are extremely important when working with electronic equipment.

The same principles apply regardless of what is being soldered.

1. Use 60/40 rosin core solder only. Never use acid-core solder for electrical connections; acid-core solder is corrosive and the joint will fail in a short time.

2. Use no more heat than necessary to get the solder to flow smoothly. Too little heat produces a "cold solder joint"; it has a dull granular appearance instead of a bright smooth appearance. Too much heat can injure the items being soldered, e.g., burn insulation on wires.

3. Keep the tip of the iron clean and tinned. Brush it off with a damp paper towel. Tin it by flowing a small amount of solder on it.

4. Hold the tip of the iron to the joint. At the same time hold solder to joint. When the joint is heated sufficiently, the solder will melt over the joint. Never apply solder to the iron as this will produce a cold solder joint.

5. Remove iron and let solder joint cool before moving it.

REPAIRING AND SPLICING WIRE

Many problems with electronic equipment are caused by loose connections between the equipment and the boat wiring. Chapter Seven describes methods for making soldered and crimped splices and connections.

REPLACING A TRANSMISSION LINE

Coaxial transmission line attenuates the transmitted signal slightly, i.e., not all the power generated by the transmitter actually reaches the antenna. With new cable, attenuation is small.

11

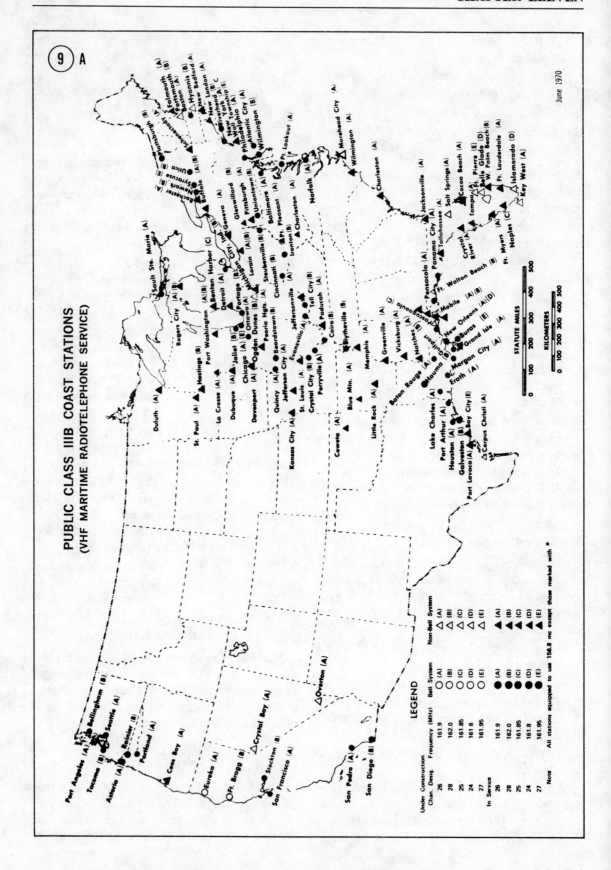

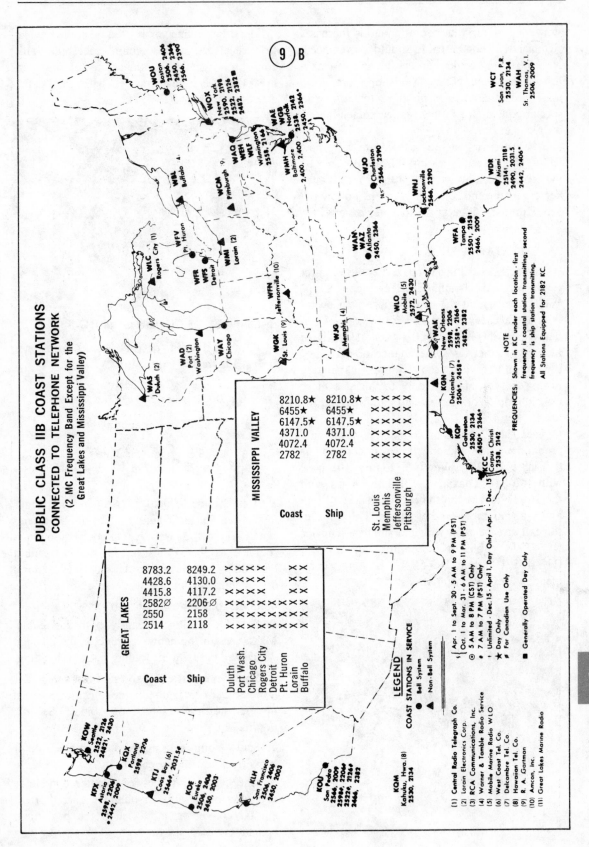

PUBLIC CLASS IIB COAST STATIONS
CONNECTED TO TELEPHONE NETWORK
(2 MC Frequency Band Except for the
Great Lakes and Mississippi Valley)

9 B

WOU Boston 2406, 2506, 2444, 2450, 2566, 2390

WOX New York 2590, 2198, 2522, 2126, 2482, 2382

WBL Buffalo 4

WAE WGB Wilmington 2143, 2558, 2142, 2558, 2450, 2366*

WEH WLF WAQ

WCM Pittsburgh (9)

WMH Baltimore NC, 2400, 2600, 2400, 2450, 2366*

WJO Charleston 2566, 2390

WCT San Juan, P.R. 2530, 2134

WAH St. Thomas, V.I. 2506, 2009

WNJ Jacksonville 2566, 2390

WDR Miami 2514', 2118', 2490, 2031.5, 2442, 2406*

WFA Tampa 2501, 2158', 2466, 2009

WLC Rogers City (1)

WFV Pt. Huron

WMI Lorain (2)

WFR WFS Detroit

WFN Jeffersonville (10)

WGK St. Louis (9)

WJG Memphis (4)

WAM WAZ Atlanta 2450, 2366

WLO Mobile (5) 2572, 2430

WAK New Orleans 2598, 2206, 2558*, 2166*, 2482, 2382

WAD Port (2)

WAY Washington Chicago

WAS Duluth (2)

KGN Delcambre (7) 2506*, 2458*

KQP Galveston 2530, 2134

KCC Corpus Christi 2450*, 2366* 2538, 2142

MISSISSIPPI VALLEY				
8210.8★	8210.8★	X X X X	
6455★	6455★	X X X X	
6147.5★	6147.5★	X X X X	
4371.0	4371.0	X X X X	
4072.4	4072.4	X X X X	
2782	2782	X X X X	
Coast	**Ship**		
		St. Louis	
		Memphis	
		Jeffersonville	
		Pittsburgh	

GREAT LAKES			
8783.2	8249.2	X X X	X X X
4428.6	4130.0	X X X	X X X
4415.8	4117.2	X X X X	X X X
2582∅	2206∅	X X X X X	X X X
2550	2158	X X X X X	X X X
2514	2118	X X X X X	X X X
Coast	**Ship**		
		Duluth	
		Port Wash.	
		Chicago	
		Rogers City	
		Detroit	
		Pt. Huron	
		Lorain	
		Buffalo	

LEGEND

COAST STATIONS IN SERVICE
● Bell System
▲ Non-Bell System

{ Apr. 1 to Sept. 30 - 5 AM to 9 PM (PST)
{ Oct. 1 to Mar. 31 - 6 AM to 11 PM (PST)
⊙ 5 AM to 8 PM (CST) Only
7 AM to 7 PM (PST) Only
† Unlimited - Dec. 15 - April 1, Day Only - Apr. 1 - Dec. 15
★ Day Only
∅ For Canadian Use Only
■ Generally Operated Day Only

(1) Central Radio Telegraph Co.
(2) Lorain Electronics Corp.
(3) RCA Communications, Inc.
(4) Warner & Tamble Radio Service
(5) Mobile Marine Radio WLO
(6) West Coast Tel. Co.
(7) Delcambre Tel. Co.
(8) Hawaiian Tel. Co.
(9) R. A. Gortman
(10) Amcon, Inc.
(11) Great Lakes Marine Radio

KQM Kahuku, Hwa. (8) 2530, 2134

KOW Seattle 2522, 2126, 2431', 2430)

KQX Portland 2598, 2206

KTJ Coos Bay (6) 2566*, 2031.5*

KOE Eureka 2506, 2406 2450, 2003

KLH San Francisco 2506, 2406, 2522*, 2124*, 2466, 2382

KOU San Pedro 2566, 2009 2598*, 2206* 2450, 2003

KFX Astoria 2598, 2206* ● 2442, 2009

NOTE

FREQUENCIES: Shown in KC under each location - first frequency is coastal station transmitting; second frequency is ship station transmitting.

All Stations Equipped for 2182 KC.

11

When exposed to weather, attenuation increases significantly and the cable should be replaced. No exact replacement interval can be established. However, after 2 years or more, have your electronics dealer measure the loss with special equipment; follow his recommendations for replacement.

When ordering a new cable, use only new RG-8/U and specify length; it is usually sold by the foot. You may have the dealer install connectors on the ends or do it yourself. Follow the procedure described in this chapter exactly.

COAXIAL CABLE CONNECTORS

Replacing a damaged coaxial cable requires removing and installing the end connectors. While not beyond the capabilities of an owner with average dexterity and a knowledge of soldering, the job is exacting. If done sloppily or incorrectly, there is some chance of damaging the transmitter when used. A sloppy installation may work fine initially, only to fail at a more crucial time. Work slowly and carefully and the job is easy.

There are 2 types of connectors commonly used on marine equipment. Most common is the large PL-259 plug (see **Figure 10**) used with RG-8/U coaxial cable. This mates with the SO-239 socket on the rear of nearly all VHF and SSB equipment on the market. This connector can also be used with the smaller diameter RG-58/U cable by installing an adaptor (UG-175/U), but RG-58/U is not recommended for these installations.

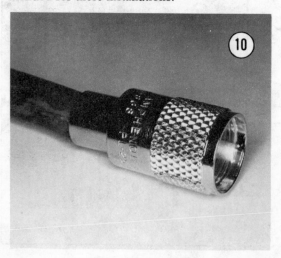

The other connector is used on some navigation receivers such as omni receivers. This connector is called a BNC connector (see **Figure 11**) and is used exclusively with small diameter coax such as RG-58/U.

Installing PL-258 Connector to RG-8/U

1. Remove 1⅛ in. of vinyl jacket from end. See A, **Figure 12**.

CAUTION
Do not nick the braided wire.

2. Bare ¼ in. of center conductor.

CAUTION
Do not nick conductor or it will break off.

3. Trim braided shield 1/16 in. beyond inner insulation. See B, Figure 12. Tin the braid and center conductor carefully. Do not use too much solder. Also, braid must not fan out, but should lay flat against inner insulation. Furthermore, do not burn insulation while soldering.

4. Slide coupling ring on cable.

5. Screw the plug assembly onto the cable. Make certain the center conductor fits through the center pin without folding back or bending.

6. Solder plug assembly to braid through solder hole. Solder center conductor to center pin. Do not use excessive heat or solder. See C, Figure 12.

7. Screw coupling ring onto assembly until it turns freely off the threads.

8. Check for short between center conductor and plug body with an ohmmeter. If shorted, cut off connector and start at the beginning, being more careful.

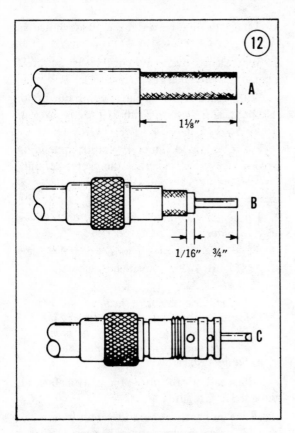

Installing PL-259 Connector to RG-58/U

This cable is not recommended for VHF and SSB transceivers, but is used on some navigation receivers. Check the manufacturer's manual.

1. Remove 21/32 in. of vinyl jacket from end. See A, **Figure 13**.

CAUTION

Do not nick the braided wire.

2. Slide coupling ring and UG-175/U adapter on cable. See Figure 13A.

3. Fan braid slightly and fold back over cable. See B, Figure 13. Compress braid around cable.

4. Position adapter to dimension shown in C, Figure 13. Press braid down over adapter and trim to ⅜ in.

5. Bare ½ in. of center conductor and tin it.

CAUTION

Do not nick conductor.

6. Screw plug assembly onto adapter. Make certain the center conductor fits through the center pin without folding back or bending.

7. Solder plug assembly to braid through solder hole. Solder center conductor to center pin. Do not use excessive heat or solder. See D, Figure 13.

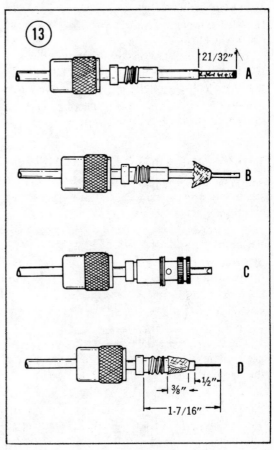

8. Screw coupling ring onto assembly until it turns freely off the threads.

9. Check for short between center conductor and plug body with an ohmmeter. If shorted, cut off connector and start at the beginning, being more careful.

Installing BNC Connector

1. Cut end of cable even.

2. Slide nut over cable. See A, **Figure 14**.

3. Remove ½ in. of vinyl jacket (B, Figure 14).

CAUTION

Do not nick braid.

4. Push braid back and remove ⅛ in. of inner insulator. See C, Figure 14.

11

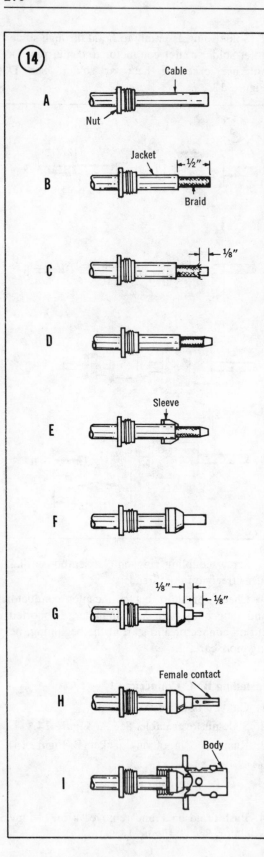

5. Taper the braid over the end as shown in D, Figure 14.

6. Slide sleeve over end until it fits squarely against end of jacket (E, Figure 14).

7. With sleeve firmly in place, comb out braid, fold back, and smooth. Trim to 3/32 in. around sleeve. See F, Figure 14.

8. Leave ⅛ in. of inner insulation extending beyond sleeve and ⅛ in. of the center conductor extending beyond insulation. See G, Figure 14.

9. Tin center conductor. Do not use excessive heat or solder.

10. Slide male pin over conductor and solder. See H, Figure 14. Remove excess solder.

CAUTION
Do not use excessive heat or inner insulation will swell, preventing it from fitting into plug body in next step. If this happens, you must start the procedure over.

11. Push end of cable into plug body as far as it will go. See I, Figure 14.

12. Slide nut into place and screw it into the body. Tighten moderately with a wrench.

CAUTION
Hold body and cable rigidly. Do not let either twist when tightening.

13. Check for short between center conductor and plug body with an ohmmeter. If shorted, cut off connector and start at the beginning, being more careful.

EMERGENCY ANTENNA

Commercial antennas are usually strong and seaworthy. But there is always a chance one could be swept away or severly damaged in a storm. Being able to improvise a substitute could mean the difference between rescue and disaster.

An antenna is a simple device, but its design is relatively exacting. Most importantly, its length must bear a precise relationship to the frequency at which it will be used. The exact design of commercial antennas is developed by formulas and careful matching to existing transmitters by experimentation.

The antenna in this section cannot be precisely matched. There is a likelihood that no accurate means is available at the time to measure its length. This will make it usable, but inefficient. In fact, if used for long periods of time, the mismatch could damage the transmitter. Therefore, it is intended only as a last resort; don't try to save money on an installation by "rolling your own."

Coaxial Antenna (VHF)

One of the simplest and most efficient of the makeshift antennas is the coaxial antenna. It is made from coaxial cable salvaged from the damaged antenna installation. To make it:

1. Cut the connector off the antenna end of the existing coaxial cable. If the end has been severed, cut the coax off cleanly at the first undamaged portion.

2. Slice off the outer insulation for the length shown in A, **Figure 15**.

3. Fold outer braid back on itself as shown in B, Figure 15.

4. Continue until the exposed braid is completely folded back over outer insulation. See C, Figure 15.

The coaxial cable connects to the transceiver in the same way as the original antenna. Raise the antenna portion as high as the length of cable will allow. Use a sail or flag halyard. See **Figure 16**. Keep the antenna as far away from metal rigging and spars as possible. The antenna portion must be as vertical as possible.

USING A MULTIMETER

A multimeter or volt-ohmmeter (VOM) is probably one of the handiest troubleshooting aids you can buy for electrical troubles. The VOM can measure voltage, e.g., when trying to determine if power is getting to an instrument. It can also measure electrical resistance. This is useful for finding short-circuits, open circuits, corroded connections, and other troubles.

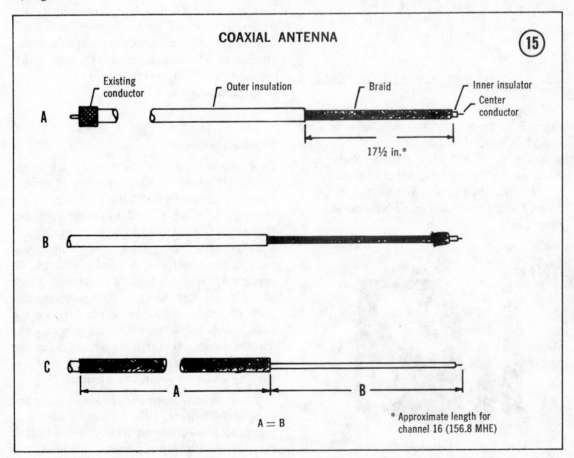

COAXIAL ANTENNA (15)

A — Existing conductor — Outer insulation — Braid — Inner insulator — Center conductor

17½ in.*

B

C

A = B

A — B

* Approximate length for channel 16 (156.8 MHE)

11

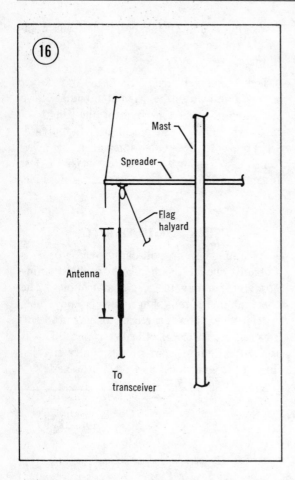

There is no need to buy a very elaborate or expensive instrument. The one shown in **Figure 17** is more than adequate for the job and sells for about $12-15. Lafayette Radio and Allied/Radio Shack have suitable instruments in this price range; there is no need to spend more. Refer to instructions with instrument for proper use.

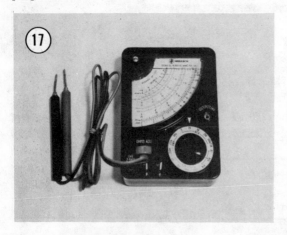

ENGINE INSTRUMENTS

Engine instruments commonly include:

a. Ammeter

b. Oil pressure

c. Coolant temperature

d. Voltmeter

e. Hour meter

f. Fuel level

Not every installation will include all of these instruments; the first 3 are usually considered the minimum necessary.

Figure 18 shows how these instruments are normally wired. Note that each instrument is independent of the others. The ammeter is connected in series between the battery and all electrical accessories except the starter. Other instruments receive 12 volts from the battery as soon as the ignition switch is turned on. The hour meter begins timing as soon as the switch goes on and the voltmeter records battery voltage. The oil sender and coolant temperature sender are mounted on the engine block. Both senders vary their resistance to change the meter indication. The fuel level sender float varies resistance according to fuel level to change fuel gauge reading.

Troubleshooting

1. *Ammeter* — Ammeters usually fail completely, giving zero reading regardless of current flow. You can easily check if it is working. Turn the ignition switch on but do not start engine. If ammeter is good, the needle will point slightly toward discharge (—). Turn on some lights and note reading increases toward discharge. If needle stays on zero, replace meter with a new one. Be sure that the new case diameter and method of mounting are the same. Wire it in the same way as the old one. Recheck new meter as described above. If everything works OK, except needle points toward charge (+) instead of discharge (—), reverse wires to ammeter.

2. *Hour meter*—Hour meters also usually fail completely. If meter fails to record time, check electrical connections to meter; ensure that it receives 12 volts on one terminal. If connections

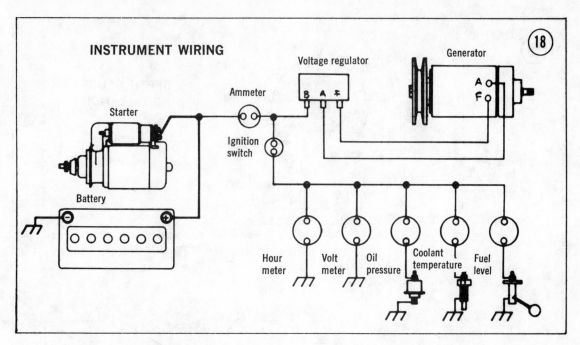

are good, but the meter still doesn't work, replace the meter. Be sure that you record hours from old meter in your log book so that correct total use can be determined at some later date.

3. *Voltmeter*—Another meter that usually fails completely, but may also simply record incorrect battery voltage. If reading is incorrect, but battery is fully charged, check the accuracy by measuring voltage with a separate voltmeter (multimeter). Replace the gauge if defective.

4. *Oil pressure*—This gauge usually becomes inaccurate, but may fail completely. If you note a significant difference in oil pressure from normal, ensure that electrical connections to gauge and sender are clean and firmly attached. If trouble persists, replace sender. If trouble still exists, replace meter.

CAUTION
Don't overlook the fact that difference in oil pressure may be caused by an engine trouble or low oil level.

5. *Coolant temperature*—Same as oil pressure gauge, except trouble shows up as difference in coolant temperature.

CAUTION
Before suspecting gauges, check symptoms in engine chapter under Cooling System Troubleshooting.

6. *Fuel level*—Same as oil pressure gauge.

WARNING
When removing sender, gasoline in tank is exposed. Do not let smoking materials (cigarettes, etc.), open flame, or electrical sparks near tank.

NAVIGATIONAL INSTRUMENTS

Navigational instruments used aboard pleasure boats normally include:

a. Knotmeter with or without log

b. Depth gauge

c. Wind speed/direction

d. Compass

The depth gauge and knotmeter consist of the instrument itself, with indicator, and a separate transducer. Location of the transducer depends on a number of factors and should be done according to the manufacturer's instructions. **Figures 19 and 20** are typical installations for troubleshooting purposes.

Windspeed/direction instruments consist of a mast top-mounted transducer assembly and a separate indicating instrument. From a troubleshooting standpoint, it is similar to a depth gauge or knotmeter. See **Figure 21**.

11

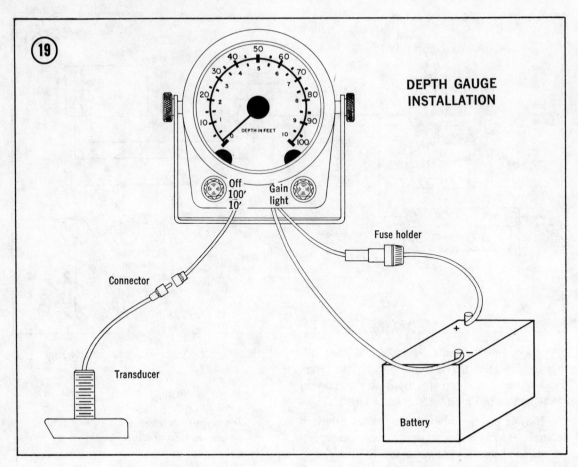

**DEPTH GAUGE
INSTALLATION**

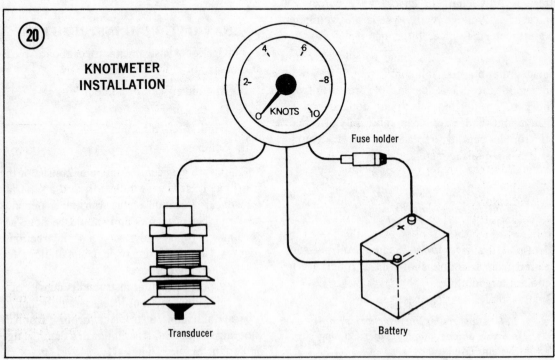

**KNOTMETER
INSTALLATION**

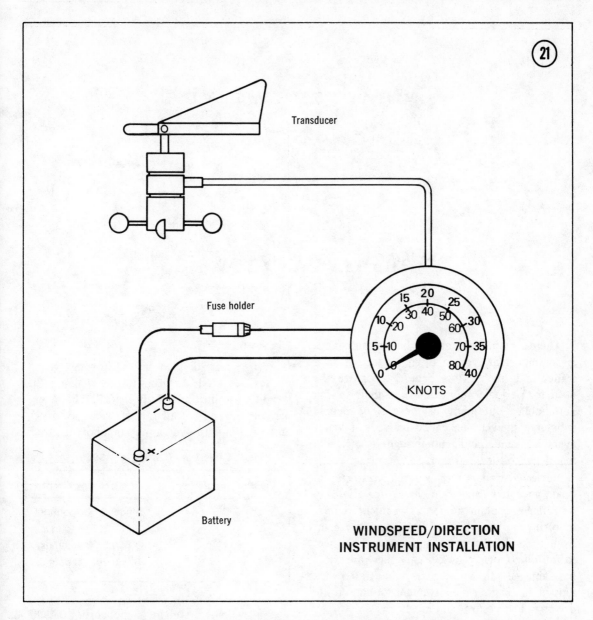

Transducer

Fuse holder

KNOTS

Battery

**WINDSPEED/DIRECTION
INSTRUMENT INSTALLATION**

If the above examination fails to show the trouble, borrow an identical indicator unit and substitute it for yours. If this solves the problem, the indicator unit was defective. If this doesn't solve the problem, replace the transducer. On some through-hull installations, this requires haul-out, though some transducers can be replaced from inside the bilge.

Erratic readings may be caused by instrument or transducer failure, poor electrical connections, or interference from the engine ignition system. See *Noise Suppression* in this chapter for possible cures for noisy ignitions.

The compass is usually completely self-contained. Follow manufacturer's recommendations for placement and installation. Defective instruments must be returned to manufacturer or compass specialist for repair.

Troubleshooting

Troubleshooting navigation instruments is fairly straightforward. If the instrument fails completely, check fuse and battery power connections. Also check condition of cable between transducer and instrument.

11

CHAPTER TWELVE

TRAILERS AND TOWING

There are not many areas where maintenance is so important, yet so often neglected, as a trailer and hitch. Most people recognize the need for periodic maintenance to their towing automobile. But many of these same people submerge their trailer in corrosive salt water every weekend, giving no thought to periodic maintenance for the trailer.

Neglected trailers are a serious hazard to the boat, your tow car, even your life. Highway Patrol files contain numerous accident reports involving trailers. A rusted axle can freeze up from lack of lubrication and cause the wheel to fall off. If you're lucky, only the trailer will be damaged. In some cases, the trailer has flipped the boat on the pavement, or caused the driver to lose control and crash.

HITCHES

A good quality, properly installed trailer hitch forms the all-important link between a trailer and its tow car. A properly designed hitch does more than merely transfer tractive effort from car to trailer. It allows the trailer to turn, yet it subdues any tendency of the trailer to sway. It must be designed so that the trailer cannot separate accidently, but if the trailer overturns, it must release so that the tow car may remain under control.

Classes

Trailers are divided into 4 towing weight classes. See **Table 1**. Gross towing weight is the weight with the trailer fully loaded. This figure includes the empty trailer, boat, water, ice, food, and anything else which may be aboard.

Table 1   TOWING CLASSES

Class	Gross Towing Weight
1	Under 2,000 pounds
2	2,000-3,500 pounds
3	3,500-5,000 pounds
4	5,000-10,000 pounds

Trailer tongue weight is the portion of the trailer's weight which is supported by the hitch ball. Trailer manufacturers design their products so that the tongue weight of a normally loaded trailer is approximately 10-15% of gross towing weight. For example, a 5,000 pound trailer should have a tongue weight of 500-750 pounds.

Types

There are 4 main types of trailer hitches. Each is designed to do a certain job.

a. Bumper hitch
b. Frame hitch

c. Weight distributing hitch

d. Axle hitch

Bumper hitches attach to the tow car by means of one or more clamps. See **Figure 1**. The strength of this system is limited by the strength of the tow car's bumper. Such hitches are used mainly for occasional towing of very small boats; those less than 1,000 lbs. gross towing weight.

Frame hitches, as the name implies, are bolted or welded to the tow car frame. See **Figure 2**. They are usually attached at several points. Frame hitches are the most popular type for all size trailers.

A load equalizing or weight distributing hitch transfers a portion of the trailer tongue weight to a point between front and rear wheels of the tow car. Remaining tongue weight transfers to the trailer wheels. Without load equalization, all tongue weight would be at a point far behind the tow car's rear axle. The rear axle becomes a fulcrum about which the entire car pivots. Tongue weight forces the rear end of the tow car

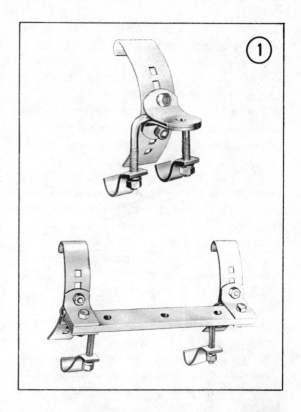

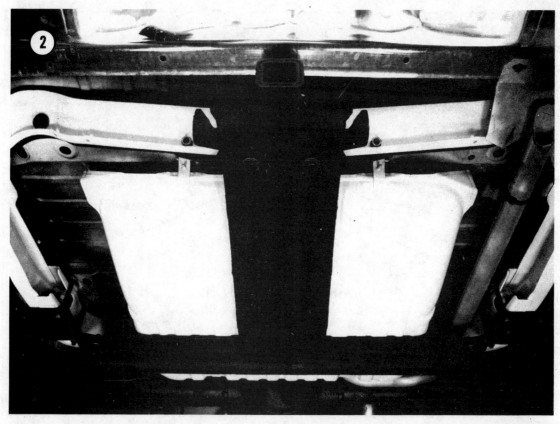

12

down. At the same time, the front end rises, up-setting front end geometry and causing various steering handling problems. Load equalizing hitches are recommended for all trailers of classes 2, 3, and 4.

Figure 3 compares load distribution using a common frame hitch used with overload springs and an equalizing hitch, using the same car and trailer. When the car and trailer are separate, weight is distributed as shown in (a). When joined to a tow car with overload springs, note that the car can remain nearly level, but weight transfers from front to rear. When an equalizing hitch is used, tongue weight is distributed between the front and rear wheels of the tow car and the trailer wheels as well.

An axle hitch is a variation of a load equalizing hitch. Instead of transferring trailer tongue weight to all 4 wheels of the tow car, it transfers it only to the rear axle. These hitches are relatively easy to install, but usually cause overloading of rear axles and wheel bearings. Many automobile manufacturers caution against axle hitches.

Installation

Hitch installation is strictly a job for professionals, except for bumper and frame hitches which are used to tow only *lightweight* trailers. Usually, each installation must be custom tailored for its individual application. Some parts may have to be cut to fit their connections; still others must be bent, *cold*, to fit, using large hydraulic presses.

Major hitch manufacturers consider proper installation so important that they operate their own service and installation centers. **Figure 4** shows a custom hitch installation. Notice that the ball mount assembly is removable when it is not needed for towing.

Maintenance

A trailer hitch is a simple, rugged device which requires no maintenance other than occasional checks to make sure that its attachment and assembly bolts are secure. Spring bars and hitch balls should be lubricated.

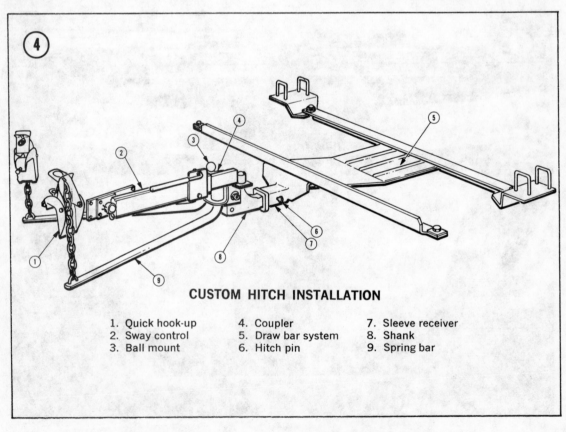

CUSTOM HITCH INSTALLATION

1. Quick hook-up
2. Sway control
3. Ball mount
4. Coupler
5. Draw bar system
6. Hitch pin
7. Sleeve receiver
8. Shank
9. Spring bar

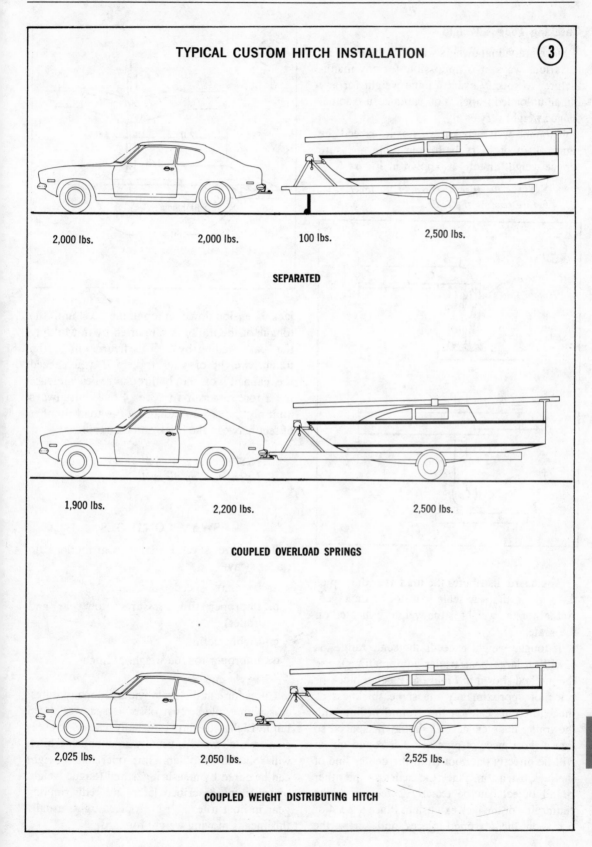

TYPICAL CUSTOM HITCH INSTALLATION

③

2,000 lbs.   2,000 lbs.   100 lbs.   2,500 lbs.

SEPARATED

1,900 lbs.   2,200 lbs.   2,500 lbs.

COUPLED OVERLOAD SPRINGS

2,025 lbs.   2,050 lbs.   2,525 lbs.

COUPLED WEIGHT DISTRIBUTING HITCH

12

Checking Tongue Weight

Since individual owners will load their trailers in various ways, it is impossible for any manufacturer to specify exact tongue weight for any but an unloaded trailer. You can measure actual tongue weight very easily.

If tongue weight is known not to exceed the range of an ordinary bathroom scale, measure tongue weight directly as shown in **Figure 5**.

NOTE: *Be sure the trailer is level before reading the scale.*

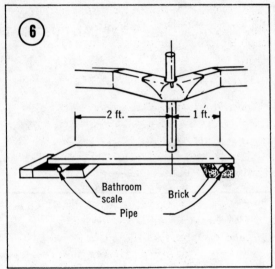

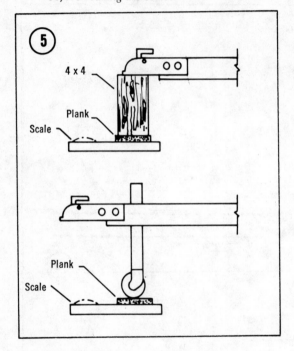

The board distributes the load over the top of the scale so that the scale will not be damaged. Actual tongue weight is the weight indicated on the scale.

If tongue weight exceeds the scale range (as it will on large boat/trailer combinations), use the method shown in **Figure 6**. Place a block or brick of approximately the same thickness as the bathroom scale on the ground in line with the trailer coupler jack. It should be spaced so that a short piece of pipe or other round object will lie directly one foot from the center line of the jack extension. Place the scales so the other round object can be exactly 2 feet from the center line of the jack extension. Place a 2 x 4 or 4 x 4 on the 2 round pieces and screw the

jack extension down on top of the 2 x 4 until the tongue of the trailer is supported by it. Multiply the scale reading by 3. This figure will be the tongue weight of your trailer. If you exceed the capacity of the bathroom scale, increase the 2 foot dimension to 3 or 4 feet, but always multiply the scale reading by the total number of feet between the brick and the scale.

NOTE: *Be sure the trailer is level before reading the scale.*

SWAY CONTROLS

There are several major contributions to trailer sway:

a. Excessive speed
b. Improper tire pressures (tow car and trailer)
c. Light steering
d. Improper tongue weight at hitch

Cures for *a* and *b* are obvious. In many states, cars with trailers must observe a slower speed limit. Light steering is usually caused by excessive hitch weight; usually an equalizing hitch will solve the problem. Improper hitch weight can be cured by measuring actual tongue weight of trailer as described later and redistributing gear in boat to establish proper weight; usually this means moving weight forward.

Several sway control systems are available to limit tendency to sway after above sources of trouble have been eliminated. These are:

a. Mechanical
b. Hydraulic

Figure 7 illustrates a typical mechanical sway control. A friction element between the tongue arm and mounting plate damps out trailer sway. This device requires no maintenance other than adjustment to each combination of car and trailer.

Hydraulic sway control systems operate much as do mechanical sway controls, except that a hydraulic cylinder similar to that of an automobile shock absorber replaces the friction element. No adjustment or service is necessary, but hydraulic units must be replaced in the event of malfunction.

LIGHTING

Lighting requirements on trailers vary from state to state. **Figure 8** shows the Federal DOT Standard 108.

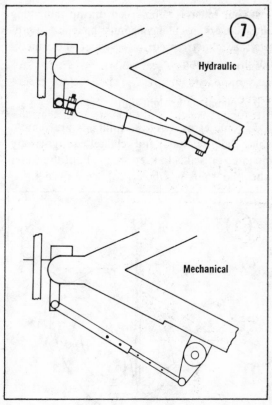

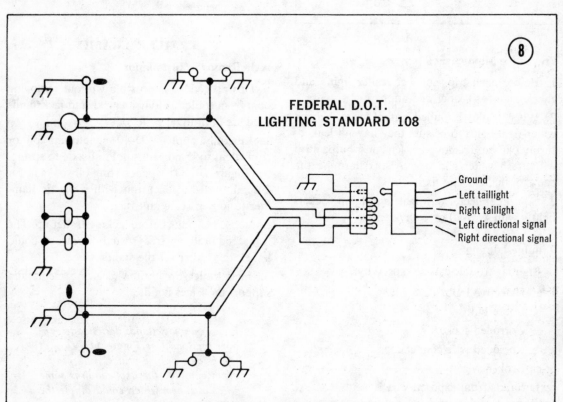

12

If the trailer is submerged during launching and recovery, some means must be made to protect the lights from corrosive water. Two methods are common:

a. Removable lights
b. Special water-tight lights

In some cases, only the taillights are removable. Side markers and clearance lights are mounted on stalks to keep them out of the water when the trailer is submerged. See **Figure 9**.

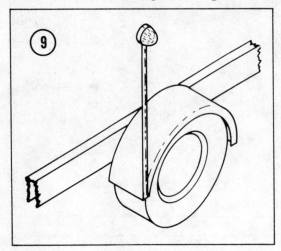

Preventive Maintenance

1. Before each trip, connect trailer lights and check each for proper operation.
2. When trailer is pulled out of water, check water-tight lights to be sure they haven't leaked. If any one has, remove the lens and bulb; flush with fresh water and dry. Also determine the cause of the leak and fix it.
3. Squirt connector terminals and lamp sockets lightly with WD-40 or equivalent.

Troubleshooting

Lighting trouble can be caused by:

a. Defective bulb
b. Loose bulb
c. Corroded sockets
d. Corroded wire connections
e. Broken wire
f. Shorts from exposed wire
g. Corroded connectors

Corrosion from salt water is one of the most common causes of lighting trouble. Particularly susceptible are connectors used for removable lights. Squirt the connector terminals with WD-40 of equivalent, then connect and disconnect plug several times to clean away corrosion.

Troubleshooting, done logically, is very simple. These procedures assume that automobile lights work when trailer is *not connected*.

1. *Single light failure*—Check bulb. Check socket for corrosion. Check connection between trailer wiring harness and individual light.

2. *Failure of both taillights, side marker and clearance lights*—Check connection between auto connector and auto wiring. Clean auto/trailer connectors of all corrosion.

3. *Erratic operation of both directional lights*—Check ground connection on trailer and auto. Clean corrosion from auto/trailer connectors.

4. *Failure of one directional light*—Check bulb. Check socket for corrosion. Clean auto/trailer connector. Clean connector on removable lights.

TRAILER FRAME

Axle Removal/Installation

This procedure is possible without removing boat from trailer as long as jacks and jackstands used are built to take the load.

1. Liberally apply WD-40 penetrating oil or equivalent to U-bolt nuts holding axle to spring. See **Figure 10**. After penetrating oil soaks in for 2-3 minutes, rap each nut with a plastic hammer to loosen scale and rust.

2. Loosen U-bolts before jacking trailer up. The force required to free rusted hardware could knock the trailer off the stands.

3. Jack trailer up until wheels are clear, and support on 4 jackstands.

> **WARNING**
> *Use proper jackstands designed to support the load (see* **Figure 11***). Do not use bricks, orange crates, milk crates, etc. Removing the axle requires some force at times, which could topple the trailer from makeshift supports.*

4. Place low jack, preferably a garage-type floor jack, under center of axle and raise it just enough to take weight of axle.

5. Remove U-bolts securing axle to springs.

6. Lower axle and remove.

7. Installation is the reverse of these steps. Use new lockwashers on U-bolts.

Leaf Spring Replacement

1. Remove axle(s) as described earlier.

2. Remove shackle bolt(s). Some springs are secured at both ends by bolts; others are bolted only at one end. See **Figure 12**.

3. Remove spring.

4. Installation is the reverse of these steps.

Inspection

Periodically check the entire trailer, looking at these areas:

1. Check tires as described in a separate section.

2. Check wheel lug nuts for tightness.

3. Check lights for proper operation.

12

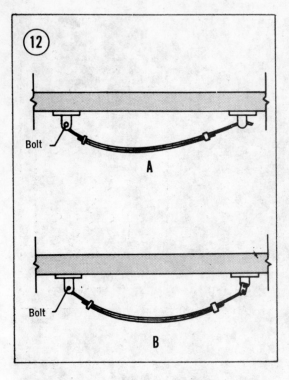

Bolt

A

Bolt

B

4. Check frame for bends and cracks, particularly at welds.

5. Wire brush large deposits of rust and scale. Check condition of exposed metal. Repaint brushed areas.

TIRES AND WHEELS

To a large extent, safety of any rig depends on its tires and wheels. This section discusses selection and service procedures for these components.

Tire Selection

Tire size should be determined by actually measuring the weight of your rig. Load the boat with all the gear you normally take aboard. Include fuel, water, ice, safety equipment, everything. Tow the loaded trailer to a public scale (check yellow pages in telephone directory). For one dollar, you can get the weight within 20 pounds. Your tires must be able to support the actual weight of the rig, plus at least a 20% safety margin.

Divide the weight plus 20% by the number of tires on your trailer. This is the required load capacity of each tire. Check the load rating on the tire sidewall to be sure that it matches or exceeds this capacity. If not, your tires are unsafe and must be replaced with larger ones.

Tire Pressure

Tire pressure is very important as it affects load capacity and tire wear.

Underinflation is one of the greatest single causes of tire failure. It causes tires to flex excessively, causing heat build-up and rapid wear. Symptoms of underinflation are excessive wear on shoulders of tread, ply separation, irregular tread wear, and greater susceptibility to bruising.

Overinflation rarely causes tire failure as does underinflation. However, overinflated tires wear very rapidly in the center of the tread, reducing useful life.

Proper inflation depends on tire size. **Table 2** shows inflation pressures for most popular tire

Table 2   TRAILER TIRES AND PRESSURES

Tire Size Tubeless	Tube-Type	Ply Rating	Load Limit and Inflation Pressures				
			20 psi	24 psi	28 psi	32 psi	36 psi
6.50-13		4	760	840			
7.00-13		8	830	920	1010	1090	1170
7.35-14		4	920	1020			
7.35-14		8	920	1020	1120	1210	1290
7.75-14		4	1010	1120			
7.75-14		8	1010	1120	1220	1330	1420
7.75-15	7.75-15	4	990	1100			
7.75-15	7.75-15	8	990	1100	1200	1290	1390
8.15-15	8.15-15	4	1060	1180			
8.15-15	8.15-15	8	1060	1180	1290	1400	1500
6.50-16	6.50-16	6	1105	1225	1330		

sizes. For greatest tire economy, select tires large enough to support maximum load measured earlier, then reduce tire pressures for lighter loads according to Table 2.

CAUTION
Tire pressure must be measured when the tire is cold. As the tire heats up in use, pressure will increase; do not reduce tire pressure to cold level.

Tire and Wheel Maintenance

Tire maintenance is simple.

a. Maintain proper pressure

b. Remove small stones imbeded in tread

c. Inspect tread and both sidewalls for wear or damage

d. Check lug nut tightness

Most auto and trailer parts suppliers have accurate, but inexpensive tire pressure gauges. See **Figure 13**. Use it when you add air at a service station.

CAUTION
Do not depend on built-in gauges on service station air hoses. These are usually grossly inaccurate.

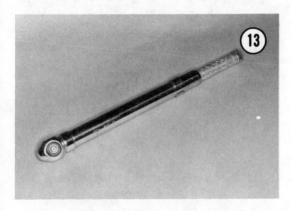

When inspecting tire tread wear, check local traffic regulations concerning minimum tread depth. Most recommend replacing tires when tread depth is less than 1/32″. Original equipment tires have tread wear indicators molded into the bottom of the tread grooves. Tread wear indicators appear as ½″ bands (see **Figure 14**) when tread depth becomes 1/16″. Tires should be replaced at this point.

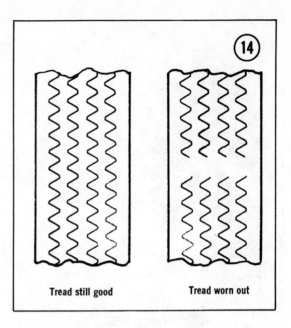

Tread still good   Tread worn out

Abnormal tire wear should always be analyzed to determine its cause. The most common are as follows.

a. Incorrect tire pressure

b. Improper driving

c. Overloading

d. Bad road surfaces

e. Incorrect wheel alignment

Figure 15 identifies wear patterns and indicates the most probable causes.

Be sure to keep wheel lugs tight. On a new vehicle, tighten them after 50 miles, then again at 200-mile intervals until they no longer loosen.

Check occasionally to be sure that wheels aren't bent. A bent wheel will result in rapid tire wear.

Wheel Balancing

Tires are normally balanced along 2 axes. To be in static balance (**Figure 16**), weight must be evenly distributed around the axis of rotation. (A) shows a statically unbalanced wheel. (B) shows the result—wheel tramp or hopping. (C) shows proper static balance.

To be in dynamic balance (**Figure 17**), the centerline of the weight must coincide with the centerline of the wheel. (A) shows a dynamically

12

Underinflation—Worn more on sides than in center.

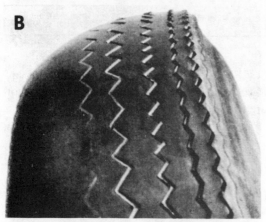

Wheel Alignment—Worn more on one side than the other. Edges of tread feathered.

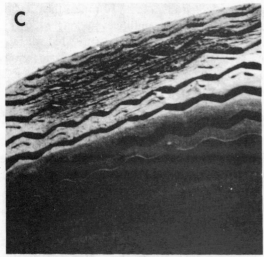

Road Abrasion—Rough wear on entire tire or in patches.

(15)

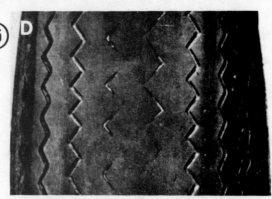

Overinflation—Worn more in center than on sides.

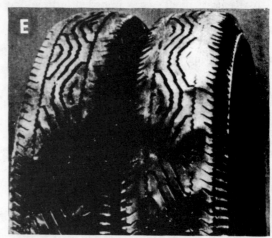

Wheel Balance — Scalloped edges indicate wheel wobble or tramp due to wheel unbalance.

Combination—Most tires exhibit a combination of the above. This tire was overinflated (center worn) and the toe-in was incorrect (feathering). The driver cornered hard at high speed (feathering, rounded shoulders) and braked rapidly (worn spots). The scaly roughness indicates a rough road surface.

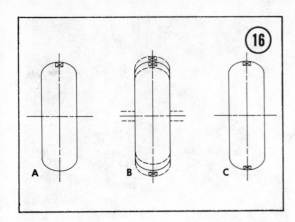

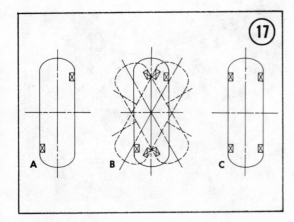

unbalanced wheel. (B) shows the result—wheel wobble or shimmy. (C) shows proper dynamic balance.

Balancing trailer wheels is not as critical as balancing tow car wheels. In nearly all cases, trailer wheels are statically balanced with a bubble-type balancer. They are rarely dynamically balanced, a procedure also called spin balancing.

Winter Lay-up and Storage

Trailers are frequently left standing idle for long periods. To prolong tire life under such conditions, jack up and block each axle just enough to take most of the weight from the tire, then reduce tire pressure to just a few pounds. Don't forget to refill the tires before the trailer is moved.

At times, such measures are impossible. If this is the case, maintain full pressure in the tires and move the trailer every week or so to place the load on a different portion of the tire.

Oil, sunlight, and ozone are among a tire's worst enemies. A canvas cover placed over the tires during storage periods helps to protect against these. Some trailer owners install snap fasteners on pieces of canvas cut to fit the wheel wells, and mating fasteners to the trailer body. Rubber preservative paint applied to both sides of the tires also helps to prolong life.

Tire Changing

Changing a tire doesn't have to be the major chore some people believe it to be. Done right, it is simple.

1. Get well off the road, especially if traffic is heavy.
2. Set out flags or flares.
3. Leave the trailer hitched to the car and set the tow car parking brake. Also, chock the opposite trailer wheel.
4. Loosen lug nuts slightly on wheel to be removed *before* jacking the trailer up.
5. Jack up trailer until bottom of tire is clear of ground. The jack should bear solidly on the rigid axle or on the trailer frame.

WARNING
Do not jack up a vehicle on an incline, loose gravel or soft surfaces.

6. Remove lug nuts and remove wheel.
7. Install good tire. It may be necessary to raise jack to get sufficient clearance.
8. Tighten lug nuts snugly.
9. Lower the trailer and tighten the lug nuts completely.

WHEEL BEARINGS

Wheel bearings should be packed with new grease periodically.

Removal

1. Jack up trailer and support on jackstands.

WARNING
Do not depend on ordinary jack to hold trailer.

12

2. Remove wheel(s).

3a. Remove dust cap, if any. Use water pump pliers as shown in **Figure 18**.

3b. Remove Bearing Buddy, if installed.

4. Remove and discard the cotter pin. Remove the adjusting nut and thrust washer (**Figure 19**).

5. Pull the wheel hub or brake drum outward about one-half inch, then push it back into position. This pulls the outer wheel bearing into position for removal.

6. Remove the outer bearing (**Figure 20**). Be careful that it doesn't drop.

7. Pull the entire hub or brake drum from the spindle.

8. Place a clean rag or newspaper under the brake drum, then place the drum on the paper so that the remaining bearing is downward.

9. Using a hammer and long drift, tap out the inner bearing. The grease seal will come out with it (**Figure 21**).

Cleaning and Inspection

1. Clean each bearing thoroughly with solvent. Do not leave any traces of old lubricant.

2. Clean out the hub cavity and be sure to remove all traces of old grease from the outer races or cups.

3. Clean Bearing Buddy (if used) throughly in solvent.

4. After cleaning, inspect each bearing for signs

of overheating, cracked rollers, pits, or other damage.

5. Pack bearing thoroughly with wheel bearing lubricant.

Installation

1. Place inner bearing in hub.

2. Install a new grease seal. Be sure that the grease seal is not cocked in its bore, then tap it gently into position.

3. Install hub on axle.

4. Install outer bearing in hub.

5. Install thrust washer and adjusting nut.

6. Adjust wheel bearing as described below.

Adjustment

1. Reassemble all parts except for the adjusting nut cotter pin and the hub dust cover.

2. Rotate the wheel in its normal running direction, and while turning the wheel, tighten the adjusting nut until it is snug.

12

3. Back off the nut ¼ to ½ turn.

4. Tighten nut by hand. *Do not use a wrench.*

5. Back off the nut until the hole in the spindle aligns with a slot in the nut.

6. Check for play in the bearing by grasping the tire at top and bottom. There should be barely perceptible looseness. If there isn't any, back off the nut one more flat, until play exists.

7. Install a new cotter pin.

> NOTE: *Roller bearings will operate properly over a wide range of adjustment. However, there must be some looseness. Under no circumstances should tapered roller bearings be adjusted to zero play.*

8. Install dust cap or Bearing Buddy.

9. Install the wheel and tire.

BEARING BUDDY

Trailering, even a short distance, heats the hubs. During launching the hubs suddenly cool and air inside contracts, forming a vacuum which draws in water through the rear seal; there is no such thing as a rotating seal which will stay perfect. Water and grit thus drawn into the hub relentlessly destroy bearings.

Bearing Buddy replaces the dust cap in the wheel hub. The hub is filled with grease through a fitting in the piston of the Bearing Buddy. This spring loaded piston holds a slight pressure inside the hub. When wheels are submerged, this pressure keeps out water. The automatic relief valve limits pressure in the hub to protect the rear seals from rupture. Since the hub is full of grease, the bearings are assured of vitally-needed lubrication and the rear seals last—they ride on a grease surface.

Installation

Remove existing dust cap from wheel hub. Hold Bearing Buddy against hub with small block of wood and drive into place with hammer. If Bearing Buddy does not stick in the hub with the first few hammer raps, STOP. Your hub is one of the few with a slightly undersize bore. If this occurs, or the Bearing Buddy is obviously too large or too small, mail your Bearing Buddys to Aquappliances, Inc., 134 Bouquet Dr., San Marcos, CA 92069. Enclose OUTER bearing OUTER race (cup) number or one of your dust caps. If hubs are threaded internally, so specify. An exchange pair of Bearing Buddys to fit your trailer will be mailed to you immediately. For Model No. 1980T (threaded), apply Permatex or other grease proof gasket cement to the Bearing Buddy threads and then screw Bearing Buddy into hub, hand tight.

Use

Initial Filling—Using grease gun, pump up the piston on the Bearing Buddy until grease appears around the retaining ring. Without removing the grease gun, apply pressure directly against the piston by grasping grease gun hose or feed tube with your hand and pushing. If piston moves in, your hub is not yet full of grease. Repeat pressure application until piston cannot be pushed inward or it springs back when pushing force is removed.

Thereafter, check at launching ramp just prior to launching. Refilling is not required if piston can be moved by touching it. Always refill the first outing of each season.

Lubricant—For best performance, a fine marine lubricant is recommended for use with your Bearing Buddy. Do not use the coarse heavy fiber grease generally used for packing wheel bearings.

TRAILER BRAKES

State laws require that all but the smallest trailers be equipped with brakes. The brakes on an average passenger car are designed to stop the car and a certain maximum safe load. If this safe load is exceeded, the brakes will fail, and a serious accident will almost certainly result.

There are 2 types of trailer brakes in common use—electric and hydraulic. Each type has its advantages and disadvantages.

ELECTRIC BRAKES

Figure 22 illustrates a typical modern electric brake. Attached to the inside and rotating with

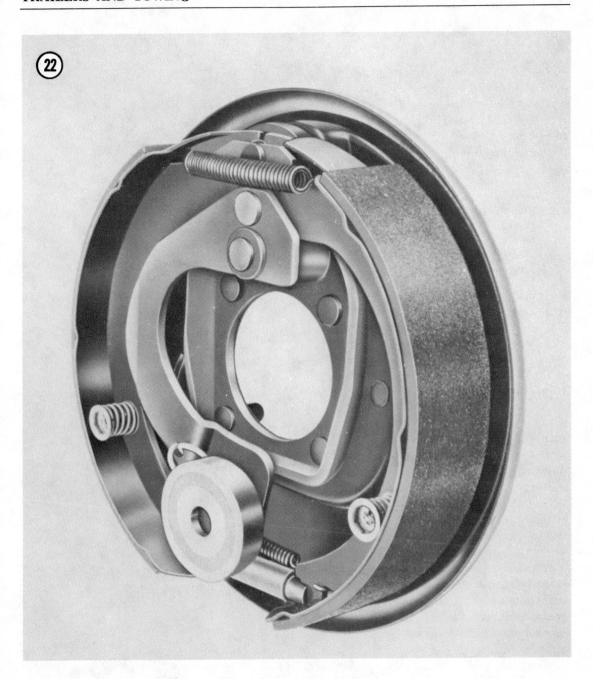

the brake drum is an armature plate. An electro-magnet bears lightly against the armature. Current through coils in the magnet causes the magnet to be attracted to the armature. Rotation of the wheel tends to carry the magnet with it. Movement of the magnet is then transmitted through the lever to the cam, which forces both brake shoes apart into contact with brake drum.

Current through the magnet, and therefore braking effort, is varied by the brake controller, which is located near the driver.

A modern Warner electric brake is shown in **Figure 23**. In this unit, the magnet is attached to the backing plate, but it is free to rotate slightly in either direction. The armature plate is bolted to, and revolves with, the brake drum.

12

Current proportional to desired braking effort is supplied by the brake controller. When the magnet is energized, it is attracted to the armature. Rotation of the armature causes the magnet to rotate slightly. The brake actuating lug on the magnet forces the brake shoes outward into contact with the brake drum.

Older Warner brakes are so designed that routine brake adjustments are not required. Newer versions are adjusted by a star wheel.

Brake Controllers

Electric brake controllers vary braking effort in accordance with brake pedal pressure, or on some models, independently, so that trailer brakes only may be applied. Brake controllers incorporate a rheostat which allows more current to flow to the brakes as the need for braking power increases.

Kelsey-Hayes (**Figure 24**) and Tekonsha (**Figure 25**) brake controllers are connected to the automobile hydraulic system so that as braking power increases, so does current to the brake magnets. In that manner, trailer and car

brakes are always synchronized. Independent operation of the trailer brakes is also possible with either of these controllers.

The latest Warner brake controller (**Figure 26**) attaches to the car's brake pedal, and may be removed quickly when it is not needed. Greater pressure on the brake pedal causes

Figure 27 is a cutaway view of an earlier Warner controller. This unit is actuated by hydraulic pressure from the tow vehicle braking system or manually by the driver.

more current to flow to the trailer brakes. Light foot pressure on the top of the controller permits only the trailer brakes to be applied.

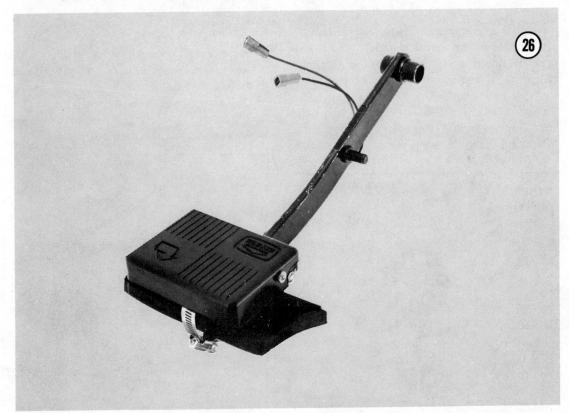

12

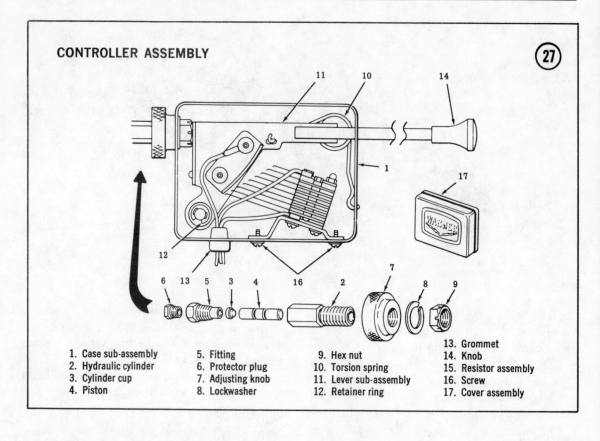

CONTROLLER ASSEMBLY (27)

1. Case sub-assembly
2. Hydraulic cylinder
3. Cylinder cup
4. Piston
5. Fitting
6. Protector plug
7. Adjusting knob
8. Lockwasher
9. Hex nut
10. Torsion spring
11. Lever sub-assembly
12. Retainer ring
13. Grommet
14. Knob
15. Resistor assembly
16. Screw
17. Cover assembly

Sure-Stop controllers (**Figure 28**) operate the trailer brakes through a signal from the tow vehicle stoplight switch. When the stoplights come on, a control relay closes, which in turn applies power to the trailer brakes through a driver-adjustable rheostat. An emergency manual control button is provided to apply the trailer brakes in the event of relay malfunction.

Controller Adjustment

Each brake controller is adjustable so that braking action may be varied to suit different driving conditions.

On Tekonsha controllers, a small thumbwheel on the lower left side may be turned to provide desired braking action (**Figure 29**).

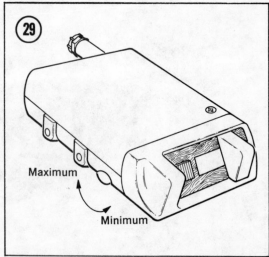

Maximum

Minimum

There are 2 adjustments on Kelsey-Hayes brake controllers. The first adjustment is stoplight switch gap. This adjustment is normally required only at initial installation or if it is inadvertently disturbed. With the trailer connected, check stoplights and turn signals for proper operation. If the stoplights are lit when the brakes are not applied, adjust controller stoplight switch gap by loosening the screw which is accessible through the hole in the bottom of the brake controller. Proper gap is 0.020 in. (**Figure 30**).

Braking action may be varied to suit driving conditions by turning the brake controller handle. Turn it counterclockwise to increase trailer braking and clockwise to decrease braking.

A knurled knob on the side of Warner controllers is used to adjust braking action. When the knob is turned clockwise, brake action is slowed.

A simple method for testing the brake controller is shown in **Figure 31**. Connect the positive terminal of a voltmeter to the "brake" lead from the controller, and the other voltmeter lead to a good ground. Connect the electric cable to the trailer. Then operate the controller through its entire range. The voltmeter should indicate steadily increasing voltage as the controller operates up to its full range. With the brakes released, the voltmeter must indicate zero.

If no voltmeter is available, connect a test lamp in place of a voltmeter. As the controller operates, the lamp should glow with steadily increasing brilliance. With no pedal pressure, the lamp should be off.

Auxiliary Valves

Automobiles since the late 1960's use a dual-circuit braking system. One circuit operates 2 wheels, e.g., the front; while the other circuit independently operates the other 2 wheels. If one circuit fails, the other circuit will operate on 2 wheels to stop the car.

The auxiliary valve insures that the trailer brakes will still work if either circuit in the tow car fails. **Figure 32** shows a typical installation for driver-controlled electric trailer brakes.

Breakaway Switch

State laws often require that trailers with brakes be equipped with a device that automatically applies the trailer brakes in the event that the tow car and trailer separate accidentally. A breakaway switch (**Figure 33**) mounted on the trailer tongue, together with an auxiliary battery carried by the trailer, accomplishes this. A strong lanyard attached to the tow car pulls a plunger from the switch in the event of accidental separation of car and trailer. Contacts in the switch then close and apply full battery power to the trailer brakes.

The breakaway switch can be handy at other times also. There have been instances where a person maneuvering a trailer by hand lost control and allowed the trailer to start rolling downhill.

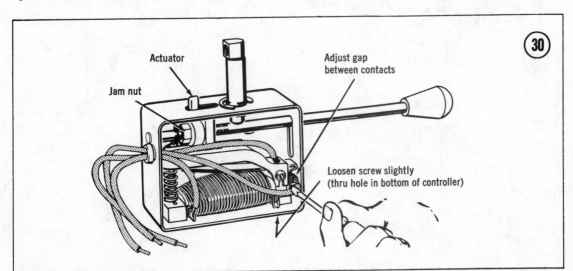

30

Actuator

Jam nut

Adjust gap between contacts

Loosen screw slightly (thru hole in bottom of controller)

12

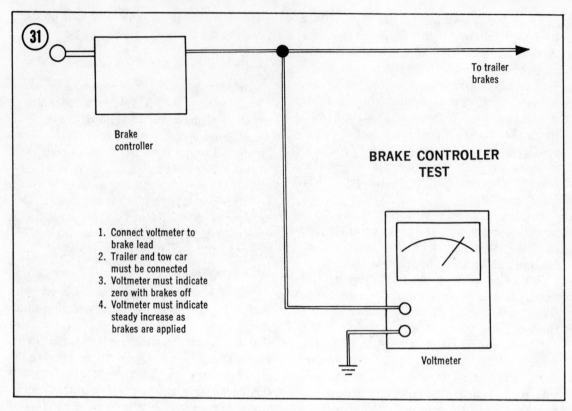

(31)

Brake
controller

To trailer
brakes

**BRAKE CONTROLLER
TEST**

1. Connect voltmeter to
   brake lead
2. Trailer and tow car
   must be connected
3. Voltmeter must indicate
   zero with brakes off
4. Voltmeter must indicate
   steady increase as
   brakes are applied

Voltmeter

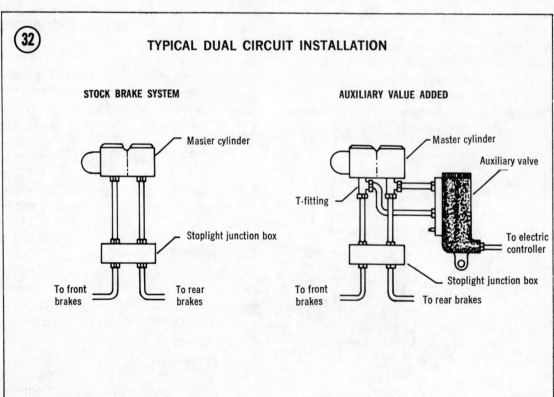

(32)

TYPICAL DUAL CIRCUIT INSTALLATION

STOCK BRAKE SYSTEM

Master cylinder

Stoplight junction box

To front
brakes

To rear
brakes

AUXILIARY VALUE ADDED

Master cylinder

Auxiliary valve

T-fitting

To electric
controller

Stoplight junction box

To front
brakes

To rear brakes

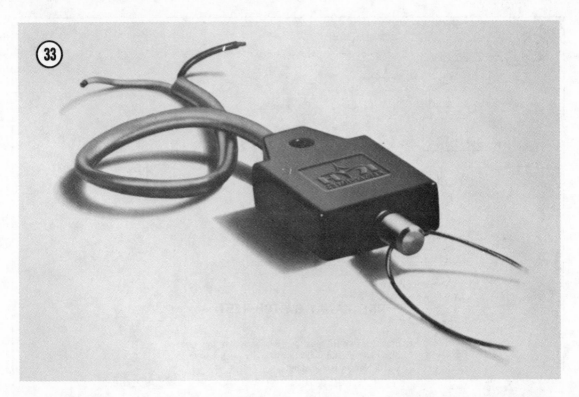

By pulling the breakaway switch lanyard, it was possible to stop the trailer and avert possible tragedy.

No maintenance is required on the switch itself. Have the battery tested periodically and replace it at once if it gets weak. **Figure 34** illustrates proper breakaway switch wiring.

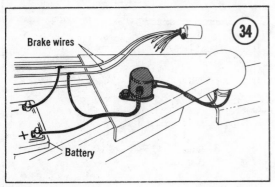

Test the breakaway switch as shown in **Figure 35**. With the switch disconnected, connect an ohmmeter or other continuity tester across its leads. The meter should indicate no continuity. Then pull out the plunger by means of the attached lanyard. With the plunger out, continuity should exist between the 2 leads.

An alternate method of testing the breakaway switch is shown in **Figure 36**. Connect the positive lead from a voltmeter to the brake terminal at the trailer connector. Connect the negative voltmeter lead to the brake return (ground) terminal. Then pull out the breakaway switch plunger. With the plunger out, the voltmeter should indicate battery voltage.

Brake Resistors

Brake resistors (**Figure 37**) limit total current supplies to the trailer brakes, and therefore provide smoother brake action. Brake resistors are usually required for lighter trailers and for all installations where a tow car with a 12-volt electrical system is connected to a trailer with 6-volt brakes. Different resistance values may be obtained by selecting various taps on the resistor or by a slider which may be moved as required.

No maintenance is required on the brake resistor other than periodic checks to be sure its connections are clean and tight.

Brake Adjustment

Trailer brakes require adjustment from time to time. The adjustment procedure is similar to

12

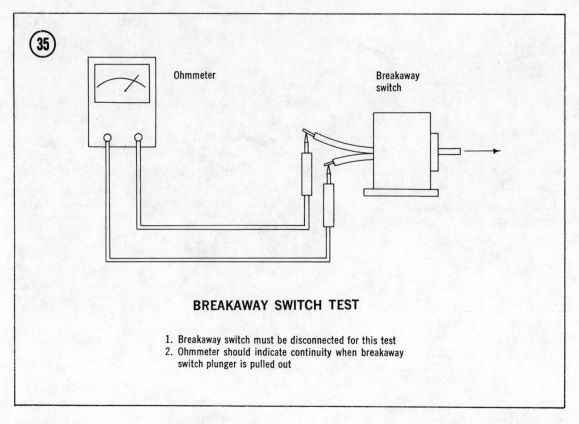

BREAKAWAY SWITCH TEST

1. Breakaway switch must be disconnected for this test
2. Ohmmeter should indicate continuity when breakaway switch plunger is pulled out

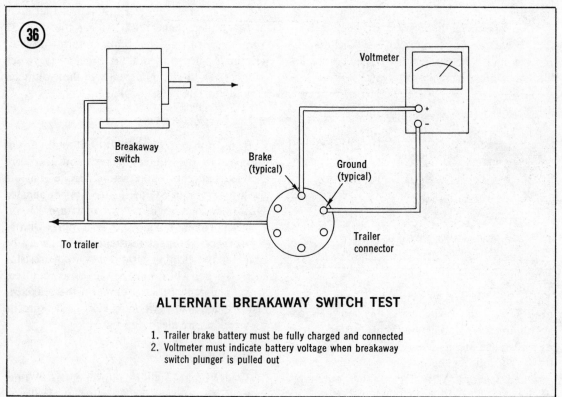

ALTERNATE BREAKAWAY SWITCH TEST

1. Trailer brake battery must be fully charged and connected
2. Voltmeter must indicate battery voltage when breakaway switch plunger is pulled out

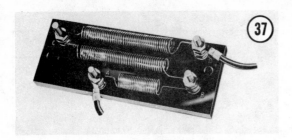

that of automobiles without self-adjusting brakes. Adjust one wheel at a time.

1. Jack up the wheel.

2. Remove the rubber access plug from the bottom of the backing plate.

3. Using a brake adjusting tool or screwdriver (**Figure 38**), turn the brake adjuster until the wheel can no longer be turned by hand. Note that for Warner spot magnet brakes, downward motion of the tool tightens the brakes.

4. Turn the adjuster in the opposite direction until the wheel turns freely. Slight grating or scratching sounds at one or two points as the wheel turns are OK, as long as the wheel turns freely.

5. Replace the rubber plug.

6. Repeat each step for the remaining wheels.

Troubleshooting

Electric brakes are simple devices and rarely give trouble. When any malfunction does occur, it is almost always an electrical, rather than a mechanical, problem. Occasionally, electric brakes will not work properly after long periods of idleness because of rust inside. After long usage, magnets and brake linings become worn and must be replaced.

Tables 3 and 4 list possible malfunctions and probable remedies. The first set of tables applies to spot magnet type brakes such as Kelsey-Hayes and recent Warner; the second set of tables applies to ring-magnet type Warner brakes.

After referring to the foregoing troubleshooting charts, it may be necessary to perform further checks on electrical components. The following sections describe bench tests that may be performed.

Checking Magnets

Test procedures are similar for all makes and styles of magnets. Two tests may be performed: current draw and short circuit. To test current draw, connect the magnet, a 0-10 DC ammeter, and a suitable battery (6-volt battery for 6-volt brakes, 12-volt battery for 12-volt brakes) as shown in **Figure 39**. Be sure to observe proper meter polarity. Current drawn by each magnet should be approximately as listed in the appropriate table.

If magnet current draw is normal, test each magnet for shorts. Connect the test circuit shown in **Figure 40**, or use an ohmmeter to determine that there is no continuity between the magnet coil and housing. Rap the magnet sharply against a hard surface during this test.

Check spot type magnets for wear as shown in **Figure 41**. If magnet faces exhibit unusually deep grooves, or if one side is worn substantially more than the other, replace the magnet.

On Warner ring-type magnets, the armature and magnet should always bear the relationship shown in **Figure 42**. Note that the magnet friction facing is undercut 0.005-0.007 in. to ensure that the magnet poles will be fully seated into their respective armature tracks before normal wear brings magnet friction facing into contact

12

Table 3   SPOT MAGNET BRAKES

Problem	Probable Cause	Remedy
Grabbing brakes	Grease on linings	Replace linings and grease seals
	Defective controller	Repair or replace controller
	No resistor in circuit	Install resistor
	Loose or broken parts	Repair
	Rusty drums or armature plate	Usually corrected by normal use. If not, clean affected parts
Weak brakes	Poor connections	Clean and tighten
	Poor ground	Do not depend on ground connection through hitch ball
	Short circuit	Repair circuit
	Incorrect resistor setting	Adjust resistor
	Worn or defective magnets	Replace magnets
	Poor adjustment	Adjust brakes
	Greasy brake lining	Replace brake lining and grease seals
	Inadequate wire size	Use larger wire
No brakes	Open circuit	Check for broken wires, loose connections, corroded connector terminals, or faulty ground connections
	Defective controller	Repair or replace controller
	Poor brake adjustment	Adjust brakes
	Defective resistor	Check for corroded connections. Replace if burned out
	Worn or defective magnets	Replace magnets
	Short circuit	Repair
Intermittent or surging brakes	Drums out of round	Turn drums
	Inadequate ground	Do not depend on ground through hitch ball
	Broken magnet wires	Test magnets. Replace if necessary
	Loose wheel bearings	Check and adjust
Dragging brakes	Incorrect adjustment	Adjust properly
	Defective controller	Repair or replace controller
	Corroded brake assembly	Check magnet levers for free movement
	Weak or broken brake shoe return springs	Check and replace
Noisy brakes	Lining worn out	Check lining, replace if worn
	Loose parts	Repair as required
	Bent backing plate or improperly located flange	Repair as required
	Grease on linings	Install new brake lining and grease seals
	Improper wheel bearing adjustment	Check and adjust if required
	Poor adjustment	A "clank" is normal as magnets drop back when brakes are released. Proper adjustment minimizes this noise

Table 4   RING MAGNET BRAKES

Problem	Probable Cause	Remedy
Weak brakes	Worn lining	Replace brake bands
	Worn drums	Reline brake bands so that there is 0.020 inch clearance between lining and drum
	Brake bands out-of-round	Check and adjust band using gauge supplied with service kit
	Grease on magnet facing	Remove grease from magnet facing. Replace magnet if necessary
	Grease on brake lining	Replace lining and grease seal
	Stop light connected in brake circuit	Wire separate circuit for stoplights
	Broken wire	Repair or replace
	Insufficient current	Check all connections. Be sure wiring is of sufficient size
Grabbing brakes	Loose wheel bearing	Adjust wheel bearing. Under normal operation, magnet poles wear a groove in the armature slightly wider than the poles. A wider groove indicates loose or badly worn bearings
	Worn or damaged bearings	Replace bearings
	Drums out-of-round	Rebore drums. Install shim stock under lining when drums are rebored
	Axle loose	Repair as necessary
	Loose brake lining	Replace lining
	Distorted bands	Round out band using gauge supplied with installation and service kit
	Only one brake working	Check wiring. Bench check magnet
	Brakes wired into stoplight circuit	Wire brakes correctly
	Poor electrical connections	Check and repair wires and connections
	Defective controller	Repair or replace controller
	Brake drum loose on hub	Tighten hub bolts. Check drum for concentricity
	Broken or weak band return springs	Replace springs. Always replace springs in pairs
	Damaged or bent backing plate	Straighten or replace backing plate
	Broken or loose parts	Replace broken parts. Check for other damage
Noisy brakes	Loose or worn wheel bearings	Adjust or replace bearings as required
	Out-of-round drums	Rebore drums. Be sure to shim brake lining
	Distorted band	Correct distortion using band gauge supplied with service kit
	Scored drums	Rebore drums. Be sure to shim lining
	Loose brake lining	Install new brake lining
Intermittent or no braking	Broken wire	Check all wiring and repair or replace as necessary
	Poor connection	Clean and tighten all connections at brakes, resistor, controller, and trailer connector
	Broken magnet wire	Replace wire
	Poor ground connection	Run separate brake ground wire. Do not depend on hitch ball for ground return
	Defective connector plug or receptacle	Check for loose connections or corroded contacts. Repair or replace as required
	Defective resistor	Replace resistor
	Defective controller	Repair or replace as required

12

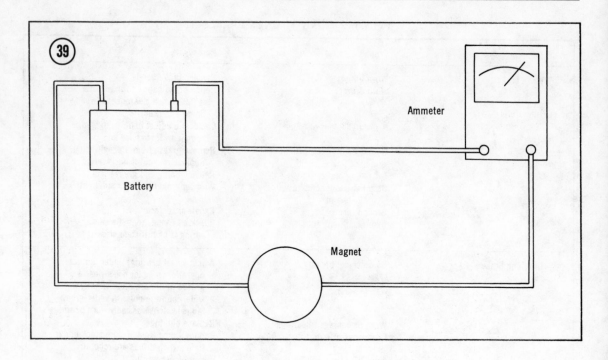

Ammeter

Battery

Magnet

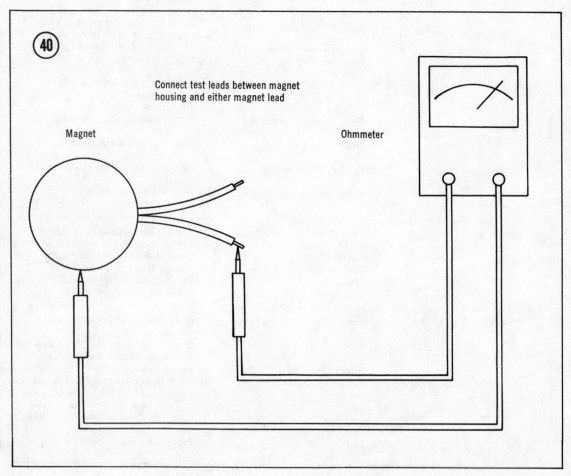

Connect test leads between magnet
housing and either magnet lead

Magnet

Ohmmeter

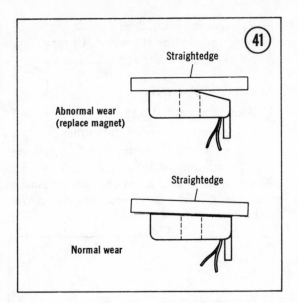

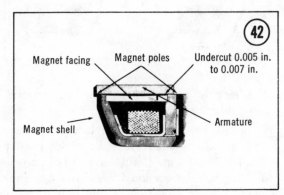

with the armature. Normal and abnormal wear patterns are shown in **Figure 43**.

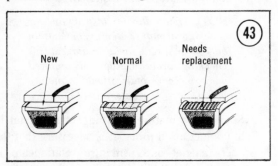

SERVICING WARNER RING-MAGNET BRAKES

Brake magnets, armatures, and linings are subject to wear and must be checked periodically and replaced when they become worn.

Replacing Magnets

1. Block the trailer securely, then jack up the trailer and remove the wheel and brake drum assembly.

2. Refer to **Figure 44**. Detach 2 magnet wires (A) from their terminals on the backing plate, or remove grommet (G) by squeezing with water pump pliers to release it from the backing plate. Remove both return springs (B).

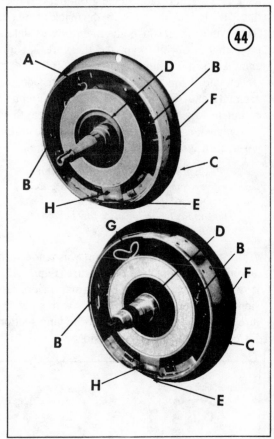

Glazed magnet facings may cause weak braking action when all other things appear to be normal. This condition may be remedied by sanding the magnet facing lightly. Do not use emery paper for this operation and be sure that no material is removed from the magnet poles.

4. Before proceeding, check brake voltage coding. All 12-volt-6-volt brakes have 4711G, 631-1100-001, or 1100-631-001 stamped on the magnet trunnion (H). Backing plate interiors (C) are painted gray. Use magnet kit 1100-7 for all 12-volt-6-volt brakes.

12

Numbers 1101-631-001, 002, or 005 are stamped on magnet trunnions (H) of 12-volt brakes. Backing plate interiors (C) are painted black. For service, use magnet kit 1101-27 (2.2 amperes) or 1101-34 (3.3 amperes).

Magnets for 10-inch, 6-volt brakes have "6-volt" stamped on magnet sides. Magnets for 10-inch, 12-volt brakes have no magnet markings.

5. Place new magnet on backing plate in same relative position as old magnet assembly. Make sure that the magnet turns freely on the backing plate hub.

6. On 12-volt brakes, connect both magnet wires (A) and replace the 2 magnet return springs (B). For 10-inch and 12-inch brakes with long magnet leads, place grommet (G) over the 2 leads into the hole in the backing plate. Rotate the magnet in both directions to determine the anchoring point for the wires. If anchored too short, they will tear off at full magnet travel, and if too long, they could catch on the armature and short out, causing intermittent or complete loss of braking. After wire length is determined, crimp the grommet into place on the wires, then insert it into the backing plate.

NOTE: *Always replace the armature when a magnet is replaced. It is good practice to replace the armature on the opposite brake also for balanced braking action.*

7. In the event that replacement was made with an old-style unidirectional armature (**Figure 45**), it will be necessary to check armature depression. This step is not necessary with new bidirectional armatures. See the following section for checking armature depression.

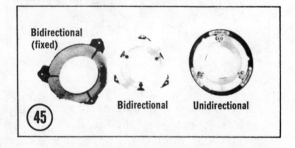

Bidirectional (fixed)

Bidirectional   Unidirectional

45

8. Check brake drum and lining condition. Turn the drum and/or install new lining as required.

9. Replace the brake drum, adjust the wheel bearing, and replace the wheel. Chapter Five describes wheel bearing adjustment.

Armature Replacement

1. Remove wheel and brake drum.

2. Remove armature from brake drum.

3. Check armature face condition. Twin grooves (A) in **Figure 46** should be only slightly wider than magnet poles. If grooves are unusually wide, check condition of wheel bearing and replace if necessary.

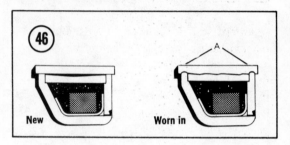

46   A

New   Worn in

4. Check drum condition. If any deep grooves exist, turn the drum.

5. Install new armature. Replacement armatures are all mounted with 3 bolts. Some older Warner brakes may still have 6-bolt armatures; 3-bolt bidirectional armatures are supplied as replacement parts and will fit older brakes, either right or left side.

6. Check armature depression if an older unidirectional armature was installed.

NOTE: *The following instructions for checking armature depression pertain only to unidirectional armatures. (This checking procedure is not required with the new bidirectional armature because of the greater travel.)*

Since the armature and magnet must run in light contact at all times, it is necessary that the proper magnet and armature relationship is maintained at all times. Because this relationship between armature and magnet constitutes a blind assembly, an armature depression gauge No. 4680 (**Figure 47**) is used. To check armature depression, follow instructions below.

1. Place the outside legs (A and B) of the gauge against the magnet friction facing. Both thumb

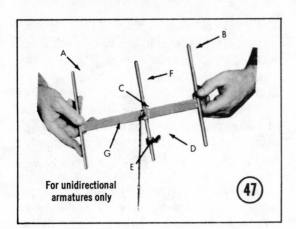

For unidirectional armatures only (47)

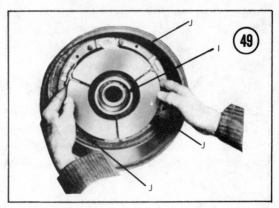

(49)

screws (C and D) should be loose and collar (E) on middle leg (F) should be on the outside of gauge crossbar (G) as shown in **Figure 48**. Push the middle, movable leg (F) into contact with the bearing shoulder (H). Make certain that gauge is held perpendicular to magnet and that magnet is flush against mounting plate.

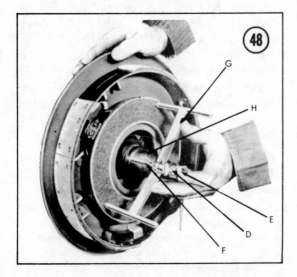

(48)

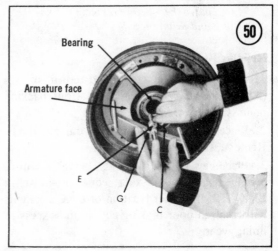

Bearing

Armature face

(50)

2. Next, tighten the thumb screw, locking movable leg (F), also shown in Figure 48. Move the collar (E) against the frame and tighten the collar thumb screw (D) fixing the collar securely on the movable leg.

3. With the wheel assembly lying so armature is horizontal, place inner bearing (I) in the hub and rotate under light pressure to make certain bearing is fully seated. Place 3 wedges (J) shown in **Figure 49**, equally spaced under the disc to hold it up against the stops.

4. Reverse the gauge so collar (E) on center leg is below gauge crossbar (G), and place the outside legs against the armature face as shown in **Figure 50**. Loosen thumb screw (C) on gauge frame and push movable leg against bearing. Retighten gauge frame thumb screw (C), fixing the movable leg in this new position. Recheck the position of the 3 legs at 3 different points, 120 degrees apart, to ensure a correct reading.

5. Measuring the distance between the gauge frame and the collar on the movable leg as shown in **Figure 51** gives armature depression. It should be between 1/8 -3/16 in.

6. For making quick checks for correct depression in the field, the armature gauge is provided with a go-no-go pin (Figure 51). The small end of the pin is 1/8 in. diameter and should slip between the gauge frame and the collar. The large end of the pin is 3/16 in. in diameter and should not slip between the gauge frame and collar.

12

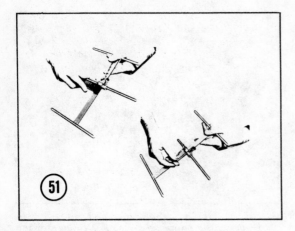

7. Adjust armature depression. If depression is less than ⅛ in., the difference must be made up by placing shims under the armature retaining ring. If depression is more than 3/16 in., place a hardened bearing spacer between the inner bearing and the bearing shoulder on the axle.

> NOTE: *If wedges were used under the armature to check depression, be sure to remove them before replacing armature and drum on axle.*

Relining Brakes

1. Pull wheel, remove 2 band-return springs (E) and detach brake band (F) from backing plate (G), shown in Figure 25.

2. Place bands in vise and drill out old rivets. Remove worn linings.

3. Place new linings on bands, being careful to arrange segments in exact sequence shown in **Figure 52**. Improper location of band segments will result in poor braking action and excessive lining wear.

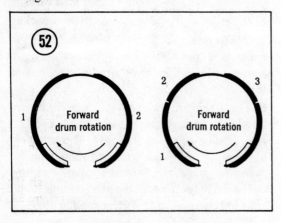

4. Rivet new linings in place.

5. Place relined band in band gauge. To assure maximum performance, the band must be uniformly round. To check for roundness, place band in Warner Electric band gauge supplied with installation and service kit. If band is free of distortion, it will contact the gauge snugly over the entire outer circumference of the gauge, with a light tension holding it in place.

Bands which are out-of-round or have flat spots should be corrected by placing them on a wooden bench top or block and striking band with ball peen hammer where necessary. Care should be taken to avoid damaging rivet holes. An out-of-round band can cause brake to act weak or grab. If the leading toe end of the band is bent away from the band gauge, braking action will be strong or grabby. When leading end is bent toward the center of the gauge, braking action will be weak.

The band gauge may also be used to check clearance between the relined band and the drum. This is done by placing the band assembly on the band gauge and fitting the band (on the gauge) into the drum. Where the diameter of the drum is more than 1/16 in. larger than overall diameter of the band assembly (on the gauge), shim stock should be used under the lining to bring it to proper fit.

6. Install band on brake. Edges of 10-inch and some 12-inch brake linings are color coded (**Figure 53**) red or green to indicate on which side of the trailer they should be mounted. If there is no color code, brake lining can be used on either side.

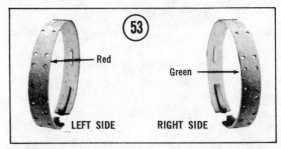

When mounting bands on the right (or curb) wheel of the trailer, green edge of band is out. For mounting on the left wheel, the red band edge should be out. This arrangement must be followed to assure proper braking action.

7. True lining and/or brake drum if required. After brakes have been relined (or a drum replaced), check the clearance between lining and drum.

Any high spots on drum should be turned down. Caution must be used when refacing drum during the relining operation as there is no definite yardstick to follow regarding how much a drum may be oversized. It is generally recommended that a drum should not be bored oversize more than ⅛ in. on the diameter, and shim stock thicker than 1/16 in. should not be used with riveted linings. In some areas, such as mountainous terrain, it is recommended that the drums be replaced before this wear situation is reached.

When brakes are relined, but the drum is not turned, the ridge left on the bell end of the drum, due to wear from the brake shoes, should be removed. This may be done with a hand grinder, using a flexible disc as shown in **Figure 54**.

CAUTION

Be careful to remove or mask bearing before grinding operation and to dust drum before replacing or unmasking bearings.

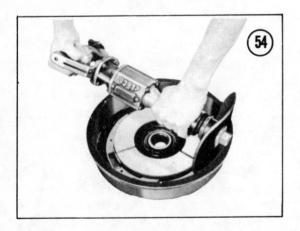

Where brake linings have high spots, special grinders are available to bring them back to concentricity with drum. These grinders mount on the axle and can be used on automobiles and trucks as well as trailers.

8. Always replace brake linings by axle, rather than by individual brake. That is, do not reline one brake unless the other brake on the same axle is relined also.

CAUTION

Since Warner ring-magnet brakes are self adjusting, clearance between drum and lining is a critical factor concerning brake operation. Brake band and lining assemblies as received from the factory are ground to provide approximately 0.020" clearance. This clearance is best controlled during initial installation or during relining and drum replacement.

If proper clearance is provided during those service operations, the brake is so designed that the lining will be worn out by the time maximum magnet travel is reached. However, if too much clearance is present initially, maximum magnet travel will occur before the lining is worn out, and loss of braking power will result. Too little clearance will cause brake drag and possible wheel lockup. Considerable variation in clearance between brakes on any unit may result in unbalanced braking.

SERVICING WARNER SPOT MAGNET BRAKES

Figure 55 is an exploded view of a Warner spot magnet brake. Refer to this illustration for assembly details. Note that some parts must be ordered as a right- or left-hand assembly.

Replacing Magnets

The magnet replacement kit includes the magnet with its detent ring in position, follow-up spring, and a new grommet.

1. Remove the brake drum and both brake shoes to gain access to the magnet lead wires.

2. Pull the old magnet outward with a rocking motion to remove it from the lever stud.

3. Compress the grommet with pliers, then pull it out from the backing plate.

4. Cut off the old magnet leads behind the backing plate.

5. Remove the old follow-up spring.

6. Install the new follow-up spring with its larger end outward.

7. Thread both new magnet leads through the round hole in the lever arm, shown in **Figure 56**.

12

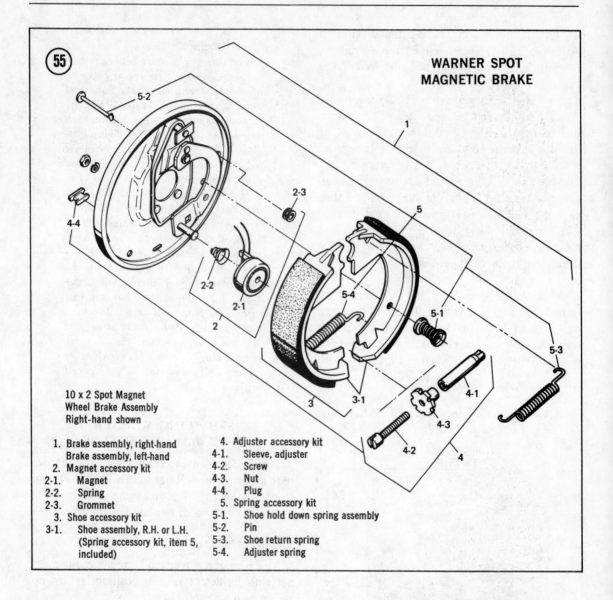

⑤⑤

WARNER SPOT MAGNETIC BRAKE

10 x 2 Spot Magnet
Wheel Brake Assembly
Right-hand shown

1. Brake assembly, right-hand
   Brake assembly, left-hand
2. Magnet accessory kit
2-1. Magnet
2-2. Spring
2-3. Grommet
3. Shoe accessory kit
3-1. Shoe assembly, R.H. or L.H.
   (Spring accessory kit, item 5, included)
4. Adjuster accessory kit
4-1. Sleeve, adjuster
4-2. Screw
4-3. Nut
4-4. Plug
5. Spring accessory kit
5-1. Shoe hold down spring assembly
5-2. Pin
5-3. Shoe return spring
5-4. Adjuster spring

8. Press the new magnet into position on its stud, using sufficient force to make the detent ring snap into place over the ridge on the end of the stud.

9. Be sure that the magnet positioning tang engages the hole in the lever arm and that the tang is between the 2 magnet leads.

10. The grommet is a right angle locking type. Lock the grommet onto the leads in such a position that the leads enter from the bottom when the grommet is in place and with the back side of the grommet approximately 5¾ in. from the far side of the hole in the lever arm (**Figure 57**). This distance provides proper slack in the leads.

Thread both leads through the hole in the backing plate, then insert the grommet.

11. Connect the new magnet leads to the brake wires, using good quality crimp connectors. Tape the wires to the axle, preferably on the back side to protect them from possible damage.

12. Replace both brake shoes and brake drum.

13. Readjust the brake.

Replacing Brake Shoes

The brake shoe replacement kit contains 2 brake shoes and all required small parts. Always install new brake shoes in left and right pairs on any one axle.

2. Remove each brake shoe hold-down spring. Although a removal tool (**Figure 59**) is available to make the job easier, it may be done by grasping the spring retainer with a pair of pliers, pushing inward to compress the spring slightly, and rotating the retainer 90° in either direction. Hold the back end of the pin by hand to prevent it from turning as the spring retainer is rotated.

Lever arm hole

Positioning tang

3. Spread the shoes by hand to remove them, as shown in **Figure 60**. Remove the lower spring and brake adjuster assembly.

4. Clean the brake adjuster assembly so that it operates smoothly over its entire range of travel.

5. Reverse the disassembly procedure to reassemble the brake, using all new small parts supplied. Be sure that the adjuster nut is located to the left, as you face the brake, and that the adjuster spring is located on the backing plate side of the brake shoes.

12

1. Using a suitable pair of pliers, remove the brake shoe return spring (**Figure 58**).

60

SERVICING
KELSEY-HAYES BRAKES

Armature Plates

Armature plates can normally be expected to wear indefinitely. However, as severe contamination may cause excessive wear, armature plates may be replaced easily. Replacement plates are supplied with all hardware necessary for installation. If the original plate is riveted into position, drill out the rivets and replace them with bolts, nuts, and lockwashers supplied with the kit (**Figure 61**).

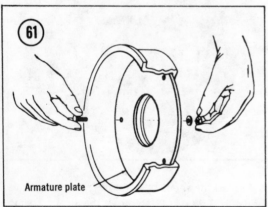

61

Armature plate

Always inspect the magnet assembly when replacing an armature plate. The same condition which caused wear to the armature plate may also have caused damage to the magnet. If the magnet is wearing flat (Figure 41), it need not be replaced unless it is worn badly. If, however, the magnet is worn at an angle or unevenly, replace it.

Brake Drums

Inspect the brake drum rubbing surface. This should have a dull gray appearance and be free from heavy scoring and/or excessive wear. One or 2 light score marks are OK, but if scoring is heavy, the drum is worn more than 0.020 in. oversize, or has more than 0.015 in. runout, rebore the drum. Discard it if it must be bored more than 0.060 in. oversize.

Since Kelsey-Hayes brakes are adjustable, it is not necessary to install shims between the brake shoes and linings. However, if a brake drum is rebored to 0.060 in., be sure to arc grind new linings so that they match the new drum diameter.

Installing Brake Shoes

Install new brake shoes as soon as any portion of the lining is worn down to the rivets, or if the lining exhibits a poor wear pattern (**Figure 62**). Poor wear patterns may be caused by improperly located flanges or a bent backing plate. Replace brake linings also in the event of oil or grease contamination.

> NOTE: *Always replace brake linings in sets. If the brake lining on one end of an axle is replaced, the brake on the other end must be relined also.*

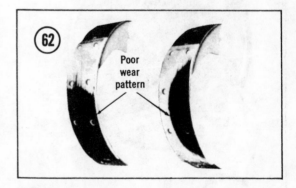

62
Poor wear pattern

1. Remove both brake shoe return springs (**Figure 63**).
2. Remove both brake shoe hold-down springs. Although a special removal tool is available, the job may be done by grasping the spring retainer with a pair of pliers, pushing inward to compress the spring slightly, then rotating the retainer 90 degrees in either direction. Hold the back end of

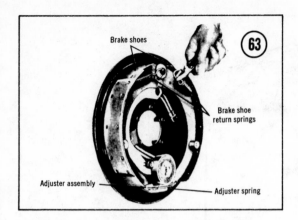

the pin by hand to prevent it from turning as the spring retainer is rotated.

3. Pull the brake shoes apart slightly, then remove the shoes and adjuster as an assembly.

4. Remove adjuster and spring from shoes.

5. Inspect all springs and replace any that are worn or stretched.

6. Clean the adjuster, then apply a very light coating of Lubriplate to it and also to the 6 places where the brake shoes bear against the backing plate.

7. Reverse the removal procedure to install the new brake shoes. Note that the shoe with the short lining segment goes toward the front of the trailer.

HYDRAULIC BRAKES

Some trailers are equipped with hydraulic brakes. Operation is no different from that on a standard passenger car. There are 2 methods for applying hydraulic brakes. Surge, or inertia, braking is most often found on smaller trailers. No brake connections to the tow car are required. In this system, when the tow car slows, inertia of the trailer operates a master cylinder, which in turn applies the trailer brakes. A spring-actuated breakaway device applies the trailer brakes in the event of accidental separation. **Figures 64 and 65** illustrate operation of an inertia braking system.

A possible disadvantage of this system is that in the event of brake failure on the tow vehicle, little or no trailer braking action is possible. Since surge-operated brakes depend entirely on towing vehicle deceleration, they simply won't work if the tow vehicle cannot slow down.

The Stromberg hydraulic brake coupler (**Figure 66**) makes synchronized hydraulic brakes possible on trailers. A complete hydraulic brake system, including a master cylinder, is installed on the trailer. A slave hydraulic cylinder is connected to the tow car hydraulic system by a flexible hose. The slave cylinder and trailer master cylinder are then connected mechanically. There is no interchange of brake fluid be-

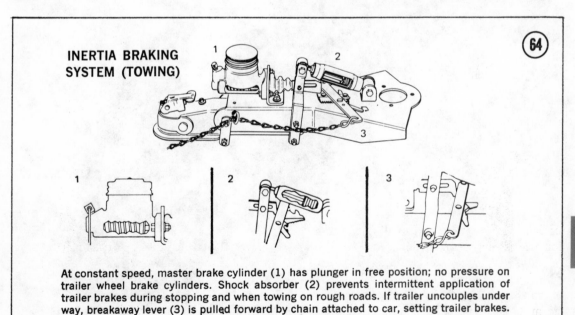

At constant speed, master brake cylinder (1) has plunger in free position; no pressure on trailer wheel brake cylinders. Shock absorber (2) prevents intermittent application of trailer brakes during stopping and when towing on rough roads. If trailer uncouples under way, breakaway lever (3) is pulled forward by chain attached to car, setting trailer brakes.

12

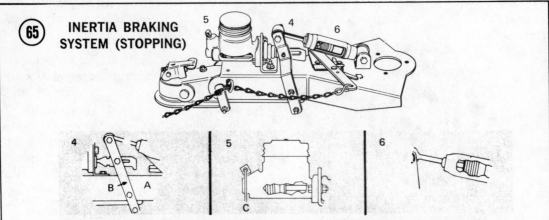

INERTIA BRAKING SYSTEM (STOPPING)

As car slows (4), trailer tongue (A) moves forward applying pressure through linkage (B) to master cylinder (5), in direct proportion to car braking. Pressure is transmitted to wheel brakes through brake lines (C). Shock absorber (6) assures smooth, even application of brakes. Atwood brakes require no connections to car's electrical or hydraulic systems, need no batteries. Fully self-contained.

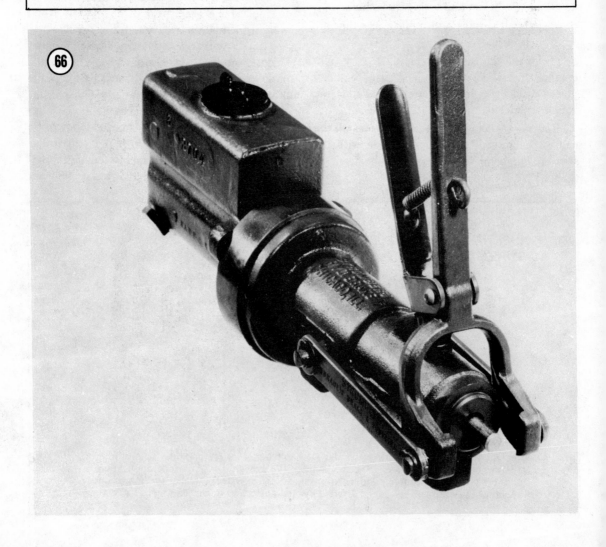

tween tow car and trailer. A spring-actuated breakaway device applies the trailer brakes in the event of accidental trailer separation.

Standard Bendix hydraulic brakes (**Figure 67**) are used with the stromberg coupler. Service on these brakes is widely available.

(67)

12

STROMBERG BRAKE MAINTENANCE

Stromberg brakes are maintained in exactly the same manner as conventional hydraulic brakes on an automobile. Replacement parts are available at most auto parts or trailer supply stores.

Every 2 weeks or so, squirt a few drops of clean brake fluid into the hole in the end of the slave cylinder. Use a screwdriver or thin punch to push the piston back in all the way, then extend it again by pumping the brake pedal. This operation prevents the piston in the slave cylinder from sticking. Do not allow dirt to enter the slave cylinder.

Never apply the breakaway mechanism when either brake drum is removed. Doing so will force the pistons from the wheel cylinders.

During periodic application of the breakaway device, examine all connections for evidence of leakage. Pay particular attention to each flexible hose. Any hose that is swollen, or exhibits any other evidence of deterioration should be replaced at once.

STROMBERG BRAKE OPERATING TIPS

Operation of Stromberg hydraulic brakes is entirely automatic once the necessary connection is made. Certain items should be kept in mind, however, to ensure satisfactory braking and long service life.

1. Keep brakes on the tow car adjusted properly, so a high pedal is maintained.

2. Adjust trailer brakes after the first 500-1,000 miles of travel.

3. After unhitching, always pump the brake pedal in the tow car once or twice. This operation is necessary to return the piston in the slave cylinder and to restore proper pedal travel in the tow car.

4. When parked for an extended period, release the breakaway lever every 2 weeks or so. This operation prevents the pistons and cups from sticking.

5. The breakaway mechanism may be used as a parking brake, but it must be released for a few moments at intervals not exceeding 48 hours.

ATWOOD SURGE BRAKES

Figure 68 is an exploded view of a typical Atwood brake actuator. Replacement parts are available from the manufacturer. Master cylinder overhaul kits are available from most auto parts stores.

Atwood Brake Maintenance

Proper lubrication of the actuator will help to ensure proper functioning (**Figure 69**). Inspect flexible hoses and other rubber parts periodically for deterioration. Keep the brakes adjusted and replace the shoes when they are worn.

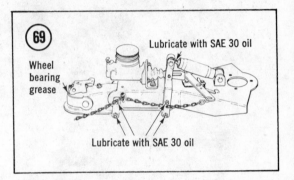

Bleeding Atwood Brakes

During any operation which requires opening the hydraulic system, air enters the cylinders and brake lines. This air must be bled to prevent loss of braking action.

1. Clean the area around the master cylinder filler cap, then remove the cap.

2. Fill the master cylinder reservoir with fresh SAE J703A brake fluid.

3. Start the bleeding procedure on the right-hand brake first. If the trailer is equipped with tandem axles, bleed the rear brakes first.

4. Connect a bleeder hose to the bleeder fitting behind the wheel cylinder. Submerge the other end in a container of clean brake fluid.

5. Loosen the bleeder fitting one turn.

6. Pull the breakaway lever fully forward, then tighten the bleeder fitting.

7. Return the breakaway lever to its rearmost position.

8. Repeat Steps 5, 6, and 7 until all fluid expelled from bleeder fitting is free of air bubbles.

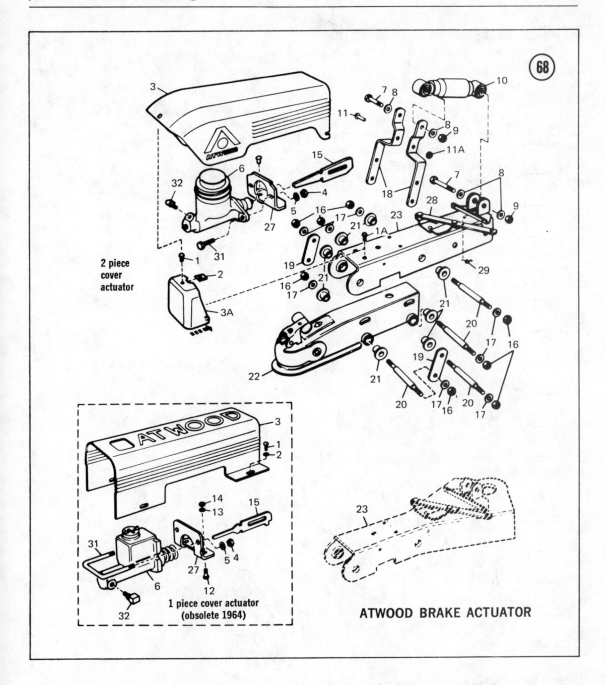

2 piece cover actuator

1 piece cover actuator
(obsolete 1964)

ATWOOD BRAKE ACTUATOR

NOTE: *Be sure to maintain the master cylinder reservoir at least half full during the entire bleeding procedure. Use only fresh fluid for replacement.*

9. After all air is expelled, close the bleeder valve securely and remove the bleeder hose.

10. Repeat Steps 4-9 for the left brake, and also the brakes on the forward axle if the trailer is equipped with tandem axles.

11. If the trailer is equipped with tandem axles, repeat the bleeding procedure for the rear axle to ensure complete air removal.

12. Breakaway lever action will be firm after all air is purged.

Atwood Brake Adjustment

There are 2 adjustment procedures, one for 8-inch brakes and the other for 10-inch

12

and 12-inch brakes. On 8-inch brakes (**Figure 70**), turn each adjusting nut simultaneously until the wheel drags heavily or locks, then back off each nut until the wheel turns freely (**Figure 71**).

To adjust 10-inch and 12-inch brakes (**Figure 72**), remove the dust plug at the lower part of the backing plate. Tighten the adjuster wheel, using a brake adjustment tool (**Figure 73**) as shown, until the wheel drags heavily. Then turn

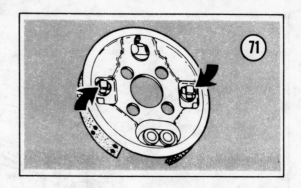

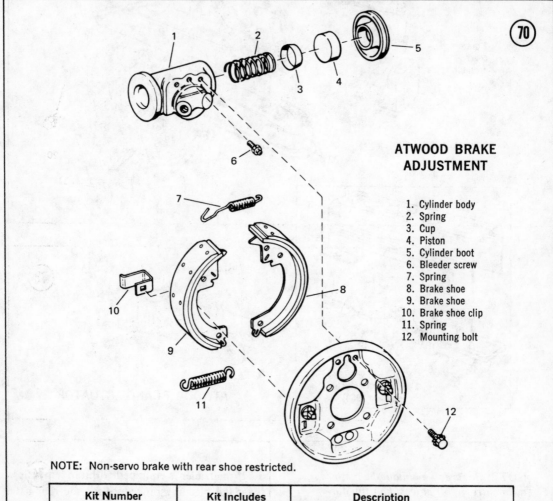

ATWOOD BRAKE ADJUSTMENT

1. Cylinder body
2. Spring
3. Cup
4. Piston
5. Cylinder boot
6. Bleeder screw
7. Spring
8. Brake shoe
9. Brake shoe
10. Brake shoe clip
11. Spring
12. Mounting bolt

NOTE: Non-servo brake with rear shoe restricted.

Kit Number	Kit Includes	Description
SK-8-1	1, 12	Wheel cylinder kit (for one axle)
SK-8-2	2, 3, 4, 5	Wheel cylinder repair kit
SK-8-3	8, 9	Shoe and lining kit (for one axle)
SK-8-4	7, 10, 11	Spring kit (for one axle)
SK-8-5	6	Bleeder nut

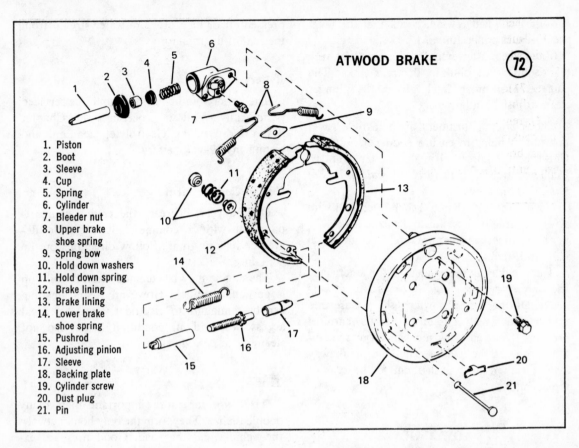

ATWOOD BRAKE (72)

1. Piston
2. Boot
3. Sleeve
4. Cup
5. Spring
6. Cylinder
7. Bleeder nut
8. Upper brake shoe spring
9. Spring bow
10. Hold down washers
11. Hold down spring
12. Brake lining
13. Brake lining
14. Lower brake shoe spring
15. Pushrod
16. Adjusting pinion
17. Sleeve
18. Backing plate
19. Cylinder screw
20. Dust plug
21. Pin

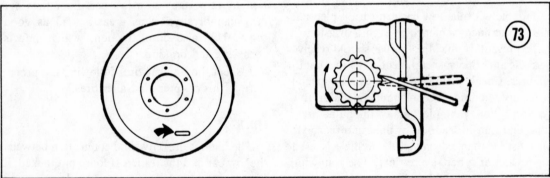

(73)

the adjuster wheel in the opposite direction until the wheel turns freely.

Atwood Brake Operating Tips

Always be sure that the breakaway chain passes through its eyelet, that it is securely attached to the tow car, and that it is long enough to permit sharp turns in either direction (**Figure 74**). Also be sure that the breakaway lever is in its rearmost position before starting to tow.

(74)

12

Periodically when towing, check that the lever has not been pulled forward.

Check the master cylinder plunger to be sure that it does not bind in the rear links. The plunger must move freely. Keep the plunger clean to avoid binding.

Check brake adjustment periodically. Proper adjustment helps to ensure good performance. Check brake fluid level in the master cylinder. Refill as required. *If there is any sudden loss of fluid, find out why.*

Never use other than a 2-inch hitch ball with Atwood surge brakes. An undersize ball results in noisy and jerky trailer braking. Keep the hitch ball lubricated.

The breakaway mechanism is for emergency use only. *Never use this device as a parking brake.* During normal towing use, be sure that that breakaway lever is pushed to its rearmost position. To release the mechanism after actuation, squeeze the locking pawl and breakaway lever together, then push them to the rear of the actuator.

TOW CAR

Trouble with the tow car can turn a pleasant trip into an inconvenience or even a disaster.

To prevent trouble, the tow car should receive periodic attention as recommended by the manufacturer. Check the owner's manual for special preventive maintenance recommended for tow vehicles. For example, many manufacturers state that transmission oil or fluid and rear axle oil must be changed only if the vehicle is used for towing or other severe duty. The following sections describe additional maintenance.

Cooling System

Once a year, for example in the spring, drain the cooling system and flush it. Many chemical cleaners are available; use as directed or the cooling system can be seriously damaged.

At the same time, check the thermostat as described in a service manual for your automobile or have it done by a competent mechanic.

Before each trip, check the radiator for bugs. You can force them out of the core with com-pressed air or high pressure water stream from the rear of the radiator.

Battery

The battery on the tow car should be serviced periodically. Follow procedures in Chapter Seven for checking electrolyte, cleaning, and testing any 12-volt battery.

Engine Compartment

Once a year, degrease the engine compart-partment with a commercially available de-greaser such as Gunk. Follow directions on the container.

The engine may be steamed clean if build up is particularly thick. However, steam cleaning can be damaging to electrical wires, electrical accessories, and air condition hoses. Do not steam clean periodically.

Tires

Tires are far more important than many people realize. They form the only bond between the vehicle and the road. Good tires are extremely important on a tow car. Poor tires not only cannot support as great a load as good tires; they also lose traction, which affects cornering and braking.

Inspect the tow car tires following the procedure in this chapter for trailer tires.

Hitch

The hitch is the only solid connection between the tow car and the trailer. If loose or cracked, it can break, causing considerable damage and even injury.

Before each trip and periodically during the trip, inspect the hitch components. Make sure that all bolts and nuts are tight. Check welds for cracks. Check coupler ball for tightness.

Brakes

Brakes should be checked periodically on any car. On a tow car, brakes should be inspected more often since stress, and therefore wear, is higher. Check brake linings (drum brakes) and brake pads (disc brakes) and adjust as described in a service manual for your car.

Oil Coolers

Engine and transmission oil performs a dual function. Obviously, oil is used as a lubricant. However, circulating oil is also used to cool the internal parts.

Oil coolers are often used to reduce oil temperatures on vehicles used for towing or other severe duty. Cooler oil increases engine or transmission life.

Oil coolers usually look like small radiators. Engine oil coolers are standard on some vehicles and optional on others. In any case, commercially available bolt-on coolers can be added to practically any car. They can even be added to cars with factory coolers to increase cooling capacity.

An automatic transmission cooler is built into the radiator of all vehicles with automatic transmission. Coolers are available to increase cooling capacity on tow cars. These coolers may replace the existing cooler or be in addition to it. In either case, capacity is increased and transmission life prolonged.

Increasing Load Capacity

There are several ways to add load carrying capacity to your tow vehicle.

- a. Leaf overload springs
- b. Coil overload springs
- c. Air shock absorbers
- d. Air bags

While all these devices will keep the car level with heavier than normal loads, in no case may the load exceed the load capacity of the tires.

Leaf overload springs simply supplement the existing springs. See **Figure 75**. They can be used only on vehicles with rear leaf springs.

Coil overload springs usually fit over the shock absorbers. See **Figure 76**. They will usually fit cars with leaf or coil rear springs.

Air bags fit inside the rear coil springs of cars so equipped. They are pumped up with air to any degree desired and effectively increase rear spring stiffness.

Air shock absorbers extend to any degree required to level the loaded car. To extend them, they may be pumped up at a service station. A small compressor can be added to the system to inflate shocks anywhere, even when driving.

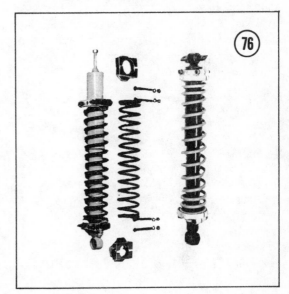

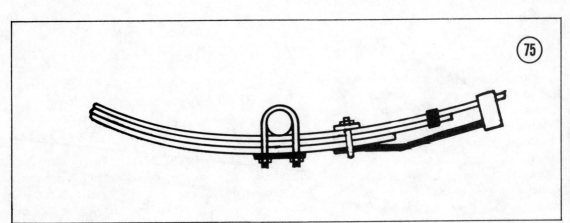

12

INDEX

NOTES

NOTES

MAINTENANCE LOG

DATE	TYPE OF SERVICE	COST	REMARKS

MAINTENANCE LOG

DATE	TYPE OF SERVICE	COST	REMARKS